NATIONAL
cycle
NETWORK

To SUSAN
THOUGHT YOU MIGHT
LIKE THIS — IT MAY HELP
TO DECIDE A HOLIDAY FOR
YOU BOTH SOMETIME

PAT & BRUCE

NATIONAL cycle NETWORK

Nick Cotton and John Grimshaw

ROUTES FOR PEOPLE

R O U T E S   F O R   P E O P L E

35 King Street, Bristol BS1 4DZ

First published by Sustrans in 2000
Second edition published 2002

Copyright © Sustrans 2002

ISBN 1-901389-35-9

Printed in Italy by G. Canale & C. Turin

Sustrans is continually improving
and refining its routes, so some of
the routes may vary from the
information currently in this book.

CONTENTS

The National Cycle Network	6
Foreword by Tony Robinson	7
Introduction	8
History of Sustrans and the National Cycle Network	8
How to Use This Guide	15
The West Country	**16**
National Cycle Network Highlights	19
City Focus	21
Traffic-Free Cycle Paths Particularly Suitable for Families	22
Useful Maps & Guides	23
Bristol & Bath Railway Path	24
Bridgwater & Taunton Canal Towpath	28
The Camel Trail – Bodmin to Padstow	32
The Plym Valley Path Towards Dartmoor	36
South East	**40**
National Cycle Network Highlights	43
City Focus	45
Traffic-Free Cycle Paths Particularly Suitable for Families	46
Useful Maps & Guides	47
Canterbury & Whitstable Cycle Path	48
South from Oxford to Abingdon	52
Cuckoo Trail – Eastbourne to Heathfield	56
London	**60**
National Cycle Network Highlights	64
Putney Bridge to Weybridge	65
Battersea Park to Greenwich	72
Victoria Park to the Thames Barrier	76
The Waterlink Way	80
Thames Barrier to Erith	82
Useful Maps & Guides	83

East of England	**84**
National Cycle Network Highlights	87
City Focus	89
Traffic-Free Cycle Paths Particularly	
Suitable for Families	90
Useful Maps & Guides	91
Wickham Market to Orford	92
King's Lynn to Shepherd's Port	96
A Circuit of Milton Keynes	100

The Midlands	**104**
National Cycle Network Highlights	107
City Focus	109
Traffic-Free Cycle Paths Particularly	
Suitable for Families	110
Useful Maps & Guides	111
Derby to Worthington	112
Doncaster to the Earth Centre/Barnsley	116
Birmingham to King's Norton Park	120

Wales	**124**
National Cycle Network Highlights	127
City Focus	129
Traffic-Free Cycle Paths Particularly	
Suitable for Families	130
Useful Maps & Guides	131
Swansea to Gowerton and the Mumbles	132
Kidwelly to the Wildfowl & Wetlands	
Centre, Llanelli	136
Cardiff to Castell Coch	140
Barmouth to Dolgellau	144
Colwyn Bay to Prestatyn	148

North of England	**152**
National Cycle Network Highlights	155
City Focus	157
Traffic-Free Cycle Paths Particularly	
Suitable for Families	158
Useful Maps & Guides	159
Along the Mersey in Liverpool	160
York to Beningbrough	164
Penrith to Keswick	168
Newcastle to Sunderland	174

Scotland	**180**
National Cycle Network Highlights	181
City Focus	183
Traffic-Free Cycle Paths Particularly	
Suitable for Families	184
Useful Maps & Guides	185
Glasgow to Loch Lomond	186
Callander to Killin or	
Loch Venachar	192
Edinburgh to the Forth Bridge	196

Northern Ireland	**200**
National Cycle Network Highlights	203
Traffic-Free Cycle Paths Particularly	
Suitable for Families	204
Useful Maps & Guides	205
City Focus	206
Castlerock to Giant's Causeway	208
Lisburn to Whiteabbey	212

Long Distance and Holiday Routes	**218**
Network Route Maps Order Form	237
The Time Trail	239
Good Cycling Code	241
Practical Advice for Cyclists	242
Cycling with Children	246
Helping Create the National Cycle	
Network	250
Other Projects	252
Millennium Miles	253
Acknowledgements	254
Join Sustrans	256

NATIONAL
cycle
NETWORK

The National Cycle Network routes open 2002

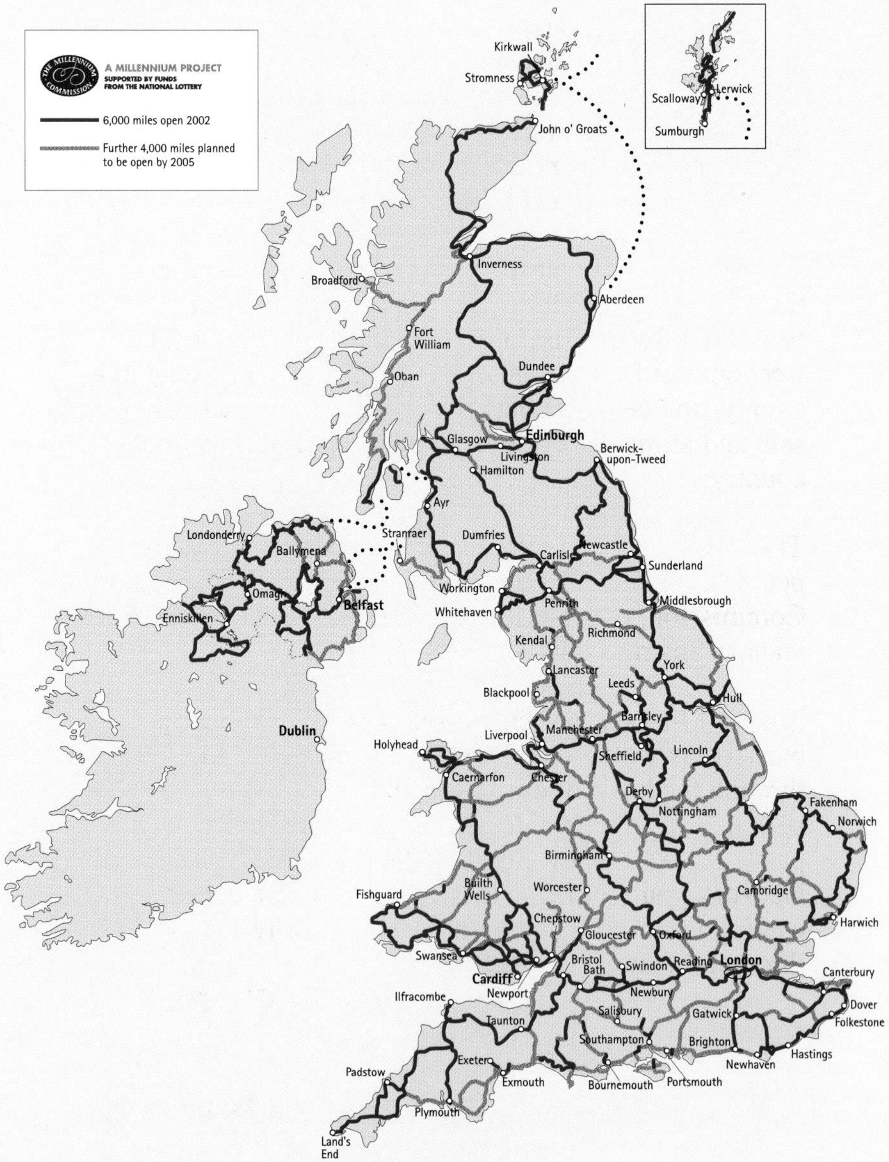

A MILLENNIUM PROJECT
SUPPORTED BY FUNDS
FROM THE NATIONAL LOTTERY

—— 6,000 miles open 2002

········· Further 4,000 miles planned
to be open by 2005

Kirkwall
Stromness
John o' Groats
Scalloway
Lerwick
Sumburgh

Broadford
Inverness
Aberdeen
Fort William
Oban
Dundee
Glasgow
Edinburgh
Livingston
Hamilton
Berwick-upon-Tweed
Ayr
Stranraer
Dumfries
Newcastle
Carlisle
Sunderland
Londonderry
Ballymena
Workington
Middlesbrough
Omagh
Whitehaven
Penrith
Enniskillen
Belfast
Kendal
Richmond
York
Lancaster
Leeds
Blackpool
Hull
Dublin
Barnsley
Holyhead
Liverpool
Manchester
Sheffield
Lincoln
Caernarfon
Chester
Derby
Fakenham
Nottingham
Norwich
Birmingham
Fishguard
Builth Wells
Worcester
Cambridge
Chepstow
Harwich
Swansea
Gloucester
Oxford
Bristol
Bath
Swindon
Reading
London
Cardiff
Newport
Canterbury
Ilfracombe
Newbury
Dover
Salisbury
Gatwick
Folkestone
Taunton
Southampton
Brighton
Hastings
Padstow
Exeter
Newhaven
Exmouth
Bournemouth
Portsmouth
Plymouth
Land's End

FOREWORD

I used to own a sepia photograph entitled 'The Trip'. Crowds of young men and women in Sunday-best clothes basked outside a pub, and in front of them, temporarily abandoned, lay hundreds of bicycles. The sun was shining, the trippers were jaunty, the photo spoke of a new modern world of independence, fun and healthy living.

A hundred years later that vision has been sullied by traffic jams and pollution. But the National Cycle Network offers us the chance to reclaim the sense of freedom our Edwardian ancestors felt, only this time in a twenty-first century context. It is weaving a network of safe and attractive cycling routes throughout the whole country.

This guide gives an introduction to the project. Many people – councils, landowners, funders, the Millennium Commission, enthusiasts, not to mention the dedicated team at Sustrans – have made this possible.

You will find extraordinary routes built to overcome barriers, as well as small details which weave their way through the heart of our towns and cities and out into the surrounding countryside. Although the project is only partly completed, by enjoying the National Cycle Network you will help create a world where once again cycling is recognised as a truly modern way of travelling through the next 100 years.

Tony Robinson

INTRODUCTION

Welcome to the Official Guide to the UK's National Cycle Network. Well over 6,000 miles of route are now open, with thousands more miles under development.

This guide will help you find and use the Network – whether you want to learn to cycle from scratch, start cycling again, or venture out to places never before reached by bike. Over one third of the Network is on traffic-free routes, often on renovated railway tracks, riversides and forest paths – ideal for those newcomers wanting safety from traffic and idyllic for experienced cyclists too.

The Network is designed for you to use straight from home. The routes pass through the middle of most major towns and cities in the UK. A continuous programme of extensions is creating links to reach more and more railway stations, schools, offices and shops, as well as other Millennium and heritage sites. By 2005, the Network is forecast to pass within two miles of over 30 million people!

Every kind of journey is possible, whether cycling to work or to school, making local shopping trips, going on family leisure rides or undertaking long-distance "green tourism" trips.

The Network is a unique national asset, completely free and open to all. It gives countless historic landmarks like old railways, canals, bridges and viaducts a new lease of life. Everyone can help their environment by driving less and cycling and walking more – and fewer cars on the roads means cleaner air for everyone! Cycling is a great way to get fit and is enjoyed by all ages.

We very much hope you enjoy the National Cycle Network. Please respect other users and follow the advice in this book. Thank you.

HISTORY OF SUSTRANS AND THE NATIONAL CYCLE NETWORK

The National Cycle Network is a magnificent visionary scheme passing through all the major urban centres of the United Kingdom and linking these cities via 10,000 miles of traffic-free routes, quiet lanes and traffic-calmed city streets to form a comprehensive cycling network right across the country. It is a traffic partnership project par excellence – hundreds of bodies are involved, including local authorities, utility companies, landowners, heritage and wildlife bodies, rail operators and central government.

The origins of Sustrans, an abbreviated form of Sustainable Transport, can be traced back to the significant date of July 7th 1977 (7/7/77) when a group of Bristol environmentalists, driven by a desire to do something about the dangers to the environment recently highlighted by the oil crisis, set up a cycling group known as Cyclebag. Within two years the group started a programme of building cycle routes which has continued unabated, although now on a vastly expanded scale, over the last 25 years.

The dismantled railway line running between Bristol and Bath was the first railway path they converted for use by cyclists and walkers. The five-mile stretch near Saltford was where Sustrans' great enterprise started, a vision initially made possible by back-breaking work undertaken by enthusiastic volunteers. Since that modest beginning, what started as a single five-mile linear route will become a 10,000-mile network covering the whole country, built at a cost of more than £400 million.

View along Bristol & Bath Railway Path looking towards Bristol Temple Meads – opened 1984.

A Community Programme team constructing the York & Selby Path, 1985.

30 years of cycle planning and Sustrans is pursuing strategies to bring cycling back into the public domain.

Following its success on the Bristol & Bath Railway Path, Sustrans made full use of the various employment schemes available in the early 1980s such as Youth Opportunities Programmes and the Community Programme with hundreds of young people helping to build more paths in other cities such as Plymouth and Glasgow. At one stage, Sustrans was in the unusual position of having just one paid employee (John Grimshaw) and 800 people working on these very useful employment programmes! Many of those who supervised the early gangs have since gone on to become Regional Managers, responsible for building the Network. No one can accuse them of lacking hands-on experience!

Negotiations with British Waterways began in 1980. Although there are 2,000 miles of canal towpaths in the country, only a portion are passable by bike and in those days the useable mileage was even smaller. The Kennet & Avon Canal near Bath was covered in a foot of impassable sludge during the winter months. This was to be Sustrans' first towpath project and such was the state of the canal banks when work began

Sustrans is motivated by a desire to find solutions to the problems caused by the huge and relentless growth of traffic. Deaths, injuries, noise, pollution, the destruction of the environment and the creation of a lost generation of unfit children who will never have known the freedom offered by the bicycle, are all problems inherent in the traffic growth over the past 25 years. Every prediction indicates that things will get worse before they get better.

At the heart of the issue is the status and safety of cyclists and pedestrians in relation to the car. Proportionately, far more people cycle in Sweden, a country which is much colder, in Germany, which has a higher car ownership, and in Switzerland, which is considerably more hilly. Mile for mile, a cyclist in Britain is eight times more likely to be hurt in an accident than in Holland or Denmark.

In 1976 Denmark had the worst child accident rate in Europe – this led to an Act of Parliament which required local authorities to build safe cycle routes to school. Denmark is now one of the safest countries for cyclists in Europe. By contrast, Britain currently has the worst child accident rate in Europe and had to wait until 1998 before a Transport Bill was introduced that even mentioned Safe Routes to School. Britain has lost

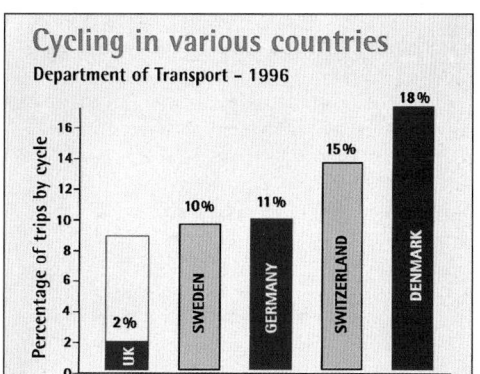

Diagram from Government's National Cycling Strategy showing cycling in various countries as a percentage of all trips. Government targets are to quadruple the low level of cycling in the UK by 2012, from 2% to +8%.

Detail from Ninth Legion by David Kemp showing use of old gas bottles and railway chairs.

that all new volunteers were told that their first job was to drive the dumper truck straight into the canal then retrieve it. The reason? The dumper truck had so often slipped into the water from the muddy 'path' that knowing how to get it out again was a most important skill to acquire! Over five years (1984-88) the path was rebuilt in stone from Bath all the way to Devizes. It is now tremendously popular as both a walking and cycling route.

Sustrans' reputation as path builders was growing year on year. More and more cities such as Derby, York, Liverpool and Sunderland had paths built through them. It became Sustrans' intention to have one quality route in each major city to show the government that the creation of attractive, safe cycle routes generated thousands of cycle journeys that might not otherwise have taken place, and enabled huge numbers of the public to learn to cycle again.

Great use was made of recycled materials in the construction of these cycle paths: bridges were made of concrete railway sleepers, sculptures were created from old JCBs and seats from wooden sleepers. Deliberate attempts were made to include attractive features such as causeways through cuttings, allowing ponds to be formed adjacent to the path, the creation of

The Ninth Legion, 17 miles from Glasgow Central on the Johnstone to Greenock Path.

Path set on causeway through deep cutting on the Lochwinnoch Loop Line south west from Glasgow.

curves to break up the monotony of dead straight lines and bending the route to weave a way through mature trees. This concept of making each ride full of interesting features became known as the 'travelling landscape'.

After 15 years' experience of building paths, Sustrans began to capture the public imagination and launched a Supporter Programme. Supporter numbers rose from 200 in 1993 to 40,000 in 2001. By 1995 Sustrans was in a position to make a realistic bid to the Lottery for Millennium funds for the National Cycle Network, a vast and visionary scheme to create a 6,500-mile countrywide network of safe cycle routes by the year 2005 with 2,500 miles of the routes built by the year 2000. (The figure of 6,500 miles has since increased to 10,000 due to the enthusiasm for the project shown by local authorities all over the country).

The bid was successful and Sustrans was awarded £43.5 million. Although this was a huge amount, it only represented 20% of the total cost of the first phase of the project and the remainder of the funding comes from a variety of sources including local authorities, development agencies, the European Union, the Highways Agency, the cycle trade and industry, and from generous contributions from Sustrans supporters.

End of the 2nd Trailblazing Ride, from Belfast to Land's End, to promote the National Cycle Network.

Advanced stop line in York.

Britain's roads are the busiest in Europe and predictions are that the situation will get worse, particularly in the countryside. Sustrans' aims in creating the Network are threefold: it should be attractive for novices, memorable for visitors and useful for everyday cyclists. The routes also promote a programme of sculpture and bring great economic benefit to many areas of the country.

The National Cycle Network is designed to encourage the public to start cycling again. Sustrans believes that to persuade non-cyclists to take up cycling it is essential to provide them with safe, traffic-free routes so they can regain confidence. These special paths can then connect (ideally) traffic-calmed urban roads with a network of routes through the countryside using quiet roads carrying less than 1,000 vehicles a day (this may sound busy but works out at less than one car a minute).

In the cities the main thrust of Sustrans' work is to increase the profile and status of the cyclist by re-allocating road space to favour the cyclist over the car, for example in the provision of Advanced Stop Lines at traffic lights, re-inforcing the idea that cyclists matter. Campaigning for lower speed limits in cities could lead to a drastic reduction in deaths and injuries to cyclists and pedestrians.

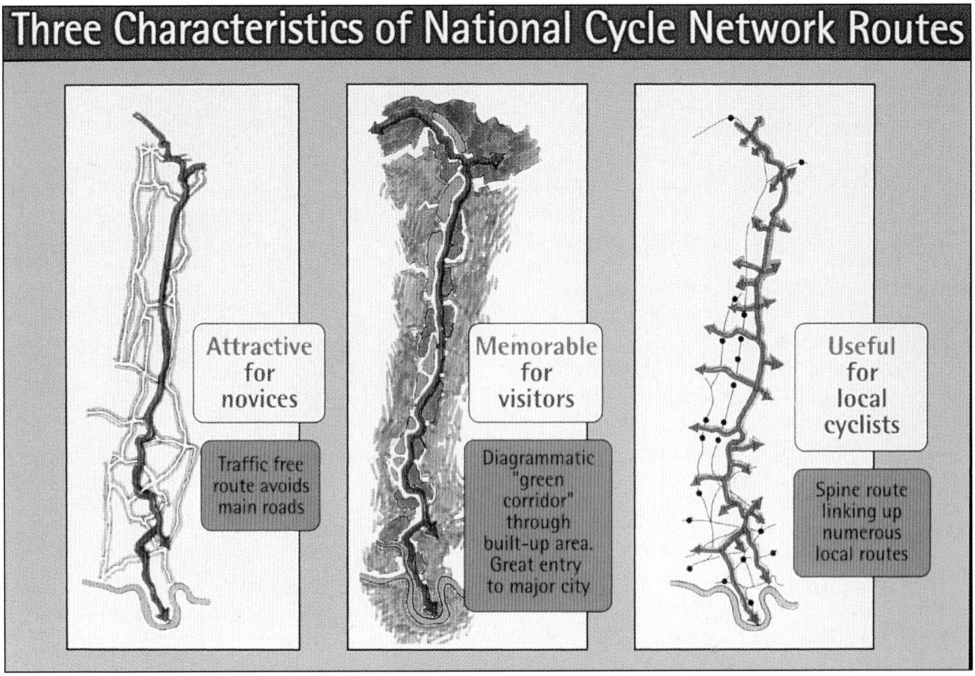

Three Characteristics of National Cycle Network Routes

Attractive for novices

Traffic free route avoids main roads

Memorable for visitors

Diagrammatic "green corridor" through built-up area. Great entry to major city

Useful for local cyclists

Spine route linking up numerous local routes

Diagram showing the three characteristics of the National Cycle Network (based on the Lee Valley Route, London).

Presentation of Millennium Milepost to the town of Odense (Denmark) to commemorate its Safe Routes to School exchange with Colchester.

The Safe Routes to Schools Project aims to change one of Britain's most shameful statistics: only 2% of journeys to school are made by bike, despite a huge majority of children wanting to get out of their parents' cars and onto their bikes. In Denmark the figure is 60%. Britain is one of the very few countries in Europe where more people cycle to work than to school. The benefits of reversing this trend are made patently clear at a school in Ipswich where 60% of the children arrive by bike. The school has won many sports competitions with other schools simply because the pupils are so much fitter.

Sculpture has come to be synonymous with the building of new sections of the Network. Starting in Consett, funded by Northern Arts, Andy Goldsworthy created the Lampton Worm, a long serpent sculpture running alongside the path. All over the country sculptures began appearing, carved from wood, sculpted from stone, welded from steel or built of brick. The Royal Bank of Scotland generously donated 1,000 mileposts with different versions designed by English, Scottish, Welsh and Irish sculptors.

Local economies have benefited enormously from the creation of Sustrans' long-distance routes. The first of these was the C2C (or Sea to Sea from the Cumbrian Coast to the North Sea) which led the way in featuring a mixture of traffic-free paths and on-road sections. Within a year of its opening 10,000 people had cycled the trail and spent over £1 million in the bed & breakfasts, Youth Hostels, pubs, cafes and shops along the way. In 1995 the C2C was the Global Winner of the 'British Airways Tourism for Tomorrow' awards. Since then many other long-distance routes have been opened and mapped, attracting many people to the idea of a cycling holiday for the first time in their lives and encouraging entrepreneurs to benefit from new business opportunities.

Sustrans has not restricted its vision to Britain alone. It is active in promoting EuroVelo, the European cycle route network, which aims to link countries throughout Europe. The first of these European routes to open was the North Sea Cyle Route taking in Norway, Sweden, Denmark, Germany, Holland and the East Coast of England and Scotland.

Route 5 – Reading to Holyhead and
Route 3 – Bristol to Land's End

HOW TO USE THIS GUIDE

This guide helps you to explore the National Cycle Network. Perhaps you would like to try out a section of the Network close to home? Maybe you are interested in planning a longer ride of several days and would like to see which of the long-distance routes best meets your requirements. Might the Network offer a safe and attractive way for you to cycle to work? Perhaps it will act as a catalyst for you to visit a nearby friend: cycle there and catch the train back or vice versa (check which way the wind is blowing!). Use your bike on the Network to explore nearby villages, towns and cities, canals, forests and country parks, ancient monuments and historic homes. From the vantage point of a bike saddle, visit Britain's rich industrial past and see how the National Cycle Network has helped regenerate derelict wasteland into corridors of greenery, dotted with specially commissioned sculptures.

The Network near you
In this guide the country has been divided into nine regional chapters, each of which starts with a map showing the Network in the area. Each route of the Network has been given a number (you may have already seen numbers on local signposts). The map will show you how close you are to the nearest part of the Network and where it goes north, south, east and west. As an introduction to the Network you may simply wish to go for a there-and-back ride on the nearest section of traffic-free trail. As you gain confidence you will no doubt want to try out other parts of the Network which make use of quiet minor lanes.

The Day Rides in the book
The 32 Day Rides in the book offer a tremendous variety of rides showing the various different aspects of the Network. Some go right through cities, including one which runs alongside the Thames in West London, others explore some of the more rugged and remote scenery of Scotland and Wales.

Planning longer trips
You may wish to start from home and make a trip to visit a friend or relative who lives on or close to the Network or perhaps you would like to

explore a different part of the country altogether. You have plenty of choice! The Network runs from Land's End to John o'Groats, from the spectacular coastline of West Wales to the Channel Ports of Dover and Ramsgate. Many of the long distance routes are covered by maps which enable you to complete a satisfying section of the Network. The most well-known of these is the C2C (Sea to Sea Route) from Whitehaven to Tynemouth but there are many others, the easiest being the Hull to Harwich route down the East Coast of the country. The hardest is probably Lôn Las Cymru (the Welsh National Route), crossing three ranges of mountains on its way from Holyhead to Cardiff. The range of award-winning Long Distance route maps published by Sustrans is detailed on page 218.

National Cycle Network Information Service
Based at Sustrans headquarters in Bristol, the Information Service offers a range of free information sheets covering many aspects of the National Cycle Network, including details about the Safe Routes to Schools Project, the Stamping Scheme, Millennium Mileposts plus a full selection of cycling literature which can be purchased. Goods for sale include the award-winning National Route Maps covering the long-distance routes within the National Cycle Network, packs of leaflets produced by local authorities and cycle guidebooks describing rides in many regions of the country.

The Information Service has an on-line mail order service so you can place a credit card order for any product available 24 hours a day from anywhere in the world via the website:
www.nationalcyclenetwork.org.uk
The website also offers detailed on-line mapping of Network routes.

National Cycle Network Information Service
PO Box 21, Bristol BS99 2HA
Telephone: 0117 929 0888

The opening times of the office are:
9.00am-5.00pm Monday to Friday excluding Bank Holidays.

Selected traffic-free paths

1. Gloucester & Sharpness Canal *2 miles* (Frampton-on-Severn)
2. Nailsworth Railway Path *5 miles*
3. Cotswold Water Park, South Cerney *9 miles*
4. Marlborough - Chiseldon Railway Path *8 miles*
5. Bristol City Centre - Pill Riverside Path *5 miles*
6. Bristol & Bath Railway Path *16 miles*
7. Kennet & Avon Canal *22 miles* (Bath - Devizes)
8. Chippenham & Calne Railway Path *6 miles*
9. Castleman Trail *8 miles* (Poole - Wimbourne)
10. Bournemouth Promenade *4 miles*
11. Bridgwater & Taunton Canal *14 miles*
12. Grand Western Canal, Tiverton *2¹/₂ miles*
13. Budleigh Salterton & Exmouth *2 miles*
14. Exeter Riverside & Canal *7 miles*
15. Okehampton to Lake Viaduct *7 miles*
16. Tarka Trail *31 miles* (Meeth - Petrockstowe - Great Torrington - Bideford - Barnstaple - Braunton)
17. Plym Valley Trail *9 miles* (Plymouth - Clearbrook)
18. Camel Trail *17 miles* (Padstow - Wadebridge - Bodmin)
19. St Austell, Pentewan & Megavissey *5 miles*
20. Mounts Bay *4 miles*

Day Rides

A. Bristol & Bath Railway Path *16 miles*
B. Bridgwater & Taunton Canal *14 miles*
C. Plym Valley Path towards Dartmoor *9 miles*
D. Bodmin & Padstow Railway Path (The Camel Trail) *12 miles*

— National Cycle Network
— Selected traffic-free sections
— Network to be completed by 2005
⊙ Selected railway stations
— Regional Cycle Routes
Route numbers
3 National **10** Regional

Ilfracombe
Braunton
31
Ba
Bidef
Gre
16
Bude **3** Holsworthy
Okehampton
Camelford
Wadebridge
Padstow **27**
D
Tavistock
Newquay **32** **18**
Bodmin
⊙ Bodmin Parkway
3 ⊙ Lostwithiel **2** **17**
19
Truro ⊙ St Austell Plymouth
Hayle Redruth Mevagissey
20 Camborne
3
Land's End Penzance

20 miles
30 km

Cheltenham

41

Gloucester

Stroud

2

Berkeley

Nailsworth

Cirencester

41

3

45

41

10

Swindon

4

Clevedon

5

Chippenham

8

Avebury

Melksham

Marlborough

Bristol

6

10

Calne

Weston-super-Mare

3

Bath

4

Devizes

4

North Wessex Downs

Burnham-on-Sea

Trowbridge

7

33

Radstock

Frome

Wells

Warminster

Exmoor

Bridgwater

Glastonbury

24

Salisbury

Taunton

B

11

Castle Cary

3

Gillingham

12

Yeovil

25

41

Tiverton

Tiverton Parkway

30

26

Sherborne

Blandford Forum

ington

33

Chard

41

leigh

Axminster

2

Wimborne Minster

Exeter

2

Seaton

Lyme Regis

Dorchester

Poole

9

10

Christchurch

14

13

Sidmouth

Bridport

Wareham

Bournemouth

oor

Budleigh Salterton

ewton Abbot

Exmouth

Weymouth

Dawlish

Teignmouth

Torquay

Totnes

Paignton

2

Salcombe

Long distance maps available

Gloucester

Severn & Thames Cycle Route

Bristol

Ilfracombe

Taunton

The West Country Way

The Devon Coast to Coast Route

© Crown copyright

Plymouth

The Cornish Way

17

THE WEST COUNTRY

On the 'first and last' section of the Cornish Way; Marazion, near Penzance, overlooking St. Michael's Mount.

The character of the West Country is largely defined by agriculture, tourism and a very extensive coastline – there is little heavy industry and Bristol and Plymouth are the largest cities. The National Cycle Network passes through many attractive towns and cities such as Bath, Wells, Glastonbury and Salisbury, visits Exmoor and Dartmoor (the two National Parks in the region) and explores much of the coastline of the Southwest Peninsula, reaching the sea at many places including Ilfracombe, Bude, Barnstaple, Padstow, Penzance, Plymouth, Exmouth and Weymouth.

Bristol is the headquarters of Sustrans and is appropriately at a major junction of the National Cycle Network Millennium Routes. Route 4 runs from West Wales across the old Severn Bridge through Bristol, Newbury and Reading to London; Route 41 runs north from Bristol to Gloucester; Route 3 (The Cornish Way and the West Country Way) stretches from Land's End to Bristol (or Bath), running the length of Cornwall, up over Exmoor, across the Somerset Levels with a final climb over the Mendips. The other Millennium Route in the West Country is the Devon Coast to Coast, connecting Plymouth on the South Coast with Ilfracombe on the North.

The Bristol & Bath Railway Path (featured on pages 24-27) was Sustrans' very first project, started in 1979 and completed in 1986. It now carries over 1.7 million journeys a year.

NATIONAL NETWORK HIGHLIGHTS

Clifton Suspension Bridge
The Clifton Suspension Bridge forms a spectacular gateway to Bristol spanning 700ft and crossing nearly 230ft above Route 4 on the riverside below. This bridge was designed by the legendary engineer Isambard Kingdom Brunel in 1829 when he was only 23, but not completed until 1864, some five years after his death.

Avebury
There is no better way of approaching Avebury than on foot or cycle. The route from Chippenham to Marlborough runs right across the stone circle, along an alignment which has been used for perhaps 3,500 years. In the distance the route climbs to join the Ridgeway which is said to be Britain's oldest 'road', thought to have been in use for 6,000 years!

Land's End Trailblazing Ride
The final day of the celebrated 1996 Trailblazing Ride from Belfast to Land's End via Holyhead, Cardiff, Bristol and Plymouth. Along the way the riders attended numerous receptions where local authorities affirmed their support for the National Cycle Network.

Severn Bridge
The first Severn Bridge takes Route 4 from Bristol to Chepstow and Newport. It opened in 1966, crossing the River Severn with a central span of 3250ft and two side spans of 1000ft each. The bridge, which has an aerofoil deck, was the first of its kind, and provides a clear deck for cyclists well separated from traffic. Four miles downstream, the second Severn Crossing makes no such provision for either pedestrians or cyclists.

Calne Millennium Bridge
Jack Konynenburg, North Wiltshire District Council's officer, has commissioned no less than three wonderful new bridges to adorn National Cycle Network Route 4 through the Calne and Chippenham area. This modern landmark designed by Mark Lovell comprises a single laminated timber arch balanced against the offset bridge deck. This 'Black Dog' bridge crosses the main A4 and completes a largely traffic-free path along the old branch line to Calne.

Meldon Viaduct
Through the boldness and vision of Devon County Council and Bordon Quarries, the spectacular Meldon Viaduct has been restored and re-used as an unforgettable gateway to Okehampton and Dartmoor.

NATIONAL NETWORK HIGHLIGHTS

Halgavor Bridge

Halgavor Bridge provides a safe crossing of the busy A30 at Bodmin and a connection to Lanhydrock House and Bodmin Parkway Station. This elegant stainless steel and carbon fibre bridge was commissioned by the Highways Agency. The connecting routes either side are built on land provided by Forest Enterprise and the National Trust, both key contributors to the National Cycle Network.

Maiden Newton Summer Work Camp 2001

One of a number of summer camps arranged by Sustrans each year, this one built the missing link, enabling Dorset County Council to open the whole of Route 26 between Dorchester and Yeovil.

Bournemouth Promenade

The opening of this promenade to cyclists is one of the National Cycle Network's most remarkable and long awaited events. The Council has taken the wholly pragmatic decision of allowing cycling for most of the day, most of the year, but not at peak times. This is an excellent arrangement, which radically improves the whole route in this area, as well as providing a valuable local resource at little cost.

Mounts Bay Promenade - Penzance to Marazion

This work, along with the traffic-free route to Mousehole, is one of the considerable achievements in the West Country. The actress, Jenny Agutter, opened the new promenade in May 2000, part of which was made through Railtrack's providing space beside their main line to Penzance Station.

River Yeo Swing Bridge

This bridge at Barnstaple has opened up the whole river frontage. Sited on the line of the former railway to Ilfracombe, the design of the Swing Bridge reflects the boating technology of the area.

Black Bridge

This bridge over the River Avon at Chippenham makes an impressive addition to the trio of bridges designed by Mark Lovell for the enterprising North Wiltshire District Council.

City Focus - South West

Maps & guides are available from National Cycle Network Information unless indicated otherwise. See page 23 for contact details.

Bath

The Severn & Thames Cycle Route Map shows Route 4 through Bath. It runs west along the Riverside Path then along the Railway Path to Bristol. To the east the Kennet & Avon Canal towpath leads to Bradford-on-Avon.

Bristol & Bath CycleCity Map. A-Z style map showing traffic-free, official and advisory routes, with plenty of extra information about cycle shops, cycling contacts, train services and relevant local publications. RC01 - £4.95.

Contacts:

Envolve, Bath Environment Centre, Green Park Station, Bath, BA1 1JB. Tel: 01225 787910. Website: www.envolve.co.uk

Bristol

The Severn & Thames Cycle Route Map shows Route 41 that goes from Bristol, past the CREATE Centre, along the Avon Gorge and Route 4, running east along the Railway Path to Bath.

Bristol & Bath CycleCity Map: see above under **Bath**. RC01 - £4.95.

Contacts:

CycleWest, 84 Colston Street, Bristol, BS1 5BB. Tel: 0117 929 0440. E-mail address: post@cyclewest.org.uk. Website at www.cyclewest.org.uk.

Exeter

The completed National Route will run south along both sides of the River Exe as part of Route 2, the South Coast Route from Plymouth to Dover.

The Exeter Cycle Guide & Map shows the traffic-free route along the Exe River and Exe Canal, National Routes, other advisory cycle routes and details of local bike shops. Available from Exeter Tourist Information Centre. Tel: 01392 265700.

Plymouth

The Devon Coast to Coast Map shows the proposed and existing National Routes through Plymouth from Torpoint Ferry to Millbay Docks and Laira Bridge, the starting point of the Plym Valley Route.

Plymouth Cycle Guide shows the Network, offroad cycle routes and onroad cycle lanes. Available from the Tourist Information Centre. Tel: 01752 304849.

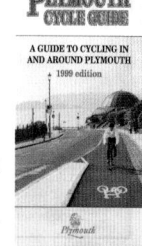

Taunton

Somerset Cycle Guide, at a scale of 1:165,000, shows Route 3 (The West Country Way) and Regional Route 30 plus street maps of Taunton, Bridgwater, Yeovil, Glastonbury, Street and Wells. RPL18 - £3.95.

The West Country Way Map shows Route 3 through Taunton, running west from the centre of town along Castle Street through Bishop's Hull and Hillfarrance towards Tiverton and northeast from the centre of town along the Bridgwater & Taunton Canal.

Other towns covered by leaflets:

Swindon Cycle Map & Guide shows existing and planned cycle routes on one side of the map and details of seven leisure rides on the other side. Available from Swindon Tourist Information Centre. Tel: 01793 530328.

NN4A - £5.99

NN27 - £5.99

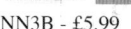
NN3B - £5.99

NN3A - £5.99

TRAFFIC-FREE PATHS PARTICULARLY SUITABLE FOR FAMILIES

St Austell to Pentewan, The Lost Gardens of Heligan and Mevagissey. 6 miles

This route is now almost entirely traffic-free. Cornwall County Council has carried out a great deal of work to make a new riverside path. The old carriageway is a relatively easy climb to Heligan Gardens and then, after great views, it's down all the way to Mevagissey.

Bristol City Centre - Pill Riverside Path. 5 miles

A riverside path running from Bristol city centre past the CREATE Centre and beneath Brunel's Clifton Suspension Bridge through the

Avon Gorge to Ham Green and Pill. A real delight in the changing autumn colours.

Exeter St Davids Station to the Quayside and Turf Lock. 6 miles

Although this route has been in existence for some years, the opening of the new bridge over the Exe, just upstream from the Mill, will create a focus of a whole network of routes radiating in all directions as well as further key links in the National Cycle Network.

Chippenham & Calne Railway Path. 6 miles

This section of the Severn & Thames Cycle Route runs along the course of the old railway that used to link the two towns and crosses the A4 on a unique timber-arched Millennium bridge.

Castleman Trail from Upton (near Poole) to Merley (near Wimborne Minster). 8 miles

A woodland railway path between Ringwood and Poole on the course of the old Dorchester to Southampton Railway Line. Two sections of four miles each.

Tarka Trail from Meeth to Bideford, Barnstaple & Braunton. 30 miles

A magnificent railway path from the heart of Devon to the north coast along the estuaries of the Rivers Taw and Torridge, passing through the historic town of Barnstaple.

USEFUL MAPS & GUIDES

For details of the full range of maps, guides and other products available contact: **National Cycle Network Information, PO Box 21, Bristol BS99 2HA. Tel: 0117 929 0888. Or visit www.nationalcyclenetwork.org.uk**
The range of National Cycle Network Maps is described in more detail on pages 218-237.

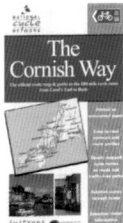 

32 Cornish Way Cycle Route (Land's End – Bude)
123 miles. NN3B - £5.99

31 27 Devon Coast to Coast Cycle Route (Ilfracombe – Plymouth)
102 miles. NN27 - £5.99

 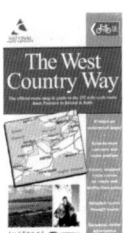

4 41 Severn & Thames Cycle Route (Gloucester – Newbury)
128 miles. NN4A - £5.99

3 West Country Way Cycle Route (Padstow – Bristol)
252 miles. NN3A - £5.99

The Ultimate Devon Coast to Coast Guide. RG58 - £5.95

The Ultimate West Country Way Guide. RG35 - £8.95

Cycling Without Traffic: South West
30 traffic-free rides described in detail in this well illustrated guide to family cycling. Includes the Camel Trail, the Tarka Trail and the Bristol & Bath Railway Path. RBA02 - £10.99

More Cycling Without Traffic: South West.
30 more traffic-free rides described in detail in this well illustrated guide to family cycling. Includes Forest of Dean, New Forest and Exe Valley routes. RBA13 - £11.99

30 South Somerset Cycle Route
80-mile signed, circular route, linking Yeovil, Castle Cary and Ilminster and connecting to National Route 3. FPR01 - FREE

41 Explore North Dorset.
73-mile circular route linking Shaftesbury, Blandford Forum and Sturminster Newton. FPR03 - FREE

20 Wiltshire Cycleway
160-mile signed circular route, taking in Salisbury, Bradford-on-Avon and Marlborough. Links to National Route 4. FPR02 - FREE

4 Bristol – Bath Railway Path
The first Sustrans cycle path – 13 miles long, now used for over 1.7 million journeys every year. FPR31 - FREE

BRISTOL & BATH RAILWAY PATH

Starting less than a mile from Sustrans' Bristol headquarters, the Bristol & Bath Railway Path was one of the charity's earliest successes and has happily and proudly stood the test of time, with each year adding something new to this extraordinarily popular route. It represents a wonderful escape from the urban heart of Bristol into the countryside and on into the centre of Bath. Even the inner city section has a green and rural feeling to it, passing through wooded cuttings with a plethora of wildflowers along the verges in the spring and early summer. The ride takes in a feast of attractions on its course from the centre of Bristol to the centre of Bath:

sculptures of wood, metal and stone (keep an eye out for the upside-down fish and the drinking giant!), the ¼-mile tunnel at Staple Hill, the old train station at Bitton complete with real, working steam engines, several crossings of the meandering, peaceful River Avon, glades of broadleaf woodland carpeted with bluebells in the late spring in Kelston Woods and finally a riverside stretch from the end of the railway path into the heart of the historic city of Bath.

The Bristol & Bath Railway Path has created a linear park into the heart of Bristol.

Starting points

1. Bristol Bridge, Castle Park in the centre of Bristol.
2. The Riverside Path, just off the A4 Upper Bristol Road in Bath.

Distance

16 miles one way, 32 miles return. If you start in Bristol, good turnaround/refreshment points are at Warmley (12 miles round trip), Bitton (17 miles round trip) and Saltford (22 miles round trip).

Grade: Easy.

Surface

Excellent surface throughout, almost all tarmac.

Roads, traffic, suitability for young children

Traffic-free path, ideal for beginners. The signposted approach roads from both Bristol and Bath city centres carry some traffic.

Hills: None.

Refreshments

Lots of choice in Bristol.
Cafes on the railway path at Warmley (seasonal) and at Bitton Station (at the weekend, all year round).
Stationmaster PH, Warmley;
Bird in Hand PH, Jolly Sailor PH, Saltford.
Lots of choice in Bath.

Leaflets

CycleCity's *Bristol and Bath Cycling Map* is an excellent publication showing the traffic-free paths, signposted cycle routes, advisory routes plus a wealth of other information. It costs £4.95 and is available from the National Cycle Network Information Service, PO Box 21, Bristol BS99 2HA (0117 929 0888) or visit: www.nationalcyclenetwork.org.uk

Silhouettes by Katy Hallett set in windows of the ruined Mangotsfield Station.

Nearest railway stations

Bristol Temple Meads, Bath Spa.

The National Cycle Network in the area

Route 4 runs from South Wales to London and uses the whole of the railway path. Routes 4 and 41 together form the Severn & Thames Cycle Route from Gloucester to Newbury. Route 3, the West Country Way and the Cornish Way, heads south west from Bristol to the furthest tip of mainland Britain at Land's End.

Other nearby rides (waymarked or traffic-free)

1. A section of the railway path (between Saltford and Mangotsfield) is used by the Avon Cycleway, an 85-mile signposted route using the network of quiet lanes around Bristol. Leaflet available from Bristol City Council. Tel: 0117 922 2000.

2. The five-mile, traffic-free Pill Riverside Path runs from the Bristol Harbourside along Cumberland Road, then alongside the River Avon to Pill, passing beneath the Clifton Suspension Bridge. There is also a link to this path through Leigh Woods.

3. The Kennet & Avon Canal Towpath from Bath to Devizes is open to cyclists free of charge.

Bath Abbey and Pump Rooms.

DAY RIDE

BRISTOL & BATH RAILWAY PATH

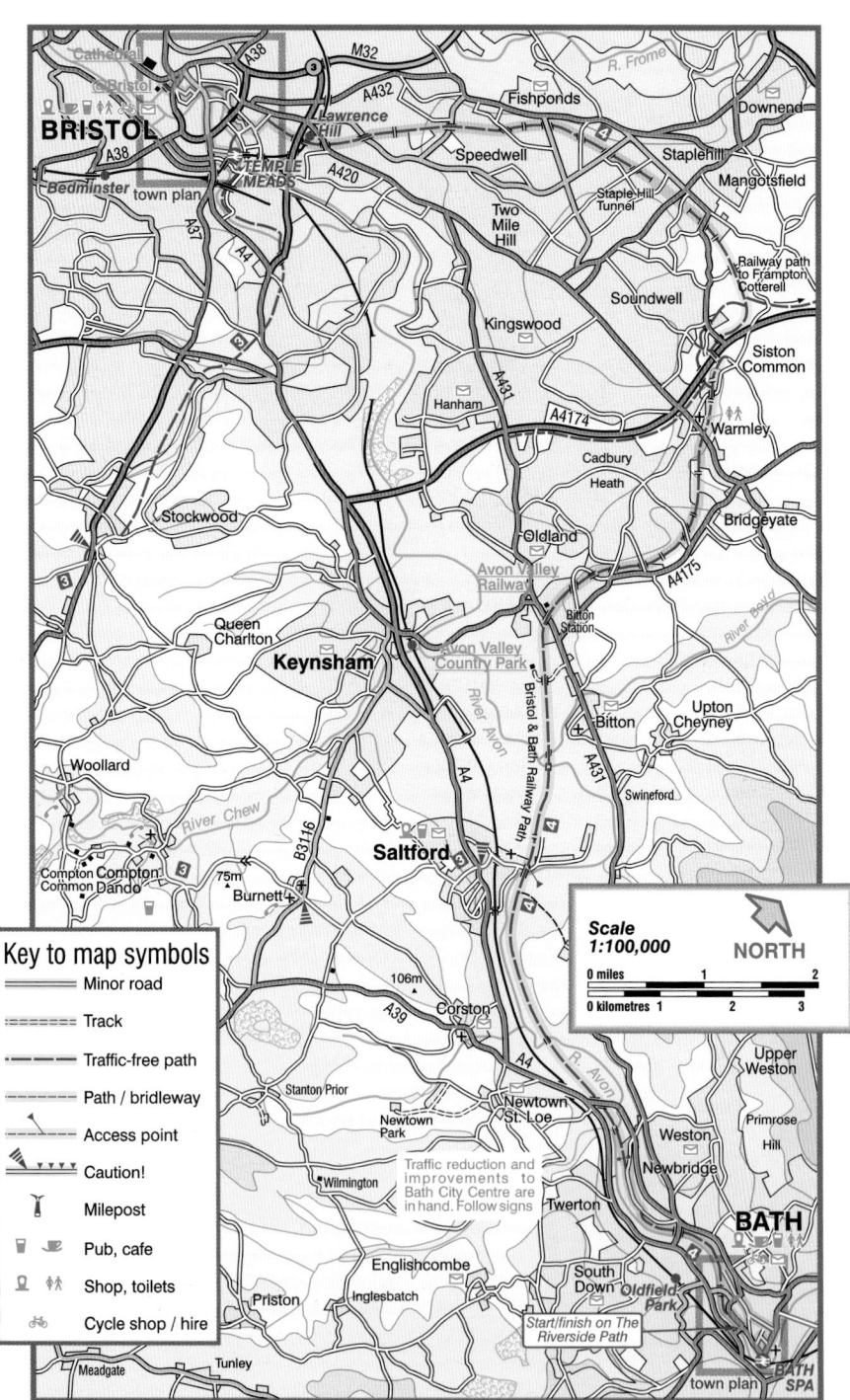

Key to map symbols

═══	Minor road
═══	Track
‒‒‒	Traffic-free path
‒ ‒ ‒	Path / bridleway
▾	Access point
▾▾▾▾	Caution!
𝟙	Milepost
▯ 🍴	Pub, cafe
𝛀 👫	Shop, toilets
🚲	Cycle shop / hire

Scale
1:100,000

NORTH

0 miles ———— 1 ———— 2
0 kilometres 1 —— 2 —— 3

Traffic reduction and improvements to Bath City Centre are in hand. Follow signs

Start/finish on The Riverside Path

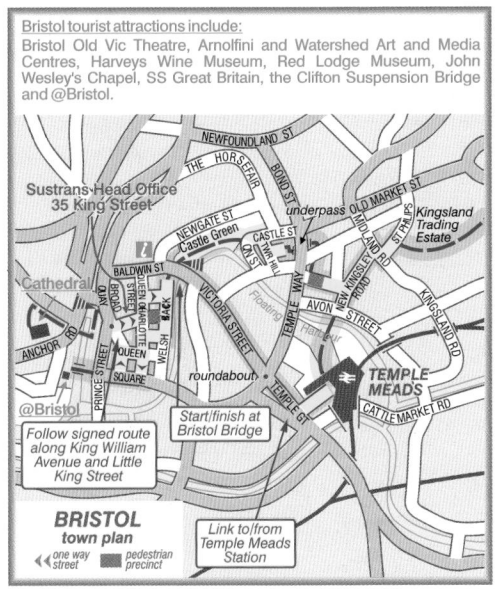

Bristol tourist attractions include:
Bristol Old Vic Theatre, Arnolfini and Watershed Art and Media Centres, Harveys Wine Museum, Red Lodge Museum, John Wesley's Chapel, SS Great Britain, the Clifton Suspension Bridge and @Bristol.

BRISTOL
town plan
‹‹ one way street   ■ pedestrian precinct

Ring Road sculpture by Jim Paulsen.

Route instructions (from Bristol to Bath)

1. From the traffic lights on the Broadmead side of Bristol Bridge in the centre of Bristol follow signs for the Bristol & Bath Railway Path on the traffic-free path alongside the River Avon across Castle Park.

2. Follow the waymarked route along Castle Street, Tower Hill and Jacob Street. Use the subway beneath Temple Way, go past Gardiner Haskins (Straight Street).

3. Turn right on Russ Street then left at the T-junction with New Kingsley Road. At the T-junction with Midland Road turn right then left onto St Philips Road. The railway path starts after 200 yards.

4. Follow the railway path for 13 miles through Staple Hill Tunnel, the new Ring Road across Siston Common, Warmley, Bitton and Saltford to its end at the Brassmill

Lane Trading Estate on the outskirts of Bath.

5. Continue along Brassmill Lane, bearing right onto the riverside path.

6. For Bath city centre, turn off the riverside path after one mile, just after Victoria suspension bridge over the river, and follow the waymarked Route 4 via Nelson Villas, King Street and Monmouth Street.

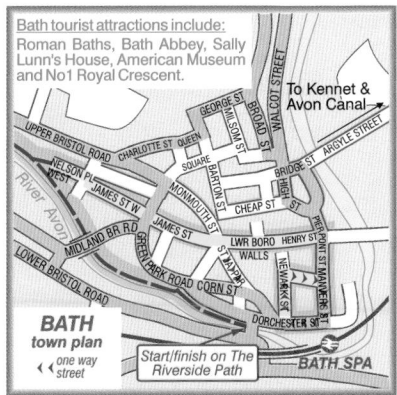

Bath tourist attractions include:
Roman Baths, Bath Abbey, Sally Lunn's House, American Museum and No1 Royal Crescent.

BATH
town plan
‹‹ one way street

Great Pulteney Street, Bath.

BRIDGWATER & TAUNTON CANAL TOWPATH

This easy ride along the towpath of the Bridgwater & Taunton Canal forms part of a much longer route; as the Cornish Way and West Country Way, National Route 3, runs for 313 miles from Land's End to Bristol. The canal was opened in 1827 as part of a grand scheme to link the Bristol Channel with the English Channel, so avoiding the dangerous passage around Land's End. Sadly, the great link never materialised in full. The Bridgwater & Taunton Canal and the Grand Western Canal near Tiverton (also used on the West Country Way) are all that remain of this ambitious project. As a cyclist along the towpath, enjoy the abundant birdlife – swans, herons and a variety of ducks can all be seen along the canal. There is also a series of stone sculptures of the planets, conceived and built by Pip Youngman in 1997. There are many options to plan your own circular rides using the wonderful network of flat lanes on the Somerset Levels as an alternative to returning along the towpath.

Bridgwater & Taunton Canal.

Starting points
1. Town Bridge, Bridgwater.
2. Bridge Street, Taunton.

Distance
14 miles one way, 28 miles return. For shorter routes (starting from Bridgwater) there are good turnaround points at the Harvest Moon PH in North Newton (10 miles round trip), the Canal Centre and Cafe at Maunsel Lock (14 miles round trip) or the pubs in Creech St Michael (21 miles round trip).

Grade
Easy.

Surface
The towpath has a variable quality gravel surface.

Roads, traffic, suitability for young children
The towpath is suitable for children, provided they know about the dangers of water. There is a three-mile road section in the middle of the ride on quiet lanes south of North Newton.

Hills
No hills along the towpath.

Refreshments
Lots of choice in Bridgwater. Boat & Anchor PH, Huntworth; Harvest Moon PH, North Newton;

A section of the towpath on the Bridgwater & Taunton Canal.

Cafe at the Canal Centre (south of North Newton), open 2.00-6.00; The Bell Inn and The Riverside Tavern, Creech St Michael. Lots of choice in Taunton.

Nearest railway stations
Bridgwater or Taunton.

The National Cycle Network in the area
This ride is part of the West Country Way (Route 3) which runs from Padstow to Bristol. Route 33, the Wessex Cycle Route, is a planned north-south route linking Taunton with the South Coast Route (Route 2) at Axminster and Seaton.

Other nearby rides (waymarked or traffic-free)
There is an excellent network of quiet, flat lanes on the Somerset Levels, to the east of Bridgwater. The South Somerset Cycle Ride is an 80-mile waymarked route around the lovely lanes and ham-stone villages of South Somerset.

The towpath through Creech St. Michael takes you right into the centre of Taunton.

DAY RIDE

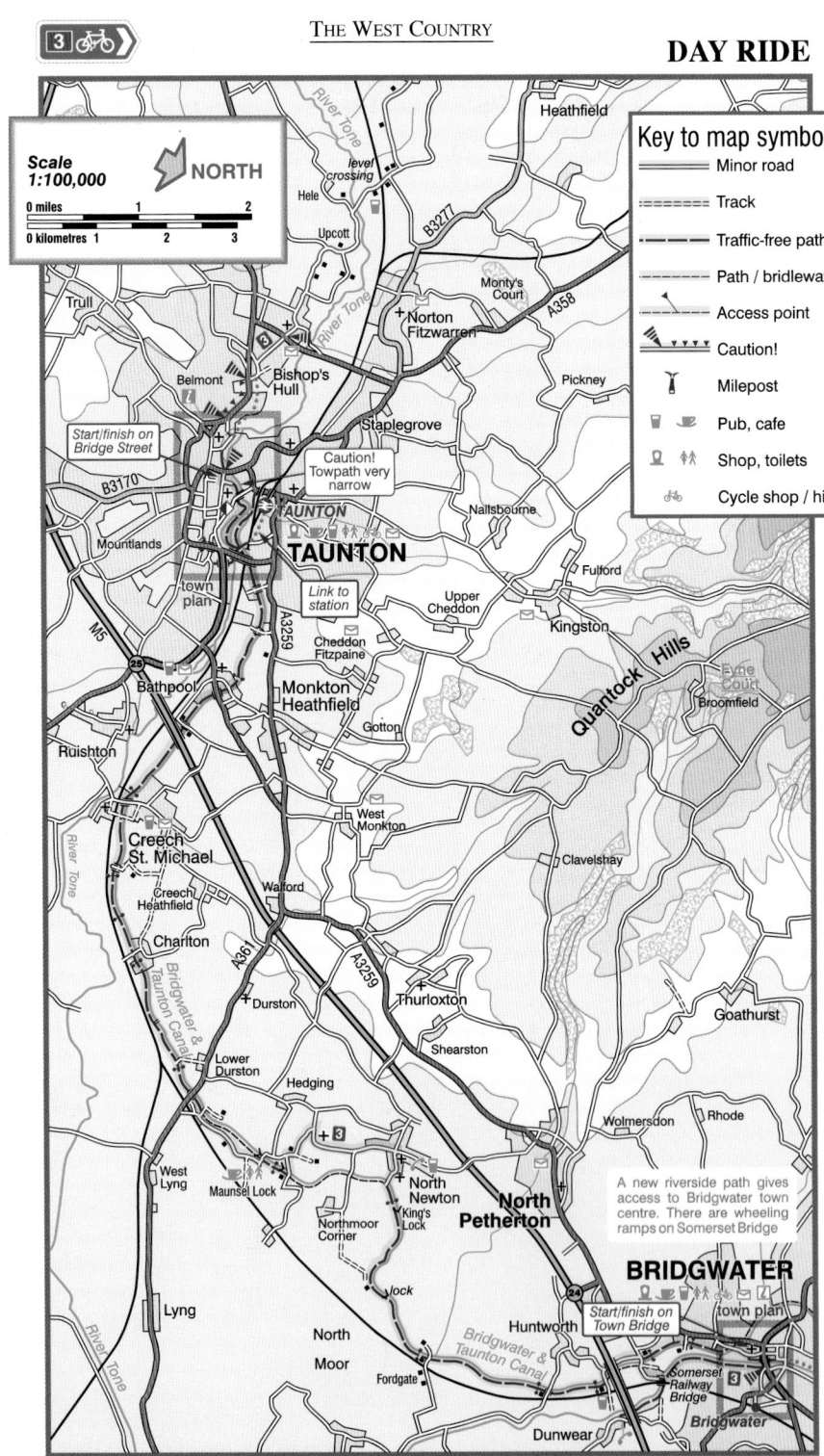

Key to map symbols

━━━━	Minor road
=======	Track
━ ━ ━	Traffic-free path
- - - -	Path / bridleway
◄- - - -	Access point
▼▼▼▼▼	Caution!
⫿	Milepost
🍺 ☕	Pub, cafe
♿ 🚶	Shop, toilets
🚲	Cycle shop / hire

Scale
1:100,000

NORTH

0 miles   1   2
0 kilometres 1   2   3

Heathfield

River Tone

level crossing

Hele

Upcott

B3277

Monty's Court

A358

Trull

Norton Fitzwarren

River Tone

Belmont

Bishop's Hull

Pickney

Start/finish on Bridge Street

Staplegrove

Caution! Towpath very narrow

B3170

TAUNTON

Nailsbourne

Mountlands

TAUNTON

town plan

Link to station

Upper Cheddon

Fulford

M5

25

Bathpool

A3259

Cheddon Fitzpaine

Kingston

Quantock Hills

Eyre Court

Broomfield

Ruishton

Monkton Heathfield

Gotton

Creech St. Michael

West Monkton

Creech Heathfield

Walford

Clavelshay

A361

Charlton

River Tone

Bridgwater & Taunton Canal

A3259

Durston

Thurloxton

Goathurst

Lower Durston

Shearston

Hedging

Wolmersdon

Rhode

West Lyng

3

Maunsel Lock

Northmoor Corner

King's Lock

North Newton

North Petherton

A new riverside path gives access to Bridgwater town centre. There are wheeling ramps on Somerset Bridge

lock

Lyng

North Moor

lock

Huntworth

Bridgwater & Taunton Canal

24

Start/finish on Town Bridge

BRIDGWATER

town plan

Fordgate

Somerset Railway Bridge

3

Bridgwater

Dunwear

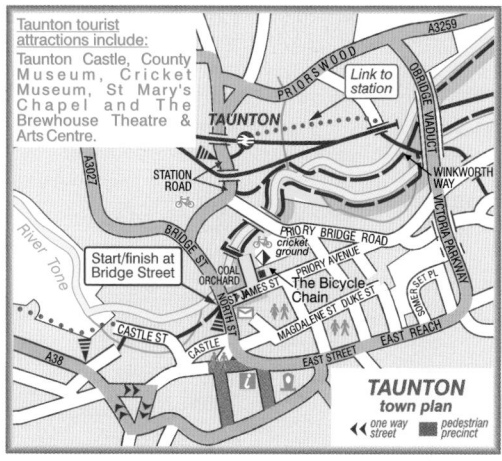

Bridgwater & Taunton Canal.

Route instructions
(from Bridgwater to Taunton)

1. From Town Bridge in the centre of Bridgwater, follow Binford Place through Goodland Gardens under the underpass, then left along the Old Taunton Road.

2. Cross the road over the canal and turn left down onto the towpath. Follow in the same direction as the track turns to a tarmac lane and passes beneath the M5. On a sharp right hand bend turn left over the wooden bridge towards the Boat & Anchor pub then turn right along the towpath.

3. Follow the towpath for four miles. Shortly after King's Lock the track turns to tarmac. Follow the road as it crosses the canal. At the T-junction by the Harvest Moon pub at the end of Church Street in North Newton turn left then shortly left again signposted 'Durston, Lyng, Canal Centre'.

4. Ignore the first road to the left (this is a no through road to Coxhill). Go past Maunsel House and take the next road left signposted 'Canal Centre'. Immediately after crossing the bridge over the canal turn right past the cafe/Canal Centre (this would be a good turnaround spot if you are looking for a short return ride).

5. Leave the towpath after ¼ mile and continue in the same direction on a minor lane. **Easy to miss**. After one mile turn right by the bridge over the canal (Outwood Swing Bridge) then left to rejoin towpath.

6. Follow the towpath for 6½ miles, passing through Creech St Michael and beneath the M5 bridge. Shortly after a second tall road bridge the waymarked route leaves the towpath and bears up to the left to a T-junction with a lane. (*To reach the station, turn right at Obridge under the railway line and first left parallel to the railway.*)

7. (Taunton town centre) Turn left, then immediately after crossing the river turn right along the riverside path onto track. This turns to tarmac then track again. Immediately after the Somerset Cricket Ground bear left through car park at the 'Route 3' sign.

8. At the mini-roundabout go straight ahead. At the T-junction just past the Bicycle Chain shop turn right along St. James Street to reach Taunton town centre (Bridge Street/North Fore Street).

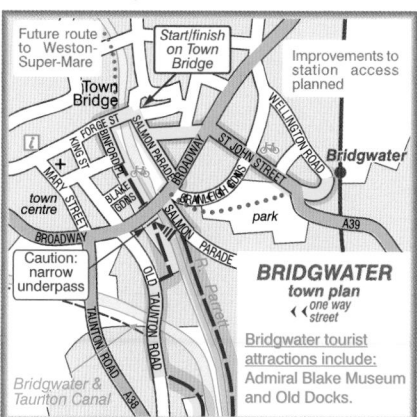

Approaching Taunton.

31

THE CAMEL TRAIL – BODMIN TO PADSTOW

The Camel Trail is the most popular tourist cycle route in the country with over 350,000 visitors a year. This superb ride follows the course of an old railway line from Bodmin along the wooded valley of the River Camel and the sandy shores of the Camel Estuary to Padstow. It also forms part of the West Country Way which runs from Padstow to Bristol. In addition to there-and-back rides along the Camel Trail there are many possible loops using the network of country lanes to explore the coastline east of the estuary at Port Isaac, Polzeath and Rock, or west of Bodmin to Ruthernbridge, Rosenannon and beyond. Bear in mind that this is a hilly part of the country and you are likely to be faced with many short sharp climbs!

Approaching Padstow along the Camel Estuary.

Starting points
1. Bodmin Parkway railway station, five miles south east of Bodmin.
2. Bodmin Jail, town centre.
3. Wadebridge town centre.
4. Padstow harbour.

Distance
The Camel Trail runs for 17 miles from Padstow to Poley's Bridge (situated between St Tudy and Blisland) ie 34 miles there and back. You have a variety of options:
1. The most popular is Wadebridge-Padstow-Wadebridge (12 miles round trip).
2. The longest would be Padstow-Bodmin-Poley's Bridge-Bodmin-Padstow (34 miles).
3. You may wish to devise your own lane routes from the ends of the trail back to Bodmin. Be warned that it is hilly around here!

Grade
The Camel Trail itself is easy, running along the course of an old railway line. The link from Bodmin Parkway to the start of the trail is fairly strenuous.

Surface
Variable gravel surface on the Camel Trail.

Roads, traffic, suitability for young children
The Camel Trail is ideal for young children, with lots to see along the way and superb cycle hire infrastructure in Wadebridge and Padstow which caters for all requirements.
1. You have to go through the centre of Wadebridge on streets but there are so many cyclists that traffic does not pose the normal threats.
2. The (hilly) route from Bodmin Parkway to the Camel Trail is mostly on-road, and includes the new Millennium bridge over the A30. Care should be taken crossing the A389 in Bodmin.

Hills
The section between Bodmin and Padstow is flat. There is a gentle 200ft climb from Bodmin north east along the Camel Trail to Poley's Bridge. The route between Bodmin Parkway station and the start of the Camel Trail is hilly with one particularly steep climb.

Refreshments
Lots of choice in Bodmin, Wadebridge and Padstow.
Tea shop near Boscarne Junction Station.

Nearest railway stations
Bodmin Parkway is linked to Route 3 via a new bridge. The Bodmin and Wenford Railway tourist line runs infrequently between Bodmin Parkway, Bodmin and Boscarne Junction.

The National Cycle Network in the area
The Camel Trail is used as part of both the West Country Way and the Cornish Way (Route 3) on its way from Land's End to Bristol. In the future, Route 2 will run from Bodmin to Plymouth.

Other nearby rides (waymarked or traffic-free)
There are forest trails in Cardinham Woods, east of Bodmin.

Cycle hire is available in Padstow and Wadebridge.

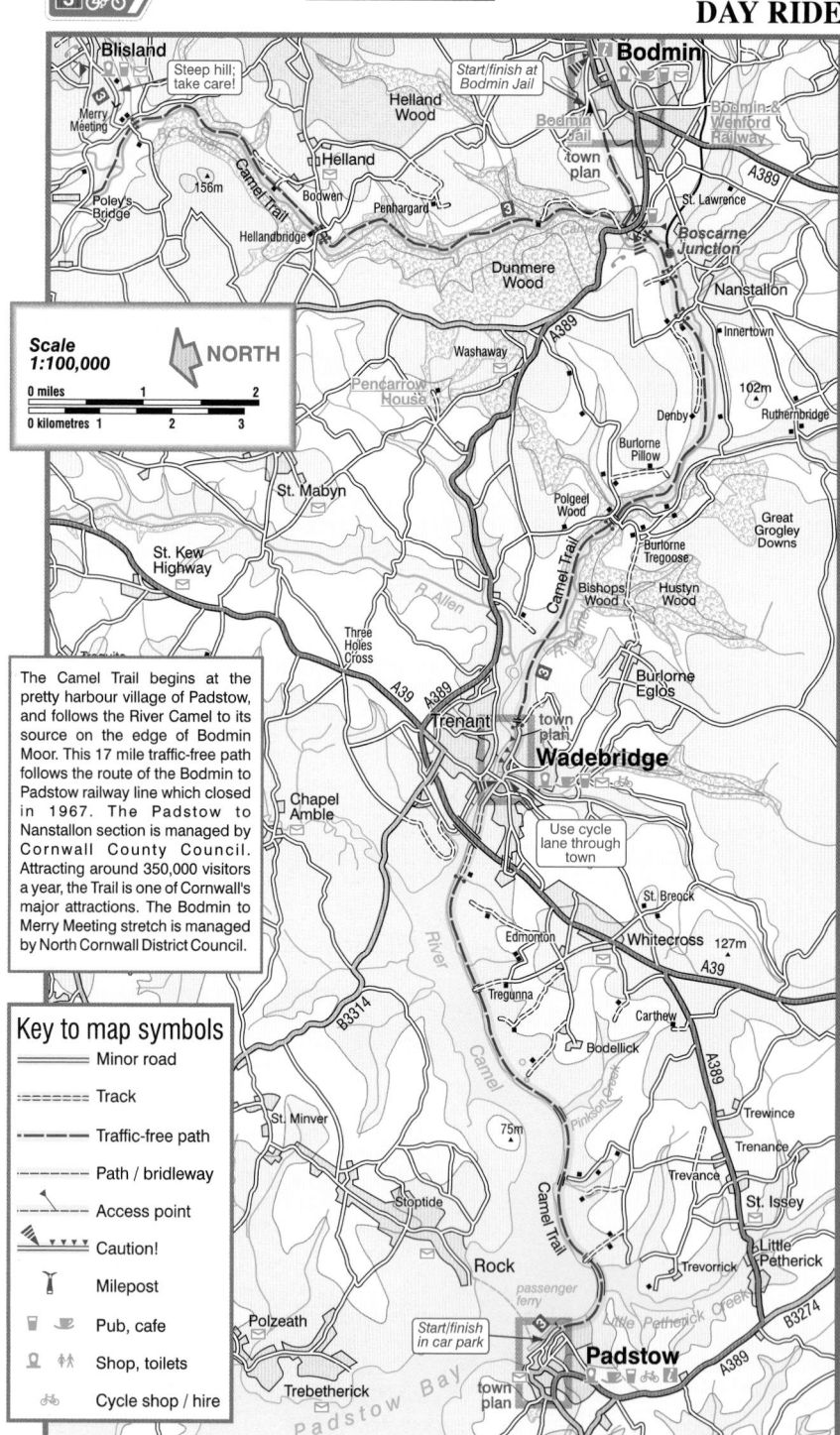

THE CAMEL TRAIL – BODMIN TO PADSTOW

THE WEST COUNTRY

DAY RIDE

3 🚲 〉

Blisland

Steep hill; take care!

Merry Meeting

Camel Trail

156m

Poley's Bridge

Helland

Bodwen

Hellandbridge

Penhargard

Helland Wood

Dunmere Wood

Washaway

Start/finish at Bodmin Jail

Bodmin

Bodmin Jail

town plan

St. Lawrence

Bodmin & Wenford Railway

A389

Boscarne Junction

Nanstallon

Innertown

102m

Denby

Ruthernbridge

Scale
1:100,000

NORTH

| 0 miles | | 1 | | 2 |
| 0 kilometres | 1 | 2 | 3 |

Pencarrow House

St. Mabyn

St. Kew Highway

R. Allen

Three Holes Cross

A39   A389

Burlorne Pillow

Polgeel Wood

Camel Trail

Burlorne Tregoose

Bishops Wood

Hustyn Wood

Great Grogley Downs

The Camel Trail begins at the pretty harbour village of Padstow, and follows the River Camel to its source on the edge of Bodmin Moor. This 17 mile traffic-free path follows the route of the Bodmin to Padstow railway line which closed in 1967. The Padstow to Nanstallon section is managed by Cornwall County Council. Attracting around 350,000 visitors a year, the Trail is one of Cornwall's major attractions. The Bodmin to Merry Meeting stretch is managed by North Cornwall District Council.

Trenant

town plan

Wadebridge

Chapel Amble

Use cycle lane through town

Burlorne Eglos

St. Breock

Edmonton

Whitecross   127m

A39

Tregunna

Carthew

Bodellick

B3314

River

Camel

Pinkson Creek

Key to map symbols

━━━━ Minor road

┄┄┄┄ Track

— – — – Traffic-free path

- - - - - Path / bridleway

——◄—— Access point

⚠▾▾▾▾ Caution!

⸸ Milepost

🍺 ☕ Pub, cafe

♒ 🚻 Shop, toilets

🚲 Cycle shop / hire

St. Minver

Stoptide

Polzeath

Rock

Trebetherick

75m

Camel Trail

passenger ferry

Start/finish in car park

Trewince

Trenance

Trevance

St. Issey

Trevorrick

Little Petherick

Little Petherick Creek

B3274

Padstow

town plan

Padstow Bay

A389

© Crown copyright

34

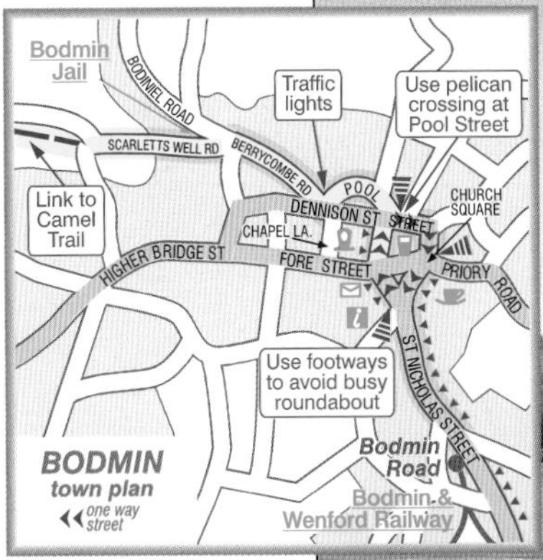

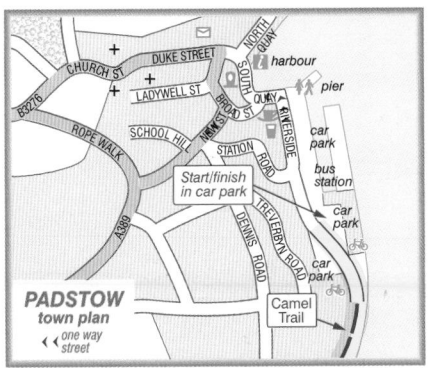

BODMIN town plan
◄◄ one way street

- Bodmin Jail
- BODMEL ROAD
- SCARLETTS WELL RD
- Link to Camel Trail
- HIGHER BRIDGE ST
- BERRYCOMBE RD
- CHAPEL LA.
- DENNISON'S ST
- FORE STREET
- POOL STREET
- Traffic lights
- Use pelican crossing at Pool Street
- CHURCH SQUARE
- PRIORY ROAD
- ST NICHOLAS STREET
- Use footways to avoid busy roundabout
- Bodmin Road
- Bodmin & Wenford Railway

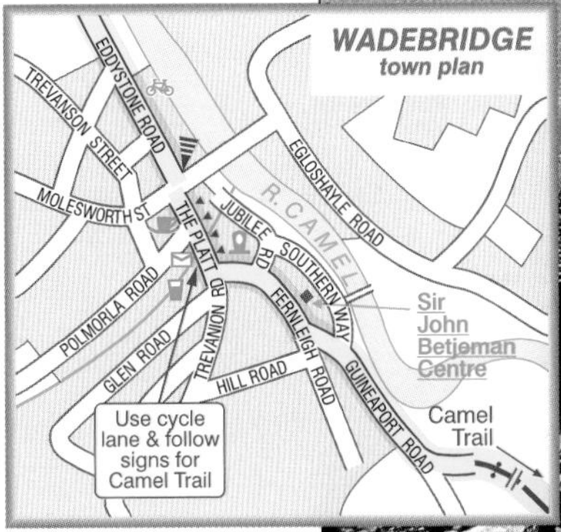

WADEBRIDGE town plan

- TREVANSON STREET
- EDDYSTONE ROAD
- MOLESWORTH S⟨T⟩
- POLMORLA ROAD
- GLEN ROAD
- EGLOSHAYLE ROAD
- R. CAMEL
- JUBILEE RD
- THE PLATT
- TREVANION RD
- SOUTHERN WAY
- FERNLEIGH RD
- HILL ROAD
- GUINEAPORT ROAD
- Sir John Betjeman Centre
- Camel Trail
- Use cycle lane & follow signs for Camel Trail

PADSTOW town plan
◄◄ one way street

- CHURCH ST
- DUKE STREET
- LADYWELL ST
- B3276
- ROPE WALK
- SCHOOL HILL
- A389
- NEW ST
- BROAD ST
- STATION
- NORTH QUAY
- SOUTH QUAY
- RIVERSIDE
- DENNIS ROAD
- TREYARNON ROAD
- harbour
- pier
- car park
- bus station
- Start/finish in car park
- car park
- car park
- Camel Trail

Overlooking the Camel Estuary.

Route instructions (from Bodmin to Wadebridge and on to Padstow)

1. From Bodmin Jail follow the signs for the Camel Trail.

2. After one mile, at a junction of tracks just past a sign for the Borough Arms PH you have a choice:
a) continue straight ahead to Wadebridge (five miles one way) and Padstow (11 miles one way);
b) turn sharp right towards Poley's Bridge (seven miles one way).

3. (Route through Wadebridge). Take care with young children on the roads through Wadebridge. Follow the waymarks and rejoin the railway path and follow for a further six miles to the harbour in Padstow.

THE PLYM VALLEY PATH TOWARDS DARTMOOR

Starting from the naval city of Plymouth, where Sir Francis Drake played bowls before defeating the Spanish Armada, the Plym Valley Path is the first section of the Devon Coast to Coast Route crossing the county from south to north and finishing at Ilfracombe. The trail runs from the heart of Plymouth alongside the River Plym, passing the magnificent 18th-century mansion Saltram House. The route continues gently uphill through thick woodland, following first the line of the Lee Moor China Clay tramway, then Cann Quarry Canal and finally the course of the old Great Western Railway (built by Isambard Kingdom Brunel) as it crosses a series of viaducts and passes through a curved tunnel. The route described below goes as far as Clearbrook on the edge of Dartmoor. On the return trip to Laira Bridge you are faced with a wonderful descent over several miles to get back to the start.

Plymbridge Woods.

Starting point
Laira Bridge or Saltram House, Plymouth.

Distance
Nine miles from Laira Bridge to Clearbrook, ie 18 miles round trip. It will be much slower climbing up to Clearbrook than coming back downhill!

Grade
Moderate.

Surface
Good gravel track from Laira Bridge to the tunnel. Rougher section from the end of the railway trail up to the Skylark Inn at Clearbrook.

Roads, traffic, suitability for young children
The traffic-free Plym Valley Trail is ideal for children. The route from the centre of Plymouth to Laira Bridge is on streets. There is a short steep lane section near Bickleigh.

Hills
Steady 500ft climb up from Laira Bridge to Clearbrook with a steep section on a quiet lane near Bickleigh.

The Plym Valley Trail, ideal for a day out.

Refreshments
Lots of choice along the seafront in Plymouth.
Skylark PH in Clearbrook.

Nearest railway station
Plymouth.

The National Cycle Network in the area
Plymouth is the starting point of the Devon Coast to Coast (Routes 31, 3 & 27) which runs to Ilfracombe and Bude. Route 2 will run west from Exeter via Plymouth to Bodmin.

Other nearby rides (waymarked or traffic-free)
1. Cycling is allowed in the forestry holdings at Bellever, Soussons and Fernworthy on Dartmoor (northeast of Tavistock).
2. A section of dismantled railway in Princetown (Dartmoor) has been converted to recreational use.

Route details at Plymbridge Woods.

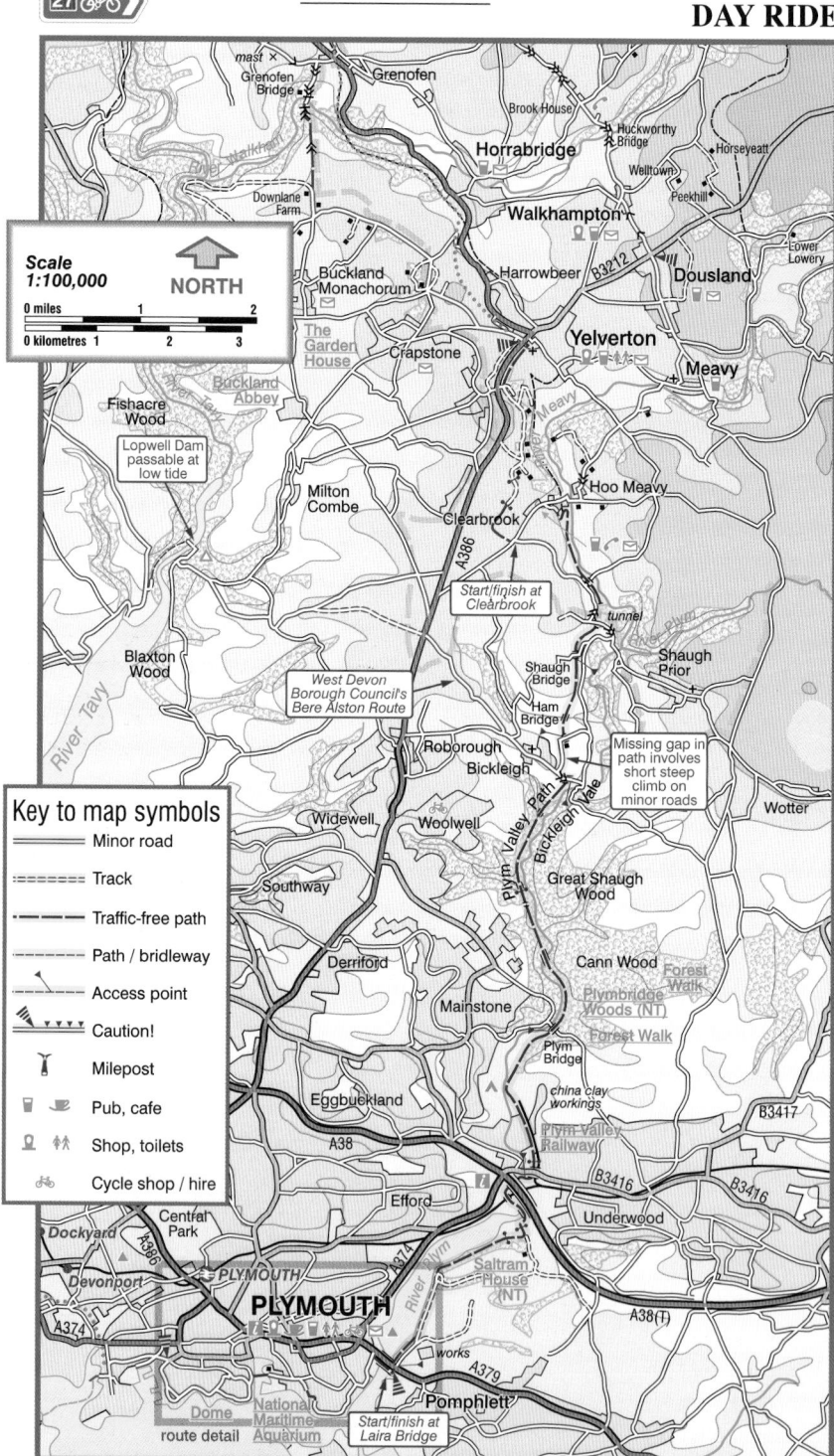

THE PLYM VALLEY PATH TOWARDS DARTMOOR

Scale 1:100,000

0 miles · 1 · 2
0 kilometres · 1 · 2 · 3

NORTH

Key to map symbols

- ═══ Minor road
- ┉┉┉ Track
- ─ ─ ─ Traffic-free path
- ─────── Path / bridleway
- Access point
- Caution!
- Milepost
- 🍺 🍽 Pub, cafe
- Shop, toilets
- 🚲 Cycle shop / hire

route detail

Cycle lanes along Plymouth Hoe.

Route instructions (from Laira Bridge, Plymouth to Clearbrook)

1. At the eastern end of Laira Bridge cross the road via traffic lights following signs for Plym Valley. Keep bearing to the left. After ½ mile, opposite a car park to the right, turn left through a wooden gate to continue close to the river.

2. At the fork of tracks beyond the next gate bear left uphill and left again at a T-junction with tarmac. (Remember this point for your return route). The narrow tarmac lane crosses a bridge over the railway. Pass beneath the A38 viaduct. Follow cycle signs for Plym Valley and Tavistock past Coypool Park.

3. After five miles, climbing gently through woodland, where the railway path comes to a T-junction with a lane, turn left steeply uphill then after 200 yds turn first right signposted 'Shaugh Prior'. Shortly after a sharp right-hand bend, turn left onto a continuation of the railway path.

4. After 1½ miles, go through a tunnel. At the end of the track follow red arrows on a steep section to climb up to Clearbrook. Turn left along the road to the Skylark Inn.

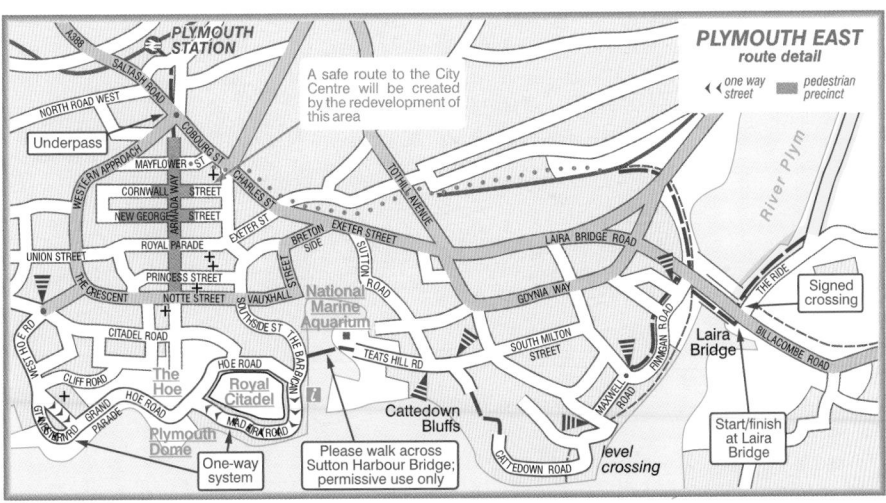

Day Rides
(A) Oxford to Abingdon *9 miles*
(B) The Cuckoo Trail *11 miles*
(Polegate - Heathfield)
(C) Canterbury - Whitstable *9 miles*

Banbury
70
20
Winslow
Bicester
5
51
6
Aylesbury
Kidlington
Thame
Princes
Risborough
Oxford
57
19
Abingdon
(A)
Chilterns
High
Wycombe
Didcot
5
Wallingford
Dagenham
2
London
6
1
Maidenhead
61
Reading
Windsor
4
4
Staines
Dartford
Newbury
4
3
Kingston
-upon-
Thames
Thatcham
4
North Wessex Downs
23
Guildford
Dorking
21
Basingstoke
22
Redhill
Roy
Tunbr
Wel
Farnham
Gatwick Airport
East
Grinstead
Stockbridge
23
Alton
Crawley
12
5
11
21
Eridge
Winchester
89
South Downs
Petersfield
20
Heathfield
Romsey
24
22
Sussex Downs
90
Eastleigh
89
Lewes
Southampton
Havant
10
89
New Forest
2
9
Chichester
2
Brockenhurst
8
Hove
Brighton
6
Gosport
Worthing
Newhaven
2
Cowes
Portsmouth
Littlehampton
7
Ryde
Newport
22
Sandown
ISLE OF
WIGHT

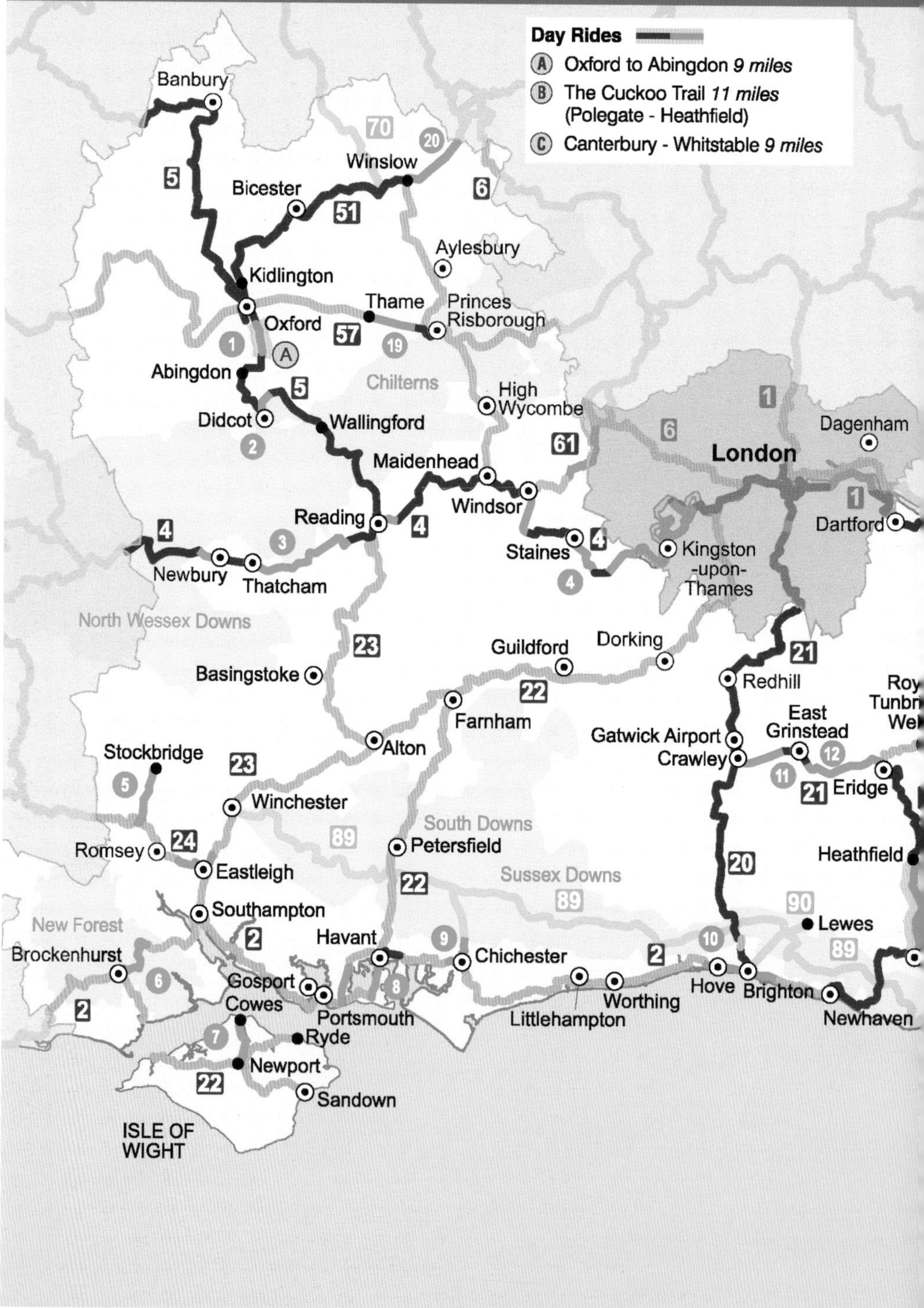

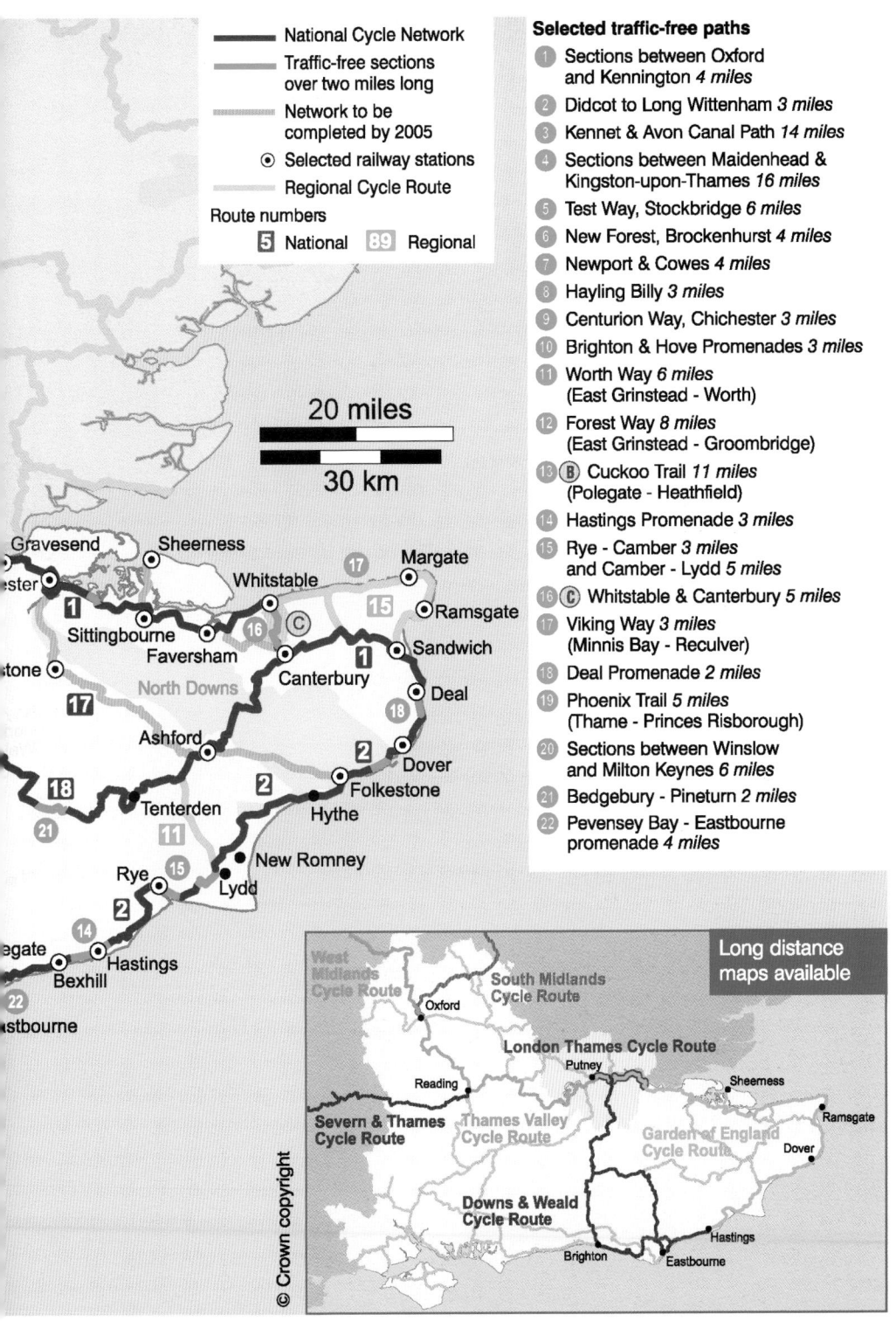

Legend:

- National Cycle Network
- Traffic-free sections over two miles long
- Network to be completed by 2005
- ⊙ Selected railway stations
- Regional Cycle Route

Route numbers
- **5** National **89** Regional

Selected traffic-free paths

1. Sections between Oxford and Kennington *4 miles*
2. Didcot to Long Wittenham *3 miles*
3. Kennet & Avon Canal Path *14 miles*
4. Sections between Maidenhead & Kingston-upon-Thames *16 miles*
5. Test Way, Stockbridge *6 miles*
6. New Forest, Brockenhurst *4 miles*
7. Newport & Cowes *4 miles*
8. Hayling Billy *3 miles*
9. Centurion Way, Chichester *3 miles*
10. Brighton & Hove Promenades *3 miles*
11. Worth Way *6 miles* (East Grinstead - Worth)
12. Forest Way *8 miles* (East Grinstead - Groombridge)
13. Ⓑ Cuckoo Trail *11 miles* (Polegate - Heathfield)
14. Hastings Promenade *3 miles*
15. Rye - Camber *3 miles* and Camber - Lydd *5 miles*
16. Ⓒ Whitstable & Canterbury *5 miles*
17. Viking Way *3 miles* (Minnis Bay - Reculver)
18. Deal Promenade *2 miles*
19. Phoenix Trail *5 miles* (Thame - Princes Risborough)
20. Sections between Winslow and Milton Keynes *6 miles*
21. Bedgebury - Pineturn *2 miles*
22. Pevensey Bay - Eastbourne promenade *4 miles*

20 miles

30 km

Gravesend Sheerness
ster Whitstable Margate **17**
Sittingbourne **15** Ramsgate
Faversham **16** Ⓒ
stone **1**
North Downs Canterbury Sandwich
17 Deal **18**
Ashford **2**
18 Dover
Tenterden **2** Folkestone
11 Hythe
Rye **15** New Romney
2 Lydd
egate **14**
Bexhill Hastings
22
stbourne

Long distance maps available

West Midlands Cycle Route South Midlands Cycle Route
Oxford London Thames Cycle Route Putney Sheerness
Reading Ramsgate
Severn & Thames Cycle Route Thames Valley Cycle Route Garden of England Cycle Route Dover
Downs & Weald Cycle Route
Brighton Eastbourne Hastings

© Crown copyright

41

THE SOUTH EAST

Southeast England is one of the most densely populated areas in Europe with over 17 million people living in or within 60 miles of London. As it is also the most affluent region of Britain, traffic levels are higher here than anywhere else in the country. Sustrans' work is all the more vital in trying to halt the growth of traffic, offering real alternatives to the car for trips to school, work, shopping and leisure.

Four routes leave London, two of which head for the South Coast. The first of these runs east along the Thames Estuary from Greenwich to Gravesend and Faversham, cutting inland to visit the architectural splendours of Canterbury and passing through Kent's 'Garden of England' fruit orchards before rejoining the coast for the journey from Deal to Dover. The other route heads south through the

Whitstable Harbour.

chalk hills of the North Downs, passing through Redhill and crossing the High Weald to East Grinstead to link with the popular traffic-free Cuckoo Trail down to Eastbourne. The coastal route running between Dover and Eastbourne completes the triangle. The third route starts in the centre of London (the Thames Valley Cycle Route) connecting the capital to the dreaming spires of Oxford via the glories of Hampton Court and Windsor and the wooded delights of the Chilterns between Reading and Wallingford. The fourth route heads northwards to reach the Lee Valley. Three further routes are planned - northwest to Watford, east to Southend and southwest to Guildford.

NATIONAL CYCLE NETWORK HIGHLIGHTS

Brighton Promenade

The promenades of the South East offer a wonderful opportunity to cycle beside the sea. Many promenades built in the heyday of rail-borne seaside holidays are now much less used by pedestrians, thus enabling the creation of traffic-free cycle routes which are an ideal place for the novice and family groups to learn to cycle again.

Shakespeare Cliffs between Folkestone & Dover

The route here climbs up from sea level at either end to run along the top of these spectacular cliffs with views out to France. Along the way you pass an early wartime listening station in the shape of a shallow parabolic concrete basin.

Milepost at Dover

This milepost at the entrance to Dover ferry announces the start of the National Cycle Network to visitors from the Continent. It is one of 1,000 mileposts marking out the Network which have been funded by The Royal Bank of Scotland.

Didcot Power Station

The power station is known as the 'Cathedral of the Vale'. Its vast cooling towers are visible from miles away in all directions. They are the despair of cyclists because they seem to be at once near yet far. Their scale distorts the distances and stretches the time of journeys to Didcot.

Portsmouth Harbour Ferry

The practical design of the Langstone Harbour Ferry from Portsmouth to Hayling Island shows total understanding of the day to day needs of cyclists.

Canterbury Cathedral

Whatever your beliefs or creed, no cycle route could be called national if it bypassed Canterbury and its ancient and magnificent cathedral. It stands on the site of a Roman church given to the monks by King Ethelbert in 597. This early church was entirely destroyed by fire but was rebuilt. The building we now see was eventually completed in 1495. The shrine of Thomas à Becket, who was murdered in 1170, was the centre of pilgrimages for centuries. These are fully described by Chaucer in his 'Canterbury Tales'.

NATIONAL CYCLE NETWORK HIGHLIGHTS

Viking Way, Minnis Bay to Reculver around the Isle of Thanet

This is a very welcome extension to the National Cycle Network - it follows the massive sea defences, which have stablilised the shoreline after centuries of retreat. Originally, Thanet was an island, and in Roman times ships sailed from their great entry port at Richborough Castle through a navigable channel to Reculver.

Hastings Promenade

Of all the seaside towns around the Network, Hastings has made one of the very best promenade routes and finds itself rewarded with considerable public acclaim. Promenade routes are particularly important sections of the Network, because they give an intimate view of the sea, something surprisingly difficult to achieve over long lengths of the National Cycle Network.

Hastings Funicular

Hastings anticipates that its East Cliff funicular will be the only such lift on the whole National Cycle Network.

A22 and A27 - Eastbourne

Progress in Polegate has been made as a result of new road schemes to the west. The busy A22 is now crossed via a bridge forming part of the Polegate Bypass. Most of the route to Eastbourne is in place, sweeping down from the ridge and over the Hastings railway, all set well back from the new road.

Royal Sovereign Promenade to Eastbourne

This new promenade has been designed wide enough to host skateboard, roller blade and other wheeled championships. It is certainly good for cycling!

Windsor Great Park

Sustrans teamed up with the Crown Estates and Guards Polo Club to put in a Pegasus Crossing over the A332. This can be used not only by cyclists, but horses as well, and has much improved this route through the Royal Park.

CITY FOCUS

Maps & guides are available from National Cycle Network Information unless indicated otherwise. See page 47 for contact details.

Canterbury

The Garden of England Cycle Map shows Route 1 through the city. *Canterbury Cycle Routes* shows other recommended routes. Tourist Information Centre. Tel: 01227 766567.

Oxford

The Thames Valley Cycle Route Map, South Midlands Cycle Route Map and *West Midlands Cycle Route Map* all cover Oxford: Route 51 heads northeast through Summertown to Kidlington. Route 5 runs north along Walton Street to Wolvercote. To the south, Route 5 runs along the Thames to Radley.

Oxford CycleCity Map. A-Z style map showing traffic-free, official and advisory routes, with information about cycle shops, cycling contacts, train services and relevant local publications. On the reverse is a map of the county showing the Oxfordshire Cycleway. RC03 - £4.95

Portsmouth

Ferries to Gosport and Hayling Island cater for cyclists, whilst the largely traffic-free National Routes run around the promontory.

Cycle Portsmouth shows advisory, proposed and traffic-free routes and details of bike shops. Tourist Information Centre. Tel: 02392 838382.

Reading

The Thames Valley Cycle Route Map Route 5 runs north through Caversham towards Wallingford. Route 4 follows the Kennet & Avon Canal towards Newbury. To the east it follows the Thames to Sonning and Maidenhead.

Cycling in Reading shows cycle paths in Reading and includes details of bike shops and useful contacts. Available from the Tourist Information Centre. Tel: 0118 956 6226

Southampton

Southampton Cyclists Guide 2000 shows existing and proposed cycle routes and icons showing the location of bike shops. Available from the Tourist Information Centre. Tel: 02380 832082

Other towns covered by leaflets:

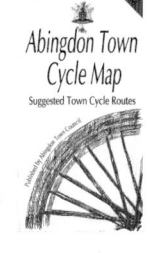

Abingdon Town Cycle Map. Tourist Information Centre Tel: 01235 522711

Cycle Chichester - Route Map. Shows offroad tracks, cycle lanes, advisory and proposed routes. Tourist Information Centre Tel: 01243 775888.

Epsom & Ewell Cycle Guide. Shows cycle tracks, signed cycle routes on road and proposed routes. Tourist Information Centre Tel: 0208 547 5992.

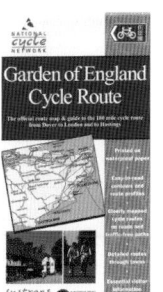
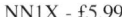
NN1X - £5.99

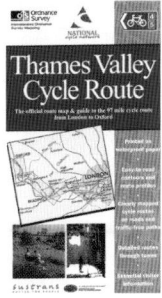
NN5A - £5.99

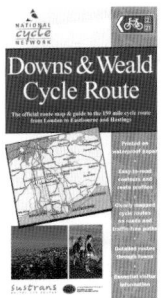
NN2A - £5.99

TRAFFIC-FREE PATHS PARTICULARLY SUITABLE FOR FAMILIES

4 **Newbury to Reading. 17 miles**
A tranquil and beautiful ride along the towpath of the Kennet & Avon Canal, resurfaced end to end with two short sections across meadows.

2 **Christchurch, Brockenhurst and the New Forest. 12 miles**
There are a number of excellent cycling routes signposted along forest roads in the New Forest. The National Cycle Network aims to join them up to make a continuous route, accessible from Christchurch or Southampton, without needing to drive to the Forest to start with.

22 **Newport to Cowes on the Isle of Wight. 4 miles**
A ride along a dismantled railway between the important sailing centre at Cowes and the island's capital in Newport. The trail runs alongside the Medina River, full of colourful moored yachts.

21 **Forest Way from East Grinstead to Groombridge. 9 miles**
An open ride on a dismantled railway passing through arable land lying between the High Weald to the south and the North Downs to the north. The countryside around Hartfield is the setting of A.A. Milne's *Winnie the Pooh*.

21 **Worth Way from East Grinstead to Crawley. 7 miles**
Starting right behind the busy commuter railway station at East Grinstead is a lovely broad wooded trail running west past the attractive old church at Worth.

2 **Rye to Camber. 4 miles**
From the historic Cinque Port of Rye near the Kent/Sussex border, a traffic-free path runs east to the holiday village of Camber, famed for its sandy beach. This provides a gateway to the quiet lane network on Romney Marsh and avoids a long detour on the busy A259.

USEFUL MAPS & GUIDES

For details of the full range of maps, guides and other products available contact: **National Cycle Network Information, PO Box 21, Bristol BS99 2HA. Tel: 0117 929 0888. Or visit www.nationalcyclenetwork.org.uk**
The range of National Cycle Network Maps is described in more detail on pages 218-237.

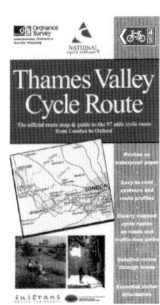

4 5 *Thames Valley Cycle Route (London – Oxford)*
97 miles. NN5A - £5.99

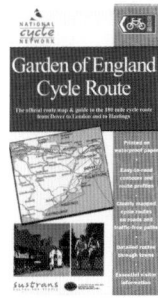

1 2 18 *Garden of England Cycle Route (Dover – London & Hastings)* 114 miles. NN1X - £5.99

20 21 2 *Downs & Weald Cycle Route (London – Hastings, via Eastbourne)* 150 miles.
NN2A - £5.99

Cycling Without Traffic: South East
30 traffic-free rides described in detail in this well illustrated guide to family cycling. Includes the Cuckoo Trail and Epping Forest.
RBA01 - £11.99

Parish Pedals - Weald of Kent
Waterproof route cards for four circular rides in the Weald of Kent.
RPL12 - £1.00

More Cycling Without Traffic: South East
A further 30 traffic-free rides described in detail in this well illustrated guide to family cycling in the South East, including the Ridgeway, the South Downs Way and the Downs Link.
RBA07 - £11.99

Great Cycle Routes in Hampshire & Dorset
Contains information on 30 routes through the Hampshire and Dorset area, including the Isle of Wight.
RBA11 - £11.99

CANTERBURY & WHITSTABLE CYCLE PATH

A short ride encapsulating all that is best about the National Cycle Network – a route starting from the centre of a beautiful, historic city, passing along traffic-calmed roads and specially-built cyclepaths into the countryside, following the course of a dismantled railway through broadleaf and conifer woodland to an attractive seaside town. Canterbury has been a place of pilgrimage for many centuries. The streets around the cathedral are a real delight. The cathedral area is best explored on foot and there is, in any case, a restriction on cycling here between 10.30AM and 4.00PM. The route climbs steadily out of the city with wonderful views opening up behind you. After passing close to the university the route soon joins a traffic-free section that runs for over four miles past fruit farms and through woodland to South Street on the edge of Whitstable. Cyclepaths and traffic-calmed streets lead right into the heart of this fine coastal town.

Canterbury beside the Great Stour.

Starting points

1. Westgate, Canterbury.
2. Whitstable town centre.

Distance

(a) Canterbury to Whitstable – nine miles one way, 18 miles return.
(b) Canterbury to Fordwich – three miles one way, six miles return.

Grade

Easy.

Surface

Streets at the start and finish, a fine stone-based path between the university and South Street, on the edge of Whitstable.

Roads, traffic, suitability for young children

The route through Canterbury and Whitstable uses traffic-calmed streets or cycle paths. The central section is on a newly-built traffic-free path through woodland, partially using the old railway line.

Hills

There is a gentle 200ft climb out of Canterbury and an undulating middle section before dropping down to the coast at Whitstable.

Refreshments

Lots of choice in Canterbury.
Lots of choice in Whitstable.

Leaflets

Canterbury Cycle Routes is an A3 leaflet showing cycle routes in Canterbury. Available from Canterbury City Council, Tel: 01227 862000, or from the Tourist Information Centre: 01227 766567.

Nearby railway stations for longer linear rides

Starting from Whitstable you could follow Route 1 west to Faversham and Sittingbourne or east to Sandwich, Deal and Dover and catch the train back.

1999 Workcamp between Canterbury and Fordwich.

Canterbury to Fordwich

Another option from the centre of Canterbury is to follow the newly-built path out to the east to Fordwich where you join a delightful network of lanes meandering across rich agricultural country eastwards to Sandwich and the coast.

The National Cycle Network in the area

Canterbury lies at a crossroads of the Network. The east-west route from London to Dover is already in place (Route 1). To the south Routes 17 and 18 will go to Ashford and Hythe respectively. To the north Route 15 will run along the North Kent Coast to Ramsgate.

Other nearby rides (waymarked or traffic-free)

The Cathedral to Coast Ride is a waymarked 50-mile circular route linking Canterbury, Folkestone and Dover. It is made up of two Regional Routes: Route 16 (Canterbury-Dover) and Route 17 (Dover-Folkestone-Canterbury). A leaflet is available from Kent Tourism, Kent County Council, Invicta House, County Hall, Sessions House Square, Maidstone, Kent ME14 1XX. Tel: 01622 696165.

Route 1 - Canterbury to Whitstable through the University of Kent.

CANTERBURY & WHITSTABLE CYCLE PATH

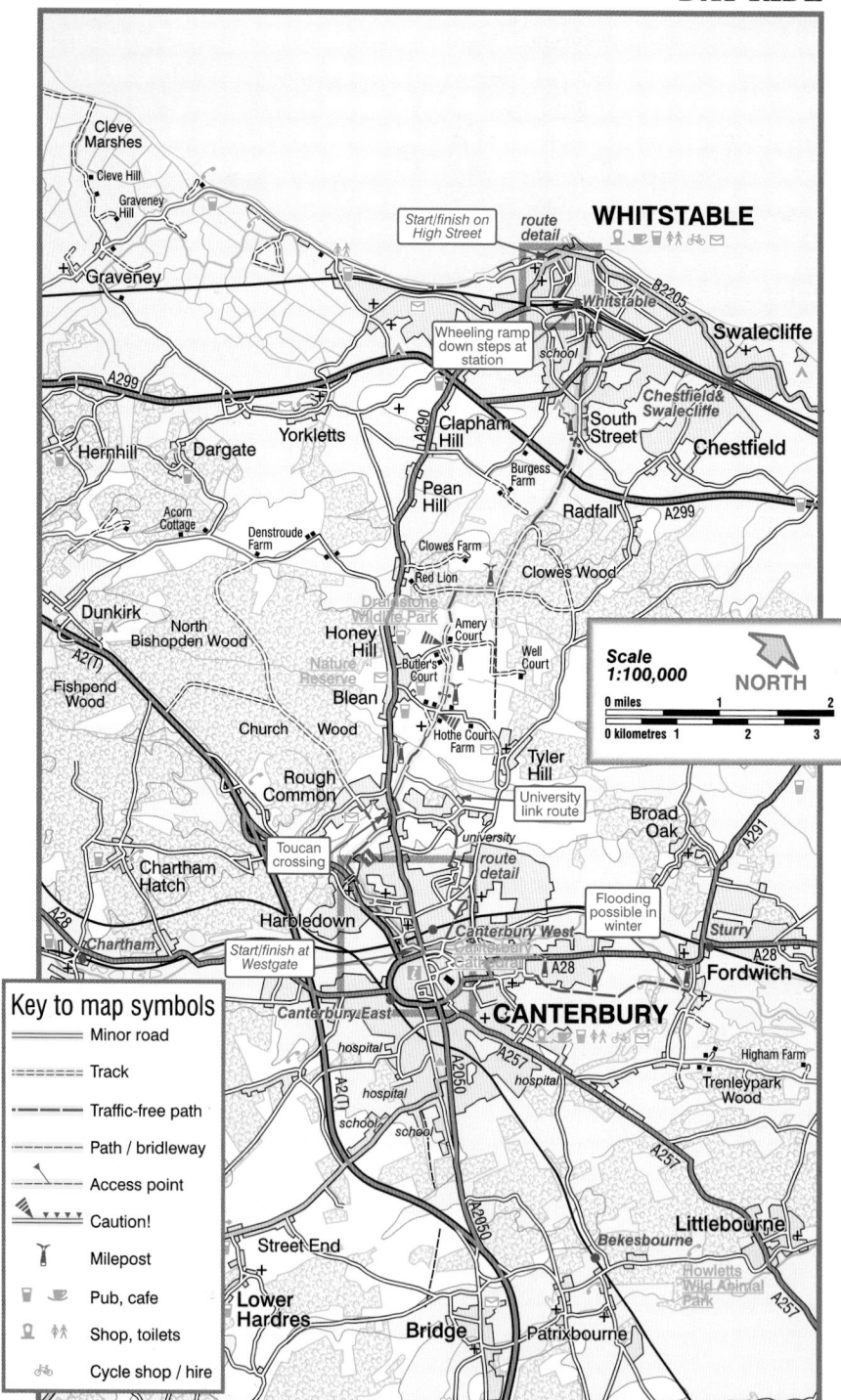

WHITSTABLE

Cleve Marshes
Cleve Hill
Graveney Hill
Graveney

Start/finish on High Street
route detail

Swalecliffe

Wheeling ramp down steps at station

Whitstable

school

Chestfield & Swalecliffe

Yorkletts

Clapham Hill

South Street

Chestfield

Hernhill
Dargate

Acorn Cottage
Denstroude Farm

Burgess Farm

Pean Hill

Radfall

A299

Clowes Farm
Red Lion

Clowes Wood

Dunkirk

North Bishopden Wood

Denstone Wildlife Park

Amery Court

Well Court

Fishpond Wood

Honey Hill

Nature Reserve

Butler's Court

Scale
1:100,000

NORTH

0 miles   1   2
0 kilometres 1   2   3

Church Wood

Blean

Hothe Court Farm

Tyler Hill

Rough Common

University link route

Broad Oak

Chartham Hatch

Toucan crossing

university

route detail

Flooding possible in winter

Sturry

Harbledown

Canterbury West

Chartham

Start/finish at Westgate

Canterbury East

+ CANTERBURY

Fordwich

A28

Key to map symbols

═══	Minor road
┄┄┄	Track
─ ─ ─	Traffic-free path
┈┈┈	Path / bridleway
─◤─	Access point
◣▼▼▼	Caution!
ⵌ	Milepost
⛫ 🍴	Pub, cafe
🛈 ♟	Shop, toilets
🚲	Cycle shop / hire

hospital
hospital
hospital
school
school

Higham Farm
Trenleypark Wood

Street End

Lower Hardres

Bekesbourne

Bridge

Patrixbourne

Howletts Wild Animal Park

Littlebourne

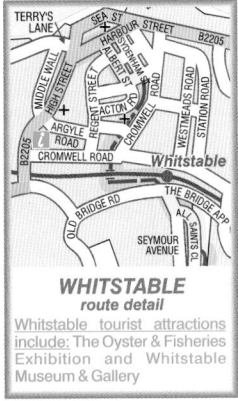

WHITSTABLE
route detail
Whitstable tourist attractions
include: The Oyster & Fisheries
Exhibition and Whitstable
Museum & Gallery

The seafront between Whitstable and Seasalter.

Route instructions – Canterbury to Whitstable

1. From Westgate, at the junction of Pound Lane and St Peter's Street in the centre of Canterbury, use the cycle island to cross the main road and follow the route waymarked 'Route 1, Harbledown' along Westgate Green and Whitehall Road.

2. Follow the 'Route 1, Harbledown' waymarks past the London Road junction and on to Blean. The route runs westwards, parallel with the A2050 then turns north through a rural setting and climbs steadily. Look behind you and to your right for fine views of Canterbury and the cathedral.

3. Go past a tall white water tower. Use the toucan crossing to cross the busy Whitstable Road (A290) onto the shared-use pavement. Opposite Kent College turn right onto a limestone path. The first sculpture on the route can be found near here. Keep straight on, pass a car park onto a track and continue northwards.

4. Descend to cross a stream, climb again passing fruit orchards and farms. Follow the

obvious track into woodland turning right at the first crossroads then left at a T-junction of forestry tracks. (To your left is a picnic site at the pond which was used to cool the winding gear on the old Canterbury & Whitstable Line).

5. After ¾ mile bear left away from the wide forestry track, descend to cross the bridge over the new A299 and follow the farm track to the road near Brooklands Farm, South Street.

6. Turn left on the road for 300 yds then immediately after passing Millstrood Road to the left bear left onto the red tarmac cycle path signposted 'Station, Town Centre Cycle Route'. At the end of the cycle path turn left then right downhill through the residential road with sea views ahead.

7. Follow the waymarked route past the station entrance into the heart of Whitstable. It is well worth visiting the harbour. (Follow: All Saints Close, railway station, Stream Walk, Albert Street, town centre and harbour).

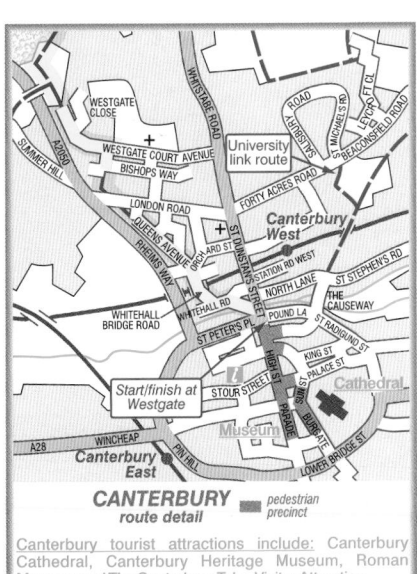

CANTERBURY
route detail
Canterbury tourist attractions include: Canterbury Cathedral, Canterbury Heritage Museum, Roman Museum and The Canterbury Tales Visitor Attraction

SOUTH FROM OXFORD TO ABINGDON

The key to linking the architectural glories of Oxford with the surrounding countryside whilst avoiding the busy roads that surround the city is to use the paths alongside its waterways. As these paths are inevitably busy, the National Route is signed via a network of minor road and cycleway links, leaving the canal and riverside for informal use. The route south to Abingdon follows the South Oxford Cycle Route through traffic-calmed streets as far as the ring road, briefly runs alongside the river, before joining a specially built path parallel with the railway line. Traffic-free paths take you across parkland into the very heart of the attractive, historic town of Abingdon.

Oxford, city of dreaming spires.

Starting point
George Street in the centre of Oxford.

Distance
8 miles one way, 16 miles return.

Grade
Easy.

Surface
Mixture of roads, tarmac cycle paths and stone-based paths.

Roads, traffic, suitability for young children
The busy roads are all crossed via toucan crossings.
The riverside path by the Thames and the path alongside the railway are ideal for children.

Hills
None.

Refreshments
Lots of choice in Oxford and in Abingdon.

Leaflets
1. CycleCity produce an excellent map of Oxford showing the traffic-free paths, the signposted routes and the advisory routes. It is available for £4.95 from National Cycle Network Information Service, PO Box 21, Bristol BS99 2HA. Tel: 0117 929 0888. Or visit: www.nationalcyclenetwork.org.uk

2. *Cycle into Oxford* is a comprehensive guide to cycle routes in and around Oxford, available from The Cycling Officer, Oxford City Council, Traffic and Design, Ramsay House, 10 St. Eddes Street, Oxford OX1 1PT. Tel: 01865 252750.

3. *Abingdon Town Cycle Map.* Large fold-out two colour leaflet showing existing and proposed cycle routes in the town. On the reverse are sections containing

1999 Summer Workcamp beside the River Thames at Kennington.

tourist information plus an inset showing the National Route between Oxford and Didcot. Contact: Abingdon Town Council, Stratton Lodge, 52 Bath Street, Abingdon OX14 3QH. Tel: 01235 522 642.

Nearest railway stations
Oxford, Radley, Didcot.

The National Cycle Network in the area
1. Oxford is on Route 5 which runs from Birmingham to Reading (where it links with Route 4 from Wales to London).
2. Route 51 heads north from Oxford and uses a new bridge to cross the A40 before reaching Kidlington where it continues north east to Bicester, Milton Keynes and Cambridge.

Other nearby rides (waymarked or traffic-free)
1. The Ridgeway Path is a broad chalk and stone track offering good off-road riding for hybrid and mountain bikes in the summer months. It runs from West Kennett (on the A4 west of Marlborough) to Goring on Thames, north west of Reading. The route can be followed beyond Goring towards Chinnor on the Icknield Way and Swan's Way.

2. The Oxfordshire Cycleway is a 200-mile waymarked ride around the county of Oxfordshire. Contact: Countryside Service, Department of Leisure & Arts, Oxfordshire County Council, Library Service HQ, Holton, Oxford OX9 1QQ.

The River Thames Path beside Iffley Lock.

SOUTH FROM OXFORD TO ABINGDON

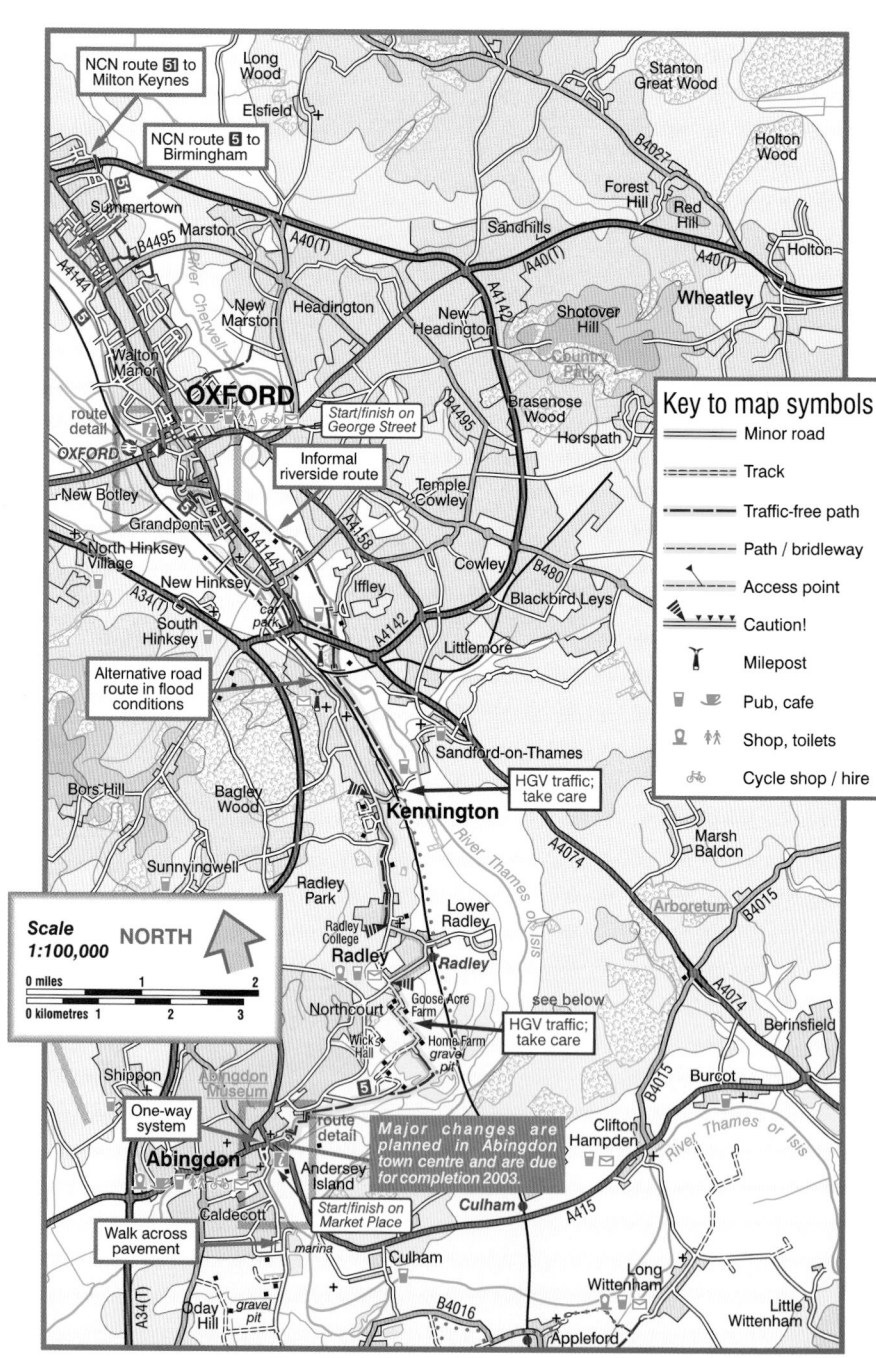

NCN route 51 to Milton Keynes

NCN route 5 to Birmingham

Long Wood

Elsfield

Stanton Great Wood

Holton Wood

Summertown

Marston

A40(T)

Sandhills

Forest Hill

Red Hill

Holton

A40(T)

A4144

B4495

River Cherwell

New Marston

Headington

New Headington

A4142

Shotover Hill

Wheatley

Walton Manor

OXFORD

Country Park

Start/finish on George Street

Brasenose Wood

Horspath

Key to map symbols

Minor road	
Track	
Traffic-free path	
Path / bridleway	
Access point	
Caution!	
Milepost	
Pub, cafe	
Shop, toilets	
Cycle shop / hire	

route detail

OXFORD

Informal riverside route

New Botley

Grandpont

Temple Cowley

A4158

North Hinksey Village

New Hinksey

A4144

car park

Iffley

A34(T)

South Hinksey

Cowley

B480

Blackbird Leys

Littlemore

A4142

Alternative road route in flood conditions

Bors Hill

Bagley Wood

Kennington

Sandford-on-Thames

HGV traffic; take care

Marsh Baldon

A4074

Sunningwell

Radley Park

Radley College

Radley

Radley

Lower Radley

River Thames or Isis

Arboretum

B4015

Scale
1:100,000 NORTH

0 miles   1   2

0 kilometres   1   2   3

Northcourt

Goose Acre Farm

Wick Hall

Home Farm *gravel pit*

see below

HGV traffic; take care

Berinsfield

A4074

Shippon

Abingdon Museum

One-way system

route detail

B4015

Burcot

Clifton Hampden

River Thames or Isis

Abingdon

Major changes are planned in Abingdon town centre and are due for completion 2003.

Andersey Island

Culham

A415

Walk across pavement

Caldecott

Start/finish on Market Place

marina

Culham

Long Wittenham

Little Wittenham

Oday Hill

gravel pit

A34(T)

B4016

Appleford

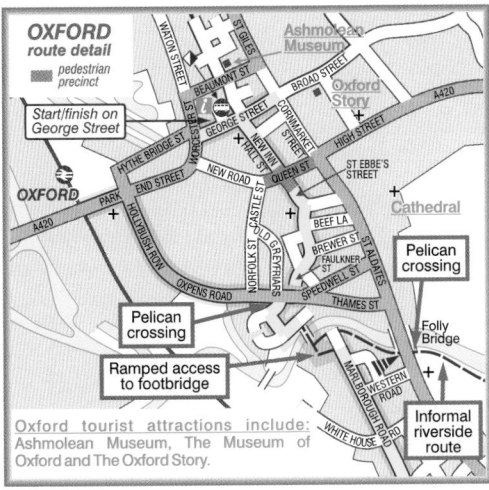

Oxford tourist attractions include: Ashmolean Museum, The Museum of Oxford and The Oxford Story.

Oxford, the city of 'Dreaming Spires'.

Route instructions from Oxford to Abingdon

1. From George Street in the centre of Oxford turn into New Inn Hall Street and follow signs for the 'South Oxford Cycle Route'.

2. Use the pelican crossing to cross the busy Oxpens Road then go over the river via a metal bridge* following signs for the 'South Oxford Cycle Route' or 'Kennington'. Follow a series of quiet residential roads and cyclepath links.

An alternative informal route runs along the riverside path (keep the water to your left) from here to the Oxford Southern Bypass.

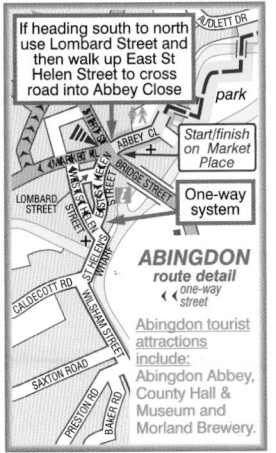

Abingdon tourist attractions include: Abingdon Abbey, County Hall & Museum and Morland Brewery.

3. Use the toucan crossings to cross to the cycleway on the east side of the busy Abingdon Road. Follow for ½ mile then immediately before the bridge over the main river use the ramp on the left to access the towpath. Turn right under the bridge and follow the newly-built riverside route to the meadows.

4. Bear right away from the river onto the newly-built path alongside the railway. At the T-junction with Sandford Lane turn right following the signed route.

5. At the T-junction with Kennington Road turn left using the shared pavement on the western side of the street. Follow this to Radley village.

6. Shortly after passing Radley College turn left signposted 'Route 5', follow the road through the village and past Radley railway station. After ½ mile turn left onto Thrupp Lane signposted 'Route 5'.

7. Follow the road round a sharp right-hand bend, a sharp left-hand bend then a second right-hand bend. Shortly, turn left onto a wide stone track. At the bottom of the gentle descent turn right along the line of the old railway.

8. The track emerges onto another new track across Barton Fields and crosses a steep footbridge before turning right along Abbey Meadows and into the park on the eastern edge of Abingdon.

9. Turn right across the bridge and through the car park. Follow this road until you see an arch on the left. This leads directly to the centre of Abingdon. **Take care at this busy junction**.

CUCKOO TRAIL – EASTBOURNE TO HEATHFIELD VIA POLEGATE

The Cuckoo Trail is one of the most popular family cycle rides in the South East. It gained its name from the Sussex tradition that the first cuckoo of spring was released at Heathfield Fair. Mostly built on the bed of a dismantled railway it offers superb traffic-free cycling through a mixture of broadleaf woodland, open grassland, arable farmland and pasture. As you head back down towards Polegate there are views of the rolling chalk hills of the South Downs ahead of you.

Along the way are metal sculptures by Hamish Black, an arch in the form of a Chinese Pagoda roof, a claw-like hand and plenty of carved wooden seats with a variety of motifs, made by the sculptor, Steve Geliot, from local oaks blown down in the Great Storm of 1987. The verges are thick with wildflowers such as willowherb and vetch. There is a gentle climb up from Polegate to Heathfield so that you can look forward to a gravity-assisted return journey! In several places bridges have been dismantled and houses have been built on the course of the railway, requiring you to cross minor roads and use short sections of estate roads through Hailsham and Horam to regain the railway path.

In 2000 a new section of route was added linking Polegate and Hampden Park in the north of Eastbourne. This is mostly traffic-free, with great views of the South Downs rising to the west. The section of the route in Polegate follows the old railway line that used to run directly eastwards to Pevensey.

One of a series of carved oak seats by Steve Geliot.

56

Starting points
1. Hampden Park Station, two miles north of Eastbourne town centre.
2. Polegate Station, four miles north of Eastbourne near the junction of the A22 and A27.

Distance
13½ miles one way, 27 miles return. The route can easily be shortened. Bear in mind that there is a 400ft climb from Polegate up to Heathfield so it is easier heading south than north!

Grade
Easy.

Surface
Tarmac and fine gravel path.

Roads, traffic, suitability for young children
The Cuckoo Trail is traffic-free and ideal for children. There are short sections on road at the start from the railway stations in Polegate and Hampden Park, and through Hailsham in the middle of the ride. There are several quiet lanes to cross. The three busy roads that need to be crossed have toucan crossings.

Hills
There is a gentle 400ft climb over 11 miles from Polegate up to Heathfield and two short, steep climbs at bridges over the railway and the A27.

Refreshments
Lots of choice in Hampden Park, Polegate, Hailsham and Heathfield. Tea shop on the trail at the Old Loom Mill Craft Centre (two miles north of Polegate, just before crossing the B2104).

Leaflets
An A3 leaflet describing the Cuckoo Trail is available from Boship Tourist Information Centre, Lower Dicker, Hailsham, East Sussex BN27 4DT. Tel: 01323 442667.

"What Was" Rio Summit 1992 Sculpture by John Harmer.

Nearest railway stations
Polegate or Hampden Park.

The National Cycle Network in the area
The Cuckoo Trail forms part of Route 21 which runs south from London through Redhill and East Grinstead to Eastbourne. From Polegate the South Coast Cycle Route (Route 2) runs east through Pevensey to Bexhill and west to Newhaven and Brighton.

Other nearby rides (waymarked or traffic-free)
The Forest Way and Worth Way are two railway paths starting in East Grinstead, running west to Crawley and east to Groombridge. There are cycle tracks along parts of the promenades in Eastbourne, Hastings, Brighton and Hove. The South Downs Way is suitable for fit cyclists on mountain bikes. There is also a route around Bewl Water (south east of Tunbridge Wells).

Jet of the Gladiators opening the Cuckoo Trail near Heathfield.

CUCKOO TRAIL – EASTBOURNE TO HEATHFIELD VIA POLEGATE

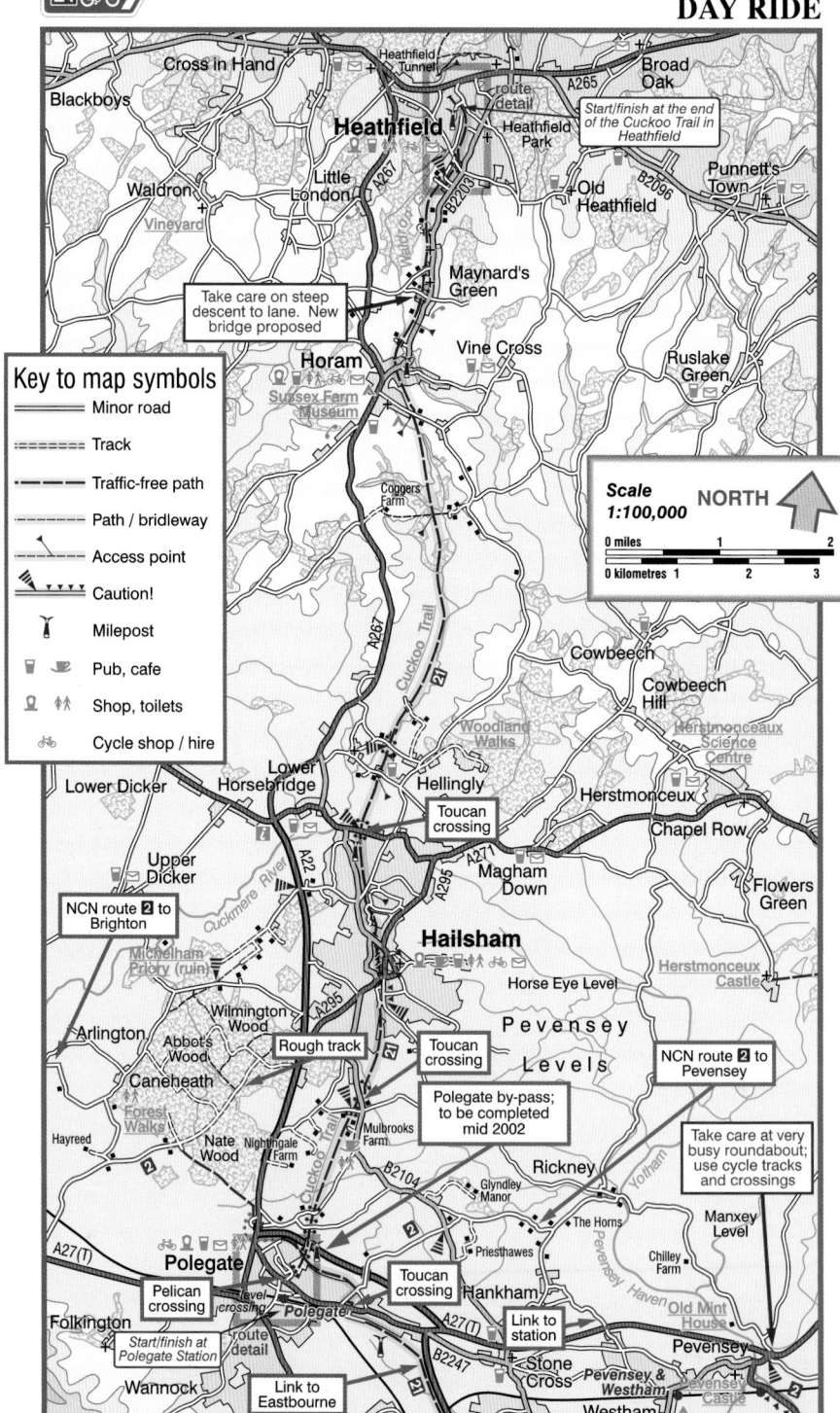

Key to map symbols

Minor road	
Track	
Traffic-free path	
Path / bridleway	
Access point	
Caution!	
Milepost	
Pub, cafe	
Shop, toilets	
Cycle shop / hire	

Scale
1:100,000

NORTH

0 miles   1   2
0 kilometres   1   2   3

Start/finish at the end of the Cuckoo Trail in Heathfield

Take care on steep descent to lane. New bridge proposed

NCN route 2 to Brighton

NCN route 2 to Pevensey

Rough track

Toucan crossing

Polegate by-pass; to be completed mid 2002

Take care at very busy roundabout; use cycle tracks and crossings

Toucan crossing

Pelican crossing

Start/finish at Polegate Station

Link to Eastbourne

Toucan crossing

Link to station

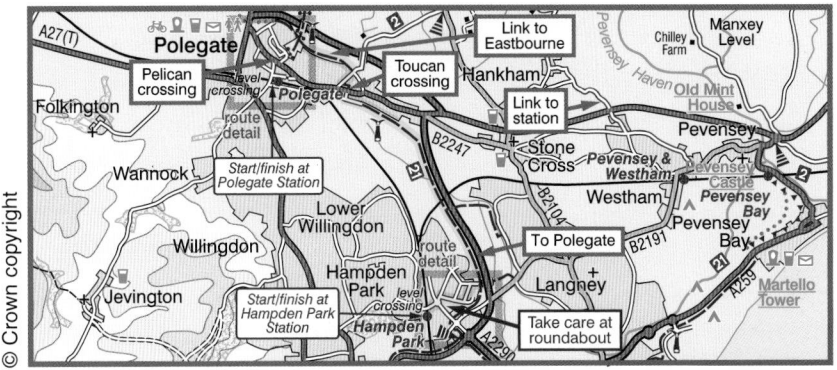

Route instructions from Hampden Park (Eastbourne) to Polegate and Heathfield

1. From the station, follow Mountfield Road east to the roundabout and cross over to the road opposite (The Hydneye). Care should be taken as this section is quite busy: you may prefer to cross the roundabout on foot. Immediately turn right into Dallington Road and go past the school.

North of Horam on a winter's day.

2. The route is then signed to the start of the path alongside the new A22. Just before the tunnel under the road, turn left over a hump-back bridge. Follow the signed route northwards through to Polegate. There is a short stretch on estate roads either side of the A27, with cycle tracks leading to a toucan crossing of the road itself.

3. At the end of Levett Road turn left onto the surfaced path north of Polegate. This brings you to the junction with the Cuckoo Trail where you turn right.

4. Follow the railway path for three miles into Hailsham. At this point the route follows estate roads so look out for 'Cuckoo Trail (bikes)' signs.

5. Rejoin the railway path and follow for five miles through to Horam. There is a second, short section on estate roads.

6. The trail ends after a further three miles in Heathfield. In this final section there are several roads to cross, mainly quiet lanes, but care should be taken none the less if you are with young children.

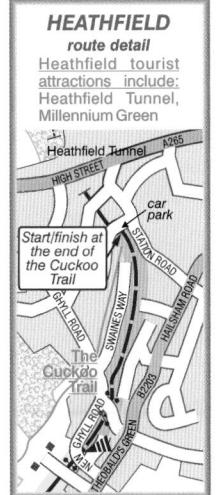

HEATHFIELD
route detail

Heathfield tourist attractions include: Heathfield Tunnel, Millennium Green

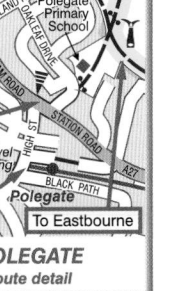

POLEGATE
route detail

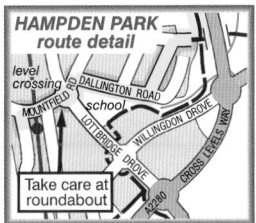

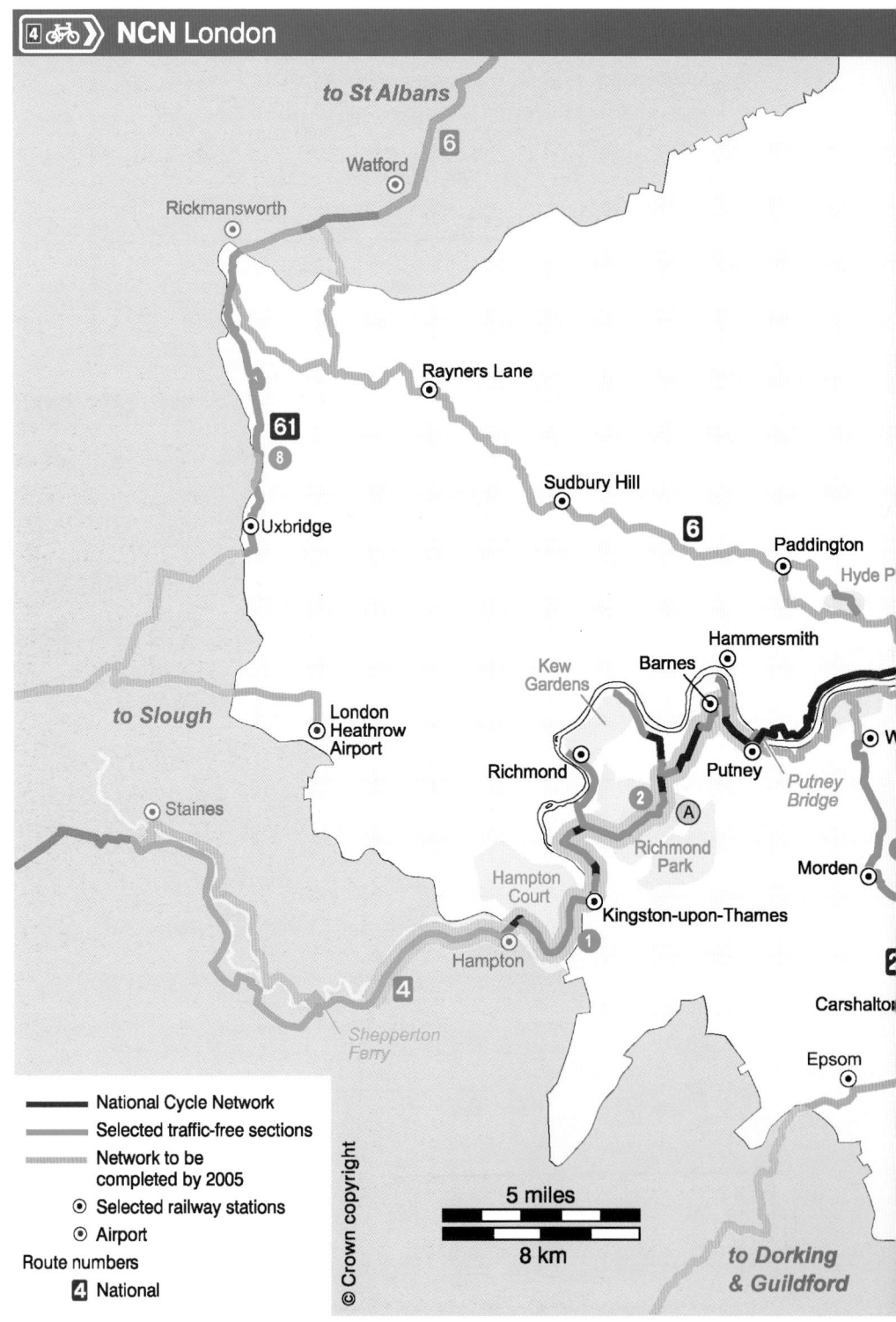

to St Albans

6

Watford

Rickmansworth

Rayners Lane

61
8

Sudbury Hill

6

Paddington

Hyde P

⊙ Uxbridge

Hammersmith

Kew Gardens

Barnes

to Slough

London Heathrow Airport

Richmond

Putney

Putney Bridge

⊙ W

⊙ Staines

2

Ⓐ

Richmond Park

Morden ⊙

Hampton Court

Kingston-upon-Thames

1

Hampton

Carshalton

4

Epsom

Shepperton Ferry

National Cycle Network

Selected traffic-free sections

Network to be completed by 2005

⊙ Selected railway stations

⊙ Airport

Route numbers

4 National

© Crown copyright

5 miles

8 km

to Dorking & Guildford

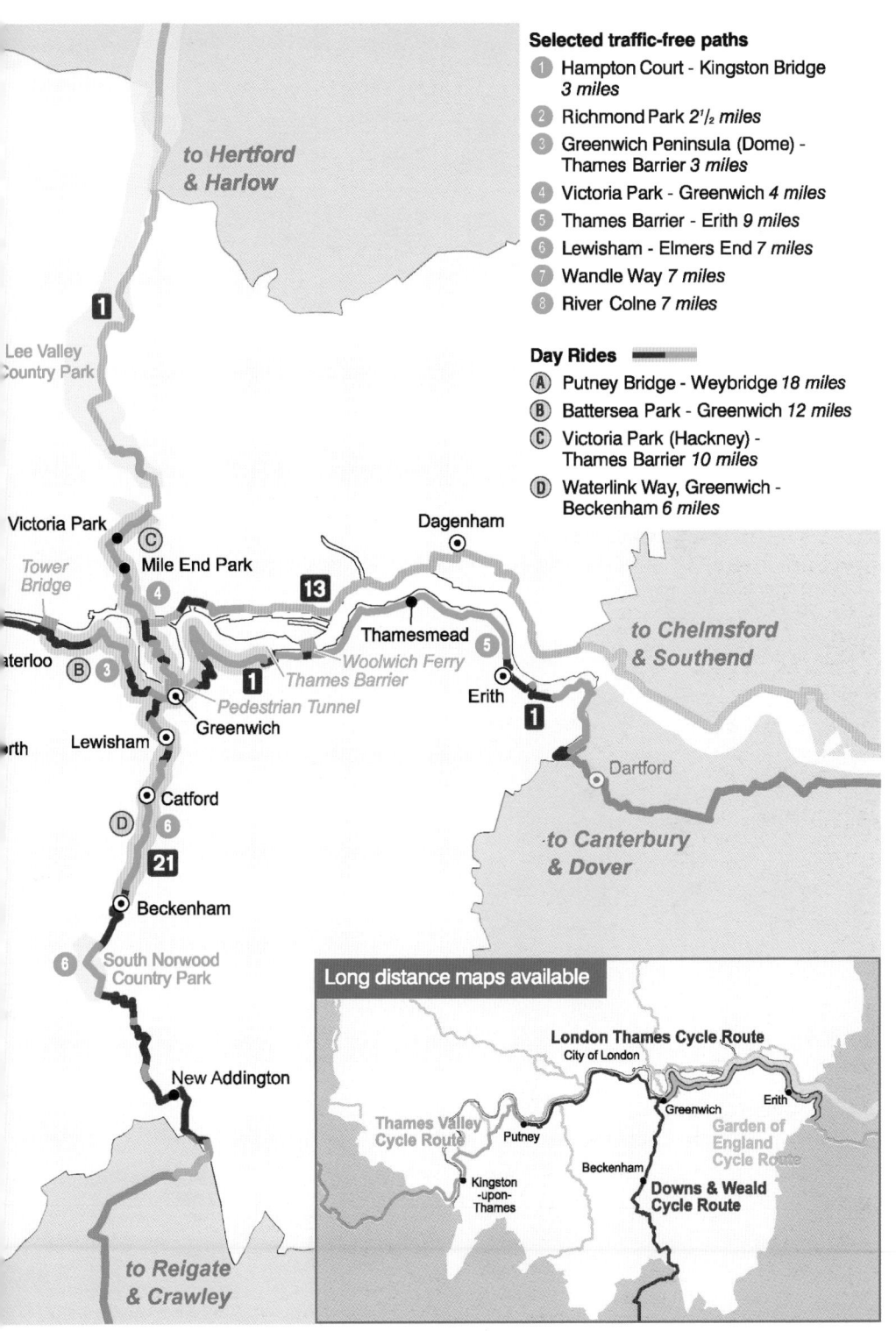

LONDON

London is the largest and busiest city in Britain so, not surprisingly, the creation of the National Cycle Network in the capital has thrown up enormous challenges to all those who have been involved in the project. Considerable effort and resources have been invested to create continuous, quality routes leading into and through London, enabling people to see and experience the city as never before.

Many main road crossings, traffic-calming measures and other features have been installed across London to improve safety and access for walkers and cyclists. These will not only make cycling more popular in London but will also ensure that one of the best ways of viewing Britain's capital city is by bike. For example, major improvements for cyclists have been installed at Blackfriars Bridge, Millbank,

Houses of Parliament.

Westminster Bridge and Lambeth Bridge. Sustrans is also working with landowners and developers to create underpasses beneath other major Thames bridges. A number of dedicated bridges have been built that provide vital links, including the new bridge over the River Lee in Hackney Marsh, and over the mouth of the River Wandle in Wandsworth.

As the Network continues to grow in London it is proposed to develop a series of additional family-friendly routes that will link together the main parks and open spaces, helping people to start cycling again.

Four routes in the National Cycle Network meet in London, crossing the Thames at Greenwich:

East from Greenwich, the Thames Cycle Route (Route 1) winds around the Dome peninsula, following a shared-use riverside promenade. From there, the route remains close to the riverbank passing the spectacular Thames Barrier, then runs along new promenades at Woolwich and Thamesmead. It continues along the riverbank to Erith where it turns south inland to Dartford and follows the northern edge of Kent.

West from Greenwich the Thames Cycle Route becomes Route 4, using the riverbank and adjacent quiet streets with breathtaking views of Tower Bridge and the City. Passing through the heart of the capital on the south bank of the Thames, Route 4 crosses over Lambeth Bridge to the north side and continues to follow the river through Chelsea before crossing back at Putney where it joins the riverside towpath. Further upstream, the main route leaves the river to cross Richmond Park and rejoin the Thames at Teddington Lock.

There are also several 'spur' routes, which use short sections of riverside path and are suitable for families with small children. These spurs offer links to the major centres of Richmond, Kew and Hammersmith. Back on the main route at Kingston, the cyclist travels past the majestic buildings of Hampton Court, continuing along a delightful long stretch of towpath through to Weybridge and Staines before a final loop through Windsor Great Park to Windsor town centre.

South of Greenwich the Waterlink Way (Route 21) follows the valley through Lewisham, Bromley and Croydon. Several new pedestrian/

cycle bridges have been specially constructed over the Ravensbourne River, joined by many new sections of cycle and walking routes following the riverbank and parkland. Route 21 continues south to Hastings, picking up the popular Cuckoo Trail at Heathfield.

North of Greenwich, the Network makes use of the Greenwich Foot Tunnel to join the Lee Valley Pathway, which, as Route 1, eventually leads all the way to Inverness. Within London itself, the route passes to the west of Canary Wharf then links together several excellent sections of riverside promenade, towpath and parkland. Innovative features include the superb 'Green Bridge', a wide, tree-lined grass bridge over the A11, within Mile End Park. Route 1 then meanders alongside waterways and through wetlands to the Lee Valley Regional Park, with all its recreational opportunities. It continues north to Waltham Abbey then runs east to join to the Harwich to Hull Route.

Three more routes are under development in London: the **Wandle Valley Way** going south west from London to Epsom (Route 22); a **north west** route to Rickmansworth (Route 6); and a **North East Thames** route to Southend (Route 13). Many sections of these new routes will be offroad, providing excellent learning grounds for novice riders close to the heart of London.

Woolwich Riverside with Thames Barrage and Dome in the background.

The London Cycle Network

The National Cycle Network in London is complemented by the London Cycle Network (LCN), which is taking shape around the capital. Started in 1995 and due for completion in 2008, the London Cycle Network will comprise 1,850 miles of routes and provide direct access to all major centres of employment, education, leisure and railway stations. Look out for the blue and white signs with route numbers and the distinctive 'London Cycle Network' logo.

London Cycling Campaign

With over 8,000 members, the London Cycling Campaign (LCC) is the largest urban cycling campaign in the world. Created in 1979, LCC has campaigned ceaselessly to implement a network of safe cycle routes in London and to raise awareness of cycling in the capital. Its campaign for a ' Thousand Mile Network' gave rise to the London Cycle Network which in 1995 gained government funding. The London Cycling Campaign has local groups in each of the 33 London Boroughs. They work locally with councils to improve conditions for cyclists and also organise rides and events. Membership benefits include discounts in many London bike shops and a regular magazine. To join telephone 020 7928 7220 or visit www.lcc.org.uk

The route runs past the Tate Britain, which is just a short ride from the Tate Modern on Bankside.

NATIONAL CYCLE NETWORK HIGHLIGHTS

Tower Bridge
The riverside is the best place from which to view the City of London, The Tower, St. Paul's, and Tower Bridge.

Hampton Court
This Palace is one of the most magnificent sights along the river, all the more memorable on account of the open riverside approach from both directions.

The London Eye
Travelling along the Thames Cycle Route, the Tate Britain, the London Eye, South Bank, Tate Modern, the Millennium Footbridge, the Globe Theatre and Greenwich, all lie within an easy cycling distance.

The Millennium Dome
A new riverside promenade has been opened up around the Greenwich Peninsula, providing spectacular views of the Dome and Canary Wharf.

Mile End Park
The A11 Green Bridge is a highlight of the Park and of this section of National Route 1. The bridge continues the thread of landscaping over the busy road below to create the illusion of an uninterrupted park.

Greenwich Foot Tunnel
The Cutty Sark frames the Greenwich entrance to the foot tunnel under the Thames leading to the Isle of Dogs and Canary Wharf. This is one of only three under-river tunnels used in the whole Network (the others being under the River Tyne and under the River Clyde).

PUTNEY BRIDGE TO WEYBRIDGE

For anyone who believes that there is no escape for cyclists from London's traffic, this ride is the answer: enjoy cycling along the green corridor that lies right on the doorstep of the capital. Putney Bridge marks the eastern end of a long stretch of the Thames riverside path which can be explored by bike. The National Cycle Network itself bears away from the river after a mile or so, past the new Wetlands Centre at Barnes, then crossing Richmond Park (where you have the option of completing a totally traffic-free circuit of the park) before rejoining the river, threading its way through Kingston upon Thames and passing the majestic buildings of Hampton Court. The Thames is followed closely for the next six miles, passing Sunbury Lock and finishing at Weybridge. This route is part of the Thames Valley Cycle Route and if you wish you could follow the ride beyond Weybridge to Windsor, Reading and Oxford.

Upstream from Hampton Court the route follows along the bank of the River Thames all the way to Shepperton Ferry.

Starting points
1. The south side of Putney Bridge.
2. The riverside path (by the pedestrian ferry) in Weybridge.

Distance
18 miles one way, 36 miles return. For a shorter trip, starting from Putney Bridge, there are good turnaround points at Richmond Park (12 miles round trip), Kingston upon Thames (18 miles round trip) or Hampton Court (24 miles round trip).

Grade
Easy.

Surface
Mixture of tarmac and good quality gravel paths.

Roads, traffic, suitability for young children
The route is a mixture of quiet streets and cyclepaths. The best traffic-free section alongside the river runs west from Kingston Bridge, crosses to the other side at Hampton Court then continues to Weybridge (a total of nine miles one way, 18 miles return).

Hills
Richmond Hill.

Refreshments
All along the way.

Leaflets
The whole of London is now covered by 19 Cycle Guides (free). They are available from London Cycling Campaign, Unit 228, 30 Great Guildford Street, London. SE1 0HS. Tel: 020 7928 7220. Website: www.lcc.org.uk E-mail: office@lcc.org.uk OR from London Travel Information. Tel: 020 7222 1234. Website: www.transportforlondon.gov.uk

Cycling the Thames. The Thames Landscape Strategy produces a pack of 10 laminated cards describing 10 rides of 5-12 miles in length between Weybridge and Hammersmith. Available for £3.50 from Thames Landscape Strategy, c/o Holly Lodge, Richmond Park, Richmond TW10 5HS. Tel: 0208 940 0654. Also available from Sustrans. See page 83 for contact details

Nearest railway stations
Putney, Barnes, Kingston upon Thames, Hampton Court.

The National Cycle Network in the area
The ride described here is the first section of the Thames Valley Cycle Route which runs from Putney Bridge to Oxford (Route 4 to Reading then Route 5 from Reading to Oxford). East from Putney Bridge the London Thames Cycle Route runs right through the heart of London to Greenwich and Dartford.

Other nearby rides (waymarked or traffic-free)
There is a traffic-free circular ride around Richmond Park.

Route instructions
1. From the south side of Putney Bridge push your bike along the pavement of Richmond Road for 100 yds then bear right downhill onto the one way street (with cycle contraflow) alongside the river.

2. Follow this to the end and continue in the same direction, as tarmac turns to gravel track. After one mile, with Fulham Football Club ground opposite you on the other side of the Thames, turn left through gates onto a tarmac track leading away from the river.

3. The track joins the sports centre access road. Continue in the same direction. Just before the crossroads with the main road bear left onto a path through the park parallel with Rocks Lane.

4. Use the toucan crossing to cross onto Ranelagh Avenue then take the first track to the left (opposite no.10) for Barnes Common. You may have to dismount and push your bike. Cross Mill Hill Road with care before continuing through the open scrubland and woodland.

5. At the junction with Rocks Lane, bear right onto the quiet road towards Barnes railway station. Immediately after passing the station on your left, bear left alongside the railings on a gravel track.

6. At the T-junction with the road, bear left to go over two level crossings. Just before the traffic lights (at the main road) bear right onto a gravel track and use the toucan crossing to cross over onto the green cycle path opposite running along Priory Lane.

7. After ¾ mile, at the end of the green painted cycle lane, turn right onto Bank Lane, then shortly first left onto Roehampton Gate. At the T-junction, turn right through the gate into Richmond Park onto a cycle lane parallel with the busy road.

8. Just before the crossroads by a white signpost, turn left at the cycle crossing to join the road towards White Lodge. Immediately after passing a car park to the right, turn right towards Isabella Plantation.

9. At the crossroads, use the cycle crossing and carry on down Ham Gate Avenue. Exit Richmond Park. At the crossroads use the toucan

PUTNEY BRIDGE TO WEYBRIDGE

DAY RIDE

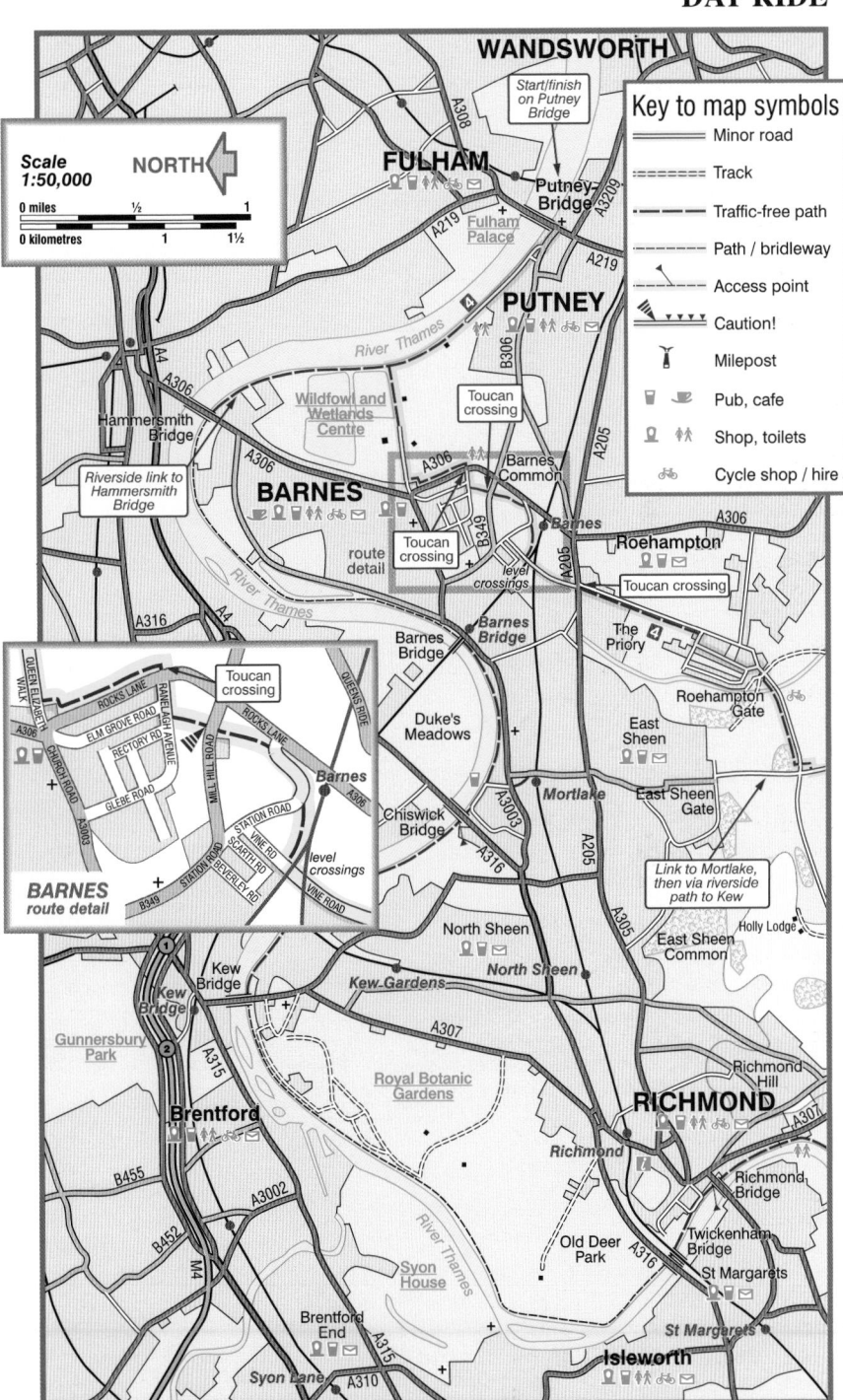

Scale 1:50,000

0 miles · ½ · 1
0 kilometres · 1 · 1½

NORTH

Key to map symbols

— Minor road
===== Track
— — Traffic-free path
– – Path / bridleway
Access point
▼▼▼ Caution!
Milepost
Pub, cafe
Shop, toilets
Cycle shop / hire

WANDSWORTH

Start/finish on Putney Bridge

FULHAM

Putney Bridge

Fulham Palace

PUTNEY

A308 · A219 · A3209 · A219 · B306 · A205

River Thames

Wildfowl and Wetlands Centre

Toucan crossing

Hammersmith Bridge

Riverside link to Hammersmith Bridge

BARNES

A306 · A4 · A316

Barnes Common

route detail

Toucan crossing

level crossings

Barnes

Roehampton

Toucan crossing

River Thames

Barnes Bridge

The Priory

BARNES route detail

QUEEN ELIZABETH WALK · ROCKS LANE · RANELAGH AVENUE · RECTORY RD · ROCKS LANE · ELM GROVE ROAD · CHURCH ROAD · GLEBE ROAD · MILL HILL ROAD · A306 · STATION ROAD · SCARTH RD · VINE RD · STATION ROAD · BEVERLEY RD · B349 · VINE ROAD · QUEENS RIDE · A306

Toucan crossing

Barnes

level crossings

Duke's Meadows

East Sheen

Roehampton Gate

East Sheen Gate

Chiswick Bridge

Mortlake

Link to Mortlake, then via riverside path to Kew

East Sheen Common

Holly Lodge

North Sheen

North Sheen

A3003 · A205 · A316 · A305 · A306 · A307

Kew Bridge

Kew Gardens

Gunnersbury Park

A315 · A307

Royal Botanic Gardens

Richmond Hill

RICHMOND

Brentford

B455 · A3002 · B452 · M4 · A315

Syon House

River Thames

Old Deer Park

Richmond

Richmond Bridge

Twickenham Bridge

St Margarets

A316 · A307

Brentford End

Syon Lane · A310

St Margarets

Isleworth

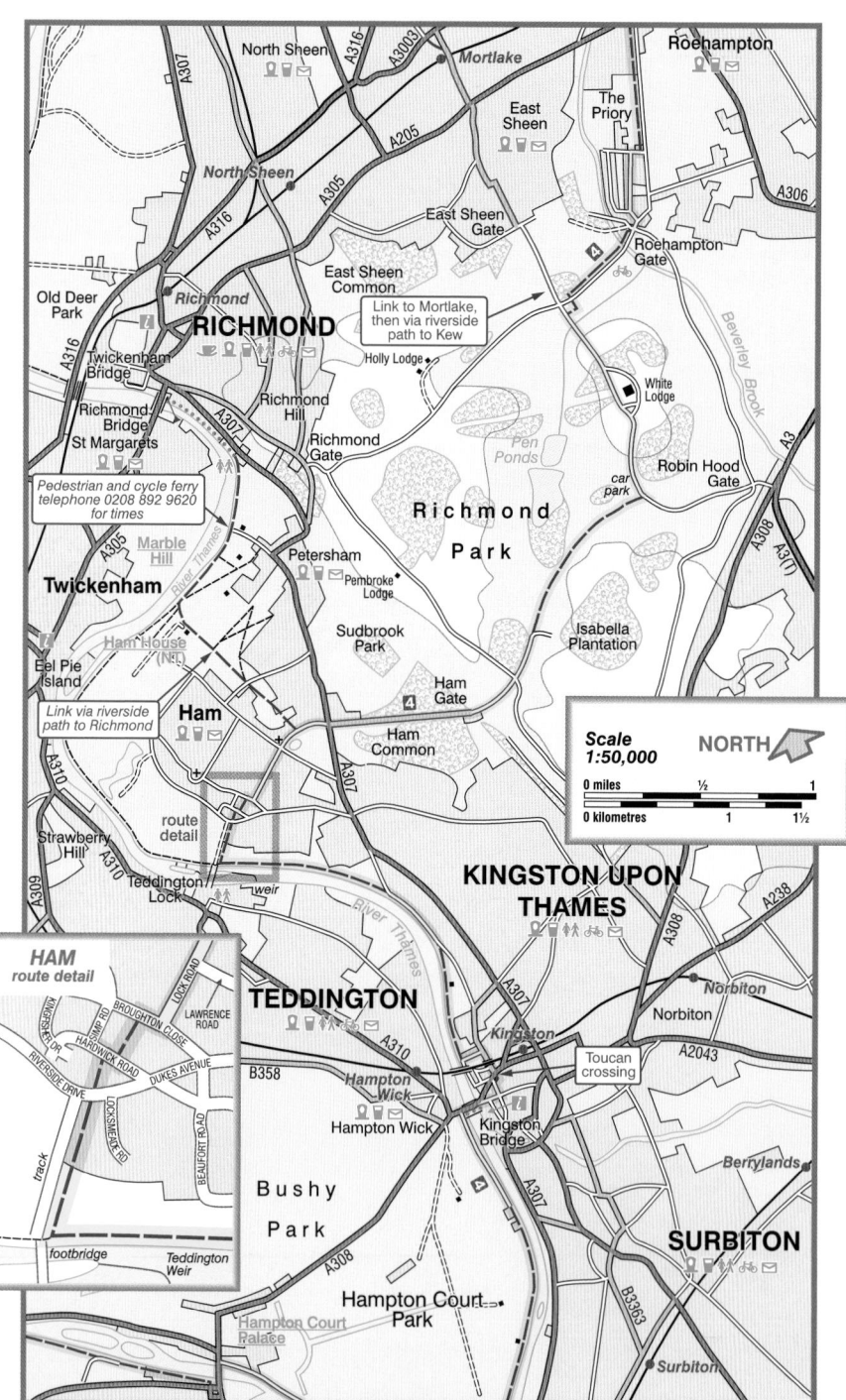

PUTNEY BRIDGE TO WEYBRIDGE

North Sheen
Mortlake
Roehampton
East Sheen
The Priory
North Sheen
East Sheen Gate
Old Deer Park
Richmond
RICHMOND
Roehampton Gate
East Sheen Common
Twickenham Bridge
Richmond Hill
Holly Lodge
Link to Mortlake, then via riverside path to Kew
White Lodge
Richmond Bridge
St Margarets
Richmond Hill
Richmond Gate
Pen Ponds
Robin Hood Gate
Pedestrian and cycle ferry telephone 0208 892 9620 for times
Marble Hill
Twickenham
Petersham
Pembroke Lodge
Richmond Park
car park
Isabella Plantation
Ham House (NT)
Sudbrook Park
Eel Pie Island
Ham
Ham Gate
Link via riverside path to Richmond
Ham Common
Scale 1:50,000

NORTH

0 miles ½ 1
0 kilometres 1 1½

Strawberry Hill
route detail
Teddington Lock
weir
KINGSTON UPON THAMES
Norbiton

HAM route detail

LOCK ROAD
BROUGHTON CLOSE
LAWRENCE ROAD
OLD CAMP
HARDWICK ROAD
DUKES AVENUE
RIVERSIDE DRIVE
LOCKSMEAD RD.
BEAUFORT ROAD

TEDDINGTON
A310
B358
Hampton Wick
Hampton Wick
Kingston
Norbiton
Toucan crossing
Kingston Bridge
Berrylands

track

Bushy Park
footbridge
Teddington Weir

SURBITON

Hampton Court Park
Hampton Court Palace
Surbiton

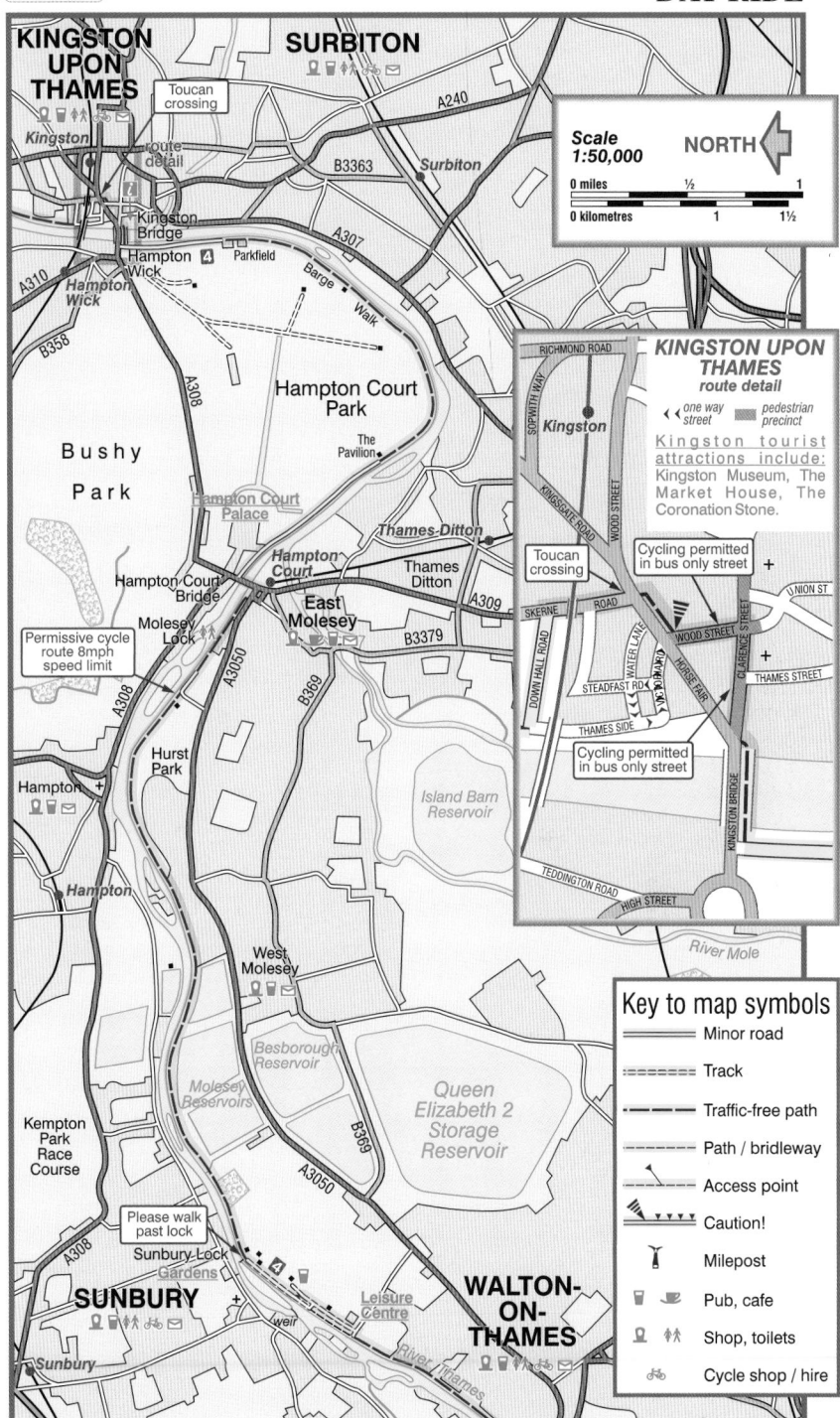

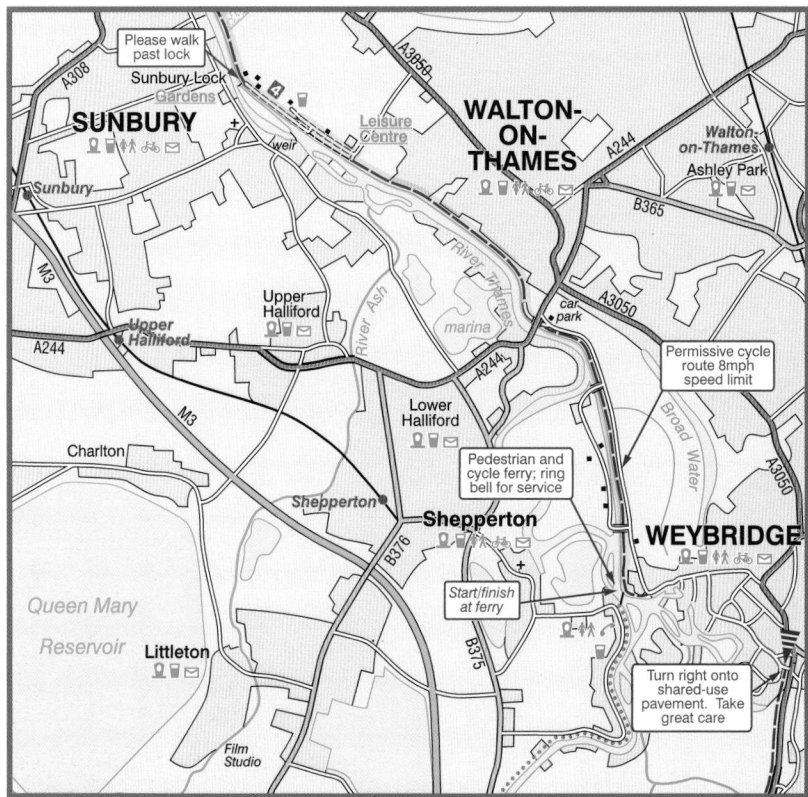

© Crown copyright

crossing and go straight ahead onto the road through Ham Common. Follow 'Teddington Cycle Route' signs.

10. Continue in the same direction, then at the T-junction at the end of Lock Road turn right then left after 50 yds onto a shared-use path. Go straight ahead at two crossroads, following the cycle path between houses and into the woods near the river. At T-junction with the riverside path, turn left.

11. At the T-junction with the road, bear right then after 400 yds leave the road and bear right again back onto the riverside path.

12. (Route through Kingston.) At the end of the riverside path, bear left down Hall Road. At the junction, cross over the busy road to a shared-use path outside Bentalls, using the toucan crossings. Follow the path to the right, leading into Wood Street (between Bentalls and John Lewis). Turn right into Clarence Street and onto the bridge.

13. Use the two-way segregated cycle path to cross Kingston Bridge, then turn left onto Barge Walk.

14. Follow the riverside path past Hampton Court. At the bridge turn

right and use the pelican crossing to cross the road. Use the segregated cycle path on the pavement to cross the bridge over the river, and turn right to rejoin the riverside path for six miles to Weybridge.

15. In Weybridge you have a choice of visiting the pubs just beyond the car park, catching the ferry across the river, or returning back towards Putney. Weybridge railway station is about 1½ miles south of this point. Alternatively, if you cross to the other side of the river via the ferry, you could catch a train from Shepperton station, which is closer and safer to get to.

Canary Wharf.

BATTERSEA PARK TO GREENWICH

One of the National Cycle Network Routes through Central London broadly follows the line of the Thames, although for the majority of this section the route is slightly set back from the river on traffic-calmed streets. The ideal time to do this ride would be on a fine Sunday morning. There is far less traffic around so not only are the roads quieter but any impromptu outside refreshment stop at a cafe or pub is likely to be more pleasant. There are so many attractions along the way that one of the best sorts of ride would link together museums and cafes, palaces and pubs, galleries and riverside views.

You may wish to warm-up for the ride to Greenwich by starting off with the easy traffic-free circuit around the perimeter of Battersea Park.

As you make your way from Battersea Park towards Lambeth Bridge you pass the Tate Gallery with its magnificent Historic British and 20th Century Collections. Once Lambeth Bridge is crossed, back to the South Bank, the National Cycle Network stays on the south side of the river to Greenwich, the main crossroads of the Network in London. If your interests lie in the past then parts of Lambeth Palace, the official home of the Archbishop of Canterbury, date back to the 13th century. If your tastes are more aligned to the present, the Museum of the Moving Image is an interactive guide to the moving image from Chinese puppets to video production. Between the two, the Jubilee Gardens would make a fine stop to appreciate views of the Thames.

Key to map:
main route
proposed route

(1) Segregated cycle lanes on Chelsea Embankment will be constructed by early 2003.

(2) An additional southern route is being developed from Putney Bridge to Lambeth Bridge, which will be constructed over the next five years.

(3) The South Bank promenade is open to walkers. Ongoing negotiations are taking place to allow family cycling on certain sections.

The Peace Pagoda in Battersea Park. A cycle around the park allows a quiet break away from the busy London streets.

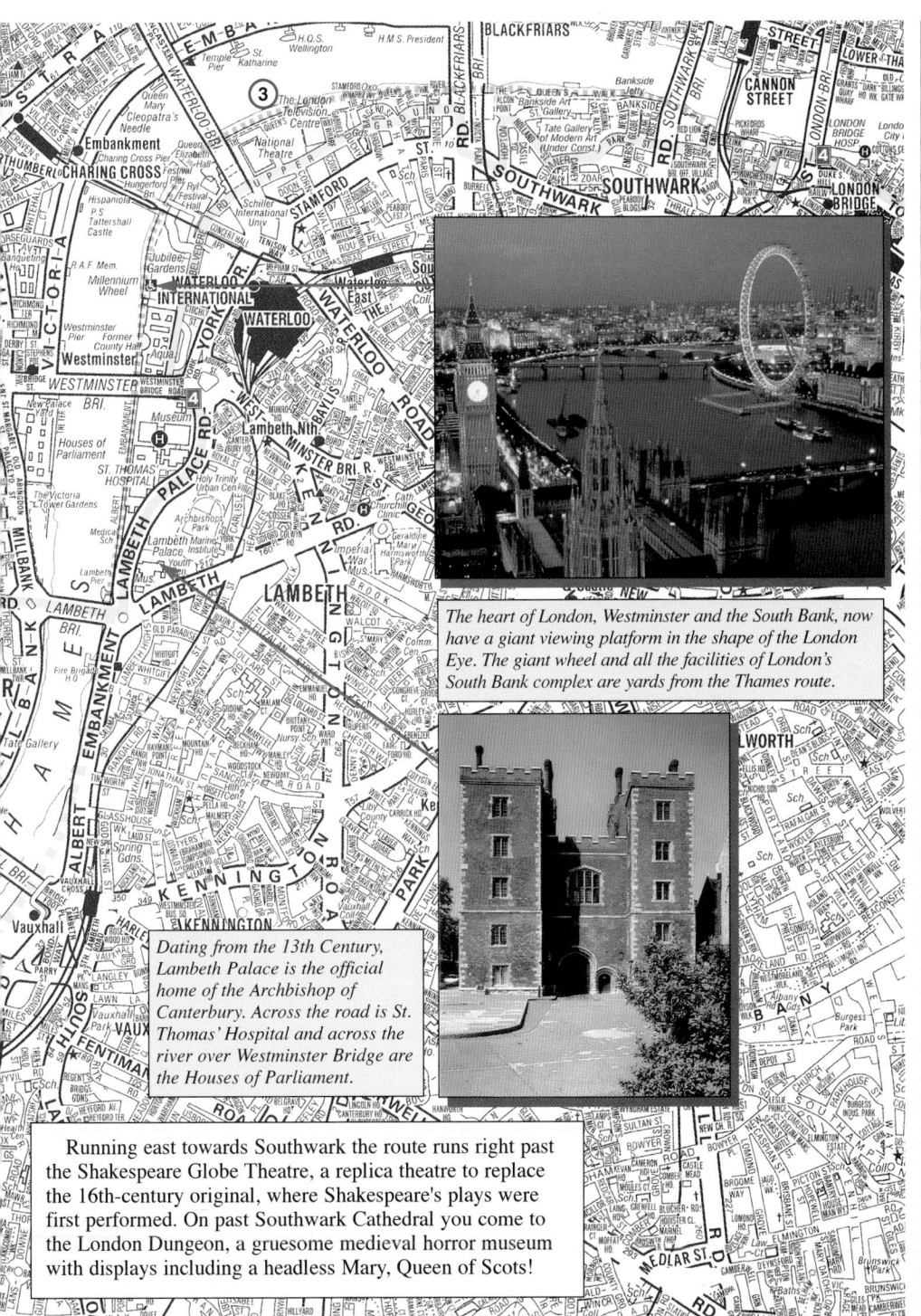

The heart of London, Westminster and the South Bank, now have a giant viewing platform in the shape of the London Eye. The giant wheel and all the facilities of London's South Bank complex are yards from the Thames route.

Dating from the 13th Century, Lambeth Palace is the official home of the Archbishop of Canterbury. Across the road is St. Thomas' Hospital and across the river over Westminster Bridge are the Houses of Parliament.

Running east towards Southwark the route runs right past the Shakespeare Globe Theatre, a replica theatre to replace the 16th-century original, where Shakespeare's plays were first performed. On past Southwark Cathedral you come to the London Dungeon, a gruesome medieval horror museum with displays including a headless Mary, Queen of Scots!

Beyond Tower Bridge, the last bridge over the Thames before Dartford, you briefly rejoin the river through Bermondsey before cutting inland through the Russia Dock Woodland and Ecological Park.

Deptford Creek is the point at which the Waterlink Way comes in from the south, linking the South Coast at Eastbourne with London via Hailsham and East Grinstead.

After a long section with few famous attractions you arrive at Greenwich and you are spoilt for choice: the Cutty Sark and Gipsy Moth IV, Greenwich Pier and the Royal Naval College, plus numerous refreshment stops. The Greenwich Foot Tunnel brings National Route 1 from the north (John o' Groats if you want to be precise!).

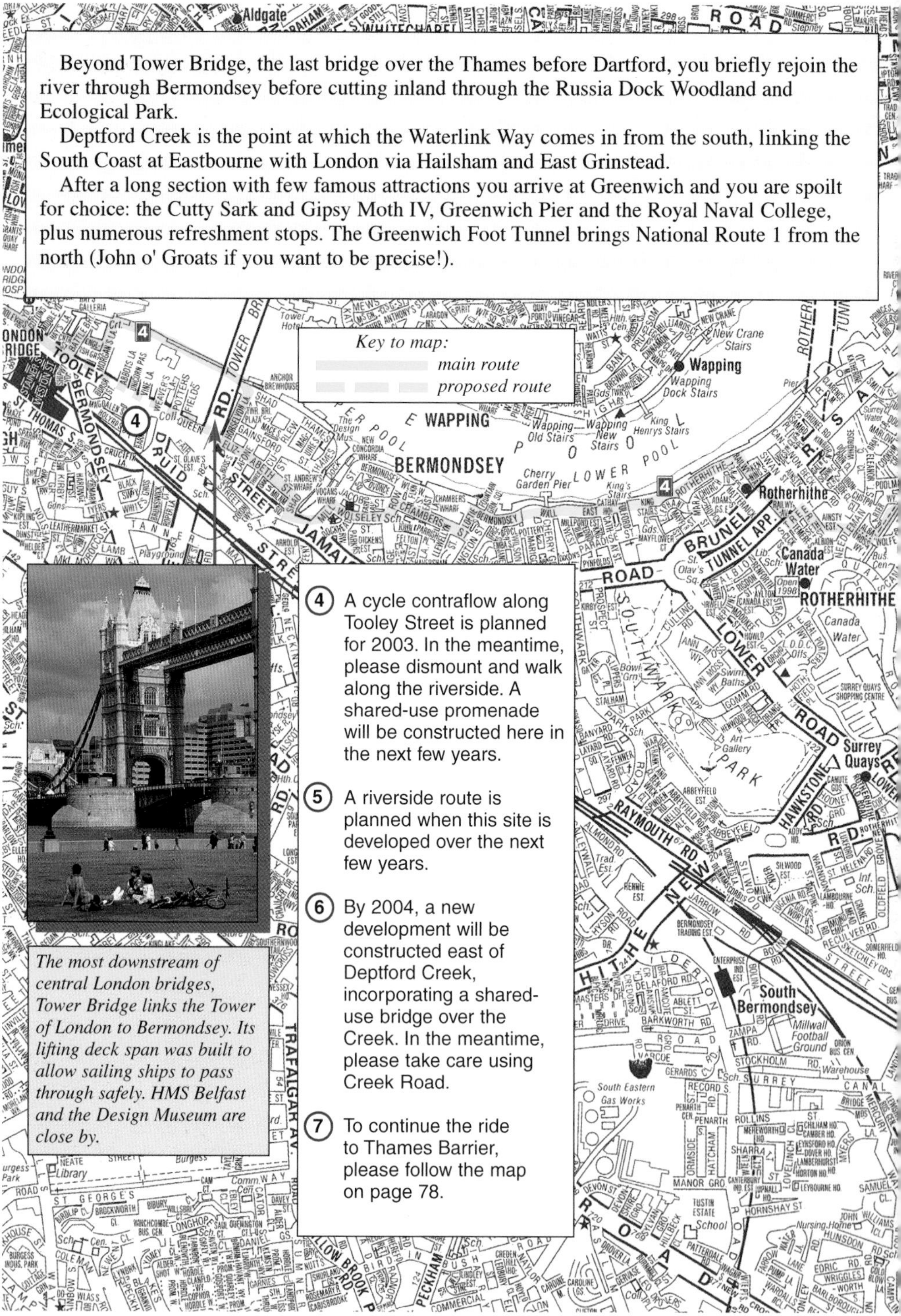

Key to map:
main route
proposed route

The most downstream of central London bridges, Tower Bridge links the Tower of London to Bermondsey. Its lifting deck span was built to allow sailing ships to pass through safely. HMS Belfast and the Design Museum are close by.

④ A cycle contraflow along Tooley Street is planned for 2003. In the meantime, please dismount and walk along the riverside. A shared-use promenade will be constructed here in the next few years.

⑤ A riverside route is planned when this site is developed over the next few years.

⑥ By 2004, a new development will be constructed east of Deptford Creek, incorporating a shared-use bridge over the Creek. In the meantime, please take care using Creek Road.

⑦ To continue the ride to Thames Barrier, please follow the map on page 78.

74

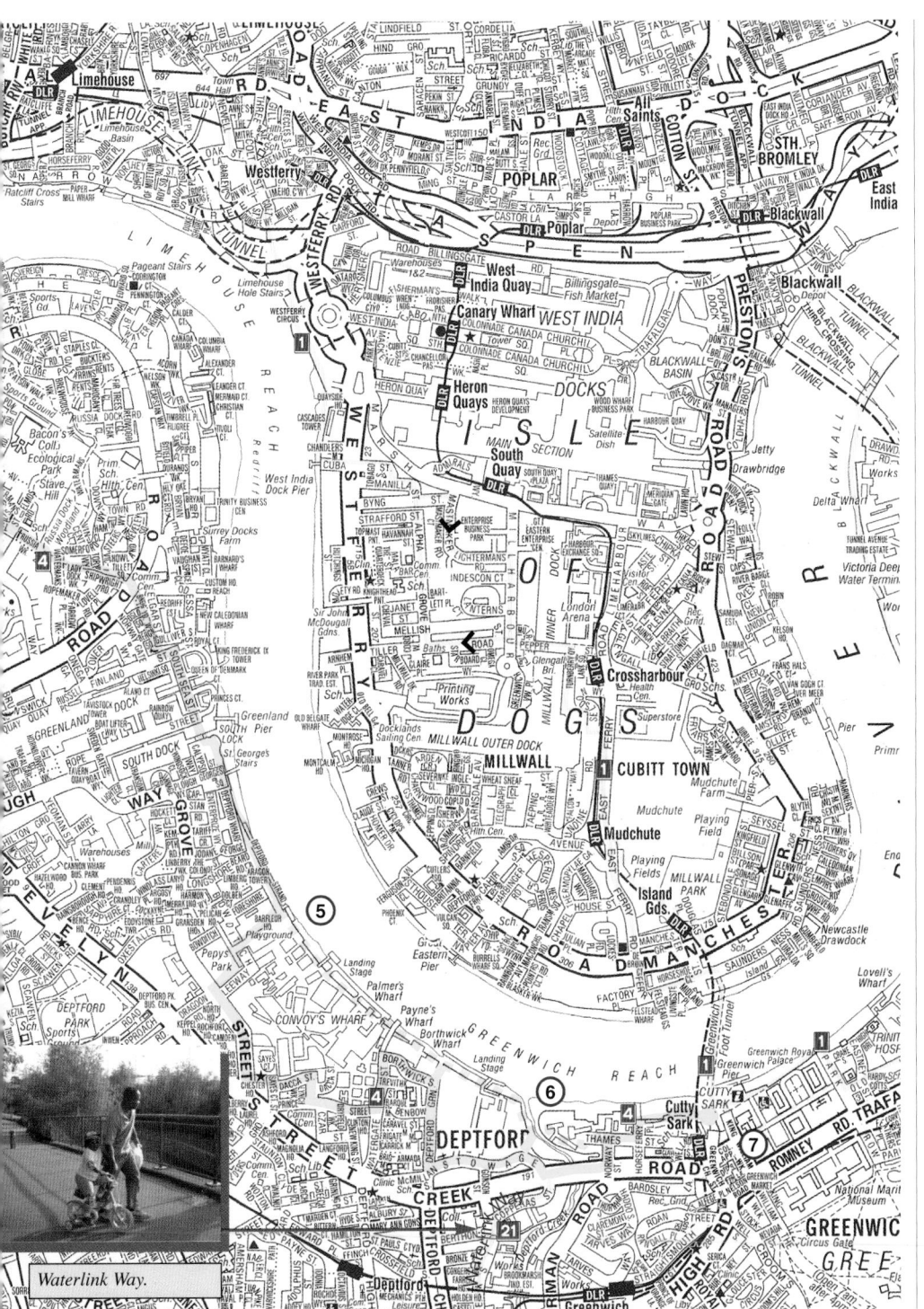

Waterlink Way.

VICTORIA PARK TO THE THAMES BARRIER

Linking together many of the most outstanding features of east London, this ride provides a fascinating way to explore an area not normally associated with sightseeing in the capital. There are myriad unexpected visual treats to be enjoyed from the traffic-free paths through Victoria Park, along the Regent's Canal (Grand Union Canal), across Mile End Park and down to the Thames at Limehouse Reach. The huge towers of Canary Wharf dominate much of the early part of the ride. After walking through the Greenwich Foot Tunnel to emerge at the Cutty Sark the route turns east in front of the Naval College. The route passes around the Greenwich Peninsula to end at the silver shell structures of the Thames Barrier, built to protect London from flooding.

Starting points
1. St Mark's Gate, Victoria Park, Hackney.
2. The Thames Barrier, Woolwich.

Distance
10 miles one way, 20 miles return.

Grade
Easy.

Surface
All tarmac.

Roads, traffic, suitability for young children
Although there are short traffic-free sections, the route is largely on traffic-calmed streets through the East End of London, so it is not really suitable for young children. If you are with older children (10+), the best time to do this ride is early on a Sunday morning.

Hills
None.

Refreshments
Lots of choice all along the way.

Leaflets
The whole of London is now covered by 19 Cycle Guides (free). They are available from London Cycling Campaign, Unit 228, 30 Great Guildford Street, London. SE1 0HS. Tel: 020 7928 7220. Website: www.lcc.org.uk E-mail: office@lcc.org.uk OR from London Travel

Information. Tel: 020 7222 1234. Website: www.transportforlondon.gov.uk

Nearest railway stations
Hackney Wick, Greenwich.

The National Cycle Network in the area
1. To the north of Victoria Park Route 1 continues up the Lee Valley corridor on broad gravel tracks, either alongside or parallel with the canal known as the Lee & Stort Navigation.
2. To the east of the Thames Barrier Route 1 continues along the Thames estuary as far as Gravesend where it heads inland through Kent then on to Canterbury and Dover.
3. Route 21 links London with the South Coast via the Waterlink Way running down through Deptford and Lewisham towards Croydon and Redhill.

Green Bridge linking Mile End Park route.

Other nearby rides (waymarked or traffic-free)
As mentioned above, there are miles of attractive traffic-free cycling in the Lee Valley Park.

Route instructions
Complicated routes through urban areas need a long and difficult set of instructions. Instead we have shown the route highlighted on street mapping so that if you ever miss a turning and lose sight of the National Cycle Network signposting and waymarks you can refer to the detailed mapping to find your way back to the route.

In broad terms you are linking the following: Victoria Park (Hackney), the Regent's Canal (Grand Union Canal), Mile End Park, Limehouse Basin, Cascades Tower, Millwall Inner Dock, Mudchute, the Greenwich Foot Tunnel, the Cutty Sark and the Thames Barrier.

1 Under the bridges, the canal towpath can be very narrow. Please dismount, or ride through them slowly.

Canal towpaths run along the southern end of Victoria Park, one of East London's most attractive and popular open spaces – an ideal starting place for a great day out.

Key to map:
main route

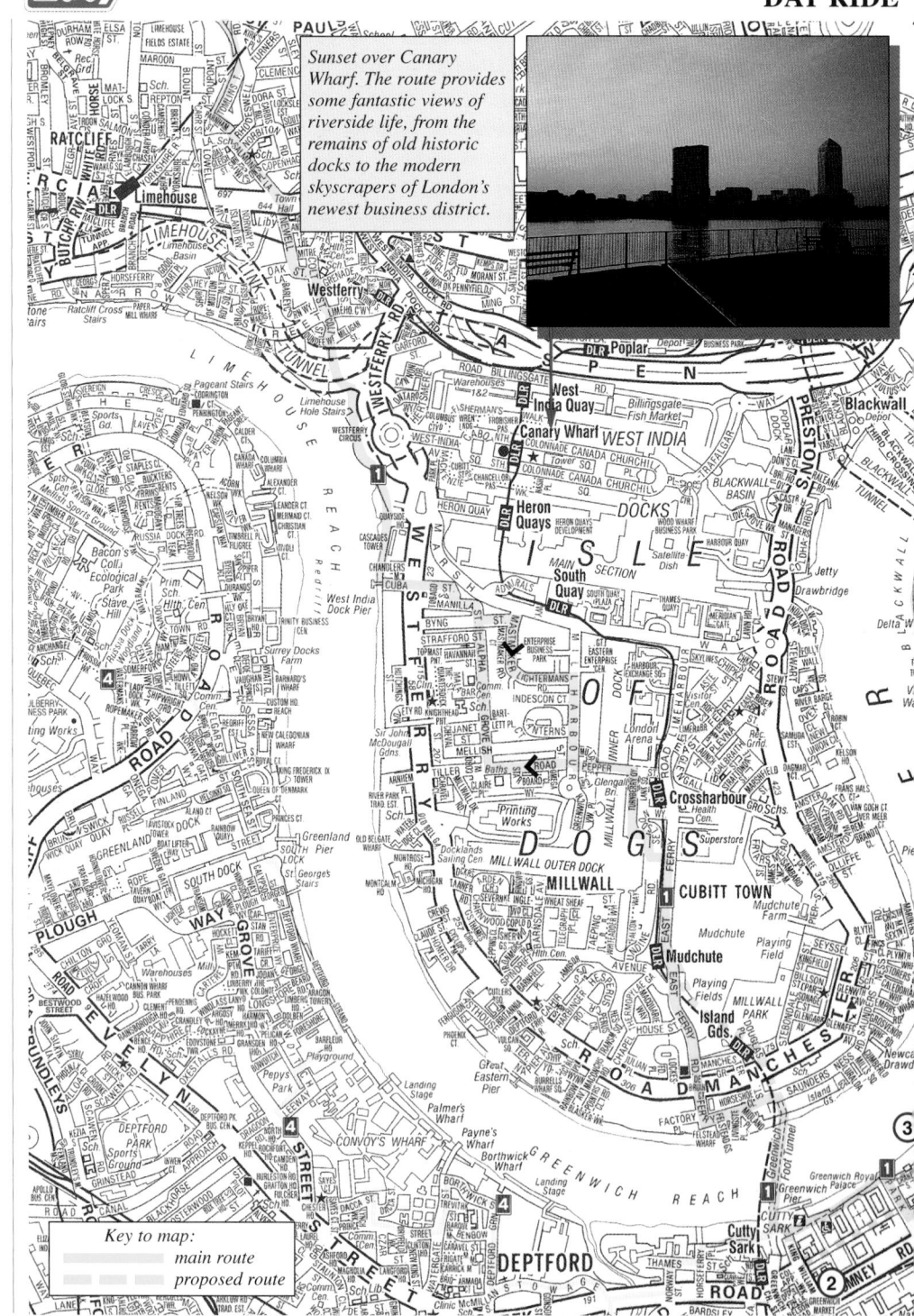

Sunset over Canary Wharf. The route provides some fantastic views of riverside life, from the remains of old historic docks to the modern skyscrapers of London's newest business district.

Key to map:
main route
proposed route

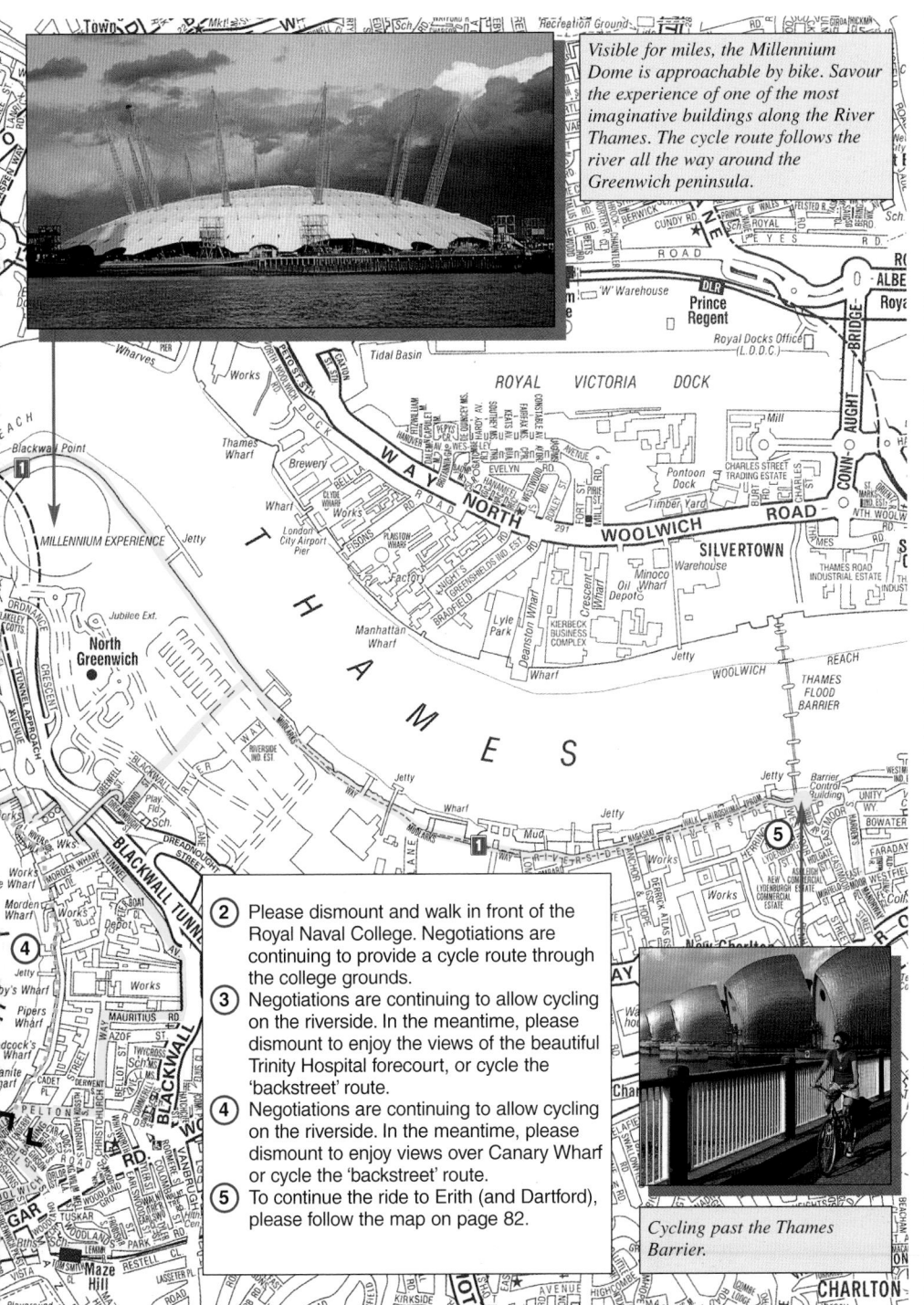

Visible for miles, the Millennium Dome is approachable by bike. Savour the experience of one of the most imaginative buildings along the River Thames. The cycle route follows the river all the way around the Greenwich peninsula.

(2) Please dismount and walk in front of the Royal Naval College. Negotiations are continuing to provide a cycle route through the college grounds.

(3) Negotiations are continuing to allow cycling on the riverside. In the meantime, please dismount to enjoy the views of the beautiful Trinity Hospital forecourt, or cycle the 'backstreet' route.

(4) Negotiations are continuing to allow cycling on the riverside. In the meantime, please dismount to enjoy views over Canary Wharf or cycle the 'backstreet' route.

(5) To continue the ride to Erith (and Dartford), please follow the map on page 82.

Cycling past the Thames Barrier.

THE WATERLINK WAY
(GREENWICH TO BECKENHAM)

Starting on the banks of the Thames at Greenwich, under the bow of the Cutty Sark, the Waterlink Way makes its way south through Lewisham, Bromley and Croydon. It follows the valley of the little-known Ravensbourne River, journeying through the pretty suburbia of London. Many new bridges and underpasses have been built for the route (as part of the new Docklands Light Railway works). There's even a suspended walkway through a tunnel over a river! The route takes you through many delightful parklands, both new and rejuvenated, making at least half of the ride traffic-free. At Catford, the route picks up the Pool River and follows it into Bromley. From park to park you hop before entering the borough of Croydon at Elmers End. Here, you can pick up a train back to London or head on south into South Norwood Country Park.

Starting Points
1. Greenwich (Cutty Sark)
2. Clockhouse Station, Beckenham Road, Beckenham.

Distance
Six miles one way, 12 miles return

Grade
Easy

Surface
All tarmac

Roads, traffic, suitability for young children
Where the route passes though parkland it is ideal for young children. However, there are also several road sections which are only suitable for older children (10+).

Hills
None

Refreshments
Lots of choice near the Cutty Sark. Various pubs near the route on the way south.

Leaflets
The whole of London is now covered by 19 Cycle Guides (free). They are available from London Cycling Campaign, Unit 228, 30 Great Guildford Street, London. SE1 0HS. Tel: 020 7928 7220. Website: www.lcc.org.uk. E-mail: office@lcc.org.uk.
OR from London Travel Information. Tel: 020 7222 1234. Website: www.transportforlondon.gov.uk

Nearest railway stations
Greenwich and Clockhouse at either end of the ride and several others in between (Lewisham, Ladywell, Catford, and Lower Sydenham).

The National Cycle Network in the area
1. The Waterlink Way is part of Route 21 (London to Hastings, covered by the *Downs & Weald Cycle Route Map*).
2. North of Greenwich, Route 1 runs across the Isle of Dogs and Victoria Park to join the Lee Valley.
3. Route 4 (covered by the *London Thames Cycle Route Map*) runs west through London to Putney Bridge to join the Thames Valley Route.
4. East of Greenwich, Route 1 runs past the Millennium Dome and the old Woolwich Arsenal on its way to Erith and Dartford (covered by the *Garden of England Cycle Route Map*).

Route Instructions
The route is well-signposted as Route 21 and by following the red and white '21' markers as well as signs for Lewisham, Catford, Bellingham, Lower Sydenham and Beckenham you should not go too far wrong. It is also (occasionally) signposted as 'The Waterlink Way'.

1. The ride starts by heading west alongside the Thames from the Cutty Sark (water to your right) before turning south to cross the main road (Creek Road) onto Copperas Street and Creek Side.

2. From Deptford Bridge the ride continues south following the Ravensbourne River and the Pool River through blocks of parkland connected by largely quiet streets.

3. The route passes Lewisham Hospital and a series of sports grounds and bowling greens, crossing and recrossing the two rivers, running mainly parallel with the Lewisham - Catford - Beckenham railway line.

4. At Beckenham Road you have the choice of catching a train back to Central London from Clock House Station or continuing south into South Norwood Country Park.

GREENWICH

South Bermondsey

River Thames

A1206

Gypsy Moth IV
Cutty Sark

Greenwich Foot Tunnel

Maze Hill

National Maritime Museum

route detail

Toucan crossing due Summer 2002.

DEPTFORD

Deptford
New Cross

Greenwich

Old Royal Observatory

Ranger's House

Toucan crossing

Start/finish at Cutty Sark

KING WILLIAM ROAD

Deptford Bridge

Route due for completion early 2003; please walk

COPPERAS STREET

THAMES STREET

CREEK RD

St Johns
St Johns

Docklands Light Railway

Greenwich

Lewisham

Blackheath

Toucan crossing

B220

Toucan crossing

Use cycle lanes across bridge

Proposed final route due late 2002.

GREENWICH
route detail

Greenwich tourist attractions include: National Maritime Museum, Cutty Sark, Gypsy Moth IV.

LEWISHAM

Ladywell

Deptford Bridge

Ladywell

Honour Oak Park

Scale
1:100,000

NORTH

0 miles   1   2

0 kilometres 1   2   3

Honour Oak Park

Catford Bridge

Use road to car park

Catford

CATFORD

A205

Key to map symbols

——— Minor road

======= Track

— — — Traffic-free path

– · – · – Path / bridleway

——◄— Access point

▼▼▼▼ Caution!

Ï Milepost

Pub, cafe

Shop, toilets

Cycle shop / hire

Forest Hill

A212

A205

Walk under station

Kent House

Cator Park

ALDERSMEAD ROAD

KINGS HALL ROAD

BECKENHAM ROAD

BARNMEAD

Use shared use cycle paths

Toucan crossing

A234

Clock House

Bell Green

Bellingham

A2218

RAVENSCROFT ROAD

BIRKBECK RD

MACKENZIE

AVENUE ROAD

BLANDFORD ROAD

ALLEN ROAD

CHURCHFIELDS ROAD

KENDALL ROAD

Final route due for completion 2003.

Follow signs around cricket pitch; final route due 2002

cricket pitch

Lower Sydenham

New Beckenham

New Beckenham

Penge East

Cator Park

Walk under station

Penge

Kent House

Use shared use cycle paths

Toucan crossing

A214

BECKENHAM

Clock House

A234

BECK LANE

DORSET ROAD

ANCASTER ROAD

ELMERS END

CLOCK HOUSE ROAD

CROMWELL ROAD

CROYDON RD

Elmers End

Elmers End

KENT HOUSE to
ELMERS END
route detail

Kent House tourist attractions include: South Norwood Country Park.

A2

A200

B207

A2210

A20

A21

B236

A21

Pool River

Waterlink Way

THAMES BARRIER TO ERITH

East of the Thames Barrier, the character of the river changes dramatically as it broadens out across the flood plains on its way to the sea. The London Thames Cycle Route follows the river all the way to Erith, inviting you to discover this magnificent, but rarely appreciated, part of the Thames.

The route is mostly offroad apart from a short section just east of the dramatic silver shells of the Thames Barrier. An offroad riverside route is under negotiation for construction in the next few years. Much of the riverside access in this eastern part of London is new, as river wharves have slowly been redeveloped. Some fine examples of this can be found along Woolwich riverside, near Woolwich Ferry. Watch out for the 'Titanic' link bridge, various pieces of sculpture and Naval artefacts along the route. Further along, the riverside

promenades lead you into Woolwich Riverside Park which marks the site of the old Woolwich Dockyard. The route continues past the Old Royal Arsenal site which supplied the battalions of Britain for much of the 19th and 20th centuries. Pop in to the Royal Artillery Museum on the site, to find out more. From here, the route launches out along the majestic sweep of Gallions Reach before connecting with the promenade at Thamesmead Town, just past the Crossness Sewage Works, where the magnificent Victorian Pumping Station is well worth a visit. The remainder of the ride makes its way through the interesting working wharves of Bexley before leading into Erith where you can catch a train back to London or Kent. Alternatively, carry on through Erith to enjoy the wildlife and wetlands of Crayford Marshes before turning south to Dartford.

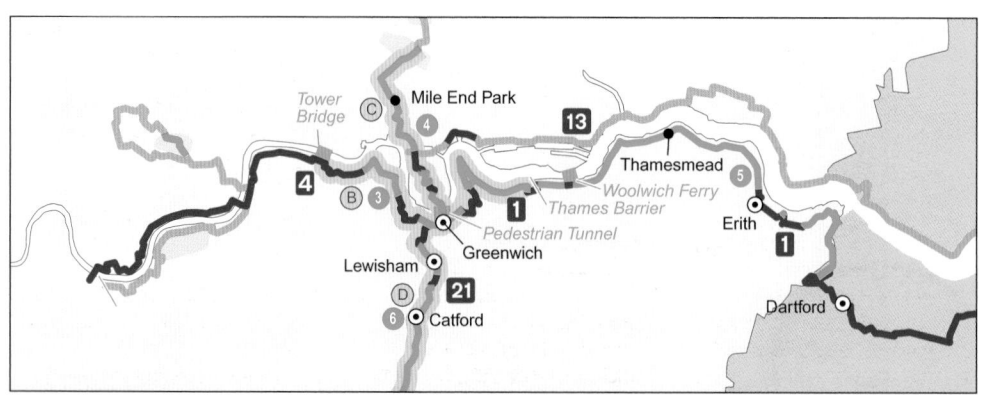

USEFUL MAPS & GUIDES

For details of the full range of maps, guides and other products available contact: **National Cycle Network Information, PO Box 21, Bristol BS99 2HA. Tel: 0117 929 0888. Or visit www.nationalcyclenetwork.org.uk**
The range of National Cycle Network Maps is described in more detail on pages 218-237.

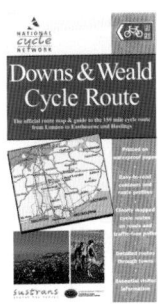

21 2 *Downs & Weald Cycle Route (London – Hastings, via Eastbourne)*
150 miles. NN2A - £5.99

4 5 *Thames Valley Cycle Route (London – Oxford)*
97 miles. NN5A - £5.99

1 2 18 *Garden of England Cycle Route (Dover – London & Hastings)*
114 miles. NN1X - £5.99

1 4 *London Thames Cycle Route (Hampton Court – Dartford)*
44 miles. LN001 - £4.99

London Cycle Guide
25 rides around the Central and Greater London areas. Includes over 125 miles of traffic-free routes.
RBH09 - £8.99

Cycling Without Traffic: London
30 leisure rides including Hampton Court and Epping Forest.
RBA09 - £11.99

Cycling The Thames
Ten route maps of easy half-day cycle rides between Weybridge and Hammersmith, including Kew Gardens, Hampton Court and Richmond Park. RPL37 - £3.50

London Cycle Guides
Transport for London in conjunction with the London Cycling Campaign has produced a series of 19 free cycle guides covering the whole of London showing signposted routes, traffic-free routes, advisory routes and proposed routes. Available from: London Cycling Campaign, Unit 228, 30 Great Guildford Street, London SE1 0HS.
Tel: 020 7928 7220.
email: office@lcc.org.uk
website:www.lcc.org.uk

Also available from London Travel Information. Tel: 020 7222 1234.
website:
www.transportforlondon.gov.uk

National Cycle Network
Selected traffic-free sections
Network to be completed by 2005
Selected railway stations
Airport
Regional Cycle Routes

Route numbers
1 National   **30** Regional

Wells-next-the-Sea

Hunstanton

Faken

1

(A)

3
King's Lynn

Stamford

63

1

Peterborough

2

Wisbech

63

Downham Market

11

13

63

March

The Brecks

12

Ely

Thetford

Huntingdon

51

11

Newmarket

51

Bury
St Edmund

Cambridge

Bedford

7

Sandy

51

12

11

Saffron Walden

13

Hadleigh

Milton
Keynes

6

6

(B)

6

Leighton Buzzard

Stevenage

Stansted

16

10

Colchester

Dunstable

Luton

6

Welwyn Garden
City

61

Braintree

1

Bishop's Stortford

Chilterns

9

Ware

Witham

Tiptree

St Albans

8

Hertford

15

1

13

Maldon

Hatfield

Harlow

Chelmsford

Watford

12

1

16

12

13

Basildon

13

14

13

Southend
-on-sea

20 miles

Tilbury

30 km

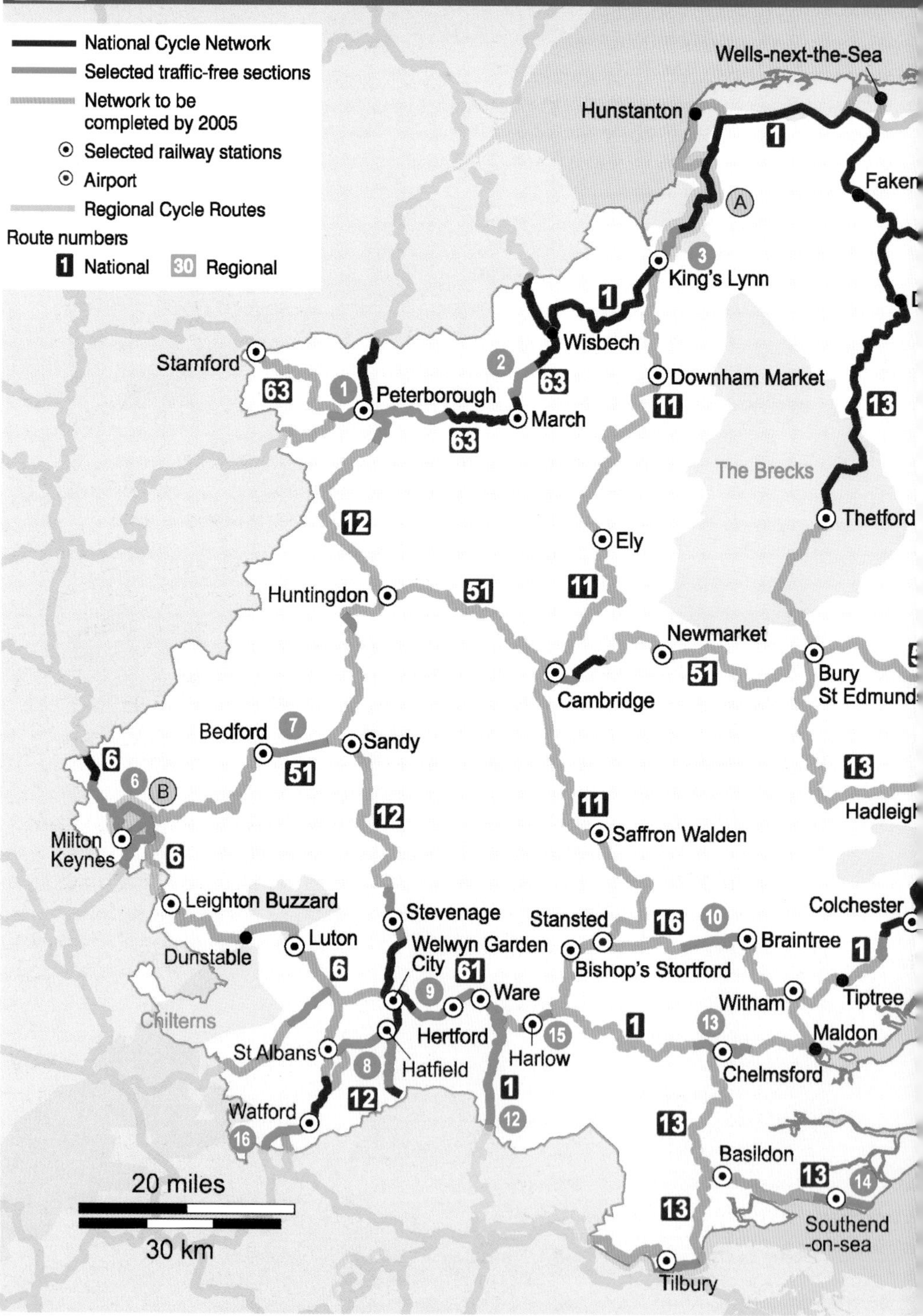

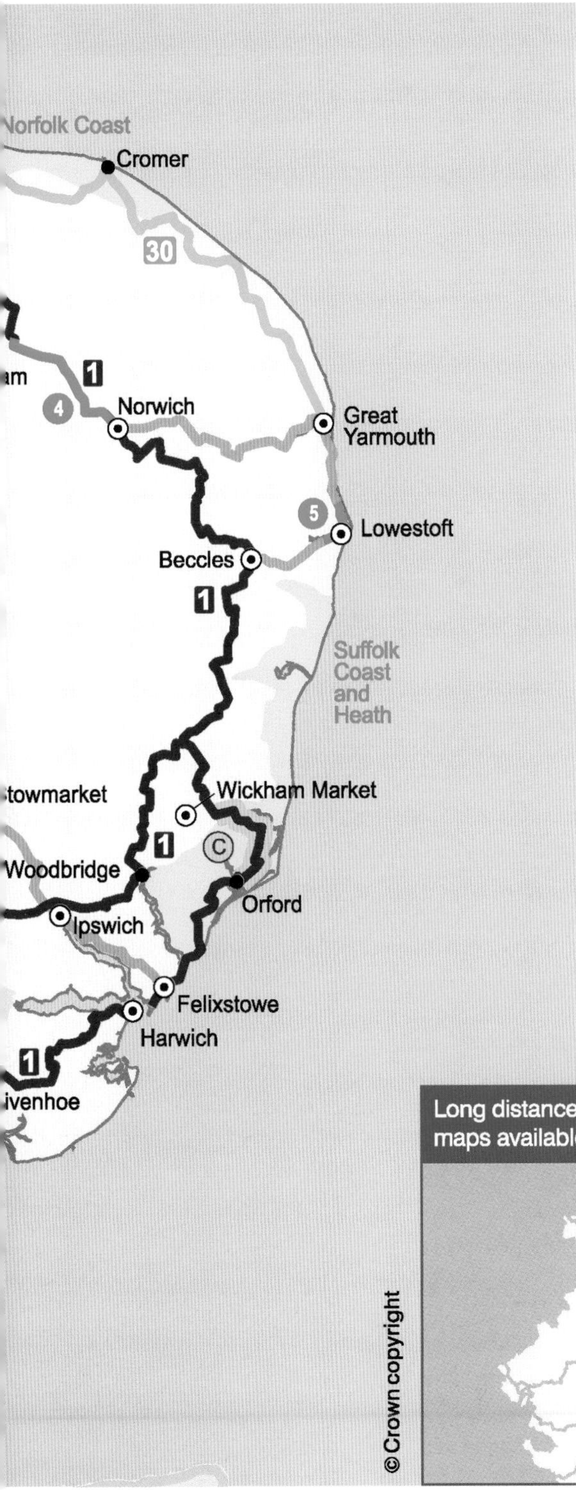

Norfolk Coast

Cromer

30

am

4 Norwich

Great
Yarmouth

5 Lowestoft

Beccles

Suffolk
Coast
and
Heath

towmarket

Wickham Market

Woodbridge

C

Ipswich

Orford

Felixstowe

Harwich

ivenhoe

Selected traffic-free paths

1. River Nene Path, Peterborough *10 miles*
   (Ferry Meadows - Whittlesey)
2. Twenty Foot River *3 miles*
3. King's Lynn Railway Path *2 miles*
4. Marriott's Way *18 miles*
   (Norwich - Reepham)
5. Great Eastern Linear Park,
   Lowestoft *1 mile*
6. The Redway Network,
   Milton Keynes *150 miles*
7. Priory Country Park and
   Willington Country Way *6 miles*
   (Bedford - Willington)
8. Alban Way *4^1/$_2$ miles*
   (St Albans - Hatfield)
9. Cole Green Way *4^1/$_2$ miles*
   (Hertford - Welwyn Garden City)
10. Flitch Way *7 miles*
    (Braintree - Little Dunmow)
11. Colchester - Wivenhoe *3 miles*
12. Hertford - Hackney *17 miles*
    (Lee Valley)
13. Chelmsford Riverside *2^1/$_2$ miles*
14. Southend sea front *1^1/$_2$ miles*
15. Pinnacles - Old Harlow *3 miles*
    (Harlow)
16. Ebury Way *2 miles*
    (Rickmansworth - Watford)

Day Rides

(A) King's Lynn to Shepherd's Port *15 miles*
(B) Milton Keynes *12 miles*
(C) Wickham Market to Orford *14 miles*

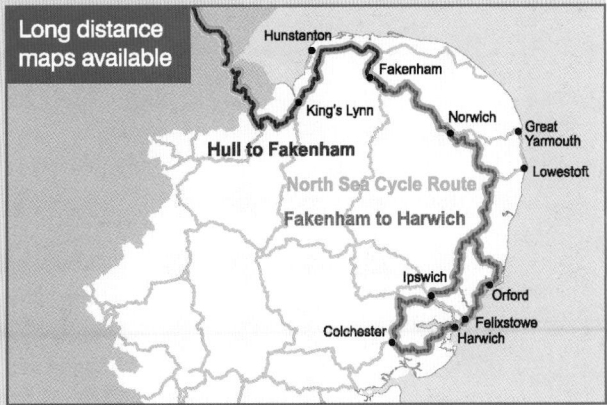

Long distance
maps available

Hunstanton

Fakenham

King's Lynn

Norwich

Great
Yarmouth

Lowestoft

Hull to Fakenham

North Sea Cycle Route

Fakenham to Harwich

Ipswich

Orford

Felixstowe
Harwich

Colchester

© Crown copyright

85

EAST OF ENGLAND

Beck's Green, Suffolk.

This is the flattest region in the whole Network – the highest point between London and the Norfolk Coast is just north of Stevenage, where the land rises to a mighty 555 ft. The highest point between Cambridge and the Wash is a mere 20 ft! The Hull to Harwich Route runs right down through the East of England and, with its easy gradients, is one of Sustrans' most popular routes for people returning to the saddle after a few years' absence.

The area is defined by intensive agriculture, particularly in the fens. The rainfall is the lowest of any region in the country, giving cyclists a greater chance of a dry ride than anywhere else.

The Hull to Harwich long-distance route has been a shining example of what can be achieved when the will power and resources of the local authorities and the Regional Tourist Board are collectively mobilised to throw their weight behind the National Cycle Network. The 369-mile route was opened seven years ahead of schedule.

NATIONAL CYCLE NETWORK HIGHLIGHTS

Cambridge

Cycling is a way of life in Cambridge, both amongst the locals and the students. Just join the throng - they are bound to take you somewhere interesting! Arriving by train, a packed crush of bikes greets you from the station entrance, whilst to the north, Britain's only covered and heated cycle bridge takes you over the railway and away from the city centre.

Shanks Millennium Bridge, River Nene, Peterborough

This new bridge, part of the Peterborough Millennium Green Wheel Project, is made from recycled steel collected at the city's recycling plant. Linking the northern and southern parts of the Green Wheel, a cycle route around the city with 'spokes' into the centre, it now forms part of the National Cycle Network, providing a much more direct and attractive alternative to the busy roads between Peterborough and Whittlesey.

Kesgrave School

This chance picture taken whilst surveying National Route 1 between Ipswich and Woodbridge, led us to Kesgrave School, which was later featured in the Safe Routes to School project. Thanks to this traffic-free green lane and some decent links, the High School enjoys the highest level of cycling in Britain with 60% of its pupils cycling each day. Consequently its pupils are relatively fit and the school successful in sports of all kinds!

Harwich and Felixstowe Ferry

This ferry has had a chequered history and its future is in doubt, despite the fact that a 10-minute ferry trip saves a journey of nearly 35 miles via Ipswich. The ferry trip is an experience in its own right, with the estuary dominated by massive container ships. The ferry has solved difficulties with docking at Felixstowe simply by landing on the beach. The service may change, so check the latest developments and use it!

Castle Rising and Sandringham Path

This new path beside the busy A149 Hunstanton Road near King's Lynn shows how, with local authority support, the Network can create vital local routes. Negotiations with the Royal Estates by Norfolk County Council allowed this path to be constructed. It links quiet minor roads and avoids the main road. Without this work King's Lynn was effectively isolated from the countryside to all but the most experienced cyclists.

Milton Keynes

Of all the British new towns Milton Keynes has the most extensive system of cycle paths, including over 150 miles of redways (red tarmac shared-use paths), plus gravel-surfaced leisure paths, giving cyclists the chance to pass through the parks and villages that are now part of Milton Keynes. The cycle network deserves to be better known but competes with an equally modern road system which leaves little advantage for the cyclist.

NATIONAL CYCLE NETWORK HIGHLIGHTS

The Peterborough Green Wheel Millennium Project

This ambitious project encircles the city with a Greenway connected to the centre by a number of 'spokes'. Much of the project has been achieved, propelling the National Cycle Network forwards.

Great North Way

The signing for the National Cycle Route in Stevenage is a real benefit: as a result, many more people can experience artist David Bickerstaff's vision of guiding cyclists through a level, direct, traffic-free route.

North Sea Cycle Route

Harwich to King's Lynn forms the southern part of the UK section of this Euroroute. Two rides left Hamburg in May 2001, one going clockwise and the other anti-clockwise. This latter reached Harwich on 23rd June and was then guided through East Anglia on the way to a grand opening in Aberdeen.

North Sea Cycle Route

Netherlands · Germany · Denmark · Sweden · Norway · Scotland · England

Tilbury Link

The National Cycle Network is made up of literally thousands of connecting paths, bridges and road crossings. One excellent

example can be found at Tilbury, where a link bridge and dedicated cycle route join the railway station and town to the liner terminal and the Gravesend ferry. From here a new riverside path takes you on to Tilbury Fort and eventually Coalhouse Fort.

Chelmsford Riverside Path

A particularly good example of the way a riverside can be used to create a route right across a town, in this case across Chelmsford from Writtle to Chelmer Village, forming the backbone of the town's cycling network.

March Station Link and River Bridge

A new link to March Station opens up direct access from a whole new part of the town. The new bridge over the river north of March offers wide views over the flat landscape.

CITY FOCUS

Maps & guides are available from National Cycle Network Information unless indicated otherwise. See page 91 for contact details.

Colchester

The Fakenham to Harwich Map
shows Route 1 through Colchester.
To the north it runs through High
Woods to Langham and Hadleigh.
To the south east it follows the
River Colne along the traffic-free
Wivenhoe Trail to Wivenhoe and on
to Harwich.

Cycling in
Colchester shows
the National Cycle
Network and
proposed routes
including the
Wivenhoe Trail.
Available from the
Tourist Information
Centre.
Tel: 01206 282920.

Milton Keynes

The South Midlands Cycle Route
Map shows Milton Keynes at a
crossroads of National Cycle
Network Routes 51 and 6. Route 51
enters the city from the southwest
(Winslow) through Tattenhoe,
passing the National Bowl. It will
continue east from Willen Lakes
towards Bedford. Route 6 enters the
city from the north (Northampton)
and passes through Wolverton then
alongside the Grand Union Canal.
It will continue south via Bletchley
to Leighton Buzzard.

Milton Keynes
Redway Map
shows the Redway,
a 150-mile network
of traffic-free cycle
tracks. Available
from the Tourist
Information
Centre.
Tel: 01908
558300

Norwich

The Fakenham to Harwich Map
shows the National Cycle Network
Route 1 through Norwich: to the
north west it runs along the Wensum
Valley on a traffic-free route
(Marriott's Way) towards Drayton
and Reepham; to the south east the
route follows the valley of the River
Yare to Surlingham and Loddon.

Peterborough

The Peterborough
Millennium Green
Wheel Cycle Map
shows the onroad
and offroad routes
that make up the
concept of a
'Green Wheel' -
a circuit around
Peterborough with
'spokes' leading into the centre of
the city. Available from the City
Trust. Tel: 01733 760883.
Or visit the website:
www.peterborough.net/pect

Ipswich

Ipswich Cycle
Map 2000 shows
the National Cycle
Network, signed
local routes,
suggested routes
(unsigned) and
traffic-calmed
routes. There is
also a wealth of
useful information
about cycle shops, 'Frequently
Asked Questions', local contacts
and leisure cycling. Available from
the Tourist Information Centre.
Tel: 01473 258070.

Other towns covered by leaflets:

Cycle Map Bedford & Kempston.
Tourist Information Centre.
Tel: 01234 215226
Bury St Edmunds Cycle Map 2000.
Tourist Information Centre.
Tel: 01284 764667.
Cambridge Cycle Route Map 2000.
Tourist Information Centre.
Tel: 01223 322640
Chelmsford Cycle Routes.
Tourist Information Centre.
Tel: 01245 283400.
Lowestoft Cycle Map 2000.
Tourist Information Centre.
Tel: 01502 523000.

NN1A - £5.99   NN1B - £5.99

TRAFFIC-FREE PATHS PARTICULARLY SUITABLE FOR FAMILIES

63 ᚛ Peterborough & Whittlesey. 9 miles

The Peterborough Green Wheel offers a number of fine rides, including one beside the River Nene. This starts at Ferry Meadows Country Park, passes the steam railway and the sculpture park, with magnificent views of the cathedral. Suddenly, in the middle of nowhere, is the new Shanks Millennium Bridge, sweeping across the river in a curve of rusting steel, which exactly mirrors the colour of the brickworks on the way to Whittlesey. This is a great day out, ending at a beautiful refurbished town square.

61 ᚛ The Cole Green Way. 4 miles (Welwyn Garden City to Hertford)

This was once a backwater of a route, cut off from Hertford by a ring-road and from Welwyn by the A414. A new bridge crossing of this road has made this railway path a delightful route, running through a quiet landscape to emerge at the end under the high arches of the mainline viaduct.

1 ᚛ Marriott's Way, Norfolk. 20 miles

This railway path is largely rural in nature and offers a wonderful way to see the Norfolk countryside. As you approach Norwich city centre you pass industrial sites between glimpses of the River Wensum. Soon after crossing the river the path emerges on the edge of the city centre.

61 ᚛ Alban Way. 6 miles

The former Hatfield to St Albans branch line of the Great Northern Railway now helps to link two of the major attractions of Hertfordshire – Hatfield House and St Albans. The route is also particularly useful for students, many of whom live in St Albans and study in Hatfield.

16 ᚛ Flitch Way. 7 miles (Braintree to Little Dunmow)

You will not find a railway path with better access by train anywhere in the UK. Braintree Station is close to the start of the Flitch Way. This seven-mile route along the former Braintree to Bishop's Stortford railway is a fine way to see the Essex countryside.

1 ᚛ The Wivenhoe Trail. 5 miles

This riverside path, squeezed between the river and the railway, gives great views of the River Colne. The path runs from the centre of Colchester to Wivenhoe Station and it is well worthwhile starting in Colchester's Dutch Quarter and finishing at Wivenhoe's attractive quay.

USEFUL MAPS & GUIDES

For details of the full range of maps, guides and other products available contact: **National Cycle Network Information, PO Box 21, Bristol BS99 2HA. Tel: 0117 929 0888. Or visit www.nationalcyclenetwork.org.uk** The range of National Cycle Network Maps is described in more detail on pages 218-237.

1 *Hull – Fakenham Cycle Route*
206 miles. NN1A - £5.99

1 *Fakenham – Harwich Cycle Route*
163 miles. NN1B - £5.99

1 *Hull – Harwich Holiday Planner*
Companion guide to Hull – Harwich Route Maps. RG14 - £4.99

10 *Explore the Norfolk Coast by Bike*
From King's Lynn to Cromer. Plus seven connecting loops. Links to National Route 1. RPR10 - £2.00

Cycling Without Traffic: East Anglia 30 traffic-free rides, including Marriott's Way, Flitch Way and Alton Water. RBA05 - £10.99

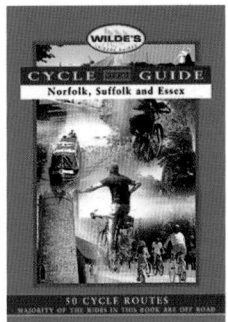

Wilde's Cycling Guide to Norfolk, Suffolk and Essex 50 circular rides all over East Anglia. RBW03 - £9.95

Cycling Without Traffic: South East 30 traffic-free rides described in detail in this well illustrated guide to family cycling. Includes Grafham Water and the Flitch Way. RBA01 - £11.99

More Cycling Without Traffic: South East A further 30 traffic-free rides, including Alton Water, the Wivenhoe Trail and Milton Keynes. RBA07 - £11.99

Cycling Discovery Packs: Cambs, Herts, Beds (6 Maps) RPP03 - £7.50
East Anglia (7 Maps) RPP02 - £9.00
Lincolnshire (6 Maps) RPP01 - £7.50
Ordnance Survey based maps describing 20-30 mile routes, mainly on quiet lanes, covering the region from Essex through Suffolk and Norfolk to Lincolnshire.

WICKHAM MARKET TO ORFORD

The gentle countryside of the Suffolk Coast provides ideal cycling for people wishing to progress from traffic-free cycle paths to the enjoyment of the wonderful network of country lanes that criss-cross Britain. These Suffolk roads carry very little traffic, the gradients are easy, the visibility is good and in Campsey Ash you have a railway station right in the middle of the countryside. This means there are no city streets to negotiate before setting out on your trip. You will cross the fertile farmland and plantations of pines to the delights of the Maltings at Snape and the wonderful village of Orford with its castle, quayside, pubs and tea rooms. There are various options to turn this into a circular ride by using a mixture of B roads and forest roads or by catching the ferry across Butley River. (Devise your own routes using Ordnance Survey Landranger maps 156 and 169.)

Orford Castle.

Starting point

Wickham Market railway station, 20 miles northeast of Ipswich. The station is not in Wickham Market itself but at the nearby village of Campsey Ash.

Distance

14 miles one way, 28 miles return. For a shorter ride, turn around at Snape Maltings (10-mile round trip).

Grade

Easy.

Surface

All tarmac.

Roads, traffic, suitability for young children

The whole route is on road, mainly on very quiet country lanes. There are a couple of short sections on B roads. There are nearby traffic-free trails in Rendlesham and Tunstall Forests.

Hills

None to mention.

Refreshments

Ship PH, Blaxhall.
Tea room, Plough & Sail PH, Snape Maltings.
Jolly Sailor PH, Crown & Castle PH, Kings Head PH, Old Warehouse Cafe, Orford.

Nearby railway stations for longer linear rides

Route 1 could be followed north to Halesworth (21 miles) or Beccles (32 miles). Alternatively head south to Felixstowe (32 miles).

The National Cycle Network in the area

The ride is part of the Hull to Harwich Cycle Route (Route 1) which runs north to Beccles and Norwich. There are two options on its course south to Harwich, either inland via Ipswich and Colchester

Views towards Orford Castle.

or along the coast via Felixstowe. The latter route uses three ferries and it is advisable to ring in advance to check the timetable:
1. Butley Ferry (south of Orford): 01394 410096 (Bryan Rogers).
2. Bawdsey to Felixstowe Ferry: 0780 347 6621 or 01394 270106 (Odd Time Ferries).
3. Felixstowe to Harwich: 07889 371138.
4. Felixstowe Tourist Information Centre: 01394 276770.

Other nearby rides (waymarked or traffic-free)

1. The Three Forest Ride is a 25-mile ride linking the Forestry Commission holdings in Rendlesham, Tunstall and Dunwich (a few miles to the north). It links traffic-free forest trails via quiet lanes. A leaflet is available from Forest Enterprise, Tangham, Woodbridge IP12 1PE.

2. The Suffolk Coastal Cycle Route is a waymarked 75-mile route. A full colour map pack (£3.50) is available from the National Cycle Network Information Service. Tel: 0117 929 0888. Or visit: www.nationalcyclenetwork.org.uk

Snape Maltings, home of the Aldeburgh Festival.

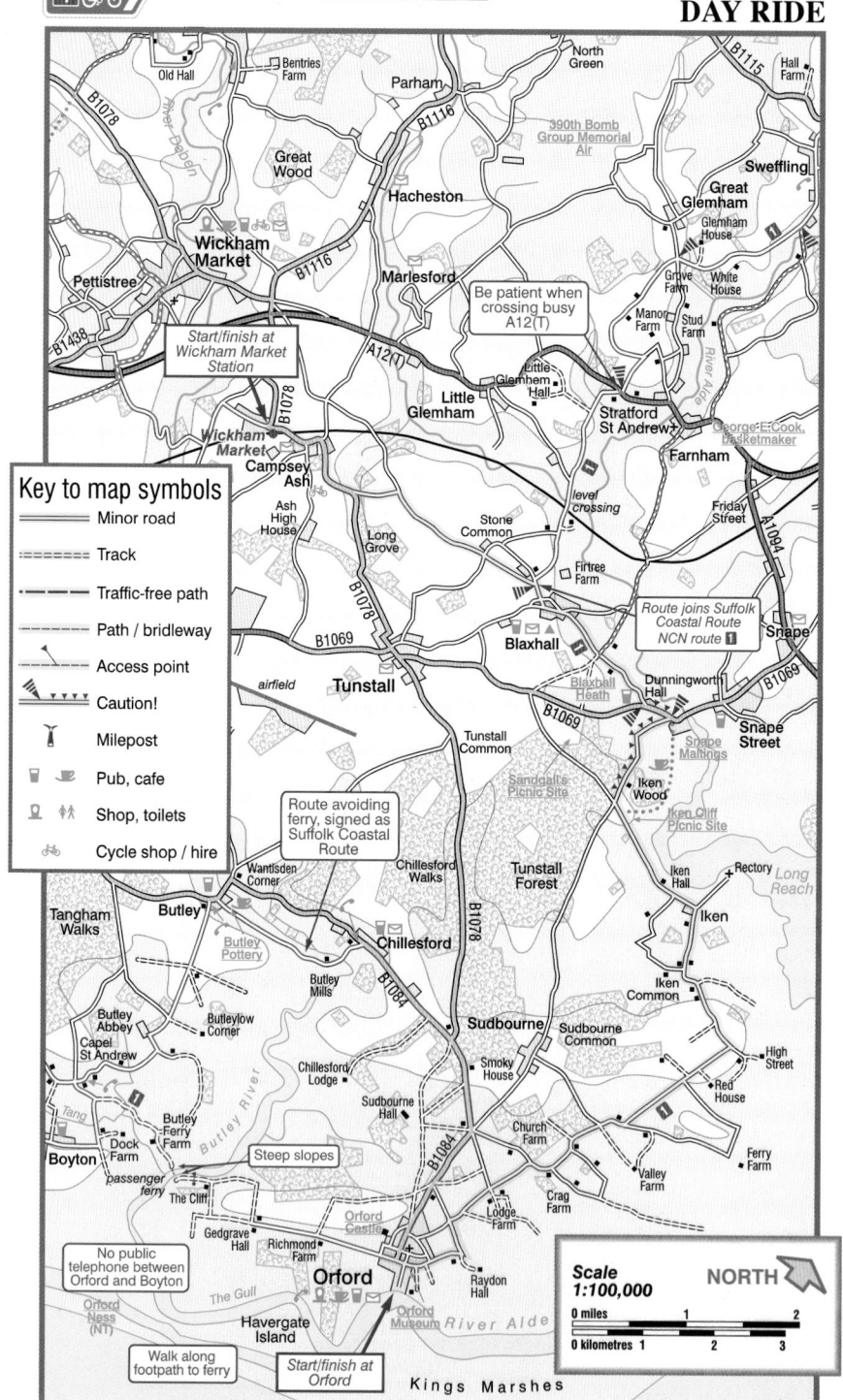

WICKHAM MARKET TO ORFORD

Key to map symbols

Minor road
Track
Traffic-free path
Path / bridleway
Access point
Caution!
Milepost
Pub, cafe
Shop, toilets
Cycle shop / hire

Start/finish at Wickham Market Station

Be patient when crossing busy A12(T)

Route joins Suffolk Coastal Route NCN route 1

Route avoiding ferry, signed as Suffolk Coastal Route

Steep slopes

No public telephone between Orford and Boyton

Walk along footpath to ferry

Start/finish at Orford

Scale 1:100,000

NORTH

0 miles   1   2
0 kilometres   1   2   3

Route instructions – Campsey Ash to Orford

1. Exit Wickham Market railway station (at Campsey Ash) and turn right. Ignore the first left to Marlesford on a sharp right-hand bend. On the next sharp right-hand bend after ¾ mile bear left signposted 'Blaxhall, Snape'.

2. At the crossroads with Red House Farm ahead, turn right. At the next crossroads (with a church to your left) go straight ahead.

3. Three closely-spaced junctions! At a crossroads by a Give Way sign go straight ahead signposted 'Snape'. At the T-junction turn left (same sign). At the next crossroads turn right (same sign).

4. At the T-junction with the B1069 turn left then take the first road to the right signposted 'Iken, Orford'

(or to visit Snape Maltings continue straight ahead for 200 yds).

5. After one mile take the first left. Follow signs for Orford for five miles.

6. **Easy to miss**. Ignore turnings to left and right. Shortly after passing two left turns signposted 'High House Farm' and 'Crag Farm' (this second left turn is by a large red-brick, thatched house) take the third left, signposted 'Orford 1½'.

7. After one mile, at a crossroads shortly after an electricity sub-station turn left. Shortly, at a junction by a triangle of grass with a no through road to Raydon Hall ahead, turn right.

8. At the crossroads in the centre of Orford, turn left for Orford Quay, turn right for the castle and pubs or go straight ahead for the Ore Estuary.

Snape Maltings now house a concert hall, shops and cafes.

95

KING'S LYNN TO SHEPHERD'S PORT

This ride is a short section of the popular long-distance Hull to Harwich Cycle Route running down the east side of the country. The whole route was opened several years earlier than planned because of the enthusiasm and support of the local authorities and the East of England Tourist Board. King's Lynn lies on the course of the River Ouse which drains much of the fertile dark earth of the Fens.

The lively port and market town is a major hub in Norfolk and boasts many fine old buildings. The ride leaves the railway station on a traffic-free path through parkland before joining the course of an old railway to arrive at the outskirts of the town. After crossing the broadleaf woodlands of Ling Common you come to the attractive village of Castle Rising with its magnificent castle and defences and old almshouses dating from the 17th century. The route continues through more woodlands and banks of rhododendrons surrounding Sandringham, country home of the Royal Family. The rhododendrons are at their best for about six weeks from mid-April to the end of May. If you have not stopped for tea at the Visitor Centre at Sandringham you are likely to be tempted by the various pubs and coffee houses in Snettisham, which also has one of the finest churches in Norfolk. If the tide is in, or if you are birdwatching, it is worth pushing on to the coast at Shepherd's Port, but be aware that when the tide is out you will be confronted by a vast expanse of mud!

North of Sandringham on the road to Snettisham.

96

Starting point
King's Lynn railway station.

Distance
15 miles one way, 30 miles return.
The ride could be shortened by
making the turnaround point either
the attractions and refreshment
stops at Castle Rising (12 miles
round trip) or Sandringham Country
Park (19 miles round trip).

Grade
Easy.

Surface
All tarmac with the exception of an
(optional) short stretch through
Sandringham Estate on good quality
gravel track.

Roads, traffic, suitability for young children
The first section, from the railway
station, across the parkland and
onto the dismantled railway is all
traffic-free. Beyond the end of the
railway path the route uses quiet
lanes as much as possible. The busy
main roads are all crossed via
central islands.

Hills
Gently undulating.

Refreshments
Lots of choice in King's Lynn.
House on the Green PH, North
Wootton.
Tea rooms at the Post Office, Black
Horse PH, Castle Rising.
Tea rooms at Sandringam Visitor
Centre.
Rose & Crown PH, Queen Victoria
PH, Compasses PH, Old Bank
Coffeehouse, Snettisham.

Railway stations for longer rides
It is 74 miles along Route 1 from
King's Lynn to Norwich or 100
miles north to Lincoln.

The National Cycle Network in the area
The ride described is part of the
Hull to Harwich Cycle Route
(Route 1).
1. East from Hunstanton, Route 1
turns inland through Ringstead and
Burnham Market to Fakenham.
2. West from King's Lynn, Route 1
crosses the Fens to Wisbech and
Boston.
3. Route 11 will run south from
King's Lynn through Downham
Market to Ely Cathedral and
Cambridge.

*St. John's Walk, King's Lynn, leads
direct to the station and to the
town centre.*

Other nearby rides (waymarked or traffic-free)
The Norfolk Coast Cycleway is a
100-mile linear route that runs from
King's Lynn to Great Yarmouth
along the North Norfolk Coast.

*The absence of traffic on the old
road from Castle Rising to
Sandringham leaves space for
fishing.*

King's Lynn to Shepherd's Port

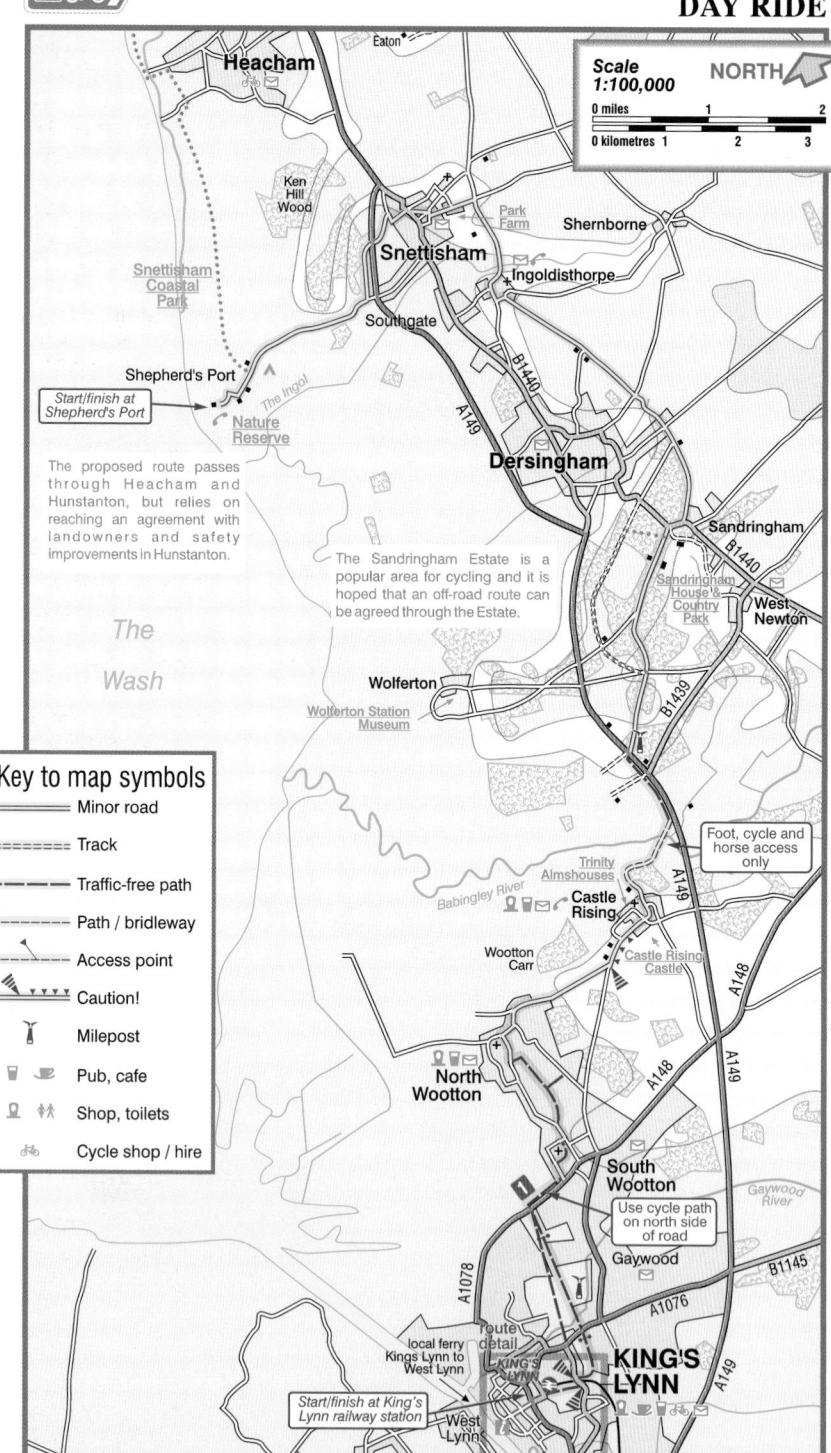

Scale 1:100,000

NORTH

0 miles | 1 | 2

0 kilometres | 1 | 2 | 3

Heacham

Eaton

Ken Hill Wood

Park Farm

Shernborne

Snettisham

Snettisham Coastal Park

Ingoldisthorpe

Southgate

Shepherd's Port

Start/finish at Shepherd's Port

The Ingol

B1440

A149

Nature Reserve

Dersingham

Sandringham

B1440

Sandringham House & Country Park

West Newton

The proposed route passes through Heacham and Hunstanton, but relies on reaching an agreement with landowners and safety improvements in Hunstanton.

The Sandringham Estate is a popular area for cycling and it is hoped that an off-road route can be agreed through the Estate.

The Wash

Wolferton

Wolferton Station Museum

B1439

Foot, cycle and horse access only

Key to map symbols

- Minor road
- Track
- Traffic-free path
- Path / bridleway
- Access point
- Caution!
- Milepost
- Pub, cafe
- Shop, toilets
- Cycle shop / hire

Trinity Almshouses

Babingley River

Castle Rising

A149

Wootton Carr

Castle Rising Castle

North Wootton

A148

A149

A148

South Wootton

Use cycle path on north side of road

Gaywood River

1

Gaywood

A1078

B1145

A1076

route detail

local ferry Kings Lynn to West Lynn

KING'S LYNN

KING'S LYNN

A149

Start/finish at King's Lynn railway station

West Lynn

Route Instructions – King's Lynn to Sandringham and the coast

1. Exit King's Lynn railway station and turn left onto the pavement/cycle path, soon turning left again at the church to pass through the park along a tree-lined avenue. Cross the road at the end of the park, turn left over the railway lines then immediately right, following signs for 'Sandringham Railway Path'.

2. Shortly bear left, go past a school on the left. At the next road (Gaywood Road) cross via toucan crossing, past the Leisure Centre.

3. At the T-junction with the main road (A1078) turn right on the cycle path alongside the road (signposted 'Woottons, Castle Rising, Sandringham') then cross the road via traffic island (**TAKE CARE**)

to continue in the same direction. Take the first road to the left (Hall Lane) then turn right along a new path beside the church to join Church Lane (a continuation of Hall Lane).

4. At the T-junction with Nursery Lane turn left, passing Meadow Road on your left. Turn into Avon Road on your right, then turn left along the edge of some grazing land on to a new path, which links to paths which take you through parkland. Head north keeping to the left and following signs to North Wootton and Castle Rising until you reach All Saints Drive. Turn right into All Saints Road then right into Manor Road and left into Ling Common Road.

5. At the T-junction at the end of Ling Common Road turn left

signposted 'Castle Rising. Route 1'. A busier road. Immediately after the Black Horse pub in Castle Rising turn left past the church onto a no through road signposted 'Route 1'.

6. Lovely old road, now shut to traffic. At the T-junction with the main road (A149) turn left onto the new cycle track. Ignore the first right on the B1439. After ¼ mile take the next right signposted 'Route 1'. **TAKE CARE** crossing this road via traffic island.

7. At cross roads go straight ahead. At the T-junction after ¾-mile bear right. Go past the Sandringham Visitor Centre (tea rooms).

8. At the T-junction with the B1140 turn right signposted 'King's Lynn' then left signposted 'Sandringham Sawmill. Route 1'.

9. At the first crossroads (your priority) go straight ahead. At the next crossroads (Give Way) go straight ahead onto Mill Road.

10. **Easy to miss**. After 1½ miles, having climbed up and over a gentle hill, take the second of two closely spaced right turns. At the next crossroads turn left* (leaving the waymarked Route 1). Aim for the distant Snettisham church spire which you pass after ½ mile.

Another option from Snettisham is to continue along Route 1 to Sedgeford then turn left on the B1454 to visit Norfolk Lavender at Heacham.

11. At the T-junction at the end of Old Church Road turn right then left onto Alma Road. At the next T-junction (with the main A149) turn left then right (**TAKE CARE**) onto Common Road. After ½ mile, at the end of Common Road, bear right and follow this no through road for two miles, passing various caravan sites, out to the coast.

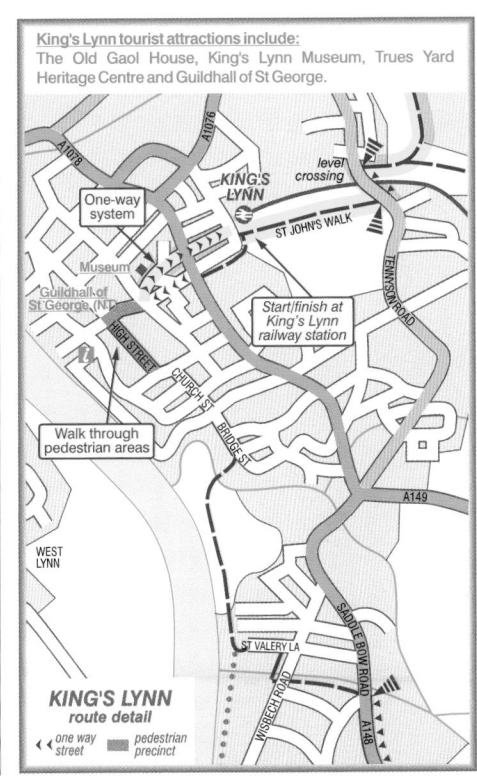

King's Lynn tourist attractions include:
The Old Gaol House, King's Lynn Museum, Trues Yard Heritage Centre and Guildhall of St George.

KING'S LYNN
route detail
◀◀ one way street   ▓ pedestrian precinct

A CIRCUIT OF MILTON KEYNES

If you have never cycled in Milton Keynes you will be astonished when you explore the place for the first time. There are a wealth of choices for the cyclist, including attractive gravel-finished paths through parks, red tarmac paths that form the famous Redway Network and many quiet roads. These will enable you to explore the city visiting lakes, canals, the Buddhist pagoda, adventure playgrounds, all the while diving in and out of stretches of broadleaf woodland. Every now and then you will come across an attractive village that is now part of urban Milton Keynes, but which still maintains its village character. The city was designed as a whole series of individual communities, and central Milton Keynes is unlike any other city centre in the country, with its wide boulevards, unusual architecture and impressive sculptures. Milton Keynes boasts probably the best collection of public art in the country.

This ride uses parts of the National Cycle Network through Milton Keynes with two links, to give a circular route through the city. The route takes in paths beside the Grand Union Canal, Campbell Park, the beautiful old stone buildings of Great Linford, a section of dismantled railway through a thickly wooded cutting and a leisure route along the Loughton Valley passing through a curious little tunnel. Last but not least there is a chance to see the famous concrete cows of Milton Keynes and the giant Head Sculpture (which forms the junction of the National Cycle Routes in Milton Keynes). The circuit has been signed as the Milton Keynes Millennium Circular Cycle Route.

'Circle Dance' by Claire Wilks. Steel frame sculpture on the Grand Union Canal.

Starting points

Central Railway Station, Milton Keynes.

Distance

12-mile circuit.

Grade: Easy.

Surface

Red tarmac or gravel paths throughout.

Roads, traffic, suitability for young children

All busy roads are crossed via underpasses or bridges. Several quiet estate roads are crossed and some quiet roads are used.

Hills

The route follows the valleys, avoiding most of the hills in Milton Keynes.

Refreshments

Lots of choice in the square by the railway station and elsewhere in central Milton Keynes.
Pub and shop in Woughton on the Green (just off the route).
Tea shop at Bradwell Abbey.
Nags Head PH, Great Linford.

Leaflets

The *Milton Keynes Redway Map* shows the full extent of the cycleway network and is indispensable when exploring the city. Available from: Milton Keynes Tourist Information Centre, Margaret Powell Square, 890 Midsummer Boulevard, Central Milton Keynes, MK9 3QA. Tel: 01908 558300.

Nearest railway stations

Milton Keynes Central, Wolverton.

The National Cycle Network in the area

Milton Keynes is at a crossroads of the National Cycle Network. Route 6 passes through Milton Keynes on

Shanks Millennium Bridge over the River Ouse at Wolverton near Milton Keynes

its way south from Leicester and Northampton to St Albans and Slough.

Route 51 runs from Oxford to Bedford, Cambridge and the coast. The circular route could be adapted by following Route 6 to Castlethorpe, an attractive village on the way to Northampton. For the more ambitious, Route 51 would take you out into the Buckinghamshire countryside to Winslow, an attractive town with a famous tea shop. If you prefer to stay within Milton Keynes, Willen Lake and Caldecotte Lake are on

the course of the second phase of the National Cycle Network (to Bedford) and are attractive destinations.

Other nearby rides (waymarked or traffic-free)

There is a comprehensive network of traffic-free paths and quiet roads with plenty of adventure playgrounds and picnic spots along the way. Use the Redway Map (see 'Leaflets' above) to explore the area at your leisure.

Cycle route around Willen Lake.

A CIRCUIT OF MILTON KEYNES

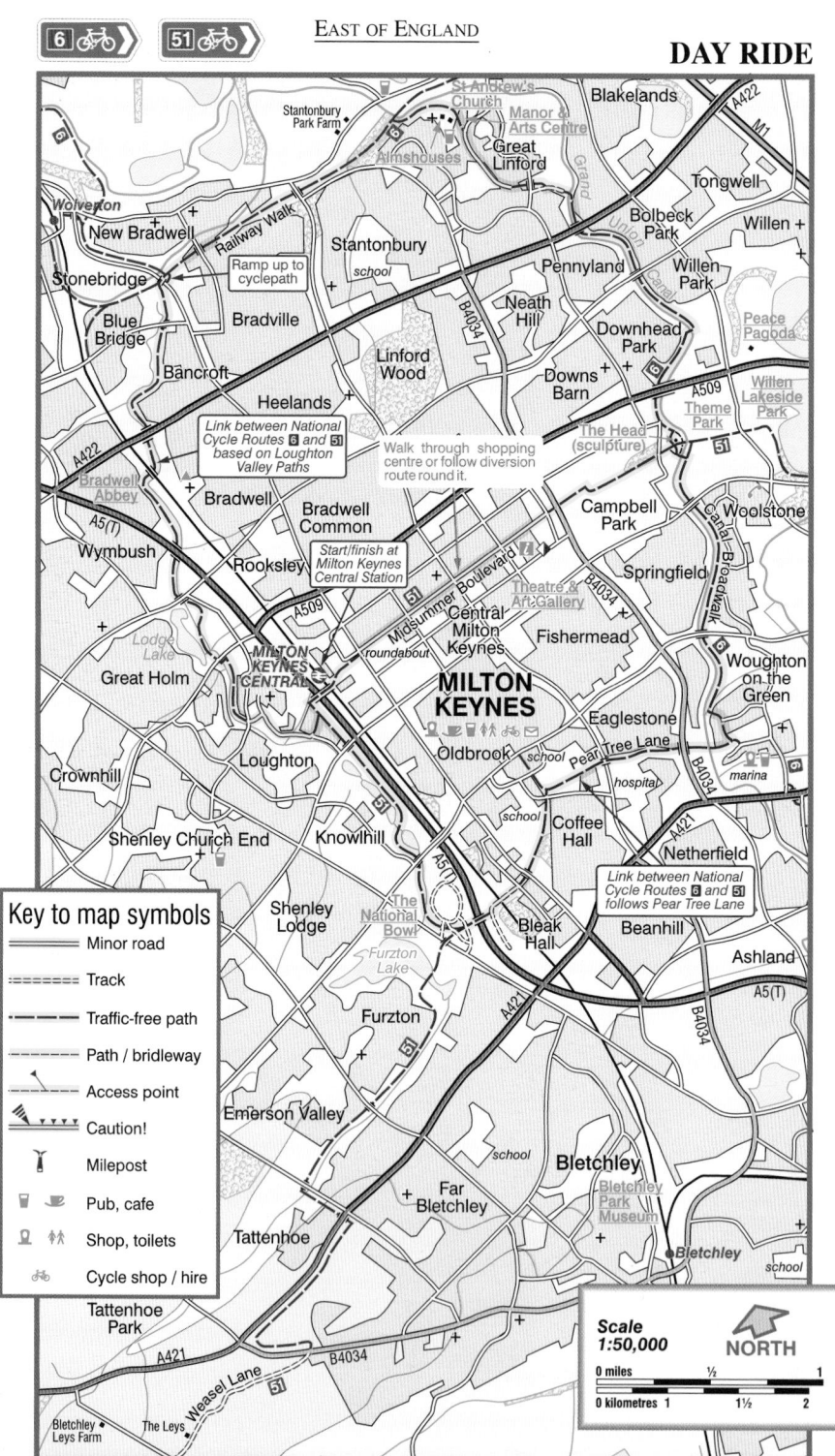

Key to map symbols

════════	Minor road
═══════	Track
▬ ▬ ▬ ▬	Traffic-free path
– – – – –	Path / bridleway
◥	Access point
⚠ ▼▼▼▼	Caution!
⅄	Milepost
⬛ ⬤	Pub, cafe
⚲ ⚤	Shop, toilets
⚙	Cycle shop / hire

Scale 1:50,000

NORTH

0 miles   ½   1

0 kilometres 1   1½   2

Ramp up to cyclepath

Link between National Cycle Routes 6 and 51 based on Loughton Valley Paths

Walk through shopping centre or follow diversion route round it.

Start/finish at Milton Keynes Central Station

Link between National Cycle Routes 6 and 51 follows Pear Tree Lane

MILTON KEYNES

Route instructions

This circular route is signed as the Milton Keynes Millennium Circular Cycle Route with red discs.

1. With your back to Milton Keynes railway station, cross over the first road then turn right then right again at the end of the glass-fronted building. Cross the bridge over the railway lines then at the T-junction turn left signposted 'Loughton, Knowlhill, Milton Keynes Bowl'.

2. Follow signs for Route 51 and Milton Keynes Bowl. Go round the outside of the Bowl past Gates 3 and 2. At the T-junction with V4 turn left signposted 'Bletchley, Route 51'.

3. At Gate 1 bear left then at the T-junction turn left (leaving Route 51) signposted 'Bleakhall, Coffee Hall'. Cross the A5 and the railway line then pass beneath a second main road. At a fork of paths bear right (there are signs for Woughton Campus a little way along the left-hand fork).

4. Gentle descent. At the crossroads go straight ahead onto 'Public Bridleway'. Cross the canal and follow the signs for 'The Green, Woughton Ouzel Valley Park'.

5. Shortly after the red-brick houses on the left, turn left alongside black railings on a tarmac path. Continue in the same direction. At the canal turn right signposted 'Woolstones, Newlands, Campbell Park'. Follow the Canal Broadwalk for 1½ miles.

6. After passing under two closely-spaced road bridges turn next left over the canal and into Campbell Park. Take the second path to the right towards and past the Head Sculpture. Rejoin the canal, now on your right.

7. Cross the canal at Bridge 80A, rejoin the Broadwalk, with the canal now on your left. At the red-brick hump-backed bridge no. 79, turn left over the bridge and follow the path away from the canal. After 300 yds turn right then left. Go past a few old houses and turn right opposite a sign for Harpers Lane.

8. Continue in the same direction along Great Linford High Street, past a telephone box and the Nag's Head pub. Go through gates into the park and bear left following Route 6 signs past lovely old buildings, a church and a stone circle.

9. Rejoin the canal then shortly bear left uphill onto the railway path. Follow for almost two miles.

10. Emerge from the wooded railway cutting and continue straight ahead, crossing the bridge over the V6 signposted 'Wolverton, Stony Stratford, Stacey Bush'. Immediately after crossing the bridge turn right and follow the path downhill and round to the right to pass beneath the bridge. The path soon runs parallel with the stream to your right. Pass beneath a curious wooden bridge.

11. The path joins the Redway near to the famous concrete cows. Bear right signposted 'Bradwell Village, Bradwell Abbey, Lodge Lake, Loughton Village'.

12. Continue in the same direction over crossroads. At a T-junction turn right to go over a narrow bridge inside a tunnel! At the end of the tunnel turn sharp left 'Lodge Lake, Loughton Village'.

13. Follow close to the stream, passing beneath two large bridges. At a T-junction turn left then right signposted 'Loughton Village, Tear Drop Lake'.

14. At the T-junction at the end of the lake turn left (same sign). Follow the path to Linceslade Grove, keeping to the right. Cross the road on the raised crossing and turn left onto the Redway. At the end of the bridge turn right and continue beside the stream.

15. At the T-junction turn right then left onto The Green. At the junction with Bradwell Road go straight ahead onto Leys Road then at the end turn left onto the Redway. Continue up Common Lane towards the railway station. Turn left then right over the A5 and the railway to take you back to Station Square.

'Head' in Campbell Park by Allen Jones.

Barnsley
5
6
4
Hadfield
62
6
67
R
Sheffield
62
67
Chesterfi
3
2
7
68
Peaks
Runcorn
56
Northwich
55
5
1
5
Macclesfield
Buxton
Chester
9
5
8
Crewe
Stoke-on-Trent
Ashbourne
Derby
Whitchurch
68
28
19
Stone
18
5
Burton-upon-
C
17
45
Stafford
Trent
15
16
W
55
54
Shrewsbury
81
Lichfield
Coal
81
Telford
Walsall
14
5
Wolverhampton
52
21
Nuneaton
Bridgnorth
Dudley
Birmingham
53
Ccoven
A
45
24
Solihull
Kidderminster
Bromsgrove
52
ort-on-Severn
Redditch
Warwick
5
Royal
25
Leamington
Great
Worcester
26
Spa
Malvern
41
Stratford-upon-Av
Evesham
5
Ban

20 miles

30 km

Southport
Trans Pennine
Trail
Hull
Doncaster
Derby
to York
Hull to
Fakenham
Lincoln
North Sea
Cycle Route
Trans Pennine Trail
West Central East
Derby
Boston
Nottingham
West Midlands
Cycle Route
King's
Leicester
Lynn
Birmingham
South Midlands
Cycle Route
Stratford-
upon-Avon

© Crown copyright

Long distance maps available

104

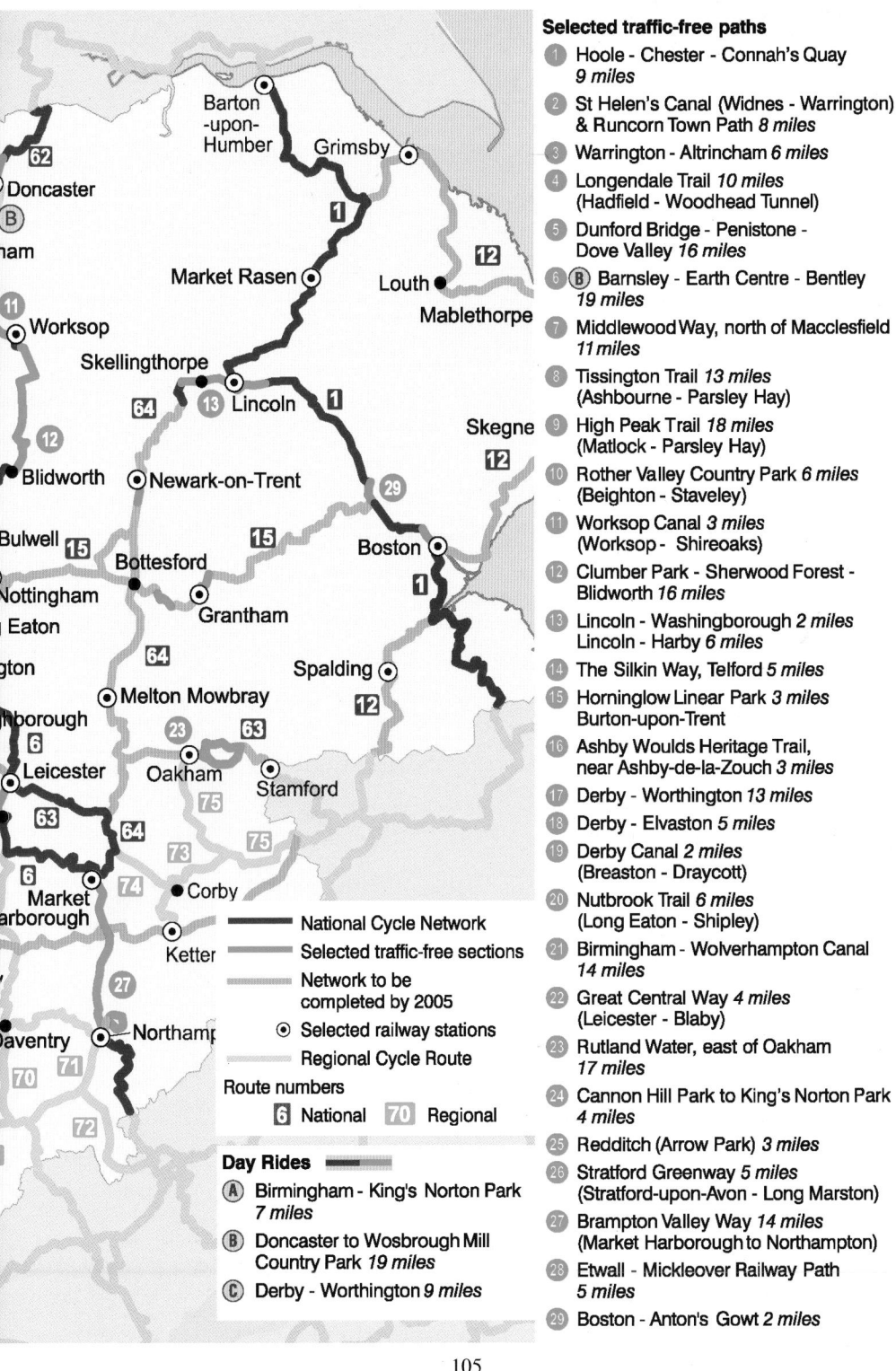

Selected traffic-free paths

1. Hoole - Chester - Connah's Quay *9 miles*
2. St Helen's Canal (Widnes - Warrington) & Runcorn Town Path *8 miles*
3. Warrington - Altrincham *6 miles*
4. Longendale Trail *10 miles* (Hadfield - Woodhead Tunnel)
5. Dunford Bridge - Penistone - Dove Valley *16 miles*
6. (B) Barnsley - Earth Centre - Bentley *19 miles*
7. Middlewood Way, north of Macclesfield *11 miles*
8. Tissington Trail *13 miles* (Ashbourne - Parsley Hay)
9. High Peak Trail *18 miles* (Matlock - Parsley Hay)
10. Rother Valley Country Park *6 miles* (Beighton - Staveley)
11. Worksop Canal *3 miles* (Worksop - Shireoaks)
12. Clumber Park - Sherwood Forest - Blidworth *16 miles*
13. Lincoln - Washingborough *2 miles* Lincoln - Harby *6 miles*
14. The Silkin Way, Telford *5 miles*
15. Horninglow Linear Park *3 miles* Burton-upon-Trent
16. Ashby Woulds Heritage Trail, near Ashby-de-la-Zouch *3 miles*
17. Derby - Worthington *13 miles*
18. Derby - Elvaston *5 miles*
19. Derby Canal *2 miles* (Breaston - Draycott)
20. Nutbrook Trail *6 miles* (Long Eaton - Shipley)
21. Birmingham - Wolverhampton Canal *14 miles*
22. Great Central Way *4 miles* (Leicester - Blaby)
23. Rutland Water, east of Oakham *17 miles*
24. Cannon Hill Park to King's Norton Park *4 miles*
25. Redditch (Arrow Park) *3 miles*
26. Stratford Greenway *5 miles* (Stratford-upon-Avon - Long Marston)
27. Brampton Valley Way *14 miles* (Market Harborough to Northampton)
28. Etwall - Mickleover Railway Path *5 miles*
29. Boston - Anton's Gowt *2 miles*

National Cycle Network
Selected traffic-free sections
Network to be completed by 2005
⊙ Selected railway stations
Regional Cycle Route

Route numbers
6 National   70 Regional

Day Rides

(A) Birmingham - King's Norton Park *7 miles*
(B) Doncaster to Wosbrough Mill Country Park *19 miles*
(C) Derby - Worthington *9 miles*

105

THE MIDLANDS

Canals near Birmingham centre.

With the exception of the Peak District in the centre of the region and the Welsh Marches to the west, the Midlands offers relatively gentle cycling with the land rarely rising above 600ft. The area described is bounded to the north by the Trans Pennine Trail, a multi-user coast to coast route from Southport/Liverpool in the west to Hull and the North Sea in the east.

Further south, the area is dominated by the vast conurbation of Birmingham and Wolverhampton (the West Midlands) and the smaller cities of Coventry, Stoke, Nottingham, Derby, Leicester and Sheffield. With the exception of Coventry and Stoke, all these cities of the Midlands are linked by the Dover to Inverness National Cycle Route, which divides into two strands at Oxford, and

becomes one again at Derby. The western route passes through Stratford and Birmingham, the eastern route through the amazing cycling infrastructure in Milton Keynes then north through Northampton and Leicester. The Midlands is blessed with the highest density of traffic-free trails in the country with hundreds of miles of railway paths, round reservoir routes and many canal towpaths. Trails include the popular Tissington and High Peak trails in the Peak District, Rutland Water and routes through Clumber Park and Sherwood Forest, and the extraordinary network of canal paths in the West Midlands.

NATIONAL CYCLE NETWORK HIGHLIGHTS

Clumber Park

A wide expanse of parkland, farmland and woodland, part of Nottinghamshire's famed 'Dukeries' and with a superb serpentine lake at its heart. There are many interesting features across the estate, including a classical bridge, temples, lodges and gate piers. Clumber House was demolished in 1938, but the fine Gothic Revival chapel survives.

Trent Viaduct, Melbourne

The Grade II listed Trent Viaduct, Melbourne was built in 1869 by the Midland Railway Company. Its cast iron parapet was recast to match when the viaduct was incorporated into the cycling route. This crossing of the Trent takes cyclists south and avoids the narrow Swarkestone causeway which was the turning point for Bonnie Prince Charlie's forces in their advance on London.

Telford Aqueduct, Smethwick

The Birmingham Main Line Canal was built between 1825 and 1838 under the direction of Thomas Telford. It cut seven miles off the distance between Birmingham and Wolverhampton. The Aqueduct took a branch off the older Smeaton Canal over the newer one, whose direct route involved massive earthworks. The cycle route follows the towpath.

The Ironbridge at Coalbrookdale

The Ironbridge at Coalbrookdale was one of the world's first iron bridges. It was opened in 1779 and spans 100ft across the River Severn to link the developing industry on both sides of the valley.

Birmingham Centenary Square

Centenary Square is evidence of Birmingham's desire to improve its image and is part of a strategic policy designed to attract people back to the city to live and work. It is a site where art is integral rather than superimposed, a place for quiet reflection as well as a square for programmed concerts and other entertainment. The high profile given to art work is tangible proof to tourist and conference visitors that Birmingham has a new-found confidence that comes from including the visual life of the environment in its overall investment programme.

Sandwell Valley Country Park

The conversion of this subway under the M5 motorway provided the crucial link between the Main Line Canal, the Midland Metro Cycle Route and Sandwell Valley Country Park – a thread of open green spaces, lakes, rivers and canals, which stretches all the way to the outskirts of Walsall. It is details of this kind which link routes together and make the whole Network possible.

NATIONAL CYCLE NETWORK HIGHLIGHTS

The Trans Pennine Trail

The Trans Pennine Trail runs across the northern part of this region. This separate Millennium Project, sponsored by 30 Local Authorities, links Southport and Liverpool to Hull and York. It was opened in 2001 and aims to provide a route for walkers and cyclists end to end, as well as horses in part. Sustrans has long links with this project dating back to the inaugural crossing in Summer 1989.

Grantham Riverside

There can be few more charming examples of a riverside route through a town than this. The path runs without a break past allotments, the town centre, an historic church, a formal park and riverside meadows, and forms part of the cycling network in the Grantham area.

Derby Canal

The former canal between Derby and Nottingham had been totally abandoned, filled in and lost. But never quite forgotten. The Canal Trust set out to recover the waterway and as a first stage teamed up with Sustrans to acquire the land, sufficient at least to construct a 'towpath' along the line of the original. This is National Cycle Network Route 6, now open from Borrowash to Breaston.

Coalville Elks

During the last Ice Age, broad-horned Irish Elk roamed throughout much of Europe. These have been commemorated by three magnificent scrap steel beasts, built by sculptor Sally Matthews, which stand overlooking Snibston Discovery Park in Coalville.

Leicester Space Centre 2001

This is a particularly notable Millennium project which incorporates the National Cycle Network in its layout, as it runs along the banks of the River Soar.

Hanley High Street

Hanley is the highest city in Britain (525ft) and one of the first to pedestrianize its centre with provision for 24-hour cycling. Although Sustrans aims to take the National Cycle Network to the very centre of each town along the route, we mostly accept 'No cycling' orders between 10am and 4pm, because this at least allows cyclists to get to work and school by the quickest and most attractive route.

CITY FOCUS

Maps & guides are available from National Cycle Network Information unless indicated otherwise. See page 111 for contact details.

Birmingham

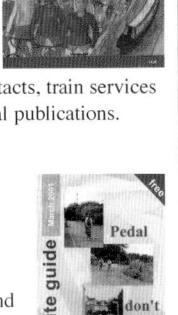

Birmingham CycleCity Map.
A-Z style map showing traffic-free and advisory routes. Lists cycle shops, contacts, train services and relevant local publications.
RC04 - £4.95

Derby

Derby Cycle Route Guide
shows offroad and onroad routes, the Network and proposed routes. Lists bike shops and contacts. Tourist Info Centre. Tel: 01332 255802.

Leicester

Leicester CycleCity Map
Layout as for Birmingham map (above). Includes Birstall, Blaby, Narborough, Thurnby, Oadby and Wigston.
RC07 - £2.95

Nottingham

The Greater Nottingham Cyclists Guide
shows the Network, existing and proposed onroad and traffic-free cycle routes. It also lists bike shops and contacts. Tourist Information Centre Tel: 0115 915 5330.

Contact: *Pedals Cycle Group.*
Tel: 0115 981 6206.
Website: www. net-space.co.uk/pedals

Sheffield

Sheffield Cycle Map 2001 shows the Trans Pennine Trail and the Network, offroad and onroad cycle lanes and tracks. Available from the Tourist Info Centre.
Tel: 0114 221 1900

Contact: *Pedal Pushers (Sheffield Cycle Campaign).*
Tel: 0114 258 1605.
Website: www.pedalpushers.org.uk

Other towns covered by leaflets:

Cheshire - The Millennium Cycle Route. Tourist Information Centre.
Tel: 01244 402111

Grimsby & Cleethorpes - Cyclist's Guide to North East Lincolnshire.
Tourist Information Centre.
Tel: 01472 323111

Rotherham - CycleCity Map.
Tourist Information Centre.
Tel: 01709 835904

Telford - Bike It Cycling Map.
Tourist Information Centre.
Tel: 01952 238008.

Walsall Cycle Map.
Tourist Information Centre.
Tel: 01922 653110

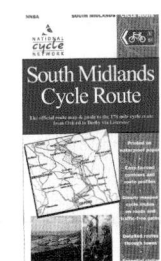

NN5B - £5.99

NN6B - £5.99

NN6A - £5.99

RPN08B - £4.95

TRAFFIC-FREE PATHS PARTICULARLY SUITABLE FOR FAMILIES

Chester to Hawarden Bridge and Connah's Quay. 8 miles

This excellent railway path has been built by Cheshire and Flintshire County Councils allowing for shared use with a guided bus way. The traffic-free route will eventually reach Flint before using minor roads over the hills to the coastal resort of Rhyl.

Tissington Trail. 13 miles

One of the most popular traffic-free rides in the country, the trail climbs 700ft over 13 miles from Ashbourne up to Parsley Hay. There are excellent cycle hire facilities. You can get to the centre of Ashbourne via a 1180ft lit tunnel.

Stratford Greenway from Stratford-upon-Avon to Long Marston. 5 miles

This five-mile railway path runs from near the centre of town, past the racecourse into open countryside via the old railway bridge over the River Avon. The route links to the Stratford-upon-Avon Canal towpath to Wilmcote.

Routes through Leicester

Leicester promotes itself as Environment City and it has made great strides in the provision of attractive and safe cycle routes passing right through the city centre and along the riverside, including the Great Central Way to Blaby.

Harby, Skellingthorpe and Lincoln. 6 miles

This path is built along a line owned by Railway Paths Limited, a charity connected to Sustrans whose aim is to hold disused railways for future transport use, in the meantime using them for walking and cycling routes. This long route has been built by Sustrans own staff over the last three years with a major Landfill Tax Credit grant and regional development funds. The last part of the route follows the Fossdyke, part of the Romans' canal scheme for recovering the Fens.

Longdendale. 6 miles

One of the finest sections of the Trans Pennine Trail runs alongside the reservoir from Hadfield Station to the Woodhead tunnels.

Even the TPT team could not contemplate a 3-mile long subterranean trek through to Dunford Bridge, so the route taken is on the old track over the moors.

Brampton Valley Way from Market Harborough to Northampton. 14 miles

A well-maintained railway path passing a collection of fine old steam locomotives at Chapel Brampton and using two tunnels to link Market Harborough with the northern edge of Northampton.

USEFUL MAPS & GUIDES

For details of the full range of maps, guides and other products available contact: **National Cycle Network Information, PO Box 21, Bristol BS99 2HA. Tel: 0117 929 0888. Or visit www.nationalcyclenetwork.org.uk**
The range of National Cycle Network Maps is described in more detail on pages 218-237.

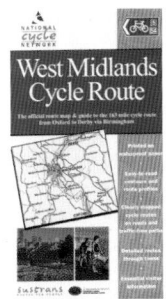

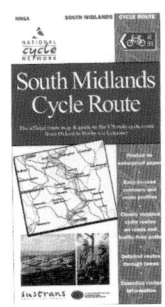

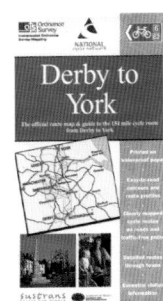

5 54 *West Midlands Cycle Route (Oxford – Derby, via Birmingham)*
162 miles. NN5B - £5.99

51 6 *South Midlands Cycle Route (Oxford – Derby, via Leicester)*
148 miles. NN6A - £5.99

6 62 *Derby – York Cycle Route*
154 miles. NN6B - £5.99

National Byway West Midlands
A 307-mile signed route from Cirencester to Chester mostly on quiet minor roads, plus 175 miles of connecting loops.
RBL38 - £3.00

More Cycling Without Traffic: Midlands & Peak District
A further 30 traffic-free routes including various sections of the Trans Pennine Trail.
RBA08 - £11.99

Derbyshire, Cheshire and North Staffordshire
35 cycle routes, the majority are offroad. Includes Carsington Water and the Ladybower Reservoirs.
RBW06 - £8.99

Grand Union, Oxford and Kennet & Avon Canals. RBW01 - £8.99

Places to Cycle in Leicestershire & Rutland. RPL66 - Free

Leisure Rides Peak District & Derbyshire. RG84 - £5.95

DERBY TO WORTHINGTON

The 13-mile ride out of Derby to the small, pretty village of Worthington is in many ways a perfect blueprint for what Sustrans would like to achieve throughout the country. An attractive traffic-free path starts in the heart of the city near where people live, work and shop. The route passes right by schools and colleges, crosses busy roads safely via toucan crossings, and uses a mixture of specially-built cycle paths, railway paths and canal towpaths to reach deep into the countryside along a green corridor, occasionally wooded and frequently punctuated with magnificent Millennium Mileposts and stone sculptures. It is a route that serves schoolchildren, commuters and leisure cyclists alike, whether they are novice cyclists, young families or more experienced cyclists looking for an attractive route out of the city to link with the network of country lanes. The Trent Viaduct is crossed near Melbourne – this is Grade II Listed, built in 1869 and repaired by Sustrans in the late 1980s. The second half of the ride has views of the limestone bluff of Breedon on the Hill, topped by a Norman church. The village of Worthington boasts an attractive church with a small wooden spire, an octagonal red-brick lock-up dating back to the 18th century, and a pub.

The Melbourne Railway Path.

Starting points
1. Derby railway station.
2. The Riverside Path in the centre of Derby (Bass's Recreation Ground).

Distance
13 miles one way, 26 miles return.

Grade
Easy.

Surface
Almost all on fine quality stone paths.

Roads, traffic, suitability for young children
Once onto the Riverside Path the route is excellent for young children. All the busy roads are crossed via bridges, subways or with toucan crossings.
There is a one-mile road section to visit Melbourne and a shorter (quieter) road section to visit Worthington.

Hills
No hills.

Refreshments
Lots of choice in Derby.
Lots of choice in Melbourne.
Malt Shovel PH in Worthington.

Leaflets
Derby City Council produces a free leaflet *Derby Cycle Route Guide*. Available from Derby City Council, Planning and Technical Services Dept., Roman House, Friar Gate, Derby DE1 1XB.
Tel: 01332 255021.

Nearest railway station
Derby.

The National Cycle Network in the area
Derby is at a major junction of the National Cycle Network:
Route 6 runs north from Milton Keynes through Northampton and

Derby town centre with the River Derwent Weir.

Leicester to Derby, then on through Nottingham to join the Trans Pennine Trail in Sheffield and Barnsley.

Route 54 runs south west from Derby through Burton-upon-Trent and Lichfield to Birmingham. From Etwall, five miles along this route, you can pick up the Pennine Cycleway (Route 68) which is open via Ashbourne and the Tissington Trail to Buxton and eventually reaches Berwick-on-Tweed.

Other nearby rides (waymarked or traffic-free)
1. The Riverside Path alongside the River Derwent runs east to Elvaston Castle Country Park where there is a circuit of the park.
2. To the north of Derby city centre (Exeter Bridge) the path continues alongside the Derwent past the Industrial Museum towards Chester Green and Darley.

DERBY TO WORTHINGTON

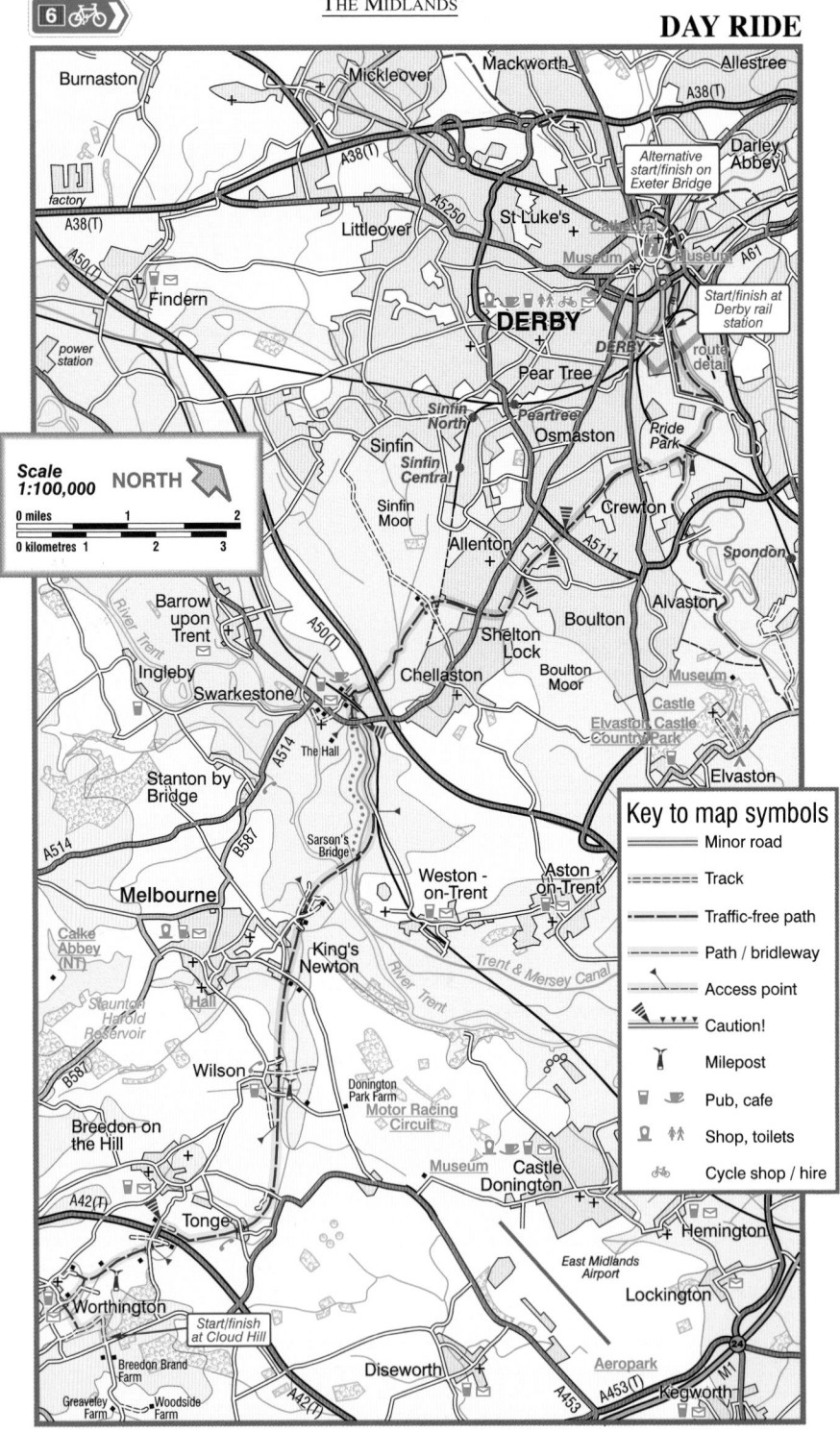

Scale
1:100,000   NORTH

0 miles   1   2
0 kilometres 1   2   3

Key to map symbols

Minor road
Track
Traffic-free path
Path / bridleway
Access point
Caution!
Milepost
Pub, cafe
Shop, toilets
Cycle shop / hire

Near Worthington.

Route instructions – Derby to Worthington

1. Exit Derby railway station and turn right. Either ride along the road (with care) or walk your bike along the pavement for 300 yds. Use the traffic lights just before the flyover to cross the road to the right and go beneath the bridge towards the Riverside Path.

If starting from the centre of Derby (Bass's Recreation Ground) follow the River Derwent east out of the city (ie keep the river on your left). Rejoin at Instruction 2.

2. Go past Pride Park (the stadium for Derby County Football Club), pass beneath a railway bridge then take the second of two closely spaced paths to the right.

3. Go past a lake then take the next right past the college buildings. Bear left to pass beneath a bridge.

4. After one mile, cross three roads in quick succession, the first and the third using toucan crossings.

5. After a further mile, near the end of the built-up area, at a crossroads with a minor lane go straight ahead signposted 'Swarkestone Lock'.

('Sinfin' is signposted to the right).

6. Pass beneath the A50, cross a bridge over the canal then turn left onto the towpath 'Melbourne'.

7. After two miles, just before the large bridge over the river, bear right and join the railway path.

After one mile, for Melbourne, cross the bridge over the river, pass beneath the power lines then fork right by the small, wooden Ranger's Hut. At the T-junction with the lane turn right. At the crossroads at the end of Trent Lane go straight ahead onto Jawbone Lane. At the T-junction at the end of Jawbone Lane, turn left then immediately right and follow this road into the heart of Melbourne.

8. For Worthington, stay on the main railway path. After four miles the path veers right and runs parallel with the A42. Cross the bridge over the dual carriageway then bear left to rejoin the railway path.

9. After 1½ miles the trail ends at Cloud Hill notable for dramatic views into an active rock quarry and for enigmatic iron birds, a pair of 'Rock Drills' and their only egg. If you wish to visit Worthington with its attractive church, octagonal lock-up and pub, turn left onto the minor lane, then at the crossroads at the end of Breedon Lane turn left onto Church Street signposted 'Griffydam, Osgathorpe'. Follow this road through the village for ¾ mile past the octagonal red-brick lock-up to the Malt Shovel pub.

DONCASTER TO THE EARTH CENTRE AND BARNSLEY

The Trans Pennine Trail crosses the country from coast to coast, starting in Southport and passing through Liverpool and South Manchester before crossing the Pennines to Barnsley, Doncaster, York, Hull and the North Sea coast. Links lead south to Sheffield and Chesterfield and north to Wakefield and Leeds. It links together many traffic-free stretches along dismantled railways, riverside paths, canal towpaths and across land regenerated after the demise of the area's heavy industries. Although an integral part of the Network, the TPT is a separately managed project and its multi-use nature means that path surfaces may vary. The section described below goes right past the Earth Centre, a 400-acre ecology park which is situated on reclaimed derelict land.

The River Don is crossed to the west of Doncaster over a viaduct high above the water, from where the railway path northwards passes Cusworth Park Museum, on the route to York. The river is then followed westwards on a delightful woodland stretch, passing the locks on the river at the Boat Inn in Sprotbrough before climbing to the northern end of the magnificent Conisbrough Viaduct. Leave yourself time to visit the Earth Centre before continuing westwards through the newly-built wetlands area to the north of Wath upon Dearne and joining the course of the old dismantled railway (the Dove Valley Trail) which will take you all the way to Worsbrough Mill Country Park (or into Barnsley).

The Trans Pennine Trail runs beside the River Don here viewed from Conisbrough Viaduct.

Starting points
Worsbrough Mill Country Park, south of Barnsley.
Doncaster Railway Station.
The Earth Centre, Conisbrough.

Distance
18 miles one way, 36 miles return. For shorter rides starting from Doncaster turn around at the Boat Inn, Sprotbrough (6 miles round trip), The Earth Centre (13 miles round trip), or the Harlington Inn (17 miles round trip).

Grade: Easy.

Surface
Tarmac and stone-based track.

Roads, traffic, suitability for young children
The route is mainly traffic-free and ideal for children. There are short road sections at the start in Doncaster and the end at Worsbrough Mill. There are also two short stretches on roads in the middle section, through Harlington and through Bolton upon Dearne.

Hills
Short climbs but no major hills.

Refreshments
Boat Inn, Sprotbrough.
Refreshments at the Earth Centre. Tel: 01709 513933 for opening times.
Harlington Inn, Harlington.

Further Infomation
Contact the TPT National Office at Barnsley MBC. Tel: 01226 772574. Or: www.transpenninetrail.org.uk

Nearest railway stations
Doncaster, Conisbrough, Barnsley, Bolton-upon-Dearne.

The National Cycle Network in the area
Barnsley is at a crossroads of the National Cycle Network: the Trans Pennine Trail (Route 62) runs from

Cyclists head west along the paved path beside the River Don.

Southport to Liverpool then east through Manchester, Barnsley and Hull to the North Sea Coast. Route 67 goes south from Barnsley to Sheffield (and on to Sherwood Forest and Nottingham by Route 6) and north to Wakefield and Leeds.

Other nearby rides (waymarked or traffic-free)
Many sections of the Trans Pennine Trail are traffic-free: from Worsbrough via Penistone and Dunford Bridge to Hadfield (near Glossop, on the western side of the Pennines) the trail is almost all traffic-free. On the southern link there is a long traffic-free stretch from the Rother Valley Park down into Chesterfield.

There is a waymarked Forestry Commission trail in Wharncliffe Woods, north west of Sheffield.

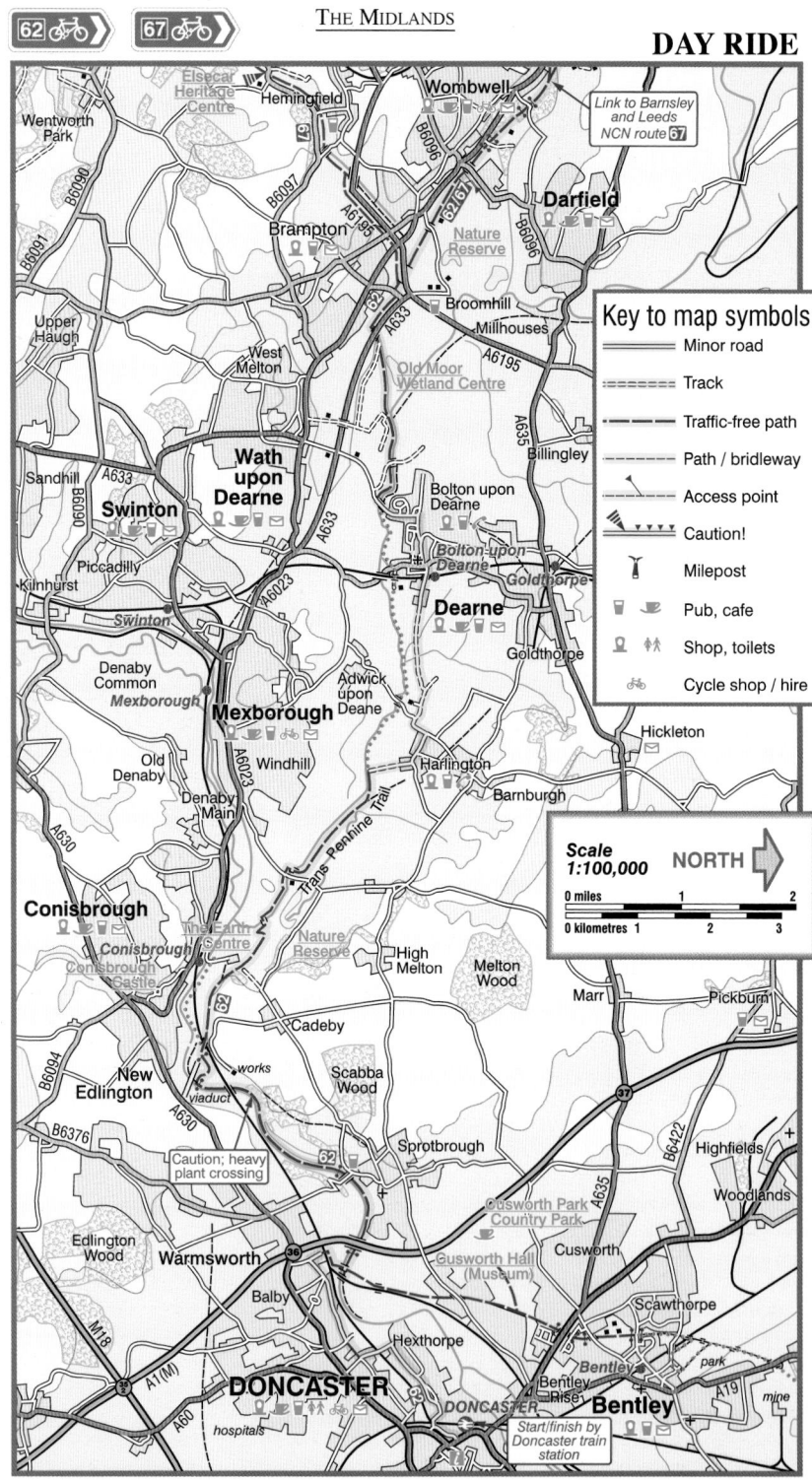

DONCASTER TO THE EARTH CENTRE AND BARNSLEY

62 67

DAY RIDE

Link to Barnsley and Leeds NCN route 67

Key to map symbols

	Minor road
	Track
	Traffic-free path
	Path / bridleway
	Access point
	Caution!
	Milepost
	Pub, cafe
	Shop, toilets
	Cycle shop / hire

Scale 1:100,000

NORTH

0 miles · 1 · 2
0 kilometres · 1 · 2 · 3

Wombwell
Hemingfield
Elsecar Heritage Centre
Wentworth Park
Darfield
Brampton
Nature Reserve
Broomhill
Millhouses
Upper Haugh
West Melton
Old Moor Wetland Centre
Billingley
Sandhill
Wath upon Dearne
Bolton upon Dearne
Swinton
Piccadilly
Kilnhurst
Bolton upon Dearne
Goldthorpe
Swinton
Dearne
Goldthorpe
Denaby Common
Mexborough
Adwick upon Deane
Mexborough
Hickleton
Old Denaby
Windhill
Harlington
Barnburgh
Denaby Main
Trans Pennine Trail
Conisbrough
The Earth Centre
Nature Reserve
High Melton
Melton Wood
Marr
Pickburn
Conisbrough
Conisbrough Castle
Cadeby
Scabba Wood
New Edlington
works
viaduct
Sprotbrough
Highfields
Woodlands
Caution; heavy plant crossing
Cusworth Park Country Park
Edlington Wood
Warmsworth
Cusworth Hall (Museum)
Cusworth
Balby
Scawthorpe
Hexthorpe
Bentley
park
DONCASTER
DONCASTER
Bentley Rise
Bentley
mine
hospitals
Start/finish by Doncaster train station

118

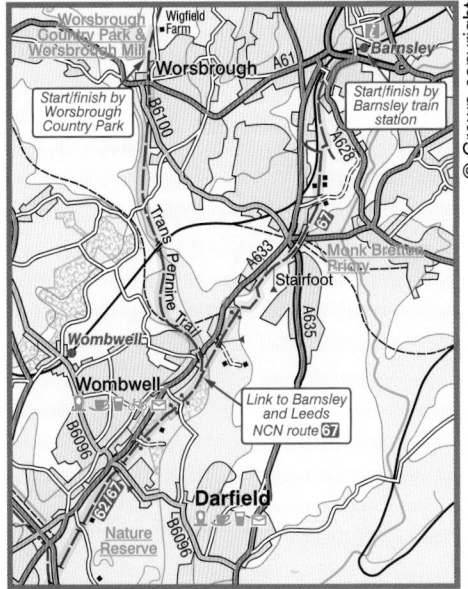

The Earth Centre.

Route instructions from Doncaster to Worsbrough Mill and Barnsley

1. With your back to Doncaster railway station, bear right on the red-brick path alongside the station car park then go through the adjoining car park. At the offset crossroads go straight ahead onto West Street then right at the T-junction with St Sepulchre Gate.

2. Continue in the same direction, past St James' Church, over the railway bridge and follow the road to the right then left. At the Rising Sun PH turn right onto Flowit St.

3. At the T-junction with Shady Side turn right then right again onto Bramworth Road. After 50 yds, as the road swings right, turn left through a small gateway onto a tarmac path. Shortly, take the third of three right turns, keeping the children's playground to your right.

4. Cross a bridge over the railway line, turn right along the road then first right signposted 'Warmsworth Cycle Route'. After almost one mile

cross the bridge over the disused railway and turn right signposted 'Trans Pennine Trail' (opposite Church Lane). Follow this to its end as tarmac turns to track, cross a bridge over the railway and follow the track round to the right.

5. Go past a cemetery, through a barrier then sharply right steeply downhill to cross the viaduct. Descend via the steps to the left (there are plans for a ramp). Follow the riverside path for three miles, passing beneath the A1 road bridge, alongside the locks and the Boat Inn at Sprotbrough.

6. Continue along the broad stone track climbing to join the road near the right-hand end of the viaduct ahead. Continue past the Earth Centre.

7. At the road cross straight ahead then turn right over the wooden bridge and join a railway path. Follow this for 1½ miles. Opposite a footbridge over the river turn right onto a track.

8. This turns to tarmac. At the T-junction (at the end of Mill Road) turn left. Go past the Harlington Inn. At the T-junction at the end of

Doncaster Road turn left signposted 'Adwick, Mexborough' then after ¼ mile, on a sharp left-hand bend turn right onto a track.

9. There are some rough sections on this stretch. The track turns to tarmac. At the T-junction (at the end of Station Road) just past the railway station, turn left then right just after the church. At the mini-roundabout turn left.

10. Shortly after crossing the bridge, turn right onto a track through the newly created wetlands area, following the Trans Pennine Trail signs.

11. Join the railway path, follow for three miles. At major fork of tracks bear left* and cross in quick succession two bridges over roads. After ½ mile at a fork of tracks bear right onto the lower track, towards a pylon.

* or bear right here and follow the signposted route into Barnsley.

12. Continue in the same direction for a further three miles. At the crossroads by the Ship PH and a sign for Wigfield Farm, leave the Trans Pennine Trail (which continues straight ahead towards Oxspring, Penistone and Dunford Bridge) turn left for 300 yds then right into Worsbrough Mill Country Park.

BIRMINGHAM TO KING'S NORTON PARK

Chamberlain Square and Victoria Square in the very heart of Birmingham are a glorious tribute to the dynamic approach that has created attractive open spaces for pedestrians and cyclists in the centre of a major city. Fine old and modern buildings stand side by side, and the whole area is enhanced by a series of huge sculptures. This ride starts from this place of vision and links with the traffic-free Rea Valley Route via a series of contraflow cycle lanes and other facilities which make life easier for the city centre cyclist. A minaret at the end of Gooch Street is testimony to the high proportion of Muslims living in this multi-cultural city and stands as a contrast to the ornate façade of Edward Road Baptist Church which you soon pass. Cannon Hill Park is an oasis of green with bright displays of flowers and marks the start of the traffic-free Rea Valley Route which is followed for four miles (for one section joining the excellent towpath of the Worcester & Birmingham Canal). This ride ends at King's Norton Park where there is a playground for children. Route 5 continues along the line of the river valley to Northfield and Longbridge, and eventually works its way out of the city southwards to Stratford-upon-Avon.

The junction of the Worcester & Birmingham Canal with the Main Line Canal at the Convention Centre.

Starting point
Tourist Information Centre, Chamberlain Square, central Birmingham.

Distance
Seven miles one way, 14 miles return.

Grade: Easy.

Surface
Mixture of road, tarmac cyclepath and stone-based tracks.

The carriage drive through Cannon Hill Park is now open for cyclists.

Roads, traffic, suitability for young children
The ride uses some traffic-calmed streets in central Birmingham, although some streets are still busy. Once out of the centre, all the busy roads are crossed via toucan crossings. The section along the Rea Valley Route through Cannon Hill Park and along the Worcester & Birmingham Canal is traffic-free and ideal for children.

Hills: None.

Refreshments
Lots of choice in Birmingham city centre.
Cafe/tea room in Cannon Hill Park.

Leaflets
CycleCity's Birmingham Cycling Map – City Centre and Suburbs is an excellent publication showing the traffic-free paths, signposted cycle routes, advisory routes and a wealth of other information. It costs £4.95 and is available from National Cycle Network Information Service, PO Box 21, Bristol BS99 2HA.
Tel: 0117 929 0888, or visit: www.nationalcyclenetwork.org.uk

Nearest railway stations
Birmingham New Street in the centre of the city.
King's Norton.

The National Cycle Network in the area
Birmingham is at a crossroads of the National Cycle Network:
Route 5 comes north from Reading through Oxford, Banbury, Stratford and Bromsgrove (and is followed in this ride into the centre of Birmingham). It continues north east via Lichfield and Burton-on-Trent to Derby.
Route 81 follows the Main Line Canal to Wolverhampton and will eventually strike into the heart of Mid Wales.
Route 44 is a long-term plan to link Birmingham to Chepstow through Worcestershire, Herefordshire and the Forest of Dean.

Other nearby rides (waymarked or traffic-free)
1. Although, as we are forever being told, Birmingham has more miles of canal than Venice, from a cyclist's point of view the towpath network is not formalised, but there is much to explore including the Worcester & Birmingham Canal towpath which is used for part of this route. For the most up-to-date information contact British Waterways: 01902 409010.
2. Sutton Park is a large park just north of Birmingham where motor traffic has been banned.
3. The Kingswinford Railway Path runs for 10 miles from Pensnett (west of Dudley) to Wolverhampton.
4. National Cycle Route 5 follows the Birmingham & Wolverhampton Canal from the centre of Birmingham to Sandwell Valley Country Park.

A good example of the high quality city centre towpath rebuilt by British Waterways.

BIRMINGHAM TO KING'S NORTON PARK

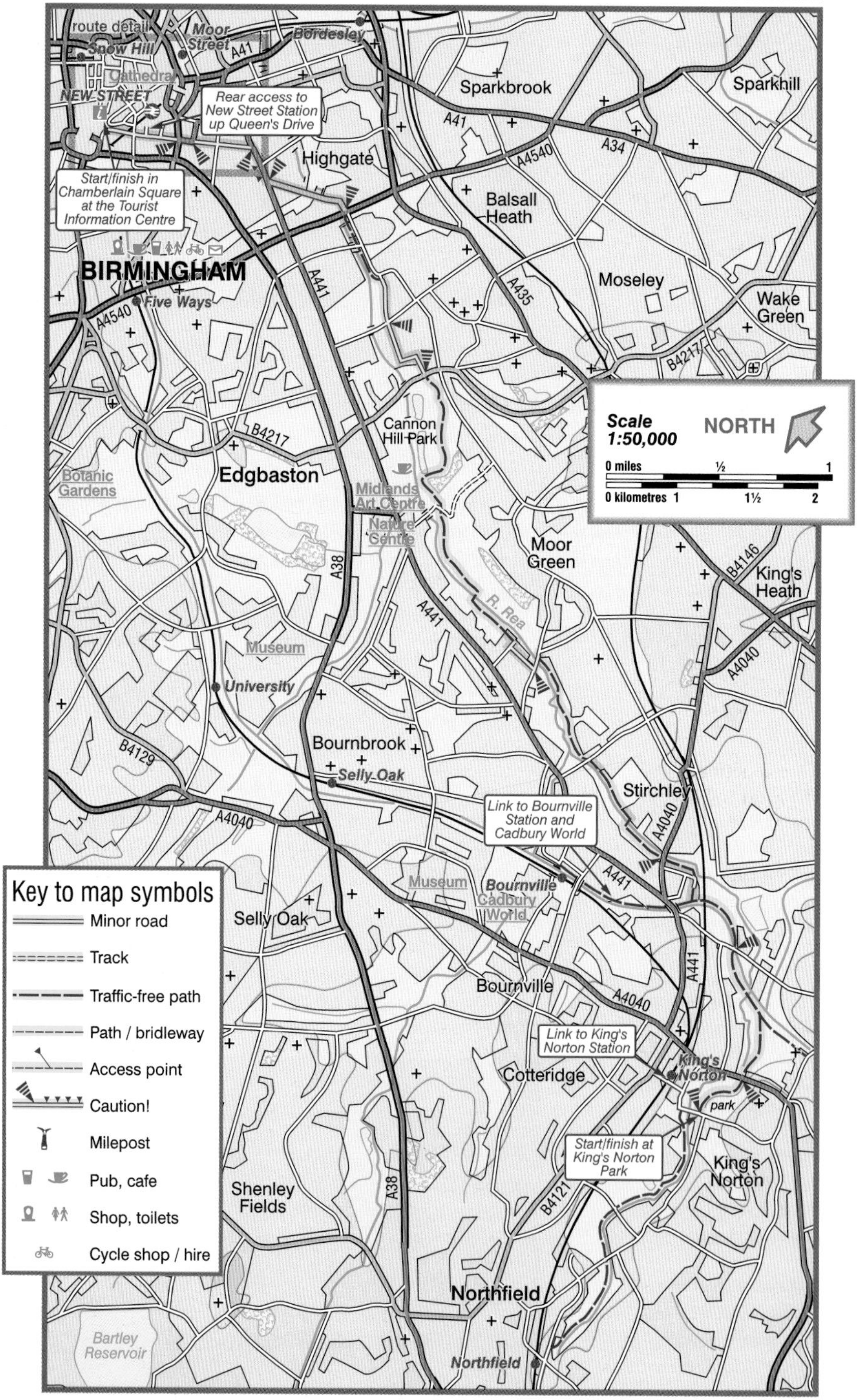

5 🚲

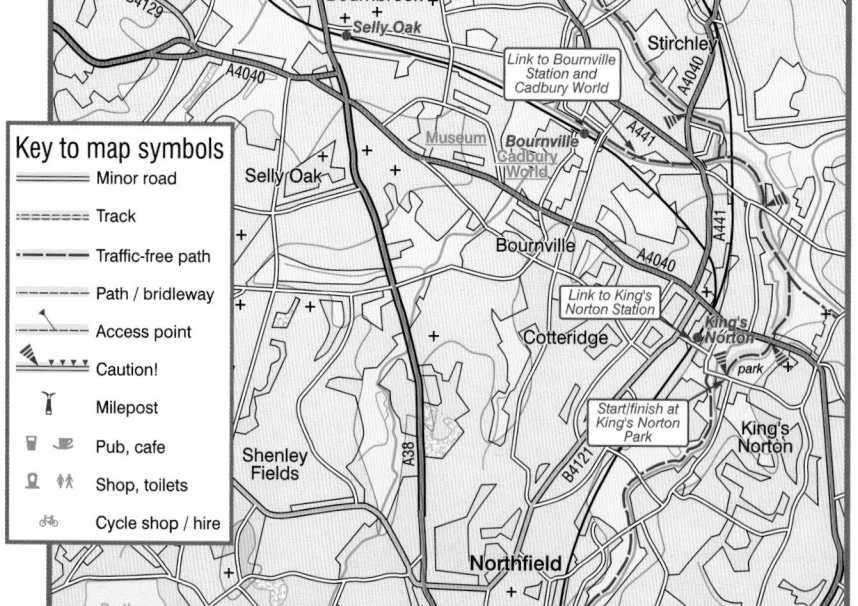

route detail

Snow Hill

Moor Street

Bordesley

Cathedral

NEW STREET

Rear access to New Street Station up Queen's Drive

Highgate

Sparkbrook

Sparkhill

A41

A41

A4540

A34

Start/finish in Chamberlain Square at the Tourist Information Centre

Balsall Heath

BIRMINGHAM

Five Ways

A4540

A441

Moseley

A435

Wake Green

B4217

Scale
1:50,000

NORTH

0 miles   ½   1

0 kilometres 1   1½   2

B4217

Cannon Hill Park

Botanic Gardens

Edgbaston

Midlands Art Centre

Nature Centre

A38

Moor Green

King's Heath

B4146

R. Rea

A441

A4040

Museum

University

A4040

B4129

Bournbrook

Selly Oak

Stirchley

A4040

A4040

Link to Bournville Station and Cadbury World

Key to map symbols

———— Minor road

===== Track

– – – Traffic-free path

- - - Path / bridleway

◄ Access point

▼▼▼ Caution!

Ȳ Milepost

🍺 ☕ Pub, cafe

⚲ 🚻 Shop, toilets

🚲 Cycle shop / hire

Museum

Bournville Cadbury World

Selly Oak

Bournville

A4040

A441

A38

Cotteridge

Link to King's Norton Station

King's Norton

park

Shenley Fields

B4121

Start/finish at King's Norton Park

King's Norton

Northfield

Bartley Reservoir

Northfield

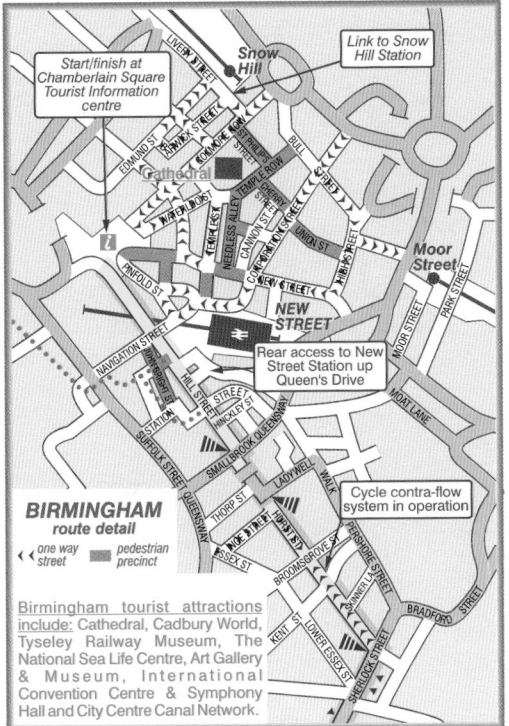

BIRMINGHAM
route detail

one way street | pedestrian precinct

Birmingham tourist attractions include: Cathedral, Cadbury World, Tyseley Railway Museum, The National Sea Life Centre, Art Gallery & Museum, International Convention Centre & Symphony Hall and City Centre Canal Network.

Route instructions from Birmingham to King's Norton Park

1. With your back to the Tourist Information Centre, go to the left of the Iron Man down Pinfold Street, left into Stephenson Street – follow round to the right into Navigation Street. Left at the traffic lights into Hill Street.

2. Go straight ahead at the traffic lights. Continue downhill. Go straight ahead on the bus/cycle lane as the traffic bears left. Go straight ahead at the traffic lights at the crossroads with Smallbrook Queensway dual carriageway.

3. Move into the cycle lane in the centre of the road to cross to the pedestrian area in front of the Hippodrome Theatre. Go straight ahead onto Hurst Street. At the traffic lights go straight ahead into a contraflow lane continuing down Hurst Street.

4. Use the cycle facility to turn right at the traffic lights onto the cycle lane in Sherlock Street. Shortly, turn left into Gooch Street.

5. At the Post Office and shops follow Gooch Street around to the right. At the traffic lights get into the cycle lane and cross straight ahead (onto Longmore Street). Just after the lights, move right and cross to the cycle track on the grassed open space alongside the road.

6. At the crossroads with Edward Road at the end of Cheddar Road, go straight ahead onto Harbury Road. At the T-junction with Willows Crescent (you can just see Edgbaston Cricket Ground to your right) turn left then shortly right onto Cannon Hill Road.

7. At the crossroads with the busy Edgbaston Road use the toucan crossing to go straight ahead through the gates into the delights of Cannon Hill Park.

8. Follow the clearly segregated cycle route through the park. Go past a Millennium Milepost on your right. At the end of the white line segregation continue straight ahead with the river on your right, following signs for Stirchley.

9. The tarmac path swings right to cross the river via a brick and metal bridge (without barriers).

10. The track joins a street with terraced houses (Kitchener Road). Turn first left onto Cecil Road then at the T-junction with Dogpool Lane turn left then immediately right onto a continuation of the riverside path.

11. Follow the Rea Valley Route and signs for 'Stirchley, King's Norton'. At the next busy road (Cartland Road) go straight ahead via a toucan crossing onto a continuation of the riverside path.

12. At the T-junction with the trading estate road turn right to cross the bridge then immediately left (with the river now on your left). At the crossroads with the busy Fordhouse Lane, use the toucan crossing to go straight ahead signposted 'King's Norton, Northfield'.

13. At the end of the cycle path by a tall wooden signpost turn left on the quiet estate road (Dacer Close) then shortly first left. Follow Rea Valley Route signs to join the Worcester & Birmingham Canal towpath and turn left.

14. At the next bridge (Lifford Lane Road Bridge) the towpath crosses to the other side of the canal.

15. After 400 yds, at the next bridge (red-brick with a '72' plaque on it) turn right just before a large red-brick house away from the towpath signposted 'Rea Valley Route. King's Norton'. Follow the path across the playing fields. Cross Pershore Road via toucan crossing.

16. The route continues along the valley to Longbridge.

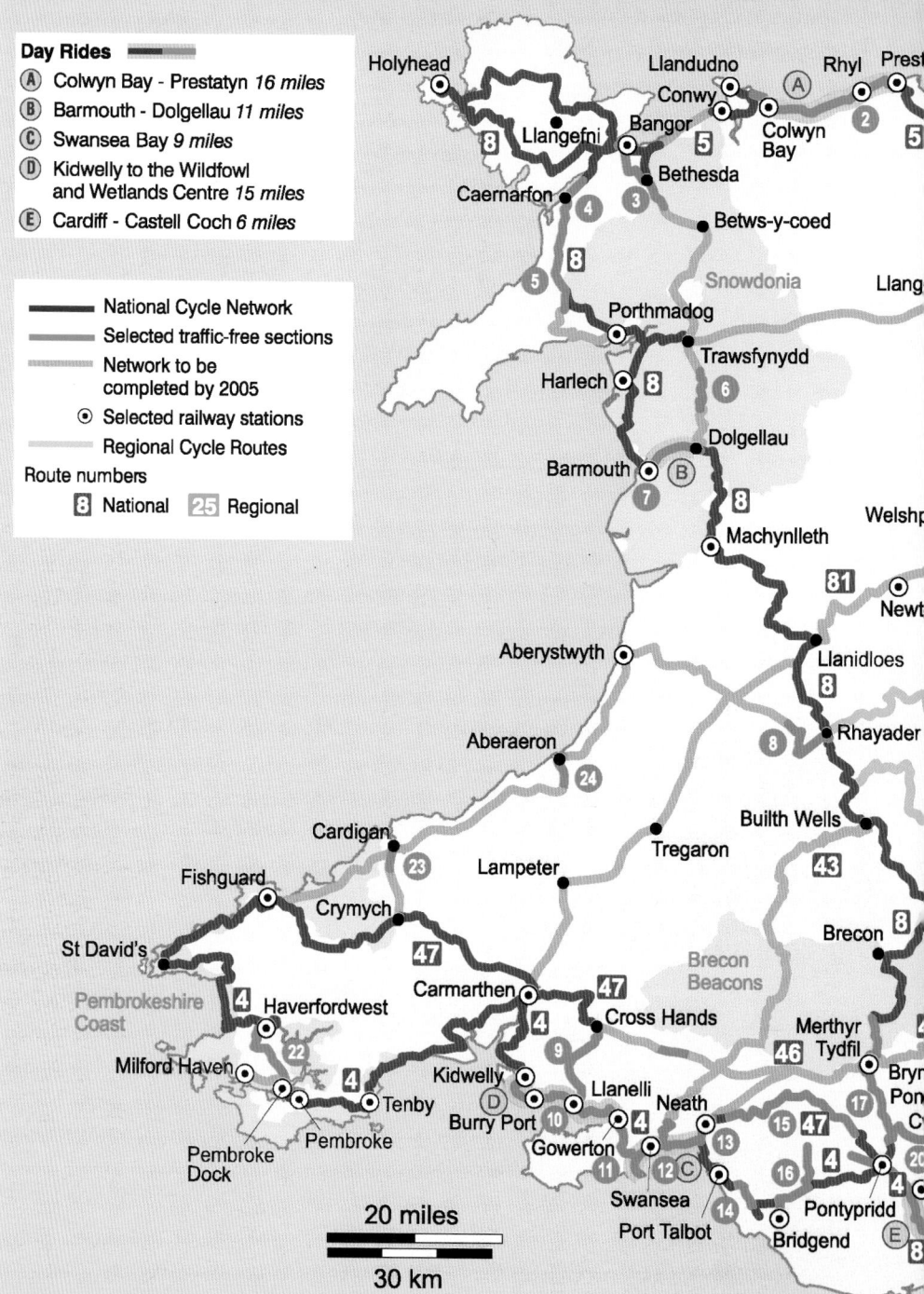

Day Rides ▬▬▬
- Ⓐ Colwyn Bay - Prestatyn *16 miles*
- Ⓑ Barmouth - Dolgellau *11 miles*
- Ⓒ Swansea Bay *9 miles*
- Ⓓ Kidwelly to the Wildfowl and Wetlands Centre *15 miles*
- Ⓔ Cardiff - Castell Coch *6 miles*

▬▬▬ National Cycle Network
▬▬▬ Selected traffic-free sections
▬▬▬ Network to be completed by 2005
⊙ Selected railway stations
▬▬▬ Regional Cycle Routes
Route numbers
8 National 25 Regional

Holyhead
Llangefni
Caernarfon
Llandudno
Conwy
Bangor
Bethesda
Colwyn Bay
Rhyl
Pres
Ⓐ
2
5
Betws-y-coed
Snowdonia
Llang
Porthmadog
Trawsfynydd
Harlech 8
6
Dolgellau
Barmouth Ⓑ
7
8
Machynlleth
Welshp
81
Newt
Llanidloes
8
Aberystwyth
Aberaeron
24
Tregaron
8
Rhayader
Builth Wells
Cardigan
23
Lampeter
43
Fishguard
Crymych
Brecon
8
St David's
47
Pembrokeshire Coast
4
Haverfordwest
Carmarthen
47
Brecon Beacons
Milford Haven
22
4
Cross Hands
4
9
Merthyr Tydfil
46
Bryn
Pon
C
Kidwelly
Ⓓ
Llanelli
Neath
17
Tenby
10
4
15
47
Burry Port
Gowerton
11
12 Ⓒ
13
16
4
Pembroke Dock
Pembroke
Swansea
14
Pontypridd
Ⓔ
Port Talbot
Bridgend
8

20 miles
30 km

Selected traffic-free paths

1. Connah's Quay - Chester - Mickle Trafford *11 miles*
2. (A) North Wales Coast Promenades *16 miles*
3. Bangor - Tregarth *5 miles*
4. Caernarfon to Y Felinheli
   Lôn Las Menai *5 miles*
5. Caernarfon to Bryncir
   Lôn Eifion *12 miles*
6. Coed y Brenin Forest Trails
7. Mawddach Estuary
   Llwybr Mawddach *7 miles*
8. Elan Valley Routes *12 miles*
9. Swiss Valley Railway *12 miles*
10. (D) Millennium Coastal Park at Llanelli *15 miles*
11. Swansea Bike Paths *11 miles*
12. Neath - Briton Ferry *8 miles*
13. Afan Forest Park *8 miles*
14. Margam Park
15. Neath to Pontypridd High Level Route *24 miles*
16. Ogmore Vale Trail *11 miles*
17. Taff Trail *53 miles*
18. Llanfoist - Govilon *2 miles*
19. Pontypool - Blaenavon *14 miles*
20. Sirhowy Country Park *5 miles*
21. Newport Canal Paths *4 miles*
22. Brunel Way *5 miles*
23. Cardigan *2 miles*
24. Aberaeron *2 miles*

Wrexham

n-Wye

18 Abergavenny
Monmouth
19 46 42 44
n 21
Newport Chepstow
Caldicot
4 Severn Tunnel
rphilly Junction
ardiff

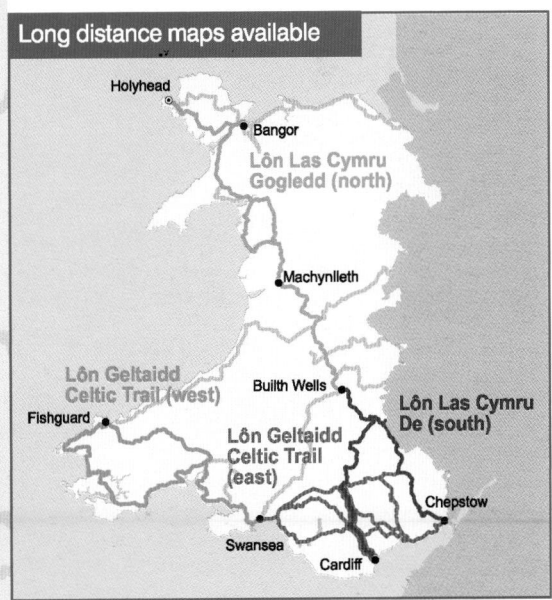

Long distance maps available

Holyhead

Bangor

Lôn Las Cymru
Gogledd (north)

Machynlleth

Lôn Geltaidd
Celtic Trail (west)   Builth Wells

Fishguard   Lôn Las Cymru
                                              De (south)
              Lôn Geltaidd
              Celtic Trail
              (east)
                                         Chepstow

       Swansea
                 Cardiff

© Crown copyright

125

WALES

Wales contains some of Britain's most beautiful countryside and some of its earliest industrial history which has left scars, particularly in the south, but also a plethora of interesting sites. Fortunately many of these scars have disappeared thanks to some of the largest land reclamation schemes in Europe. This juxtaposition of beauty and industry includes the untouched farmland and moors on the ridges between the old coal mining valleys and the dramatic contrast of the heavy industrial complexes at Port Talbot overlooked by sheep-dotted rolling hills.

The Welsh National Cycle Route, also known as Lôn Las Cymru, runs the length of Wales from the Bristol Channel to the island of Anglesey. Highlights along the way include the magnificent development around Cardiff Bay, the fairy-tale

Route 8 from Cardiff to Holyhead follows the remains of the Glamorgan Canal into Merthyr Tydfil under this impressive railway relic.

castle at Castell Coch, the dramatic beauty of the Brecon Beacons, the mountains of Mid Wales, the broad and scenic Mawddach Estuary and the solid splendour of Caernarfon Castle.

Two other Millennium routes cross Wales from east to west. The Bangor to Liverpool route skirts along the North Coast; in South and West Wales the Celtic Trail/Lôn Geltaidd links the port of Fishguard, via the attractions of Pembrokeshire, to the old coal mining valleys, crossing the Welsh National Route in Pontypridd before running east through Newport and Chepstow to the old Severn Bridge.

NATIONAL CYCLE NETWORK HIGHLIGHTS

Menai Bridge
Telford's suspension bridge across the Menai Straits and a ferry service from Caernarfon provide the links onto Anglesey. The two National Routes in North Wales (5 & 8) combine here to cross over this stretch of water at Menai Bridge.

Newport Transporter Bridge
The Newport Transporter Bridge is the largest of a number built by Ferdinand Arnodin. The bridge took four years to build at a cost of £98,000 and was opened by Viscount Tredegar on 12 September 1906. It has a clear span of 592 ft and a height of 177 ft to the underside of the boom. The bridge never paid its way, and once the George Street Bridge was opened in 1964 it fell into dereliction. Eventually Newport Borough had to close the bridge until major funding was found to refurbish this wonderful structure over the years 1992-1995, when it was reopened.

The A55 Route: Conwy to Abergwyngregyn
One of the hardest routes Sustrans has built runs parallel with the North Wales Coast Expressway at Llanfairfechan, hemmed in by road, rail and precipitous headlands.

Caerphilly Castle
Caerphilly Castle is the largest castle in Wales. In 1268 building began on the site of an earlier Roman Fort, by the Anglo-Norman Gilbert de Clare in his struggle with the Welsh ruler Llewellyn ap Griffydd. The Castle's ownership passed to and fro until 1648 during the English Civil War when it was partially destroyed and the moat drained. The National Cycle Route passes close by the moat and lakes which were reflooded in 1958.

Cefn Coed Viaduct
The magnificent Cefn Coed Viaduct, spans the Afon Taf Fawr in a gentle curve south west of Merthyr Tydfil. The viaduct is a 15-bay structure, 770 ft long, and was completed in 1866 as part of a complex detour insisted on by the owner of Cyfarthfa Castle, who did not want to see the new Brecon and Merthyr Tydfil Junction Railway from his windows.

Colwyn Bay Promenade
Conwy and Denbighshire's superb promenade route links Colwyn Bay and Rhyl and Prestatyn along a largely traffic-free path overlooking the sea. It runs parallel to the North Coast Railway and has involved heavy engineering to create a continuous route almost entirely separate from traffic.

NATIONAL CYCLE NETWORK HIGHLIGHTS

Swiss Valley, Llanelli

This 10-mile route takes you most of the way from the Millennium Coastal Park at Llanelli to the National Botanic Garden of Wales at Middleton Hall. It follows the line of a railway which itself was built on the course of a former tramway, which can be seen snaking off from side-to-side in various locations.

Millennium Coastal Park, Llanelli

This Millennium Project was opened in 1999 and forms one of the highest quality sections on the whole of the Network. It includes a number of major bridges, two landscaped tunnels over the mainline railway and some bold coastal protection works to stabilize the sand dunes.

Machynlleth River Dyfi Bridge

This Millennium Bridge, built on the line of the former Corris Tramroad includes balustrades by the sculptor, Jon Mills. The route now avoids the main road north to Dolgellau. The Centre for Alternative Technology is connected to Machynlleth just three miles away.

Bethesda to Llyn Ogwen

The new path from Bethesda runs along the foot of the slate heaps and joins the old road up to Llyn Ogwen. The trail follows the floor of Nant Ffrancon on the opposite side to Telford's A5 road.

The Cob at Porthmadog

Any reader who was on the Trailblazing Ride from Belfast to Land's End will remember the joy of cycling across The Cob at Porthmadog with the traffic held back. The Environment Agency is now constructing a new bank to reinforce The Cob on the landward side, which will carry a traffic-free route for cyclists across to Boston Lodge.

Cardiff Bay Barrage

The first phase of the Barrage was opened on 2nd June 2001. When finally linked to the Norwegian Church at Cardiff Bay, the Barrage will make a memorable finale to Lôn Las Cymru from Holyhead.

CITY FOCUS

Maps & guides are available from National Cycle Network Information unless indicated otherwise. See page 131 for contact details.

Cardiff
Lôn Las Cymru (South) Map
shows Route 8 on its way through
Cardiff, on a largely traffic-free
course from Cardiff Bay past the
Millennium Stadium and alongside
the River Taff to Tongwynlais and
Castell Coch. Just north of here, at
Nantgarw, Route 8 meets Route 4
(the Celtic Trail). A railway path
runs east into Caerphilly. The map
also shows the proposed route
development across the Cardiff
Bay Barrage, through Penarth to
Barry and on to Cardiff airport.

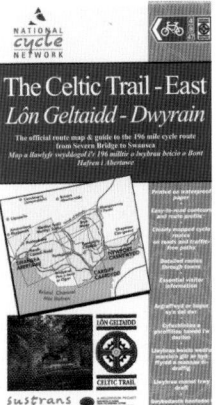

Newport
The Celtic Trail (East) Map
shows Newport at the junction of
three National Routes: Route 46
follows the canal and then a
railway path north through
Malpas and Cwmbran to
Pontypool and Blaenavon; Route
47 follows the other branch of the
canal past the Fourteen Locks to
Crosskeys and into Sirhowy
Valley Country Park; Route 4 is
being developed to the west
alongside the A4042 (Docks Way)
and across Tredegar Park to
Bassaleg and the minor road
network to Draethen; to the east
Route 4 crosses the splendid
Transporter Bridge onto the
network of lanes south of the M4.

Swansea Bay Cycling, a leaflet
produced by the City of Swansea,
shows three traffic-free routes in
and near Swansea and lists cycle
shops and cycle-friendly
accommodation. Available from the
Tourist Information Centre.
Tel: 01792 468321.

Swansea
The Celtic Trail (West) and the
Celtic Trail (East) Maps both show
Swansea and the course of Routes
4 and 43. Route 4 runs west along
the Promenade towards Mumbles
and Clyne Valley Country Park.
To the east the route is still being
developed parallel with the A483
towards Briton Ferry and the start
of the Neath Canal.

TRAFFIC-FREE PATHS PARTICULARLY SUITABLE FOR FAMILIES

46 **Pontypool to Blaenavon. 6 miles**

This railway path connects the Brecon Canal at Pontypool with the Blaenavon Mining Museum and Ironworking complex, which has been recently awarded World Heritage status. Beyond Blaenavon the route continues to a summit 1400ft above sea level and then drops down to pick up the spectacular Clydach Gorge route to Abergavenny.

8 **Caernarfon – Bryncir also known as Lôn Eifion. 12 miles**

Two railway paths start in Caernarfon, both are used on the Lôn Las Cymru route as it crosses Wales from Cardiff to Anglesey. This, the longer of the two, runs south for 12 miles to Bryncir, north of Criccieth. Minor roads lead to Porthmadog.

8 **Elan Valley Trail. 6 miles**

A beautiful route along the line of the old Birmingham Corporation Railway in the very heart of Mid Wales with panoramic views of four of the Elan Valley Reservoirs, built at the turn of the 20th century to provide a water supply for Birmingham.

4 **Neyland. 4 miles**

At one stage Brunel had the idea of turning Neyland into a major transatlantic terminus. The now disused railway is almost all that remains of this aspiration and makes a magnificent trip linking Johnston to the estuary. At the lower end, the route runs on a causeway through the tidal Nature Reserve.

47 **Neath – Llanwonno (Pontypridd) High Level Route. 20 miles**

The traffic-free section of this route follows wide gravel roads through the largest forest area in South Wales. From the top of Fairylands Road, north east of Neath, to Llanwonno, north west of Pontypridd, enjoy 20 miles of forest roads climbing to a highpoint of almost 2,000 ft. *NB. Not suitable for young children - too strenuous!*

47 **Newport – Crosskeys Canal towpath. 8 miles**

One of the best canal towpaths in Wales – a wide gravel track runs alongside what was once a major artery carrying coal down to the docks at Newport. There are views of wooded hills rising to over 1,000 ft either side of the canal as you approach Crosskeys.

USEFUL MAPS & GUIDES

For details of the full range of maps, guides and other products available contact: **National Cycle Network Information, PO Box 21, Bristol BS99 2HA. Tel: 0117 929 0888. Or visit www.nationalcyclenetwork.org.uk** The range of National Cycle Network Maps is described in more detail on pages 218-237.

4 47 8 *Celtic Trail East (Swansea – Chepstow)* 84 miles. NN4B - £5.99

4 47 *Celtic Trail West (Fishguard – Swansea)* 143 miles. NN4C - £5.99

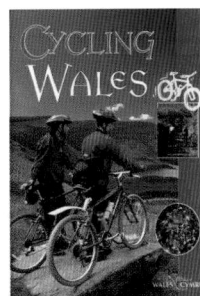

Cycling Wales Guide Excellent guide with information about cycling in Wales. FG08 - FREE

8 42 *Lôn Las Cymru South (Chepstow/Cardiff – Builth Wells)* 83 miles. NN8A - £5.99

8 *Lôn Las Cymru North (Builth Wells – Holyhead)* 175 miles. NN8B - £5.99

25 *Radnor Ring* Map and accommodation list for this 84-mile route around Radnor Forest and Llandridnod Wells. Links to Route 8. RPR12 - £4.99

The Brecon Beacons.

Cycling Without Traffic: Wales Thirty traffic-free rides throughout Wales. RBA06 - £10.99

SWANSEA TO GOWERTON & THE MUMBLES

The wide sweep of Swansea Bay provides a dramatic start to both rides, starting from the heart of Swansea, the 'ugly, lovely town' described by Dylan Thomas, who was born here. It is the second largest city in Wales, after Cardiff, with much of it rebuilt after suffering heavy bombing during the Second World War. In the 19th century Swansea was swept along by the rapid industrialisation of South Wales, serving as a port for the local tinplate, copper and coal industries. In the 20th century the docks fell into decline, but have recently been regenerated with the creation of the new Maritime Quarter, the centrepiece of which is a 600-berth marina at the old South Dock. The Mumbles is a busy sailing and watersports centre which has nevertheless kept its character as a Victorian seaside resort. If you are feeling energetic you may wish to climb up to Mumbles Head for excellent views back over the bay. From Swansea, leading north towards Gowerton, the climb up through the 725 acres of Clyne Valley Country Park is a wooded delight, especially lovely in the changing autumn colours. The gentle three-mile descent on the return trip is a joy for weary legs!

Swansea Waterfront.

Starting point
The seafront by the Marina/County Hall in Swansea.

Distance
Swansea – The Mumbles, five miles one way, 10 miles return.
Swansea – Gowerton, eight miles one way, 16 miles return.

Grade
Easy.

Surface
Tarmac throughout.

Roads, traffic, suitability for young children
The two routes are ideal for children. The one busy road crossing (the A4067 at Black Pill) has a cycle crossing.

Hills
Flat ride to The Mumbles. There is a gentle 200ft climb up through Clyne Valley Country Park to the highpoint at Dunvant on the Gowerton ride.

Refreshments
Lots of choice in Swansea and The Mumbles.
Pubs and stores in Gowerton.

Nearest railway stations
Swansea.
There is a restricted service at Gowerton.

Mumbles Pier at the end of the former Oystermouth railway.

The National Cycle Network in the area
The ride described here is part of Route 4, also known as the Celtic Trail/Lôn Geltaidd, which runs from Fishguard to Chepstow.
Route 43 will link Swansea to Builth Wells where it joins Lôn Las Cymru from Cardiff to Anglesey (Route 8).

Other nearby rides (waymarked or traffic-free)
1. Neath Canal.
2. The High Level Forestry Route from Fairylands Road, east of Neath to Llanwonno, north west of Pontypridd.
3. There are many routes in Afan Argoed Country Park, north east of Port Talbot.

Swansea Harbourside boasts an ambitious series of sculptures including Captain Cat, the blind seafarer in Dylan Thomas' Under Milk Wood.

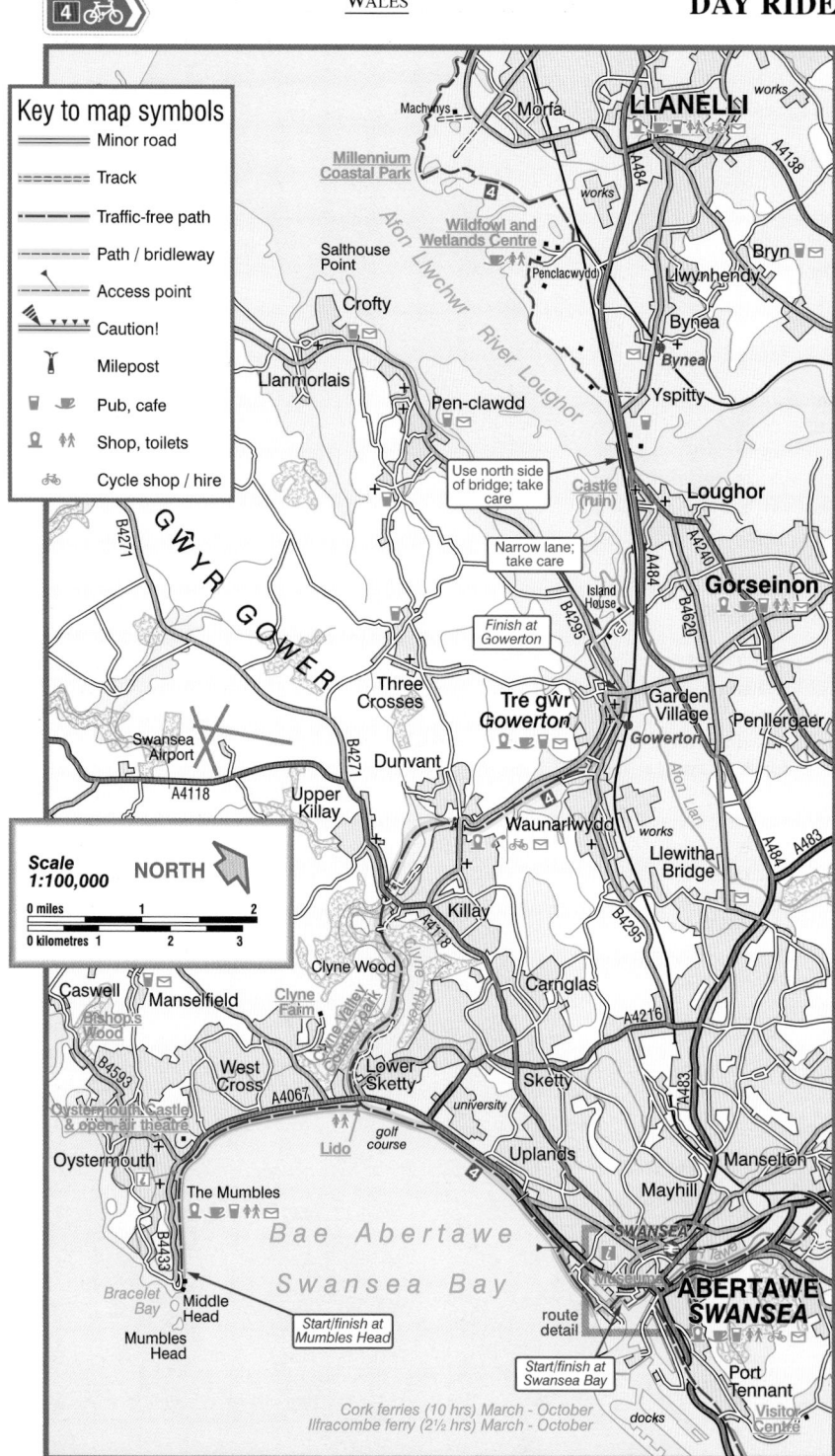

SWANSEA TO GOWERTON & THE MUMBLES

Key to map symbols

═══	Minor road
▭▭▭	Track
━ ━ ━	Traffic-free path
┈┈┈	Path / bridleway
◀━	Access point
▬▬▬	Caution!
Ⅰ	Milepost
🍺 ☕	Pub, cafe
🚻 🚹🚺	Shop, toilets
🚲	Cycle shop / hire

Machynys

Morfa

LLANELLI

works

A4138

Millennium Coastal Park

4

works

Afon Llwchwr

Wildfowl and Wetlands Centre

Penclacwydd

River Loughor

A484

Bryn

Llwynhendy

Bynea

Bynea

Salthouse Point

Crofty

Yspitty

Llanmorlais

Pen-clawdd

Use north side of bridge; take care

Castle (ruin)

Loughor

A240

Narrow lane; take care

A484

A484

Island House

B4295

Gorseinon

A4620

GWYR GOWER

B4271

Finish at Gowerton

B4271

Three Crosses

Tre gŵr **Gowerton**

Garden Village

Penllergaer

Swansea Airport

Dunvant

Gowerton

A4118

Upper Killay

B4271

Waunarlwydd

works

Afon Llan

A483

Llewitha Bridge

A484

A483

Scale 1:100,000

NORTH

0 miles — 1 — 2
0 kilometres 1 — 2 — 3

Killay

A4118

4

B4295

Carnglas

A4216

Clyne Wood

Clyne River

Caswell

Manselfield

Clyne Valley Country Park

Bishop's Wood

Clyne Farm

B4593

West Cross

A4067

Lower Sketty

Sketty

university

A483

Oystermouth Castle & open-air theatre

Lido

golf course

Uplands

Manselton

Oystermouth

Mayhill

The Mumbles

4

SWANSEA

Museum

route detail

B4433

Bae Abertawe

Swansea Bay

ABERTAWE SWANSEA

Bracelet Bay

Middle Head

Start/finish at Mumbles Head

Start/finish at Swansea Bay

Port Tennant

Mumbles Head

Visitor Centre

docks

Cork ferries (10 hrs) March - October
Ilfracombe ferry (2½ hrs) March - October

Swansea Bay.

Route instructions

A. Swansea to The Mumbles

Keeping Swansea Bay to your left, follow the cycle path along the promenade/seafront for five miles, passing both the university and the golf course.

The route stops in The Mumbles where a number of good refreshment stops can be found.

B. Swansea to Gowerton

1. Follow the cyclepath along the promenade/seafront for three miles, passing Swansea University.

2. At the end of the golf course on the right, bear right away from the sea front and cross the main A4067 via the traffic lights. Enter Clyne Valley Country Park and start climbing steadily.

3. Climb almost 200 ft to the highpoint at Dunvant. Descend. At the housing estate at the end of the railway path bear left to continue in the same direction, soon rejoining a tarmac track.

4. This becomes a residential road (Woodlands Road). At the cycle crossing (with the busy B4295) turn left for the shops and the centre of Gowerton.

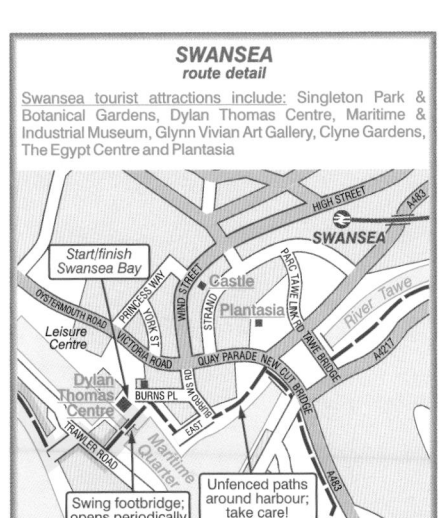

The Clyne Valley Path.

KIDWELLY TO THE WILDFOWL AND WETLANDS CENTRE, LLANELLI

Starting from Kidwelly with its dramatic castle, you soon join a traffic-free path that continues more or less unbroken to the Wildfowl & Wetlands Centre south of Llanelli. Throughout the ride there are many views of estuaries that flood in exceptionally high tides. The first, Gwendraeth, has a backdrop of rounded green hills rising up over 600 ft from the shoreline. You soon enter the sandy woodlands of Pembrey Forest, where there are many tracks which you could explore based around the Country Park Visitor Centre. Beyond Pembrey Forest there are long sections of newly-built cycle paths with wonderful views out over the estuary that separates the Gower Peninsula from the mainland. Between Burry Port and Llanelli the railway line is crossed twice via huge land bridges covered with earth and grass, a wonderful piece of landscaping. Indeed along the whole length of the route millions of tons of earth have been moved to regenerate what was once a derelict wasteland. At the Wildfowl & Wetlands Centre you have the option of pressing on to Swansea and catching the train back, or cycling all or part of the way back as far as the stations at Llanelli or Burry Port.

Llanelli Promenade from the landscaped park over the Fishguard Railway.

Starting points
1. The centre of Kidwelly.
2. The Wildfowl & Wetlands Centre, southeast of Llanelli.

Distance
18 miles one way, 36 miles return. For a shorter ride you might go as far as Pembrey Country Park (14-mile round trip).

Grade
Easy.

Surface
Mixture of tarmac and gravel paths.

Roads, traffic, suitability for young children
There is a short road section at the start in Kidwelly where care should be taken. Very minor roads are used through Burry Port. Otherwise this is an excellent route for young children (as long as you take account of the wind!).

Hills
None.

Refreshments
Lots of choice in Kidwelly.
Cafe at Burry Port.
Cafe at North Dock, Llanelli.

Cafe at Pembrey Country Park (just off the route).
Cafe at the Wildfowl & Wetlands Centre at the end of the ride.

Nearest railway stations
Kidwelly, Burry Port, Llanelli.

The National Cycle Network in the area
The ride described here is part of Route 4 also known as the Celtic Trail (Lôn Geltaidd) which runs from Fishguard to the old Severn Bridge near Chepstow. Route 43 will link Swansea to Builth Wells where it joins Lôn Las Cymru from Cardiff to Anglesey (Route 8).

Construction work on the Llanelli Coastal Park Project.

Other nearby rides (waymarked or traffic-free)
1. There are many more tracks to explore in Pembrey Forest, around the Country Park.
2. Route 4 runs west from Swansea, to Gowerton and The Mumbles – see page 132.
Route 47 runs north from Llanelli via Swiss Valley – see page 128.
3. You can now cycle offroad from the Wildfowl & Wetlands Centre to Bynea around the Loughor estuary.

KIDWELLY TO THE WILDFOWL AND WETLANDS CENTRE, LLANELLI

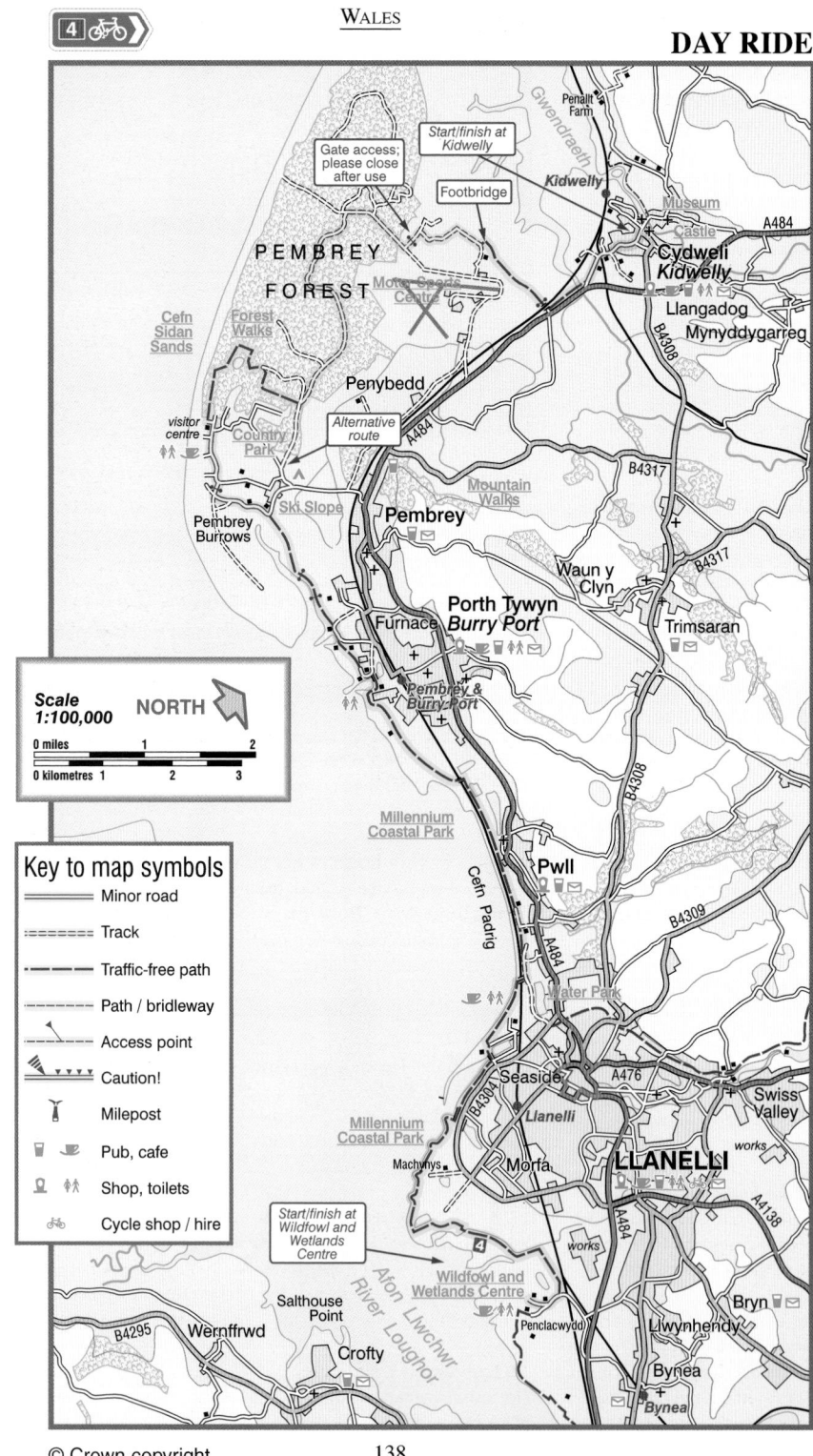

Gwendraeth

Penallt Farm

Gate access; please close after use

Start/finish at Kidwelly

Footbridge

Kidwelly

Museum

Castle

A484

PEMBREY FOREST

Moto-Sports Centre

Cydweli *Kidwelly*

Llangadog

Mynyddygarreg

Cefn Sidan Sands

Forest Walks

B4308

visitor centre

Penybedd

Country Park

Alternative route

A484

B4317

Ski Slope

Pembrey

Mountain Walks

B4317

Pembrey Burrows

Waun y Clyn

Trimsaran

Scale 1:100,000

NORTH

0 miles   1   2
0 kilometres   1   2   3

Furnace

Porth Tywyn *Burry Port*

Pembrey & Burry Port

Millennium Coastal Park

Cefn Padrig

Pwll

B4308

B4309

Key to map symbols

———— Minor road

========= Track

– – – – Traffic-free path

– · – · – Path / bridleway

⊤ Access point

⚠ Caution!

🏁 Milepost

🍺 ☕ Pub, cafe

🛍 🚻 Shop, toilets

🚲 Cycle shop / hire

Water Park

Seaside

A476

Swiss Valley

Millennium Coastal Park

Llanelli

works

Machynys

Morfa

LLANELLI

A4138

Start/finish at Wildfowl and Wetlands Centre

4

works

Llwynhendy

Afon Llwchwr

River Loughor

Wildfowl and Wetlands Centre

Bryn

Salthouse Point

Wernffrwd

Penclacwydd

Bynea

B4295

Crofty

Bynea

Route instructions from Kidwelly to the Wildfowl & Wetlands Centre

1. From the church in the centre of Kidwelly follow the B4308 south towards the main road (A484) and Burry Port.

2. Climb then descend. Immediately before the roundabout cross the B4308 onto the pavement/cycle path and follow this round to the right, parallel with the main Llanelli road (A484) for ½ mile.

3. Where the pavement ends, opposite a road turning on the left to Pinged, turn right to pass under a low railway bridge and join a path along the raised embankment with the estuary to your right.

4. At the end of the track turn left down steps, cross the small bridge over the drainage ditch, turn right onto the concrete track and then bear right towards the forest, following 'Route 4' signs.

This bench is made from recycled greenheart timber on the link to Pembrey Forest.

5. Ignore two left turns, following the main track round a left-hand then right-hand bend to arrive at a T-junction. Turn left through the gate. At the next T-junction (with a tarmac lane) turn right, signposted 'Route 4'.

6. After ¾ mile take the first broad gravel track to the left ('Route 4') and follow this in the same direction, ignoring turnings to left and right for four miles.

7. Exit the forest at the T-junction with tarmac, turn right then left (or keep bearing right to visit Pembrey Country Park for refreshments).

8. Bear to the left of the red-brick buildings. At the end of the fence to the right, on a sharp right-hand bend, turn left between tall stone pillars onto a wide gravel path.

9. At the crossroads at the end of the cycle path go straight ahead and follow the road to the left past the caravan park. At the T-junction at the end of Heol Vaughan turn right.

10. Turn left before the dock and follow the path around the dock to the seafront. Straight on leads to the harbour, Burry Port and lighthouse.

11. Follow this track for four miles roughly parallel to the railway line which you have to cross twice.

12. At the cafe/Visitor Centre turn left, then right and cross to the new cycle path and bridge over the creek, then just before the roundabout turn right.

13. Immediately after Copper House roundabout and a wooden plank bridge over the creek turn right by tall wooden posts to continue alongside the water's edge.

14. The tarmac surface turns to good gravel track. Follow this for three miles towards the steel works (Trostre Tin Plate).

15. At the T-junction turn right then shortly fork right for the Wildfowl & Wetlands site. At this point you have a choice:
(a) go on to Swansea (another 14 miles) and catch the train back to Kidwelly;
(b) cycle all the way back to Kidwelly;
(c) cycle back only as far as Llanelli or Burry Port and catch the train back to Kidwelly.

CARDIFF TO CASTELL COCH

Opened in 1993 and running from Cardiff Bay through Merthyr Tydfil to Brecon, the 55-mile Taff Trail forms part of Lôn Las Cymru (Route 8) which continues beyond Brecon right the way up though Wales to Anglesey. The six-mile section described here (Cardiff to Castell Coch) offers a magnificent exit from the very heart of Cardiff and links together some fine traffic-free trails alongside the River Taff, passing right beneath the splendid new Millennium Stadium. Between Llandaff and Tongwynlais you will pass the Mellingriffith Water Pump, considered to be one of the most important industrial monuments in Europe: a water-powered beam engine erected in 1807 to lift water 11 feet up from the river to the Glamorganshire Canal. The pump worked for 140 years until 1948 when the canal was closed and filled in. Castell Coch, reached after a short road section through Tongwynlais and a very steep climb up the drive, is a Grade 1 listed building described as 'one of the most fascinating surviving relics of Victorian Medievalism'. With its conical turrets rising above the surrounding beech woodland, it is an outstanding landmark.

Cardiff Castle from Bute Park.

Starting points
Cardiff railway station or Cardiff Castle.

Distance
Six miles one way, 12 miles return.

Grade
Easy, with one steep climb up to Castell Coch itself.

Surface
Mixture of tarmac and good quality gravel paths.

Roads, traffic, suitability for young children
The route is almost entirely traffic-free from Cardiff to Tongwynlais. There is a short section on road through Tongwynlais and up the steep drive leading to Castell Coch.

Hills
The route is flat as far as Tongwynlais then there is a short steep climb up to Castell Coch.

Refreshments
Lots of choice in Cardiff centre. Lewis Arms PH in Tongwynlais. Cafe in Castell Coch (you will need to pay to enter the castle).

Nearest railway station
Cardiff.

The National Cycle Network in the area
The Taff Trail forms part of Route 8 which links with a number of city centre cycle routes and extends to Holyhead in North Wales. Just north of Castell Coch the Taff Trail joins the Celtic Trail/Lôn Geltaidd (Route 4) which runs from Fishguard to Chepstow.

Taff Trail Cardiff.

Other nearby rides (waymarked or traffic-free)
1. The Taff Trail continues north from Castell Coch (starting with an exceedingly steep climb!) along dismantled railways through Nantgarw and Rhydyfelin to Pontypridd. The low level alternative drops back down to Tongwynlais and heads north from the Lewis Arms to join a traffic-free path north of Taffs Well Station. South from Cardiff centre the trail runs to Cardiff Bay and the Barrage.
2. There are good quality towpaths along the canals leading from Newport north west to Crosskeys and north to Cwmbran and Pontypool.

The University link, Cardiff.

CARDIFF TO CASTELL COCH

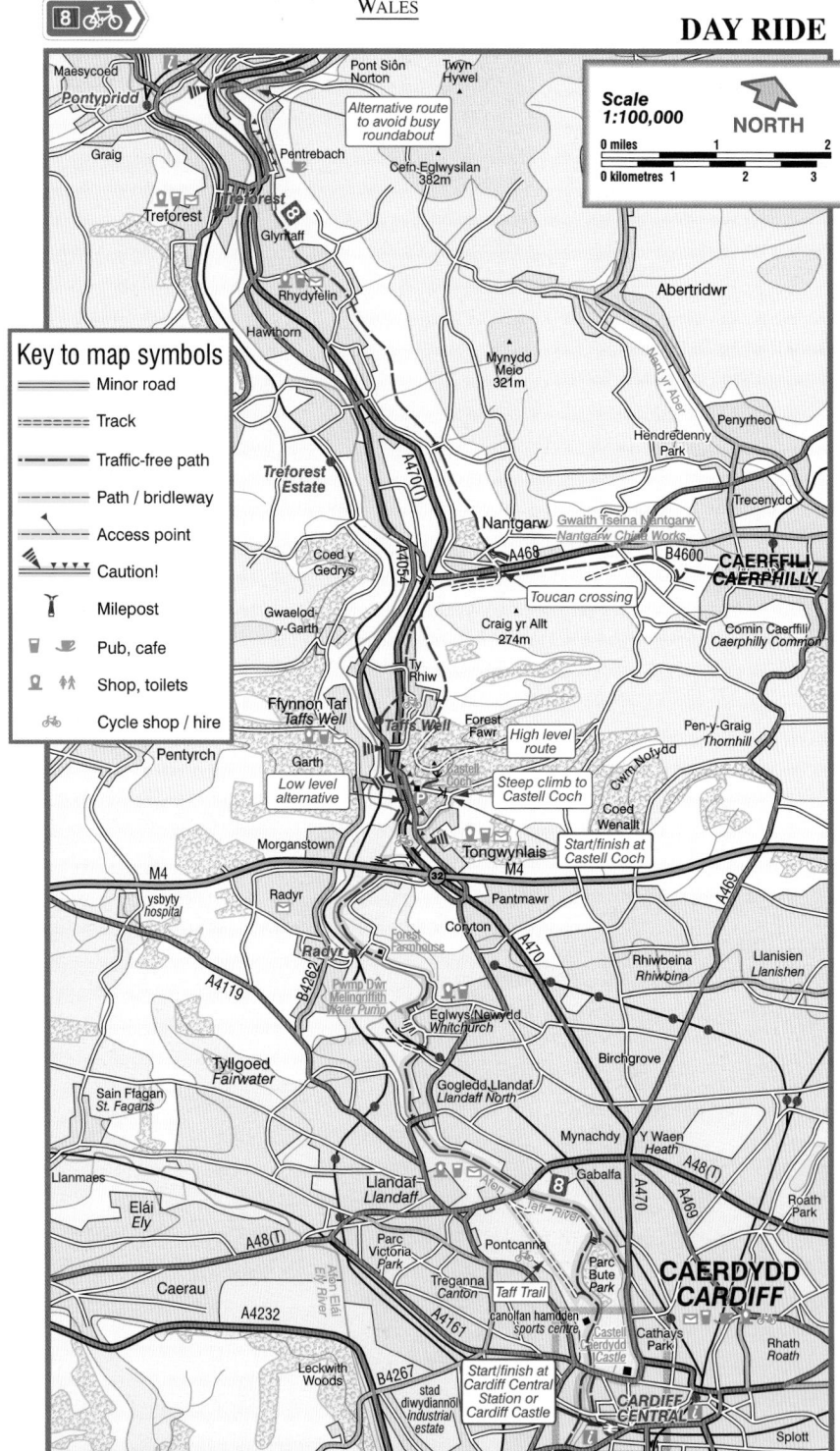

Key to map symbols

	Minor road
	Track
	Traffic-free path
	Path / bridleway
	Access point
	Caution!
	Milepost
	Pub, cafe
	Shop, toilets
	Cycle shop / hire

Scale
1:100,000

NORTH

0 miles   1   2

0 kilometres   1   2   3

Maesycoed
Pontypridd
Graig
Pont Siôn Norton
Twyn Hywel
Alternative route to avoid busy roundabout
Pentrebach
Cefn Eglwysilan 382m
Treforest
Treforest
Glyntaff
Abertridwr
Rhydyfelin
Hawthorn
Mynydd Meio 321m
Nant yr Aber
Penyrheol
Hendredenny Park
Trecenydd
Treforest Estate
Nantgarw
Gwaith Tseina Nantgarw
Nantgarw China Works
A468
B4600
CAERFFILI CAERPHILLY
Coed y Gedrys
Toucan crossing
Comin Caerffili Caerphilly Common
Gwaelod-y-Garth
Craig yr Allt 274m
Ty Rhiw
Forest Fawr
Pen-y-Graig Thornhill
Ffynnon Taf Taffs Well
Taffs Well
High level route
Cwm Nofydd
Garth
Castell Coch
Steep climb to Castell Coch
Coed Wenallt
Pentyrch
Low level alternative
Start/finish at Castell Coch
M4
Morganstown
Tongwynlais
M4
A4119
ysbyty hospital
Radyr
Pantmawr
Coryton
A470
A469
Llanisien Llanishen
Radyr
Forest Farmhouse
Rhiwbeina Rhiwbina
B4262
Pwmp Dŵr Melingriffith Water Pump
Eglwys Newydd Whitchurch
Birchgrove
Tyllgoed Fairwater
Gogledd Llandaf Llandaff North
Sain Ffagan St. Fagans
Mynachdy
Y Waen Heath
A48(T)
Llanmaes
Llandaf Llandaff
Gabalfa
A470
Roath Park
Elái Ely
A48(T)
Parc Victoria Park
Pontcanna
Parc Bute Park
CAERDYDD CARDIFF
Rhath Roath
Caerau
A4232
Afon Elái Ely River
Tregganna Canton
Taff Trail
Castell Caerdydd Cardiff Castle
Cathays Park
A4161
A4161
canolfan hamdden sports centre
Leckwith Woods
B4267
stad diwydiannol industrial estate
Start/finish at Cardiff Central Station or Cardiff Castle
CARDIFF CENTRAL
Splott

142

Route instructions from Cardiff to Castell Coch

1. Exit Cardiff railway station* and turn left. At the traffic lights, by the Millenium Stadium and multiplex cinema, turn left then immediately after crossing the bridge over the river turn right (use the toucan crossing) and follow the pavement northwards alongside the river. During the course of the ride you will be following 'Taff Trail' and 'Route 8' signs.

*Alternative start from near Cardiff Castle. From the College of Music and Drama on North Road (just north of Cardiff Castle on the A470 towards Merthyr Tydfil) follow signs for Route 8 parallel to and to the east of North Road. You will soon find yourself alongside the River Taff. At a fork of tracks after ¾ mile, pass to the left of a black and white timbered lodge house and follow the riverside path. Rejoin at Instruction no.3.

2. At a round stone pillar and Taff Trail sign continue along the river. Cross Blackweir Bridge and turn left to head north on the riverside track.

3. Go past Llandaf Weir and alongside playing fields, bear right away from the river at the Taff Trail signs then briefly use the shared-use pavement alongside the road. After ¾ mile, as the road starts climbing on a right hand bend immediately after passing the old metal and wooden Mellingriffith water pump, turn left onto a tarmac track between newly-built houses to return to the track alongside the river.

4. Briefly use a minor road, continuing in the same direction alongside the river. At a T-junction of tracks by a pylon turn left and pass beneath the M4. Join a minor lane and follow this beneath a bridge (the A470). At the T-junction at the end of Iron Bridge Road in Tongwynlais turn left then after 400 yards turn right by the Lewis Arms pub onto Mill Road to follow the high level route.

5. Follow for ¾ mile then turn left at the sign for Castell Coch. Steep climb on tarmac.

A new low level route is now open. At the Lewis Arms PH carry straight on and follow the tarmac track to the right of

Taff Trail marker by Angharad Jones.

the A4054. Follow the route to Cemetery Road. From Taff's Well Station the route continues on a new railway path to the toucan crossing at the A468 at Nantgarw.

(If you wish to extend your ride, opposite the castle itself turn right onto the track signposted 'Taff Trail' that soon becomes a very steep push. At the T-junction at the top, turn left to continue climbing gently before a fast descent through woodland. Keep following 'Taff Trail'/'Route 8' signs.)

CARDIFF route detail

Canolfan hamdden sports centre
Bute Park
Cardiff Castle
Cardiff Bridge
River Taff
CATHEDRAL ROAD
WELLINGTON STREET
FITZHAMON EMB
TUDOR STREET
CASTLE ST
DUKE ST
WESTGATE STREET
PARK ST
WOOD STREET
CENTRAL SQUARE
CARDIFF CENTRAL
KING EDWARD VII AVE
COLLEGE RD
NORTH ROAD
MUSEUM AVENUE
CITY HALL ROAD
THE FRIARY
QUEEN STREET
HIGH ST
ST MARY STREET
CHURCHILL WAY
BRIDGE ST
CUSTOMHOUSE ST
BUTE TERR
Start/finish at Cardiff Central station or Cardiff Castle
pedestrian precinct

Cardiff tourist attractions include: Cardiff Castle, The Millennium Stadium, Techniquest, Cardiff Cathedral, National Sports Centre and The National Museum of Wales

Castell Coch lies at the top of an exceedingly steep hill.

BARMOUTH TO DOLGELLAU
LÔN MAWDDACH TRAIL

The Mawddach Estuary is surely one of the most beautiful in the country, and exploring it by bike is by far the best way to see it. The wooded hills to the north of the estuary rise to over 1000 ft providing a stunning backdrop to the lovely waters of Afon Mawddach. The ride runs south from the seaside resort of Barmouth crossing the estuary on the wonderful wooden railway bridge carrying trains down the coast from Pwllheli to Aberystwyth. This links to the seven-mile railway path along the estuary which follows the course of the old line from Barmouth to Ruabon. The railway was opened in 1869 and became popular with Victorian holiday makers, particularly those from North West England visiting the fashionable resort of Barmouth. The line was closed in 1965. Halfway along you will pass an excellent refreshment stop at the George III pub at Penmaenpool. Dolgellau is the final destination, solidly built of stone with an attractive square and lots of pubs and tea shops.

Barmouth Bridge.

Starting points

1. Barmouth railway station (on the west coast of Wales, to the north of Aberystwyth).
2. The Tourist Information Centre, Dolgellau.

Distance

11 miles one way, 22 miles return.

Grade

Easy.

Surface

Tarmac and gravel track.

Roads, traffic, suitability for young children

The trail itself (the railway path) is ideal for children. Care should be taken on the road sections linking the trail with the centres of Dolgellau and Barmouth, particularly on the right turn from Barmouth onto the bridge over the estuary.

Hills

One short climb between Barmouth and the bridge over the estuary.

Refreshments

Lots of choice in Barmouth and Dolgellau.
George III pub at Penmaenpool (also does cream teas).

Nearest railway station

Barmouth.

The National Cycle Network in the area

The ride is part of Lôn Las Cymru, the Welsh National Route (Route 8) that runs from Cardiff to Anglesey.
1. North from Barmouth the route uses a four-mile stretch of the busy A496 (interim route) before turning inland on a network of quiet (and hilly!) lanes. To avoid the A496, cycle along the beach at low tide.
2. There is an alternative to the coastal route that runs north from Dolgellau through Coed-y-Brenin

Cyclists on Barmouth Bridge.

Forest and Trawsfynydd. This follows a new offroad path around the north east side of the lake and west of of the power station to Gellilydan.
3. South of Dolgellau the route uses a rough section of coach road to link with a minor road through Aberllefenni and Corris to link with Dyfi Bridge in Machynlleth.
4. There is a tough off-road option south from the Mawddach Estuary to Machynlleth that climbs from Arthog on an old stone track before dropping down Happy Valley.

Other nearby rides (waymarked or traffic-free)

1. Coed-y-Brenin Forestry rides.
2. Traffic-free railway paths run north and south from Caernarfon.
3. Small offroad section from Hafod y Meirch to Gwerngraig in Cwm-hafod-oer.

The Barmouth to Dolgellau railway path.

BARMOUTH TO DOLGELLAU

Brithdir
Caerynwch
B4416
Tabor
giât
gate
Hafod-y-meirch
Gwerngraig
Cross Foxes Inn
A487(T)
225m
Hafod-oer
Waenllefenni
400m
296m
Bwlch Llyn Bach
Route to Machynlleth NCN route 8
Very rough and steep. Use A487 with care as an on-road alternative.
Minffordd
Dol-y-cae
Dolffanog
Llyn Arran

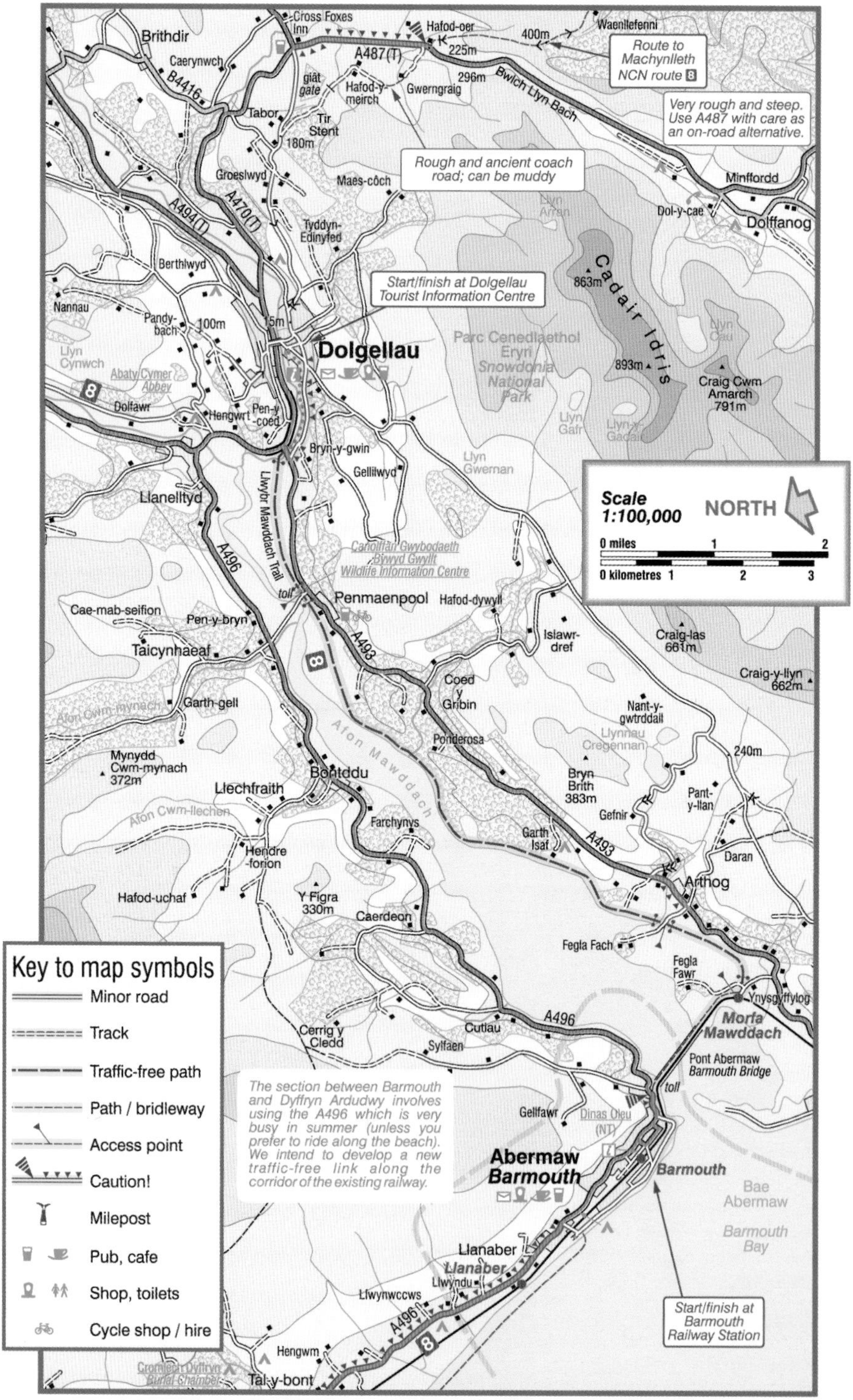

Groeslwyd
Tir Stent 180m
Maes-côch
Rough and ancient coach road; can be muddy
Cadair Idris
863m▲
Berthlwyd
Tyddyn-Edinyfed
893m▲
Llyn Cau
Craig Cwm Amarch 791m

A494(T)
A470(T)
Nannau
Pandy-bach
100m
Start/finish at Dolgellau Tourist Information Centre
Parc Cenedlaethol Eryri Snowdonia National Park
Craig-las 661m

Llyn Cynwch
Abaty Cymer Abbey
8
Dolfawr
Hengwrt
Pen-y-coed
Dolgellau
Llyn Gafr
Llyn-y-Gadair
Craig-y-llyn 662m

Llanelltyd
Bryn-y-gwin
Gellilwyd
Llyn Gwernan
Llwyr Mawddach Trail
Cae-mab-seifion
Pen-y-bryn
Taicynhaeaf
Llanelltyd
A496
Canolfan Gwybodaeth Bywyd Gwyllt Wildlife Information Centre
toll
Penmaenpool
Hafod-dywyll
Islawr-dref
240m

A493
Coed
Coed Gribin
Nant-y-gwtrddail
Llynnau Cregennan
Pant-y-llan

Garth-gell
Afon Cwm-mynach
Mynydd Cwm-mynach 372m
Bontddu
Llechfraith
Ponderosa
Afon Mawddach
Bryn Brith 383m
Gefnir
Daran

Afon Cwm-llechen
Farchynys
Garth Isaf
A493
Arthog

Hendre-forion
Hafod-uchaf
Y Figra 330m
Caerdeon
Fegla Fach
Fegla Fawr
Ynysgyffylog

Scale 1:100,000
NORTH
0 miles 1 2
0 kilometres 1 2 3

Key to map symbols
Minor road
Track
Traffic-free path
Path / bridleway
Access point
Caution!
🍸 Milepost
Pub, cafe
Shop, toilets
🚲 Cycle shop / hire

The section between Barmouth and Dyffryn Ardudwy involves using the A496 which is very busy in summer (unless you prefer to ride along the beach). We intend to develop a new traffic-free link along the corridor of the existing railway.

Cerrig y Cledd
Cutiau
Sylfaen
A496
Gellifawr
Dinas Oleu (NT)
Morfa Mawddach
Pont Abermaw Barmouth Bridge
toll
Abermaw Barmouth
Barmouth
Bae Abermaw
Barmouth Bay

Llanaber
Llanaber
Llwyndu
Llwynwccws
Start/finish at Barmouth Railway Station

8
A496
Hengwm
Cromlech Dyffryn Burial Chamber
Tal-y-bont

Route instructions from Barmouth to Dolgellau

1. From Barmouth railway station go to the seafront then left past the Leisure Centre.

2. At the T-junction after passing beneath the railway bridge, turn right. Shortly at the brow of the hill turn right onto a path towards the bridge signposted 'Route 8'. **TAKE CARE** on this right turn.

3. Cross the bridge, continue along the gravel track parallel with the railway lines and follow the cycle path as it swings round to the left, at first parallel with the minor lane.

4. Follow the old railway path for seven miles, passing the George III pub at Penmaenpool after five miles. The ride will arrive at Bontywernddu where the original offroad route terminates.

5. At the crossroads with the A493 go straight ahead down to the gate.

Aerial view of the Mawddach Estuary and Barmouth Bridge.

Continue alongside the River Wnion for ½ mile. At path junction bear right over bridge to the other side.

6. Emerge from trees onto the Marian Fawr with Dolgellau in sight. The track continues along the flood bank to arrive at the car park.

The wooden bridge at Penmaenpool.

COLWYN BAY TO PRESTATYN

Enjoy this wonderful open breezy ride along the wide sea promenade that stretches almost unbroken for 16 miles from Colwyn Bay to Prestatyn. The ride has a background of wooded hills rising to over 600 ft behind Abergele.

The ride runs along the bustling seafront of Colwyn Bay before passing the curious concrete anchors that have been dumped in great heaps along the coast to prevent erosion from the sea. Two short climbs take you up and over the jetties carrying stone from the quarries out to sea. Up in the wooded hills between Llanddulas and Abergele you will catch a glimpse of the atmospheric Gwrych Castle. The ride continues along the coast past the extensive caravan sites of Towyn to cross the River Clwyd. Rhyl's ice cream stalls will give you the boost you need to complete the last few miles to journey's end at Prestatyn.

NB. This is an open coastal ride where you should be very aware of the wind (normally from the west). If you are going to cycle there and back it is best to cycle into the wind at the start, while you are fresh, and have the wind help you on the return journey. Alternatively, contemplate catching the train then doing a one way trip, blown back to the start!

Colwyn Bay promenade with cycle route.

148

Prestatyn.

Starting points
1. Prestatyn railway station (or the Tourist Information Centre on Prestatyn seafront).
2. Colwyn Bay railway station.
3. The Tourist Information Centre at Rhos-on-Sea.

Distance
16 miles one way, 32 miles return.

Grade
Easy but take good note of the wind direction! Catch the train into the wind and cycle with the wind behind you.

Surface
Tarmac or good stone-based track.

Roads, traffic, suitability for young children
The route is almost entirely traffic-free.

There are short road sections from Prestatyn railway station to the seafront and at the western end of Rhyl over the Blue Bridge.
There are no difficult road crossings along the seafront. The ride is ideal for children.

Hills
None.

Refreshments
Lots of choice in Colwyn Bay, Rhyl and Prestatyn.

Nearest railway stations
Colwyn Bay, Abergele, Rhyl and Prestatyn.

The National Cycle Network in the area
The ride is part of Route 5, which runs east-west from Runcorn to

Bangor. At its eastern end Route 5 connects with the Southport to Hull Trans Pennine Trail; at its western end it links with Lôn Las Cymru, (Route 8) from Holyhead to Cardiff.

Other nearby rides (waymarked or traffic-free)
1. There are two railway paths starting from Caernarfon, one heads south to Bryncir, the other runs north east towards Bangor.
2. A railway path will run south from Porth Penrhyn (near Bangor) to Bethesda.
3. There are waymarked forestry routes in the woodlands around Betws-y-Coed.

DAY RIDE

COLWYN BAY TO PRESTATYN

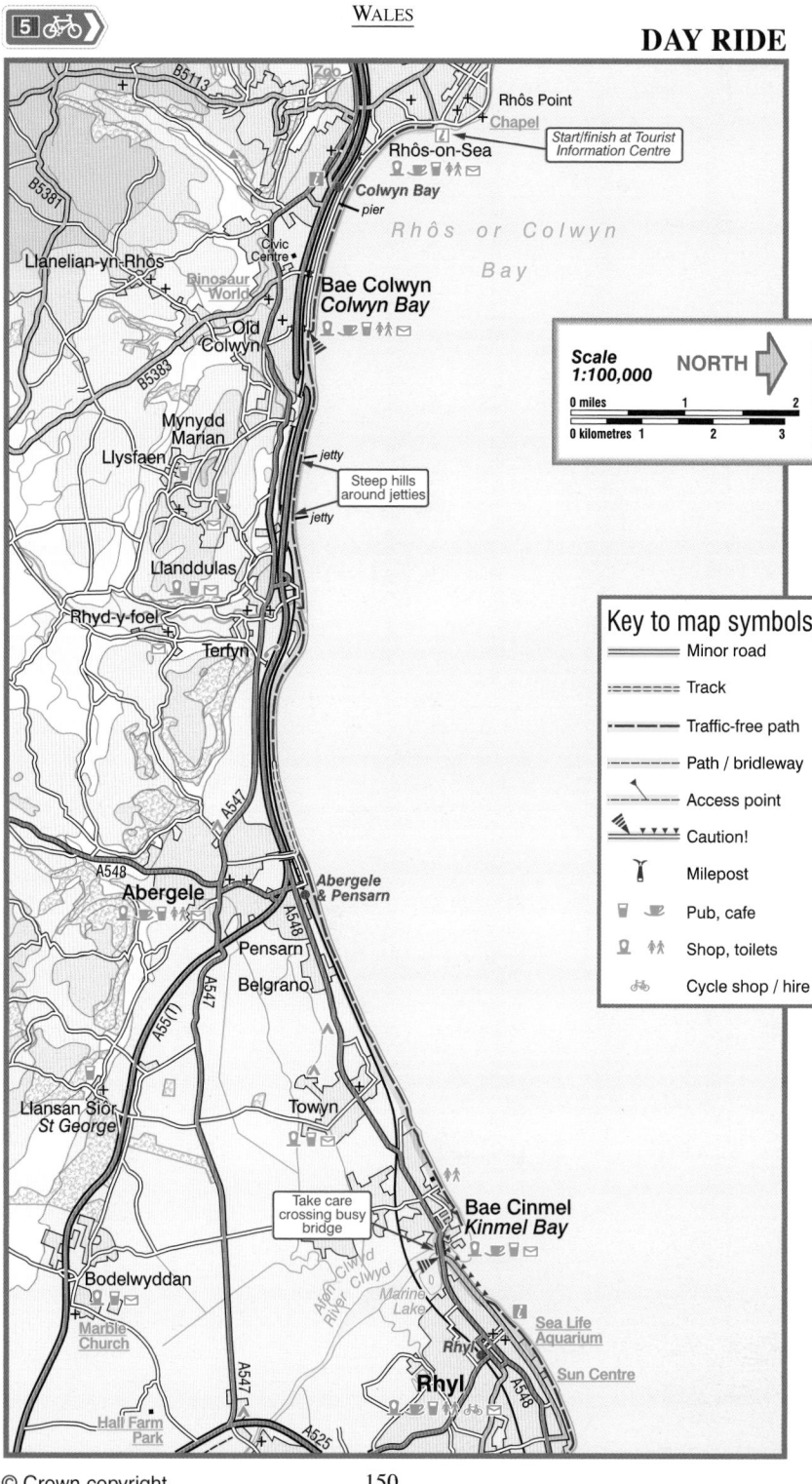

5 🚲 ▶

Start/finish at Tourist Information Centre

Rhôs Point
Chapel
Rhôs-on-Sea
Colwyn Bay
pier

Rhôs or Colwyn
Bay

Civic Centre
Llanelian-yn-Rhôs
Dinosaur World
Bae Colwyn
Colwyn Bay
Old Colwyn
B5383

Scale
1:100,000

NORTH ▶

0 miles   1   2
0 kilometres   1   2   3

Mynydd Marian
Llysfaen

jetty
Steep hills around jetties
jetty

Llanddulas

Rhyd-y-foel
Terfyn

Key to map symbols

═══════ Minor road
═ ═ ═ ═ Track
▬ ▬ ▬ Traffic-free path
– – – – – Path / bridleway
⌐⌐⌐⌐ Access point
▀▀▀▼▼▼ Caution!
⊥ Milepost
🍺 ☕ Pub, cafe
🛈 🚻 Shop, toilets
🚲 Cycle shop / hire

A548
Abergele
Abergele & Pensarn

Pensarn

Belgrano

A547
A55(T)

Llansan Siôr
St George

Towyn

Take care crossing busy bridge

Bae Cinmel
Kinmel Bay

Bodelwyddan

Afon Clwyd
River Clwyd
Marine Lake

Marble Church

Sea Life Aquarium

Rhyl
Sun Centre

A547

Rhyl

A548

Hall Farm Park

A525

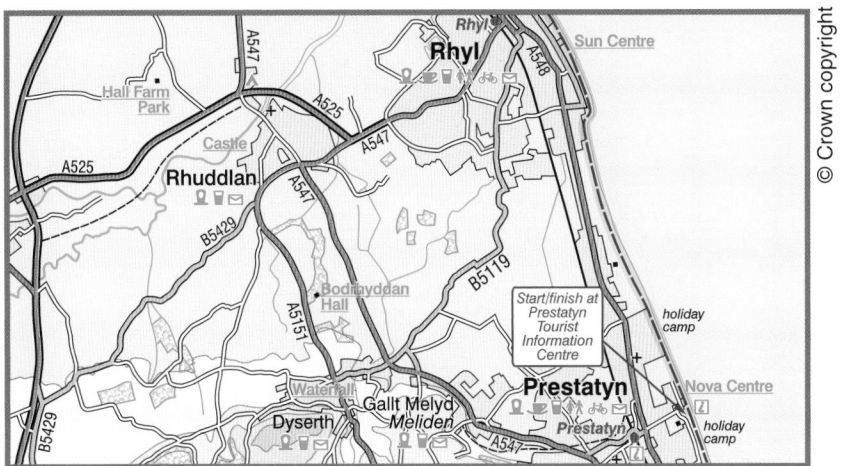

Route instructions from Rhos-on-Sea to Prestatyn

1. From the Tourist Information Centre in Rhos-on-Sea (at the western end of Colwyn Bay), with the sea to your left, follow the green cycle path along the seafront.

2. There are two short steep climbs up over the jetties serving the quarries to your right.

3. Towards the end of the road alongside the caravan park the path bears left to join the wide red seafront path.

4. Leave the seafront path at the railway station and follow the path to the right of the wall.

5. Descend to the broad track below the sea wall. Go past the huge sea defence works. Towards the end of Kinmel Bay, turn right away from the seafront at a footpath signpost onto a tarmac path. **Easy to miss.**

6. At the T-junction with wide track turn left then right onto Berwyn Crescent. At the T-junction with Bryn Avenue turn left and follow this round to the main road.

7. Turn left by the Ferry pub and walk your bike along the pavement to cross the metal bridge.

8. Go along the seafront to the end of Rhyl. Continue for a further three miles to end at Prestatyn Tourist Information Centre.

9. For Prestatyn Station, turn right by Prestatyn Tourist Information Centre and follow the road leading directly away from the beach. At the traffic lights go straight ahead to the station.

Colwyn Bay is suitable for young and old.

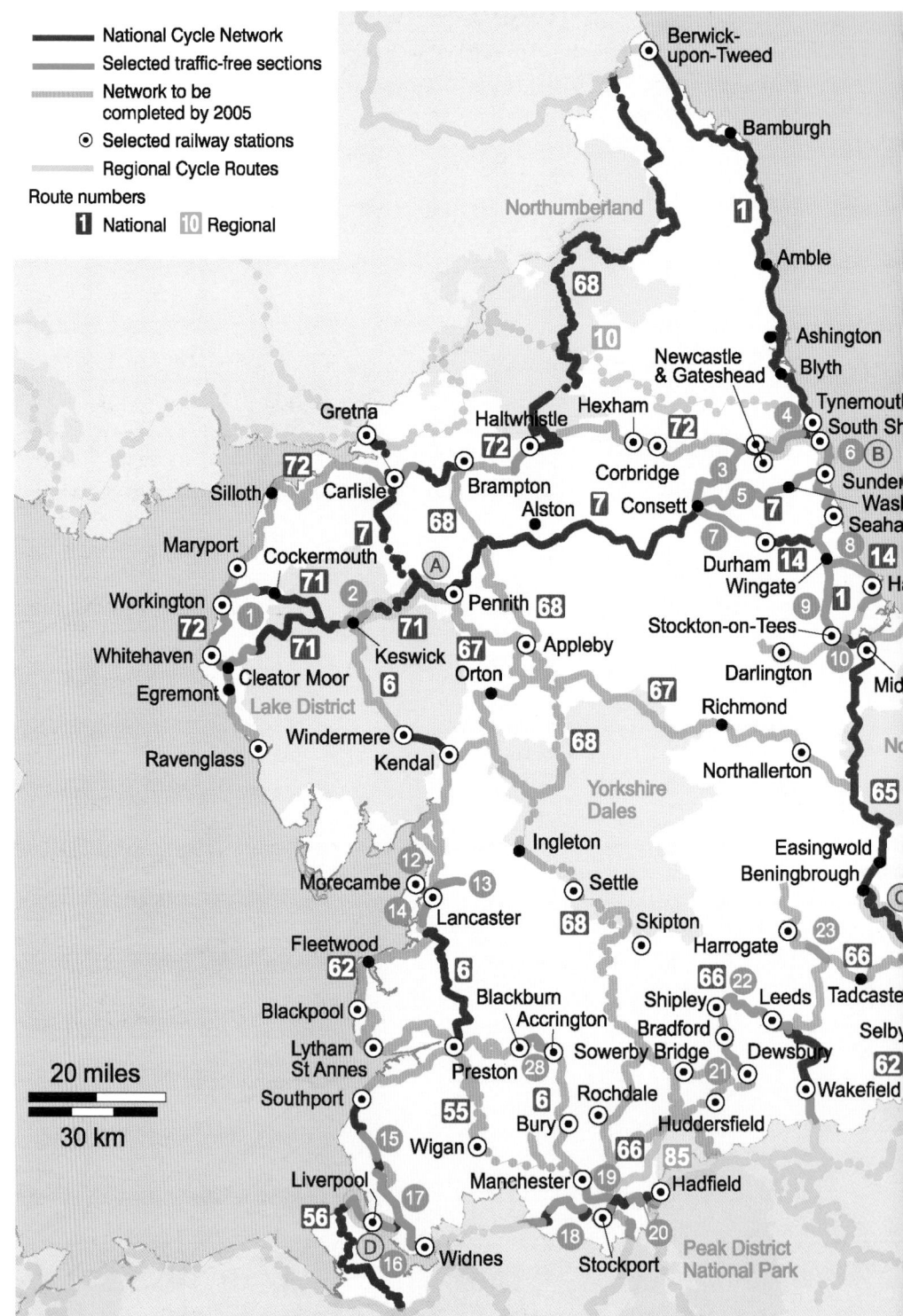

National Cycle Network
Selected traffic-free sections
Network to be completed by 2005
⊙ Selected railway stations
Regional Cycle Routes
Route numbers
1 National **10** Regional

Berwick-upon-Tweed
Bamburgh
1
Amble
Ashington
Blyth
68
10
Newcastle & Gateshead
Tynemouth
South Sh
Northumberland
Gretna
Haltwhistle
Hexham
72
4
6 (B)
Silloth
72
Carlisle
Brampton
Corbridge
3
Sunder
Was
Maryport
68
Alston
Consett
5
7
Seaha
Cockermouth
7
7
Durham
14
14
Workington
71
2
Penrith
68
Wingate
H
72
1
Whitehaven
71
71
Appleby
9
1
Keswick
67
Stockton-on-Tees
Cleator Moor
6
Orton
Darlington
10
Mid
Egremont
Lake District
67
Ravenglass
Windermere
68
Richmond
No
Kendal
Northallerton
Yorkshire Dales
65
Ingleton
Easingwold
Beningbrough
12
Settle
C
Morecambe
13
68
23
14
Lancaster
Skipton
66
Fleetwood
62
6
Harrogate
66 **22**
Blackpool
Blackburn
Shipley
66
Leeds
Tadcaste
Accrington
Bradford
Selby
Lytham St Annes
28
Sowerby Bridge
Dewsbury
62
Preston
21
Wakefield
Southport
55
Rochdale
Huddersfield
15
Wigan
6
Bury
66
Liverpool
17
Manchester
19
Hadfield
85
56
D
18
20
Peak District National Park
16
Widnes
Stockport

20 miles
30 km

Selected traffic-free paths

1. West Cumbria Railway Paths *20 miles*
2. Keswick - Threkeld *4 miles*
3. Consett - The Tyne & Wylam *11 miles*
4. Walker to North Shields *5 miles*
5. Consett - Sunderland *21 miles*
6. Sunderland - South Shields *11 miles*
7. Consett - Durham *14 miles*
8. Haswell/Hart Railway Path *9 miles*
9. Stockton to Wingate *8 miles*
10. Middlesbrough to Stockton via Barrage *5 miles*
11. Whitby - Scarborough *18 miles*
12. Lancaster - Morecambe *3 miles*
13. Lancaster to Caton *5 miles*
14. Lancaster to Glasson Dock *5 miles*
15. Cheshire Lines Path *10 miles*
16. Wirral Promenade *5 miles*
17. Liverpool Loop Line *10 miles*
18. Sale Water Park *6 miles*
19. Fallowfield Loop *7 miles*
20. Apethorne - Godley *2 miles*
21. Spen Valley Greenway *7 miles*
22. Leeds & Liverpool Canal to Shipley *13 miles*
23. Wetherby - Spofforth *3¹/₂ miles*
24. Through York to Riccall *15 miles*
25. Walmgate Stray & Foss Island Railway *2¹/₂ miles*
26. Beverley - Market Weighton *11 miles*
27. Hull - Hornsea Line *13 miles*
28. Baxenden Railway Path, Accrington *1¹/₂ miles*

Day Rides ▬▬▬

- Ⓐ Penrith - Keswick *24 miles*
- Ⓑ Newcastle - Sunderland *20 miles*
- Ⓒ York - Beningbrough *9 miles*
- Ⓓ Wallasey & Liverpool Promenades *11 miles*

Long distance maps available

© Crown copyright

153

THE NORTH

The Tynemouth railway provides an impressive backdrop to Route 72 on its way to the Tyne Tunnel.

The North of England, defined here as the area south from the border with Scotland to a line from Liverpool to Hull, is a region of great contrasts. There are the densely populated areas around Tyneside, Teesside and along the industrial corridor running from Liverpool to Leeds and yet Northumberland is the most lightly populated county in England. The scars of the old heavy industries of coal, steel and shipbuilding and of course the textile mills of Yorkshire and Lancashire lie within a few miles of England's most rugged scenery, its highest mountains and five of its National Parks – The Peak District, The Lake District, The Yorkshire Dales, The North York Moors and Northumberland.

The five National Cycle Network Routes in the region each present a very different aspect of the Network. The Sea to Sea Route (C2C) from Whitehaven or Workington on the Cumbrian Coast to Tynemouth or Sunderland on the North Sea is Sustrans' most popular long-distance route, cycled by thousands of people every year as they cross the country from the Lake District, over the Pennines to the East Coast. The Trans Pennine Trail, a multi-user trail for walkers, cyclists and horse riders, threads its way through one of the most urbanised areas of Britain between Liverpool and Manchester before crossing the Pennines and reaching the North Sea beyond Hull at Hornsea. The White Rose Cycle Route runs north from Hull along the flat expanse of the Vale of York, then passes through the lush western fringes of the North York Moors before reaching the industrial port of Middlesbrough. The Three Rivers Route (Tees, Wear and Tyne) from Middlesbrough to Newcastle and the Coast and Castles Route (from Newcastle to Edinburgh) complete the picture. These last two also form part of a route all the way up the east coast from Harwich to John o' Groats and the Shetlands, covered by seven long-distance maps.

154

NATIONAL CYCLE NETWORK HIGHLIGHTS

Pier Head - Liverpool
From the deck of the Mersey Ferry en route from the Wirral at Wallasey, Liverpool presents a memorable frontage. The twin towers of the Liver Building mark the headquarters of the once prestigious Atlantic Passenger trade, whilst on the horizon is the tower of the huge Anglican Cathedral finished in 1924.

Gateshead Millennium Bridge

The stunning new pedestrian and cycle bridge, just downstream from the landmark Tyne Bridge, weighs 600 tonnes and was created from a pair of graceful steel arches linked by thin suspension rods that open like a giant lid of a closed eye to form a gateway arch under which ships can sail.
The bridge, designed by Wilkinson Eyre Architects and Gifford & Partners, joins the routes that run along the north and south banks of the Tyne.

York Millennium Bridge
This is one of the most innovative new links on the Network. The design by Whitby, Bird & Partners is largely built from stainless steel. It not only joins riverside paths on both sides of the Ouse, but also acts as a focus for a citywide network of purpose-built cycle routes.

Terris Novalis

This stainless steel sculpture by Tony Cragg is a 20 times life-size version of the theodolite and level used in the construction of a mainline railway. It is positioned on the site of the former Consett Steelworks and is both a memorial to this extraordinary industry (which made the Sydney Harbour Bridge) and to the two instruments which set out the lines, levels and directions of our present transport system.

Stadium of Light
Sunderland FC's football ground, the Stadium of Light, towers above the River Wear – a veritable cathedral on the Wear. The new football stadium was opened on 30 July 1997 when 40,000 supporters watched Ajax FC of Amsterdam, and was voted the best in England in 1998. This magnificent building marks the start of a modern riverside route culminating at St. Peter's Quay.

Bamburgh Castle
Bamburgh Castle is one of a chain of spectacular castles along the route from Newcastle to Berwick. The basalt outcrop on which it sits has been occupied since the first century. The castle you see as you cycle past today is the product of centuries of rebuilding with considerable work by the first Lord Armstrong at the end of the 19th century. Despite its strength the castle was the first in England to succumb to artillery fire when it was attacked during the War of the Roses.

NATIONAL CYCLE NETWORK HIGHLIGHTS

Bridge over the River Lune

Designed by Whitby, Bird & Partners to remind one of ships' spars, this bridge divides on the Lancaster side, with one branch going down to the quayside and the other up to the railway path, running for six miles along the banks of the Lune. The completion of this bridge links Lancaster to Morecambe and takes the Network over another major obstacle.

Larpool Viaduct

This crosses the Esk Valley 120ft above the river. The line from Scarborough to Whitby was one of the most scenic in the country but it was never economic. After standing closed for 30 years, Scarborough Borough Council opened it to the public in 2000 as the first stage of its ambitious plan to renovate the whole 20-mile route to Scarborough.

Greta Boardwalk - Keswick

At Greta, on the approach to Keswick, the line of the disused railway was blocked by the construction of the A66 main road viaduct above. Solving the problem involved creating a 300ft timber boardwalk, perched on the face of a steep hillside above the Greta. Designed by John Naylor of Groundwork West Cumbria, it used 40 tonnes of English Oak, making a vast improvement to this route.

Waverley Line Bridge - Longtown

This 50ft span bridge was built by volunteers during the Summer 2000 Work Camp to make a route avoiding the main A7 road between Carlisle and Longtown.

Fallowfield Loop - Manchester

Work started in April 2001 to build 12 miles of traffic-free routes to the Commonwealth Games and Vélodrome sites in Manchester. This route follows the line of the former railway, the dried-out Stockport Canal and the restored Ashton Canal. Altogether, the route passes under or over 32 bridges.

County Durham Gateway Bridge

Rivers are not the only barriers to cyclists. Sometimes busy roads are almost impossible to cross, at least for novices. This bridge, opened by the Prime Minister, Tony Blair, completes the Castle Eden Walkway to make a splendid path from Stockton to Wingate.

CITY FOCUS

Maps & guides are available from National Cycle Network Information unless indicated otherwise. See page 159 for contact details.

Bradford

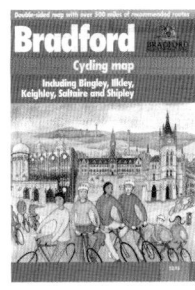

Bradford & Ilkley CycleCity Map A-Z style map showing traffic-free, official and advisory routes, with plenty of extra information about cycle shops, cycling contacts, train services and relevant local publications. Includes Bingley, Ilkley, Keighley, Saltaire and Shipley. RC10 - £2.95

Leeds

Leeds CycleCity Map Layout as for Bradford map (above). Features the route along the Leeds & Liverpool Canal and the Aire & Calder Navigation. The map covers the area bounded by Yeadon, Scarcroft, Morley and Rothwell. RC08 - £2.95

Liverpool

Liverpool Cycle Map shows suggested routes, traffic-free routes, signed routes, the Network and the Trans Pennine Trail. Available from the Tourist Information Centre. Tel: 0906 680 6886.

Manchester

Greater Manchester CycleCity Map. Layout as for Bradford map (see left). Covers city centre, suburbs, Stockport and Salford. Includes River Mersey routes and Tameside Trail. RC06 - £4.95

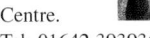

Teeside (Stockton & Middlesbrough)

Cycling in Stockton shows the Network, traffic-free paths and proposed routes. Tourist Information Centre. Tel: 01642 393936

Tyne & Wear (Newcastle & Sunderland)

Tyneside CycleCity Map Layout as for Bradford map (see above left). Shows National Routes along both sides of the Tyne. Includes Newcastle, Gateshead and North & South Tyneside. RC05 - £4.95

Other towns covered by leaflets:

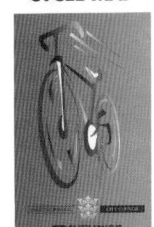

Hull Cycle Map. Shows the Network, offroad tracks and advisory routes. Tourist Information Centre. Tel: 01482 223559.

Cycling in Sunderland. Shows Route 1 and the C2C Route. Tourist Information Centre. Tel: 0191 553 2000.

York Millennium Cycle Route Map. Shows signed cycle routes, on and offroad. Tourist Information Centre. Tel: 01904 621756.

The following National Cycle Network Maps also show information about cities in the North:
Derby to York
Hull to Fakenham
Sea to Sea Cycle Route
Three Rivers Cycle Route
White Rose Cycle Route

TRAFFIC-FREE PATHS PARTICULARLY SUITABLE FOR FAMILIES

Spen Valley Greenway 7 miles

This railway path links the outskirts of Bradford to Cleakheaton, Liversedge, Heckmondwike, Ravensthorpe and the Calder Navigation for Dewsbury. It is a particularly fine example of a railway path, built by Dave Jackson who has been building routes since the first Sustrans path (York/Selby) opened in 1984. Working closely with Kirklees Council, Sustrans has made the most of this green corridor running through the industrialised valley of West Yorkshire.

West Cumbria Railway Paths 22 miles

Many of the old mineral tramways have been converted to good cycle routes in this old industrial area of West Cumbria. Workington and Whitehaven are the two starting points for the famous Sea to Sea (C2C) cycle route. The Groundwork Trust projects make extensive use of wayside sculpture.

Lancaster to Morecambe via the new Millennium Bridge. 12 miles

The new Millennium Bridge over the River Lune makes the key connection between a number of excellent railway paths and links Lancaster to Morecambe seafront with its memorable new promenade filled with mosaics and sculpture.

Calder Valley Cycleway. 13 miles

This trail, part of Route 67 from Manchester to Hull, is based around the Rochdale Canal corridor and links the east Pennine towns of Sowerby Bridge, Mytholmroyd, Hebden Bridge and Todmorden.

Consett to Sunderland. 24 miles

This is one of the two options for finishing the Sea to Sea (C2C) Route. The railway path drops 1,000 ft on its way from the crossroads of four railway paths at Consett down to the North Sea in Sunderland. This early Sustrans route, built throughout with a Manpower Services Community Programme team, has a number of major sculptures including earthworks by Andy Goldsworthy.

Leeds to Saltaire along the Leeds & Liverpool Canal. 14 miles

The canal follows the valley formed by the River Aire (Airedale) offering a safe and attractive route through this highly built-up area to the north west of Leeds, with views of the 12th-century Cistercian Abbey at Kirkstall.

USEFUL MAPS & GUIDES

For details of the full range of maps, guides and other products available contact: **National Cycle Network Information, PO Box 21, Bristol BS99 2HA. Tel: 0117 929 0888. Or visit www.nationalcyclenetwork.org.uk**
The range of National Cycle Network Maps is described in more detail on pages 218-237.

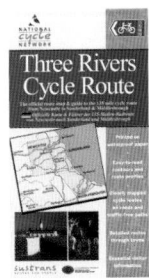

1 *Coast & Castles Cycle Route (Newcastle - Edinburgh)*
200 miles. NN1C - £5.99
65 66 *White Rose Cycle Route (Hull - Middlesbrough)*
123 miles. NN65 - £5.99

Cycling Without Traffic: North
30 traffic-free rides. Includes the Liverpool Loopline, York to Selby and the Durham railway paths. RBA04 - £9.99

7 71 *Sea to Sea Cycle Route (Whitehaven & Workington - Sunderland & Newcastle)*
140 miles. NN7AA - £5.99
7 14 72 1 *Three Rivers Cycle Route (Newcastle - Middlesbrough)*
135 miles. NN14 - £5.99

10 *Reivers Cycle Route (Newcastle - Whitehaven)*
RPR07 - £4.50

C2C & Reivers B&B Guide
RG08D - £5.99

Great Cycle Routes: Yorkshire
describes 30 routes away from traffic in Yorkshire. RBA12 - £11.99

Great Cycle Routes: North West
30 routes in the Lake District, Cumbria and North Lancashire. An excellent guide for family cycling. RBA10 - £11.99

56 62 *Trans Pennine Trail West: Irish Sea - Pennines*
Southport, Liverpool, Warrington, Stockport, Peak District and Barnsley. RPN08A - £4.95

62 67 *Trans Pennine Trail Central: Derbyshire & Yorkshire*
Doncaster, Leeds, Wakefield, Barnsley, Sheffield, Rotherham and Chesterfield. RPN08B - £4.95

62 65 *Trans Pennine Trail East: Yorkshire to North Sea* Doncaster, Selby, York, Hull & Hornsea. RPN08C - £4.95

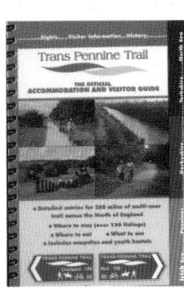

Official Trans Pennine Trail Visitor Information and Accommodation Guide
Pocket-size guide to the Trans Pennine Trail which includes accommodation listings and lots more. RG86 - £4.95

ALONG THE MERSEY IN LIVERPOOL

Here is a ride taking in the best of Liverpool's tourist attractions: the famous Liver Buildings loom over the wide open square at Pier Head, a little way down the Mersey is Albert Dock with the Beatles Museum. Linking the two parts of the ride is the quintessential experience for the visitor to the city, the ferry across the Mersey. Liverpool has made giant steps in improving the riverside area, and the promenade from Otterspool to Pier Head is a wide attractive path with big open breezy views across to the Wirral. At every stage there are signs of regeneration: Albert Dock had fallen into disuse but is now the largest group of Grade 1 listed buildings in Great Britain – a quayside complex with many museums, galleries and restaurants. The views are just as good from the Birkenhead side as you make your way north to New Brighton.

Pier Head from the Wallasey Ferry.

The Royal Albert Docks now house the Tate Gallery.

Starting point
Pier Head Ferry Terminal (by the Liver Buildings), Liverpool.

Distance
(a) Seacombe Ferry Terminal to New Brighton – four miles one way, eight miles return.
(b) Pier Head to Otterspool Promenade – five miles one way, 10 miles return.

Grade
Easy.

Surface
All tarmac.

Roads, traffic, suitability for young children
Both sections of the ride are ideal for children and they will love the crossing on the ferry!

Hills
No hills.

Refreshments
Lots of choice around Pier Head and Albert Dock.
Plenty of choice in New Brighton.

Nearest railway stations
James Street Station, Cressington Station, New Brighton.

The National Cycle Network in the area
The Trans Pennine Trail starts in Southport and runs south east along the traffic-free Cheshire Lines Path and the Liverpool Loop Line through Ainsdale, Maghull, Aintree and Halewood to Widnes (and thence eastwards towards South Manchester and the Pennines). Route 56 runs down through the Wirral to Chester and joins the North Wales Route at Queensferry/Connah's Quay.

Other nearby rides (waymarked or traffic-free)
1. The Cheshire Lines Path, the Liverpool Loop Line, and St Helen's Canal through Sankey Valley Park are all traffic-free sections of the Trans Pennine Trail.
2. The North Wirral Coastal Park continues west from New Brighton along the edge of the Wirral.
3. It is hoped that in the future there will be a good quality path all the way around the outside of the Wirral, connecting up with the Wirral Way through West Kirby, Heswall and Neston to Hooton. (At present only short sections are appropriate for cyclists.)

The Mersey Ferry.

ALONG THE MERSEY IN LIVERPOOL

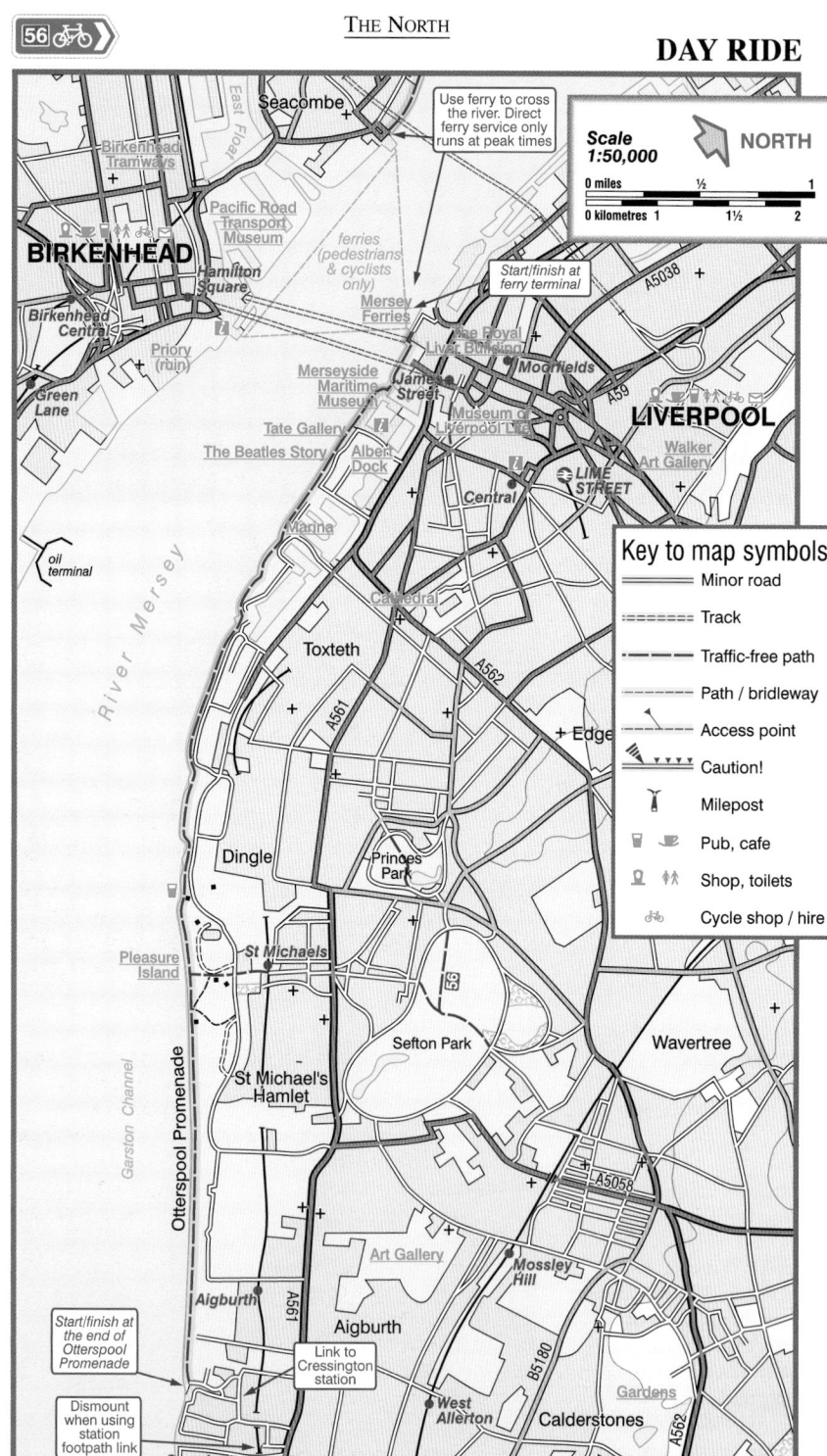

Use ferry to cross the river. Direct ferry service only runs at peak times

Start/finish at ferry terminal

Scale 1:50,000

NORTH

0 miles ½ 1

0 kilometres 1 1½ 2

Seacombe

Birkenhead Tramways

Pacific Road Transport Museum

BIRKENHEAD

Hamilton Square

Birkenhead Central

Priory (ruin)

Green Lane

ferries (pedestrians & cyclists only)

Mersey Ferries

The Royal Liver Building

Moorfields

A5038

A59

LIVERPOOL

Walker Art Gallery

Merseyside Maritime Museum

(James Street)

Museum of Liverpool Life

Tate Gallery

The Beatles Story

Albert Dock

Marina

Central

LIME STREET

oil terminal

River Mersey

Cathedral

Toxteth

A562

A561

Edge

Key to map symbols

————	Minor road
========	Track
– · – · –	Traffic-free path
– – – –	Path / bridleway
↘	Access point
▼▼▼▼	Caution!
⌶	Milepost
🍺 ☕	Pub, cafe
⚲ 🚹	Shop, toilets
🚲	Cycle shop / hire

Dingle

Princes Park

Pleasure Island

St Michaels

56

Sefton Park

Wavertree

Otterspool Promenade

Garston Channel

St Michael's Hamlet

A5058

Art Gallery

Aigburth

A561

Mossley Hill

Aigburth

Start/finish at the end of Otterspool Promenade

Link to Cressington station

B5180

Gardens

A562

Dismount when using station footpath link

West Allerton

Calderstones

Cressington

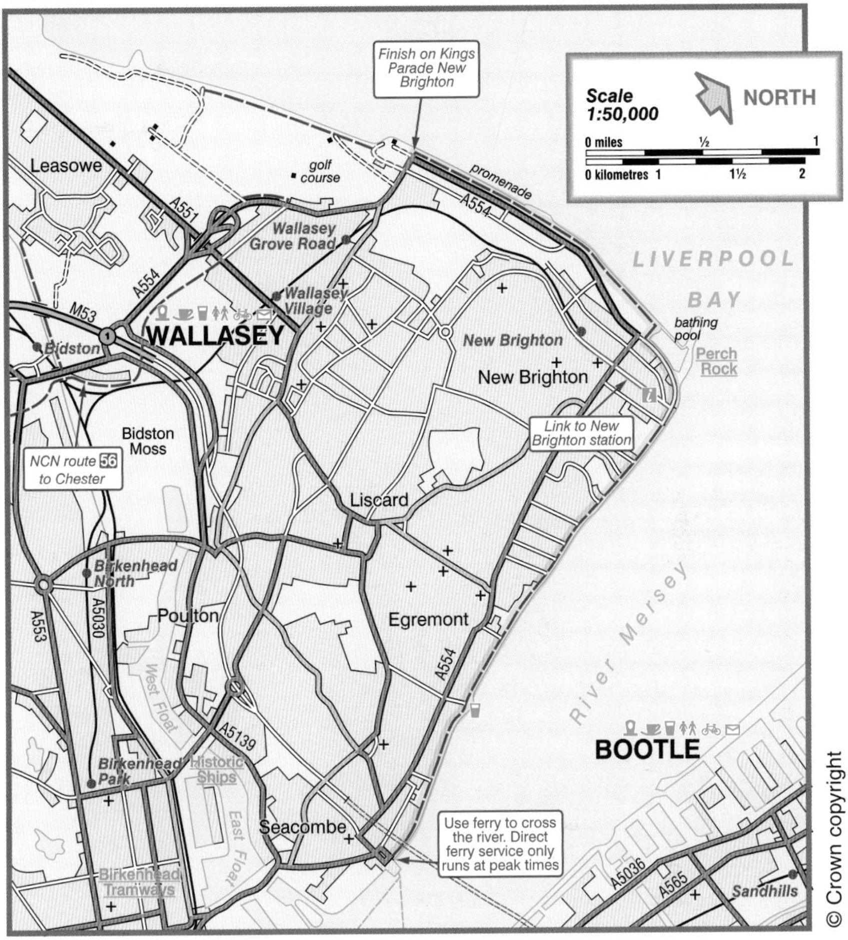

Scale 1:50,000

NORTH

0 miles — ½ — 1
0 kilometres 1 — 1½ — 2

Finish on Kings Parade New Brighton

Leasowe

golf course

promenade

A554

Wallasey Grove Road

LIVERPOOL BAY

Wallasey Village

bathing pool

WALLASEY

Bidston

New Brighton

New Brighton

Perch Rock

M53

A554

A551

Bidston Moss

NCN route 56 to Chester

Link to New Brighton station

Liscard

Birkenhead North

Poulton

Egremont

A5030

A553

A554

West Float

A5139

River Mersey

Birkenhead Park

Historic Ships

BOOTLE

East Float

Seacombe

Use ferry to cross the river. Direct ferry service only runs at peak times

Birkenhead Tramways

A5036

A565

Sandhills

© Crown copyright

Route Instructions

From Pier Head you have two choices:

1. New Brighton. Catch the Mersey Ferry to Seacombe Terminal, Birkenhead and turn right along the promenade for four miles to New Brighton. You may wish to continue west along the promenade on the North Wirral Coastal Park. Alternatively, Route 56 turns inland after passing the outdoor bathing pool and before the golf course. It runs down through the west side of Birkenhead to Neston and Chester.

2. Otterspool. Stay on the Liverpool side of the Mersey and turn south (keep the Mersey to your right) along the promenade for five miles to Otterspool, passing Albert Dock and the marina.

The Mersey Ferry
Monday to Friday there is a half-hourly service until 10.00AM and after 4.00PM. In the middle of the day (10.00AM to 4.00PM) there is an hourly service. At the weekends there is an hourly service.

There is plenty to do around Albert Dock, including the Beatles Museum,

allowing you to fill the time while waiting for the ferry.
For further information about ferries call 0151 630 1030 or 0151 236 7676.

New Brighton Promenade.

YORK TO BENINGBROUGH

York has done more than most cities in Britain to cater for the needs of the cyclist and although its achievements may still be some way behind Holland and Denmark, a start has been made in the acceptance of the role the bike can play in helping to solve traffic congestion. The ride starts near the heart of the beautiful walled city and runs parallel with the broad, slow-moving River Ouse. Be warned that after heavy winter rains the riverside path can completely disappear under water! The ride crosses the grazed Rawcliffe Meadows – a managed 25 acres of wildflowers and birdlife. You will pass several curious sculptures – seats looking like horse-drawn carriages and farm implements, a weather vane with a bicycle and dog, and a metalwork globe with depictions of York Cathedral and the walled city. The ride joins the network of quiet lanes and crosses the flat and fertile land of the Vale of York. This is the route of the East Coast Main Line and a sign alongside the railway indicates that you are 200 miles south of Edinburgh and 200 miles north of London. The National Trust property of Beningbrough Hall offers a view of life in an English country house from Georgian to Victorian times. It is open from Easter to October. If you wish to push on to a pub, you have a choice of two in Newton-on-Ouse, a small village just beyond Beningbrough.

York Minster is a focus for the National Cycle Network. It is visible for miles and a cycle route passes right outside its walls.

Starting point
The riverside path at the end of Marygate in the centre of York.

Distance
Nine miles one way, 18 miles return. For a longer linear ride you could follow Route 65 to Thirsk (36 miles one way) or to Northallerton (46 miles one way) and catch the train back to York.

Grade
Easy.

Surface
Sealed riverside paths and quiet lanes.

Roads, traffic, suitability for young children
The four miles at the start of the ride are traffic-free and flat, thus offering an ideal ride for young children. Five miles of the route (from Overton to Beningbrough) are along quiet lanes.

Hills
None.

Refreshments
Lots of choice in York.
The Sidings Hotel & Restaurant, Shipton (open for coffee, lunch, tea).
The cafe at Beningbrough Hall is open from Easter to October.
Downay Arms pub, Blacksmith Arms pub, Newton-on-Ouse (just beyond Beningbrough).

Leaflets
A superb map of cycle facilities in York is produced by York City Council. It is available from: The Cycling Officer, York City Council, Directorate of Development Services, 9 St Leonard's Place, York YO1 2ET. Tel: 01904 613161.

Nearest railway station
York.

The National Cycle Network in the area
York is at a crossroads of the Network. The north-south section from Middlesbrough to Selby is signed and mapped (Route 65) as is the route from Beverley and Pocklington to the east (Route 66). The western section to Harrogate and Leeds (a continuation of Route 66) will be completed in the future.

Other nearby rides (waymarked or traffic-free)
York has two other waymarked, traffic-free routes, both used in the

Beside the River Ouse just upstream from Scarborough Bridge.

National Cycle Network. To the south, a route runs alongside the River Ouse, past the new Millennium cycle/foot bridge, the racecourse then down the course of the former Selby railway to Riccall. Crossing the Millennium Bridge a route crosses Walmgate Stray past the University to the Foss Island Railway Path and on to Stamford Bridge.

Bridge across Hurn's Gutter modelled on the Forth Bridge!

65 🚲 ❯

DAY RIDE

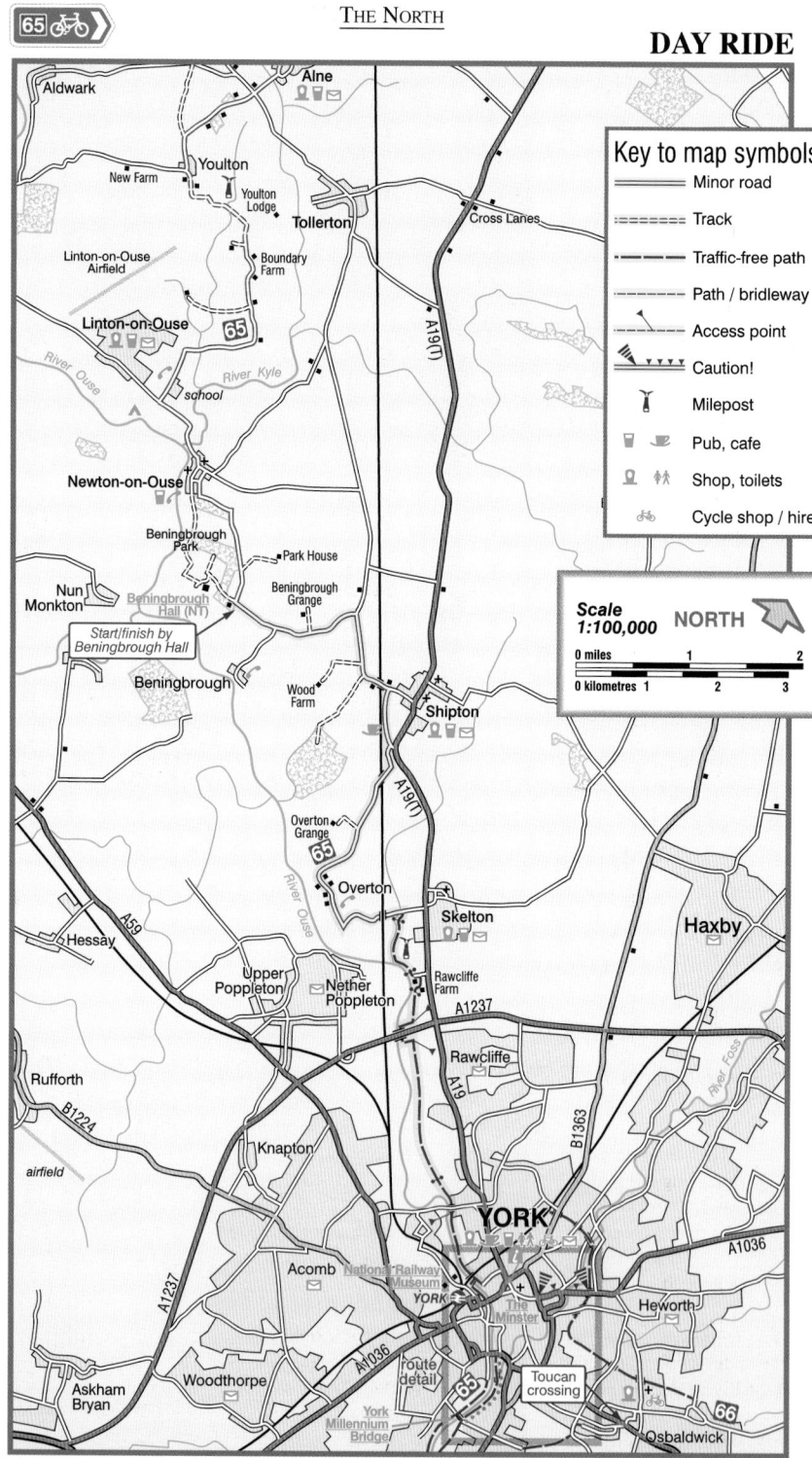

Key to map symbols

═══	Minor road
╪╪╪╪╪	Track
▬ ▬ ▬	Traffic-free path
─ ─ ─	Path / bridleway
↘	Access point
▨ ▾▾▾▾	Caution!
⚑	Milepost
🥛 ☕	Pub, cafe
⚲ 🚹🚺	Shop, toilets
🚲	Cycle shop / hire

Scale
1:100,000   NORTH ↗

| 0 miles | | 1 | | 2 |
| 0 kilometres | 1 | | 2 | 3 |

Aldwark
Alne
Youlton
New Farm
Youlton Lodge
Tollerton
Cross Lanes
Linton-on-Ouse Airfield
Boundary Farm
Linton-on-Ouse
65
River Ouse
River Kyle
school
A19(T)
Newton-on-Ouse
Beningbrough Park
Park House
Nun Monkton
Beningbrough Hall (NT)
Beningbrough Grange
Start/finish by Beningbrough Hall
Beningbrough
Wood Farm
Shipton
Overton Grange
65
River Ouse
Overton
Skelton
Haxby
Hessay
A59
Upper Poppleton
Nether Poppleton
Rawcliffe Farm
A1237
Rufforth
Rawcliffe
A19
B1363
B1224
River Foss
airfield
Knapton
A1237
York
Acomb
National Railway Museum
YORK
A1036
Heworth
The Minster
A1036
route detail
65
Toucan crossing
66
Askham Bryan
Woodthorpe
York Millennium Bridge
Osbaldwick

© Crown copyright

166

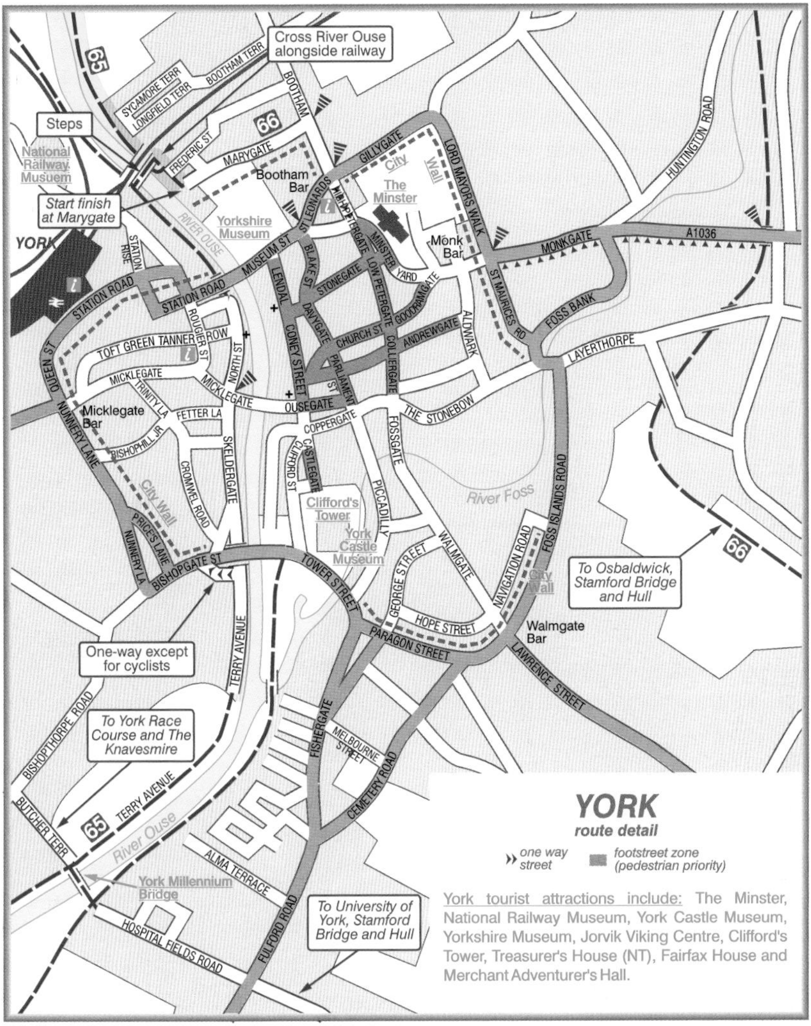

Map labels

Cross River Ouse alongside railway

85

66

BOOTHAM

SYCAMORE TERR
LONGFIELD TERR

FREDERIC ST

Steps

National Railway Museum

MARYGATE

GILLYGATE

City Wall

Lord Mayor's Walk

HUNTINGTON ROAD

Bootham Bar

Start finish at Marygate

Yorkshire Museum

The Minster

YORK

MUSEUM ST

STATION RISE

STATION ROAD

STATION ROAD

RIVER OUSE

BLAKE ST

STONEGATE

STONEGATE

LENDAL

CONEY STREET

ST LEONARD'S

PETERGATE LOW PETERGATE

CHURCH ST

COLLIERGATE

Monk Bar

ST MAURICE'S RD

MONKGATE

A1036

FOSS BANK

LAYERTHORPE

66

TOFT GREEN TANNER ROW

RUGDER ST

NORTH ST

MICKLEGATE

MICKLEGATE

QUEEN ST

TRINITY L'A

FETTER LA

BISHOPHILL JR

NUNNERY LANE

Micklegate Bar

OUSEGATE

SPURRIERGATE

COPPERGATE

DOWNGATE

PARLIAMENT ST

ANDREWGATE

THE STONEBOW

PICCADILLY

FOSSGATE

River Foss

FOSS ISLANDS ROAD

To Osbaldwick, Stamford Bridge and Hull

City Wall

BRUCE LANE

CROMWELL ROAD

SKELDERGATE

CLIFFORD ST

BISHOPGATE ST

NUNNERY L.

Clifford's Tower

York Castle Museum

TOWER STREET

GEORGE STREET

WALMGATE

NAVIGATION ROAD

Walmgate Bar

TERRY AVENUE

FISHERGATE

PARAGON STREET

HOPE STREET

LAWRENCE STREET

One-way except for cyclists

BISHOPTHORPE ROAD

To York Race Course and The Knavesmire

TERRY AVENUE

BUTCHER TERR

65

River Ouse

ALMA TERRACE

MELBOURNE STREET

CEMETERY ROAD

York Millennium Bridge

HOSPITAL FIELDS ROAD

FULFORD ROAD

To University of York, Stamford Bridge and Hull

YORK
route detail

» one way street

footstreet zone (pedestrian priority)

York tourist attractions include: The Minster, National Railway Museum, York Castle Museum, Yorkshire Museum, Jorvik Viking Centre, Clifford's Tower, Treasurer's House (NT), Fairfax House and Merchant Adventurer's Hall.

Route instructions from York to Beningbrough

1. From the end of Marygate follow the riverside path alongside the River Ouse away from the centre of York (ie keep the river to your left).

2. Pass through Rawcliffe Meadows.

3. After four miles, having passed beneath the bridge carrying the ring road over the River Ouse, at the T-junction by a row of terraced houses, turn left to rejoin the riverside path.

4. At the end of the cycle path by the National Cycle Network sign turn left. At the T-junction near to the main road turn left signposted 'Beningbrough, Newton-on-Ouse'.

5. At the next T-junction turn left to cross the railway bridge (same sign).

6. After one mile turn left by the 'Coaches only' signpost (Route 65). After 1½ miles go into Beningbrough Park to visit the Hall. If you wish to visit the pubs in Newton-on-Ouse, go past the hall to the further entrance.

Waymarking by Andy Hazell at the Skelton Lane/Overton turning.

PENRITH TO KESWICK

Forming part of the popular Sea to Sea (C2C) Cycle Route which crosses the country from coast to coast, this section from Penrith to Keswick takes you right into the heart of the Lake District, with much of the ride dominated by the majestic outline of Blencathra, rising to almost 3000ft. Once out of the busy town of Penrith the ride links together a series of small hamlets and villages built of stone, almost all of which have a pub, so that if you wish to shorten the ride there are several good turnaround points. This is a land of drystone walls and sheep grazing, with solid farmhouses and the occasional fortified hall (the ride runs across the southern end of what was once a vast lawless area between England and Scotland, frequently raided by the Reivers in the 15th and 16th centuries).

If you make it as far as Keswick there are scores of possibilities for refreshments from cafes to fine restaurants. With luck the prevailing westerly winds should help blow you back to Penrith! There is a tough alternative heading east from Keswick which passes the magnificently located Castlerigg Stone Circle then climbs steeply on a challenging off-road section using the course of an old coach road that ascends to almost 1,500 ft.

N.B. The old coach road should only be undertaken by fit cyclists on mountain bikes in good weather.

It's worth the climb to Castlerigg Stone Circle, east of Keswick.

Starting points
1. Stricklandgate (the A6 Scotland Road) in the centre of Penrith.
2. Keswick Tourist Information Centre in the centre of Keswick.

Distance
24 miles one way, 48 miles return. For shorter rides, starting from Penrith, there are pubs at Newton Reigny (7 miles round trip), Blencow (11 miles round trip), Greystoke (15 miles round trip) or Troutbeck (24 miles round trip).

Grade
Moderate (with challenging off-road options).

Surface
Almost all on road except a short section of farm track on the outskirts of Penrith and a three mile stretch of gravel-based railway path at the Keswick end. The challenging and adventurous off-road option along the old coach road is rough and should only be undertaken by fit cyclists on mountain bikes in good weather.

Roads, traffic, suitability for young children
The ride is almost all on minor roads. There is a short section on busy streets from Penrith to the start of the minor road network. A good option for young children would be to follow the course of the dismantled railway from Keswick to Threlkeld alongside the River Greta. This route crosses and recrosses the river as it runs through its wooded gorge.

Hills
There is a steady climb of over 500 ft from Penrith to the highpoint of the ride just north of Troutbeck. If you return to Penrith via the coach road you will be faced with a climb of almost 1,000 ft from crossing St John's Beck to the highpoint of the old road.

Refreshments
Lots of choice in Penrith.
Sun Inn, Newton Reigny.
Crown Inn, Great Blencow.
Boot & Shoe PH, Greystoke.
Sportsmans Inn, Troutbeck Inn, Troutbeck.
Salutation Inn, Horse & Farrier PH, Threlkeld.
Lots of choice in Keswick.

Nearest railway station
Penrith.

The National Cycle Network in the area
The ride forms part of the C2C Cycle Route (Routes 7, 71, 72) from Whitehaven/Workington to Newcastle/Sunderland. Route 1 branches off through Skelton and Dalston to Carlisle to link with the Lochs & Glens Route (Carlisle – Glasgow – Inverness, Route 7). In the future Route 67 will link

The Coach Road to Matterdale End provides a wonderfully remote route on fine days.

Penrith across the Pennines to Richmond, Northallerton and York. South from Keswick, Route 6 will pass through Kendal, Lancaster and Preston to Manchester.

Other nearby rides (waymarked or traffic-free)
In Cumbria, the Reivers Cycle Route runs from Carlisle south west towards the Cumbrian Coast, passing around the north side of Caldbeck Fells to Cockermouth, Workington and Whitehaven. This offers the possibility of a signposted, circular ride of 150 miles linking Whitehaven, Penrith and Carlisle.

The Munsgrisdale Road from Scales.

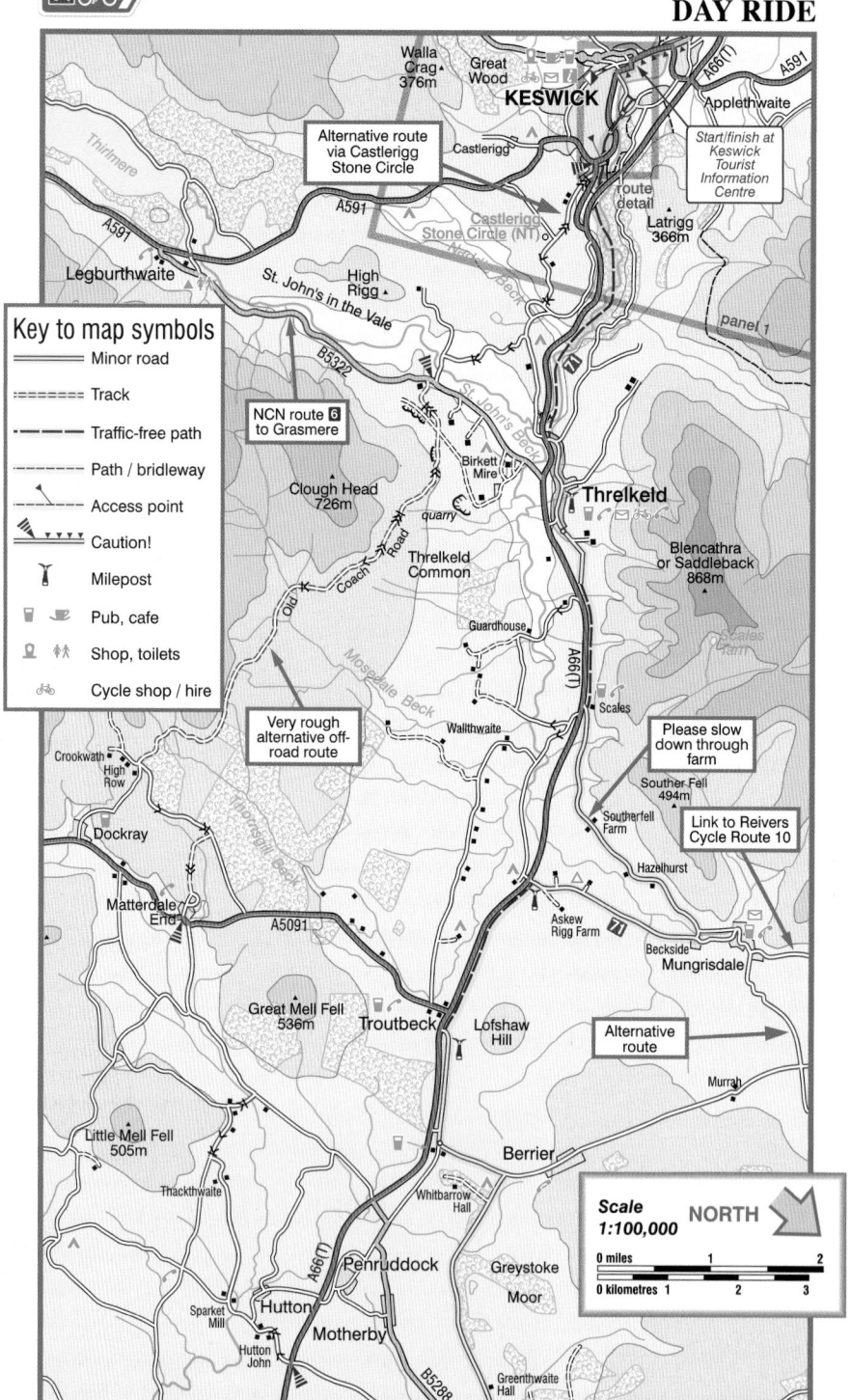

71 🚲

DAY RIDE

PENRITH TO KESWICK

Walla Crag 376m
Great Wood
KESWICK
A66(T)
A591
Applethwaite

Thirlmere

Alternative route via Castlerigg Stone Circle
Castlerigg

A591
Castlerigg Stone Circle (NT)
route detail

Start/finish at Keswick Tourist Information Centre

Latrigg 366m
Panel 1

Legburthwaite
A591
St. John's in the Vale
High Rigg

B5322

Key to map symbols

═══	Minor road
═════	Track
━ ━ ━	Traffic-free path
─ · ─ ·	Path / bridleway
⟵	Access point
▼▼▼	Caution!
⚲	Milepost
🍺 ☕	Pub, cafe
♨ 🚻	Shop, toilets
🚲	Cycle shop / hire

NCN route 6 to Grasmere

Birkett Mire

Threlkeld

Clough Head 726m

quarry

Threlkeld Common

Blencathra or Saddleback 868m

Old Coach Road

Guardhouse

A66(T)

Mosedale Beck

Very rough alternative off-road route

Wallthwaite

Scales

Please slow down through farm

Crookwath
High Row

Souther Fell 494m
Southerfell Farm

Link to Reivers Cycle Route 10

Dockray

Hazelhurst

Matterdale End
A5091

Askew Rigg Farm
71

Beckside
Mungrisdale

Great Mell Fell 536m
Troutbeck

Lofshaw Hill

Alternative route

Murrah

Little Mell Fell 505m

Thackthwaite

Whitbarrow Hall

Berrier

Greystoke Moor

Scale 1:100,000

NORTH

0 miles / 1 / 2
0 kilometres / 1 / 2 / 3

A66(T)
Penruddock

Sparket Mill
Hutton

Motherby

Hutton John

Greenthwaite Hall

B5288

© Crown copyright

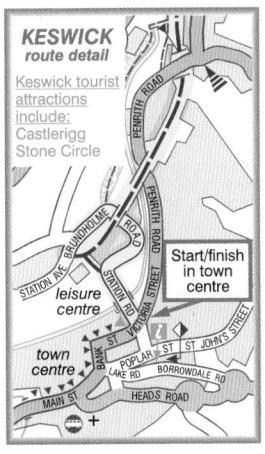

KESWICK route detail

Keswick tourist attractions include: Castlerigg Stone Circle

Route instructions from Penrith to Keswick

1. Take care on the busy roads through Penrith and follow signs for 'A6 (north)'. Shortly after passing petrol stations to the right then left, bear left by the Grey Bull pub signposted 'Caravan Park'.

2. The tarmac turns to track by the farm. Go past barns and alongside the M6 then turn left through the subway beneath the motorway. Ignore the turning to the right. Climb the hill.

3. At the fork of tracks by the group of college buildings bear left onto the concrete track to pass through the college itself. Shortly at a crossroads go straight ahead signposted 'Residents only. No exit'. At the road turn right.

4. Follow signs for Skelton and Laithes through Newton Reigny. Go through the hamlet of Laithes. At a crossroads by a Give Way sign turn left signposted 'Blencow, Greystoke'.

5. Follow signs for Greystoke. At the crossroads in the village turn right signposted 'Berrier'. Steady climb.

6. Long fabulous descent. At T-junction turn left signposted 'Troutbeck, Keswick'. At the next T-junction by the Sportsmans Inn turn right signposted 'Keswick' then on a sharp left-hand bend bear right onto a minor lane running parallel with the main road.

7. At the T-junction with the A66, turn right onto the cycle path alongside the main road. After 150 yds take the first road to the right by Hillcrest B&B. Fine descent. At the T-junction with the main road turn right on the cycle lane.

8. Second fine descent. Take the next road to the right 'Mungrisdale, Caldbeck C2C'. Turn left on the second drive/track signposted 'Southerfell.'

9. At the T-junction with a minor road turn left. At the end of this gated road turn right past the White Horse Inn. At the T-junction with the A66 turn right. Follow the cycle lane up to the right away from the A66 to go through a bridlegate onto the old road.

10. At the T-junction at the end of the old road (Fellside) turn right. Go past the pubs in Threlkeld. Just before rejoining the A66 turn right onto the cyclepath. Tarmac turns to gravel track.

11. Follow the Cockermouth, Keswick & Penrith (1869) railway path for three miles. This crosses the River Greta on a number of impressive bridges, and towards the end creeps around the hillside below the A66 viaduct on a newly built boardwalk.

12. At the end of the railway path continue straight ahead then bear to the left of the Leisure Centre and descend to the road. Turn right then at the crossroads at the end of Station Road go straight ahead for Keswick town centre.

Keswick to Greystoke (challenging offroad option via the old coach road)

13. With your back to Keswick Tourist Information Centre go straight ahead towards Keswick Lodge Hotel. At the crossroads go straight ahead onto Station Road.

14. On a sharp right-hand bend bear left up towards the Leisure Centre. Pass to the right of the building then bear right onto the railway path and past the old station.

Coach road near its junction with St. John's in the Vale.

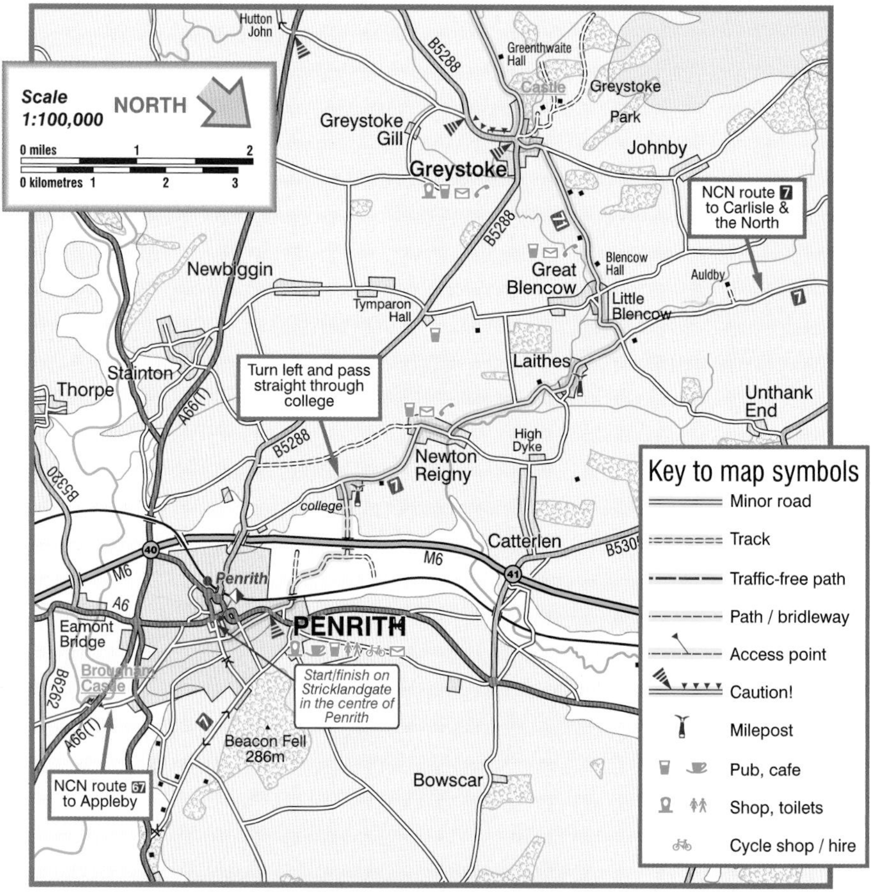

**Scale
1:100,000**

NORTH

0 miles   1   2

0 kilometres   1   2   3

Hutton John

B5288

Greenthwaite Hall

Castle

Greystoke Park

Greystoke

Greystoke Gill

Greystoke

Johnby

NCN route 7 to Carlisle & the North

7

Newbiggin

Great Blencow

Blencow Hall

Little Blencow

Auldby

7

Tymparon Hall

Stainton

Thorpe

A66(T)

B5288

Turn left and pass straight through college

Laithes

Unthank End

High Dyke

college

Newton Reigny

7

Catterlen

B5305

B5320

M6

40

Penrith

A6

M6

41

Eamont Bridge

B6262

PENRITH

Start/finish on Stricklandgate in the centre of Penrith

Brougham Castle

A66(T)

Beacon Fell 286m

Bowscar

NCN route 57 to Appleby

Key to map symbols

═════	Minor road
═════	Track
─ ─ ─	Traffic-free path
─ ─ ─	Path / bridleway
	Access point
▼▼▼▼	Caution!
⍓	Milepost
	Pub, cafe
⚲ ⚶	Shop, toilets
⚲	Cycle shop / hire

© Crown copyright

Blencathra towers over the route between Threlkeld and Scales.

15. Immediately after passing beneath the first bridge, leave the railway path, turn left up the steps then left on the road. Take the first road left then the first road to the right signposted 'Castlerigg, C2C'.

16. Climb steeply and go past the Castlerigg Stone Circle. Fast descent. At the T-junction at the bottom of the hill turn right signposted 'C2C, Grasmere Bike Route'. At the next T-junction turn right again (same sign).

17. Take the first road to the right signposted 'Shundraw, St John's in the Vale'. At the T-junction with the B5322 turn right signposted 'Thirlmere' then left 'Matterdale. C2C'. Climb steeply.

18. At a fork of tracks by a farm bear left. At a diagonally offset crossroads (with a level tarmac path) go straight ahead. Follow the old coach road for five miles, climbing to almost 1,500 ft.

19. At the crossroads at the end of the old coach road, turn left signposted 'Troutbeck'. Climb then descend past a wood on the left. Shortly after the start of a second wood, close to a stone barn, turn sharp right onto a broad stone track signposted 'Bridleway to Matterdale End'.

20. At the road (A5091) turn left then right 'Penruddock, Penrith'. Ignore a right to 'Dockray, Ullswater'. Take the next right after 1¼ miles 'Thackthwaite C2C'.

21. Steep climb. Follow the road round a sharp left-hand bend. Descend. **Easy to miss**. Take the first road left 'Thackthwaite'.

22. At T-junction by Sparket Mill turn left 'Penrith, Greystoke'. At the crossroads with the A66 go straight ahead 'Greystoke'. At the T-junction with the B5288 turn right 'Greystoke, Penrith'.

23. At the crossroads by the stone cross in the centre of Greystoke take the road signposted 'Johnby, Blencow, C2C'. Rejoin the outward route.

Spanning the River Greta, Brundholme Bridge is one of the bowstring bridges designed by Sir Thomas Bouch and built in 1862-64.

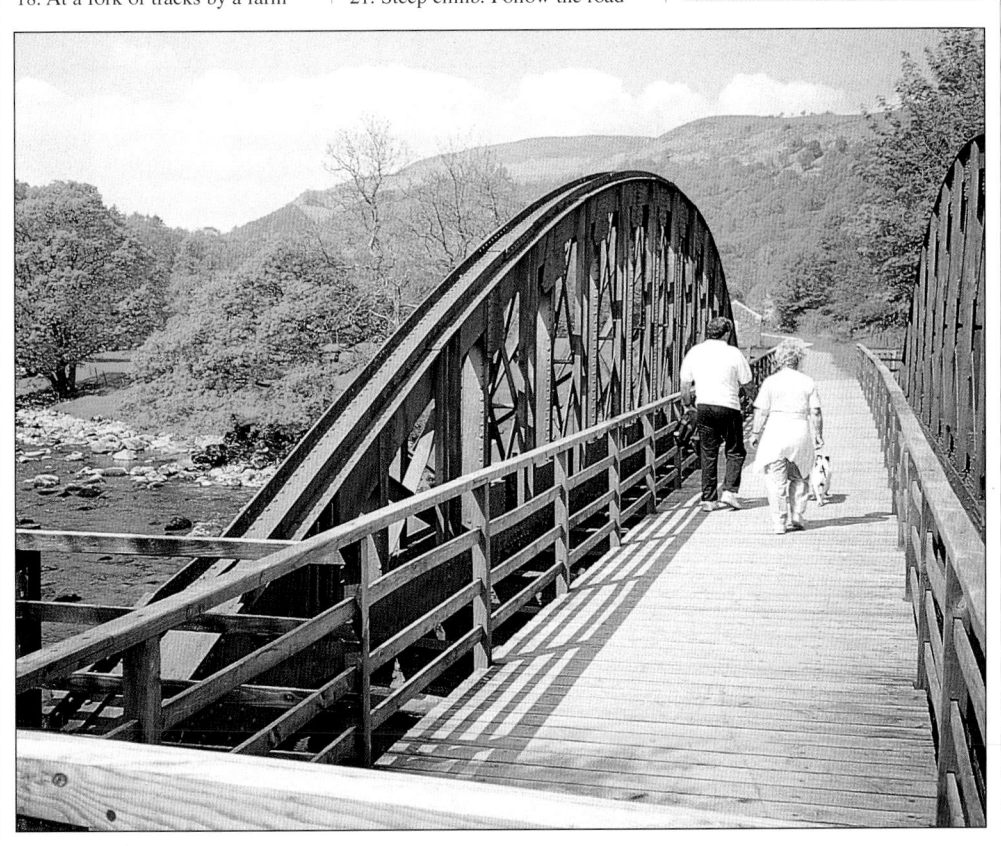

NEWCASTLE TO SUNDERLAND

Tyne & Wear has seen the creation of a highly developed network of cycle routes in the past few years, much of it tied in closely with the overall regeneration of the industrialised area alongside the River Tyne. Many loops are possible using the cycle routes on either side of the river and crossing via the bridges in the centre of the city, including the magnificent new Gateshead Millennium Bridge, at Blaydon in the west or via the foot and cycle tunnel near Jarrow to the east. Using a mixture of quiet streets, riverside paths and railway paths the route described here runs along the north side of the Tyne to the ferry terminal at North Shields, crosses the water via the ferry then soon joins the shared-use path alongside the A183 with fine views out to the North Sea. Along this section you pass Souter Lighthouse, built in 1871 and the first lighthouse specifically constructed to use electric light. As with the Tyne, so too the River Wear has seen attractive regeneration and development along the waterfront, including many fine sculptures and the National Glass Centre.

Tyne Ferry.

Starting point

The Quayside in the centre of Newcastle upon Tyne.

Distance

19 miles one way, 38 miles return. For shorter rides, starting from Newcastle, there are good turnaround points at the Segedunum Heritage Centre at Wallsend (10 miles round trip), North Shields Ferry Terminal (18 miles round trip), Souter Lighthouse (28 miles round trip).

Alternatively you may wish to push on beyond North Shields to Tynemouth and then return to Newcastle (23 miles round trip).

Grade

Easy.

Surface

Mixture of tarmac and stone cycle path.

Roads, traffic, suitability for young children

Traffic-free paths are mixed with sections along quiet streets all the way from Newcastle to Sunderland. There is a long stretch of shared-use pavement alongside the A183 between South Shields and Sunderland but care should be taken crossing the many side roads.

Hills

No major hills.

Refreshments

Plenty of choice in the centres of Newcastle, South Shields, North Shields and Sunderland. There is a tea room at Souter Lighthouse, to the south of South Shields.

Leaflets

1. *CycleCity's Tyneside Cycling Map* is an excellent publication showing the traffic-free paths, signposted cycle routes, advisory routes plus a wealth of other information. It costs £4.95 and is available from the National Cycle Network Information Service, PO Box 21, Bristol BS99 2HA. Tel: 0117 929 0888. Or visit www.nationalcyclenetwork.org.uk

2. *Leisure Cycling in South Tyneside* – South Tyneside MBC, Development Services Dept, Town Hall and Civic Offices, Westhoe Road, South Shields, Tyne & Wear NE33 2RL. Tel: 0191 427 1717.

Nearest railway stations

Newcastle upon Tyne, Sunderland. Two bikes are allowed on each train. From Monday to Friday you are not allowed to travel with your bike before 0900 or between 1600 and 1800. No bikes (except folding bikes) are allowed on the train on Saturdays. There are no restrictions on Sundays.

The National Cycle Network in the area

1. The C2C has two possible endings: Consett to Tynemouth and Consett to Sunderland. The latter uses 18 miles of railway path between the two points, passing through Stanley, Washington and Roker on its way to the North Sea Coast.
2. Route 1 links South Shields with Sunderland and Seaham and runs further south to Teeside and the White Rose Cycle Route (Routes 65 & 66).
3. Hadrian's Way (the North Tyne Cycleway) continues west from Blaydon to Wylam.
4. The Reivers Cycle Route runs from Tynemouth to North Shields then turns north through Seaton Burn and Ponteland towards Bellingham and Kielder.
5. The Three Rivers Route (Routes 1, 14, 7) links Middlesbrough, Stockton, Hartlepool, Durham, Consett, Newcastle, Gateshead and North and South Tyneside.
6. The Coast & Castles Route (Route 1) runs north along the coast of Northumberland from Tynemouth to Berwick-on-Tweed then through the Scottish Borders to Edinburgh.

Other nearby rides (waymarked or traffic-free)

You are spoilt for choice for traffic-free routes in the North East: there are all the Durham Railway paths such as the Lanchester Valley and the Waskerley Way plus the routes on either side of the Tyne such as Keelman's Way and Hadrian's Way. See the Regional Map on page 152 and the 'Traffic-free paths' section on page 158.

Along the railway path at Walker.

DAY RIDE

NEWCASTLE TO SUNDERLAND

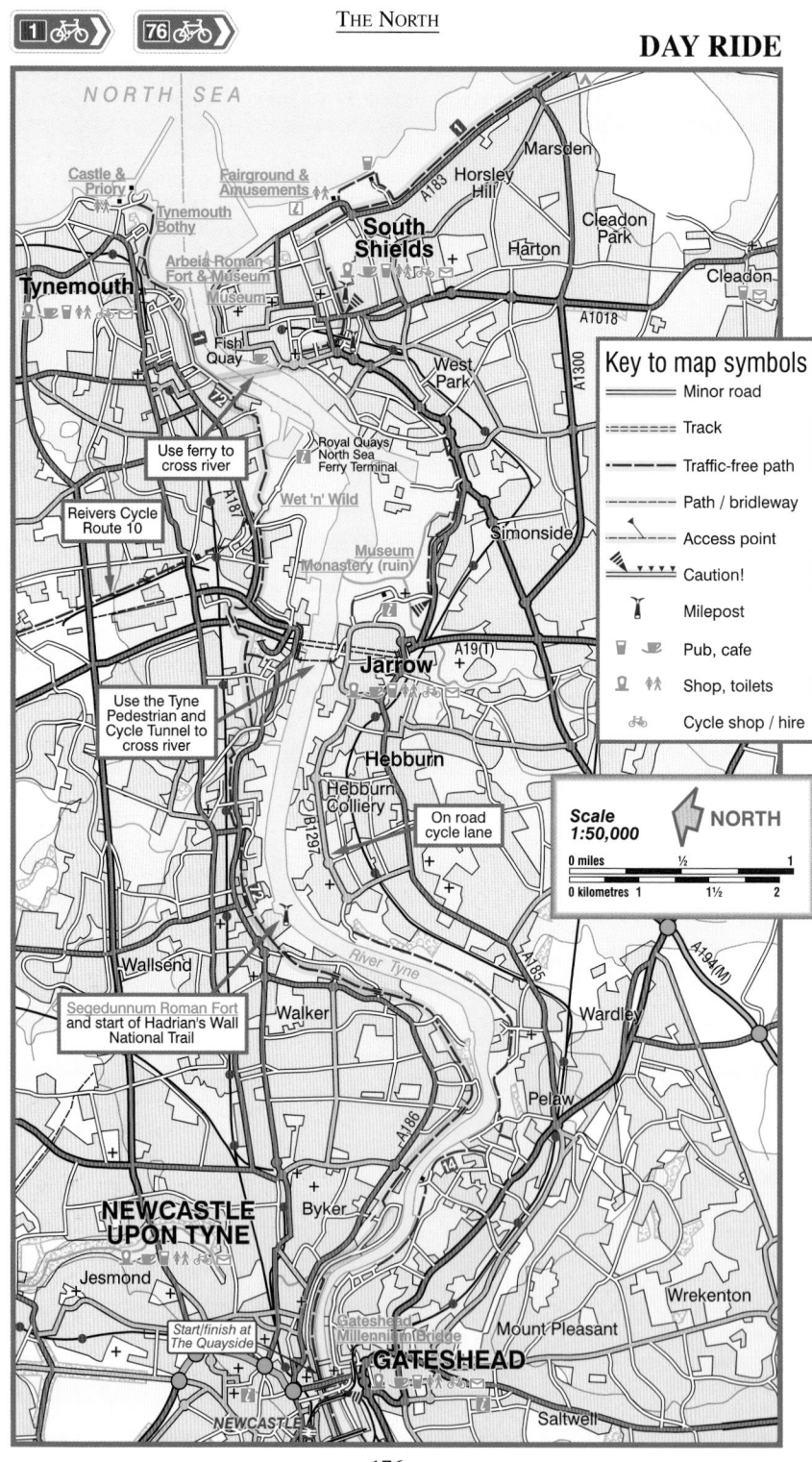

The North

1 🚲 ›   76 🚲 ›

Key to map symbols

═══════	Minor road
╍╍╍╍╍	Track
▬ ▬ ▬	Traffic-free path
─ ─ ─	Path / bridleway
⌐	Access point
▲▲▼▼▼▼	Caution!
⌇	Milepost
☕ 🍺	Pub, cafe
♀ ♟	Shop, toilets
🚲	Cycle shop / hire

Scale
1:50,000

NORTH

0 miles   ½   1
0 kilometres 1   1½   2

Use ferry to cross river

Reivers Cycle Route 10

Use the Tyne Pedestrian and Cycle Tunnel to cross river

On road cycle lane

Segedunnum Roman Fort and start of Hadrian's Wall National Trail

Castle & Priory

Tynemouth Bothy

Fairground & Amusements

Tynemouth

Arbeia Roman Fort & Museum

South Shields

Marsden

Horsley Hill

Cleadon Park

Cleadon

Harton

Fish Quay

West Park

Royal Quays/ North Sea Ferry Terminal

Wet 'n' Wild

Museum Monastery (ruin)

Simonside

Jarrow

Hebburn

Hebburn Colliery

River Tyne

Wallsend

Walker

Wardley

Pelaw

NEWCASTLE UPON TYNE

Byker

Wrekenton

Jesmond

Start/finish at The Quayside

Gateshead Millennium Bridge

Mount Pleasant

GATESHEAD

NEWCASTLE

Saltwell

176

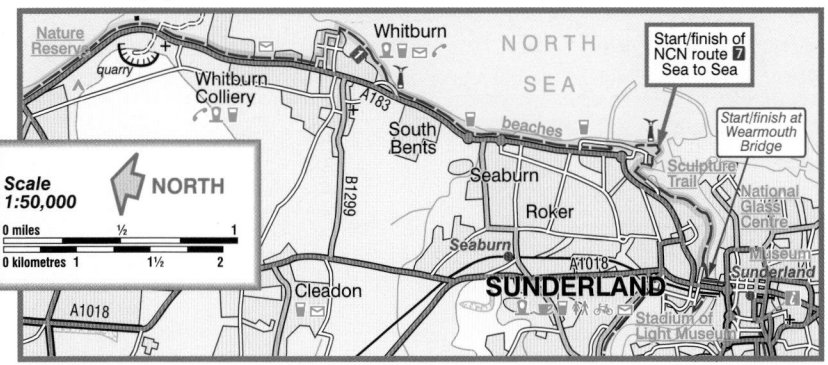

obvious cycle
lane through
several barriers.

10. Cross the
busy Westoe
Road, climb
past a big, tree-
filled cemetery.
Sea views open
up at the top of
the rise.
Continue in the
same direction
downhill. At the T-junction at the
end of Sea Way, turn right then left
onto cyclepath.

11. At the roundabout, go straight
ahead signposted 'Two Rivers
Cycleway, Route 1, Sunderland,
Souter Lighthouse'.

12. Go past Souter Lighthouse and
through an area where there are
houses on both sides of the road.
Easy to miss. Opposite small
chapel by Whitburn Cemetery on
the right, turn left signposted
'Route 1', follow signs to the sea.

13. Lovely section along the cliffs.
Rejoin the road. After two miles, as
the main road swings sharp right
away from the coast turn left
sharply back on yourself down
towards the beach signposted 'City
Centre, C2C, Route 1'.

14. At the bottom of the hill follow
the cyclepath close to the water and
alongside the marina. 'Route 7' is
signposted. Go past the National
Glass Centre and along the riverfront.

15. It is suggested you go as far as
the end of the riverside path just
beyond the metal tree sculpture.
For Sunderland station bear right,
away from the river soon after the
metal tree, signposted 'C2C, Route
7'. At the T-junction turn left on the
green cycle lane to cross bridge.
Follow one-way system to station.

Route instructions from Newcastle upon Tyne city centre to North Shields (Tynemouth) and Sunderland

1. From the Swing Bridge in
Newcastle city centre follow the
riverside path east (ie river to right).

2. At the Spillers building bear left
uphill away from the river. At the
mini-roundabout continue straight
ahead. After the car park on the left,
turn left opposite Foundry Court,
pass between stone barriers onto the
railway path. Follow for four miles.

3. At the T-junction with Hadrian
Road (A187) in Wallsend, at the
end of the railway path, cross to the
cycle path on the other side of the
road. Shortly, bear left downhill
away from the main road, cross the
bridge over the small river then at
the T-junction turn right.

4. Before rejoining the main road
(Hadrian Road/A187) turn left onto
Bewicke Road immediately before
the PH, then left onto cycle path.

5. Cross the open ground then the
bridge over the A19, bearing right.
Follow the cycle signs (and the C2C
signs) then turn right down towards
the shops at the Royal Quays.

6. Just before the second
roundabout turn left onto Redburn
Dene signposted 'C2C. Route 72'.

Follow this downhill through a
landscape of boulders and timbers
and bear left at the bottom. At the
roundabout go straight ahead.

7. Follow the waymarking closely
as there are few street names.
At a second roundabout go straight
ahead then shortly turn left then
first right between warehouses.
At a T-junction turn right then left.
Follow 'Route 10' signs down the
wheeling ramp parallel with a
flight of steps and either push your
bike or cycle down the ramp to the
ferry terminal*.

Side trip to Tynemouth
(a) At the bottom of the ramp
follow New Quay, Clive Street,
Liddell Street and Bell Street (all
the same road!) to Union Quay.

(b) Go through the car park and
along the promenade above
Tynemouth harbour and pier.

Main Route to Sunderland
8. Cross the Tyne on the ferry.
From the South Shields Ferry
Terminal go up ramp, then right at
T-junction with Ferry St signposted
'Sunderland, Souter Lighthouse,
Seafront Cycle Route'.

9. At the first roundabout, go
straight ahead. At the second
roundabout, turn left onto the cycle
lane then first right onto Old
Coronation Street. Follow the

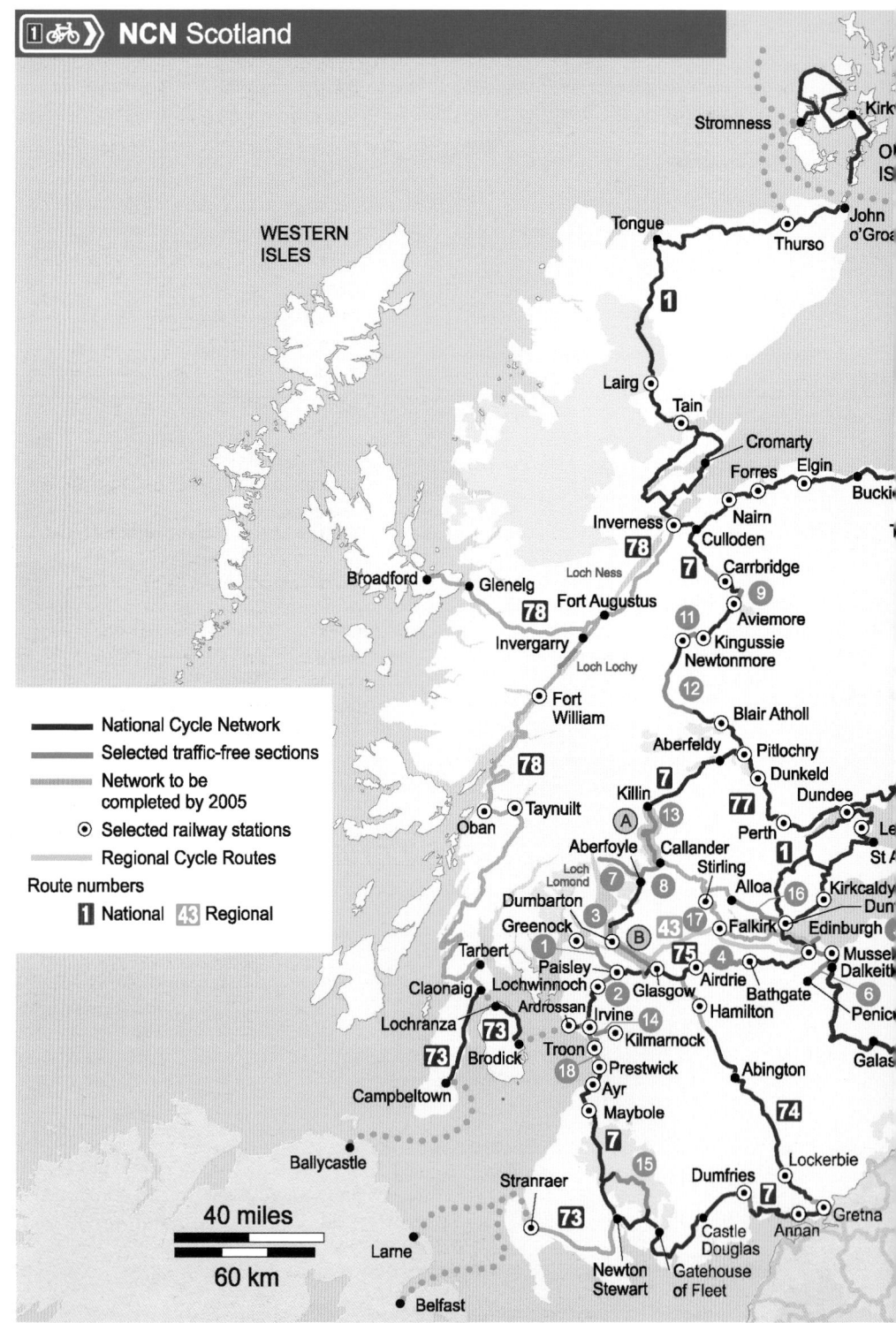

WESTERN ISLES

Stromness   Kirk
O
IS

Tongue   John o'Groa
Thurso

1

Lairg
Tain

Cromarty
Forres   Elgin
Bucki

Inverness   Nairn
78   Culloden

Broadford   Glenelg
Loch Ness
Carrbridge
7   **9**
Fort Augustus   **11**   Aviemore
78
Kingussie
Invergarry   Newtonmore
Loch Lochy   **12**

Fort William   Blair Atholl

Aberfeldy   Pitlochry
78   Dunkeld
Killin   **7**   Dundee
77
Taynuilt   **A**   **13**   Perth   Le
Oban   Aberfoyle   Callander   St A
1
Loch   **7**   **8**   Stirling
Lomond   Alloa   **16**   Kirkcaldy
Dumbarton   **3**   **17**   Dun
Greenock   **B**   **43**   Falkirk   Edinburgh
1   Paisley   **7** **5**   Musse
Tarbert   **2**   Glasgow   **4**   Dalkeith
Claonaig   Lochwinnoch   Airdrie   **6**
Ardrossan   Irvine   Bathgate   Penic
Lochranza   **73**   Kilmarnock   Hamilton
73   Brodick   Troon   **18**   Galas
Prestwick
Campbeltown   Ayr   Abington
Maybole
Ballycastle   **7**   **74**
15   Lockerbie
Stranraer   Dumfries   **7**
73   Gretna
Castle   Annan
Larne   Douglas
Newton   Gatehouse
Stewart   of Fleet
Belfast

Legend:

— National Cycle Network
— Selected traffic-free sections
▨ Network to be completed by 2005
⊙ Selected railway stations
— Regional Cycle Routes

Route numbers
1 National   **43** Regional

40 miles
60 km

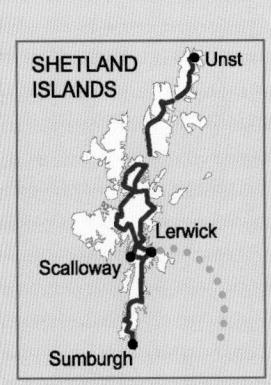

SHETLAND ISLANDS

Unst
Lerwick
Scalloway
Sumburgh

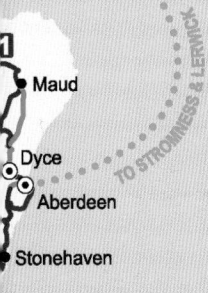

Maud
Dyce
Aberdeen
Stonehaven
ntrose
ath

Berwick-upon-Tweed

TO STROMNESS & LERWICK

Selected traffic-free paths

1. Johnstone - Greenock *14 miles*
2. Johnstone - Kilbirnie *11 miles*
3. (B) Glasgow - Loch Lomond *20 miles*
4. Airdrie - Bathgate Railway Path *15 miles*
5. Edinburgh Urban Railway Paths *15 miles*
6. Dalkeith - Penicuik Railway Path *15 miles*
7. Loch Katrine *10 miles*
8. Aberfoyle - Callander - Strathyre *23 miles*
9. Aviemore to Slochd *13 miles*
10. Formartine and Buchan Way *21 miles*
11. Kingussie - Newtonmore *2 miles*
12. Drumochter Pass *11 miles*
13. Glenogle *9 miles*
14. Irvine - Kilmarnock *9 miles*
15. Galloway Forest Park *20 miles*
16. Dunfermline - Alloa Railway Path *11 miles*
17. 43 Millennium Link *55 miles*
    (Glasgow - Edinburgh via canal towpaths)
18. Irvine - Troon - Prestwick
    several sections over 12 mile stretch

Day Rides ▬▬▬

(A) Callander - Loch Venacher - Balquhidder - Killin *24 miles*

(B) Glasgow - Loch Lomond *20 miles*

(C) Edinburgh - Forth Bridge *11 miles*

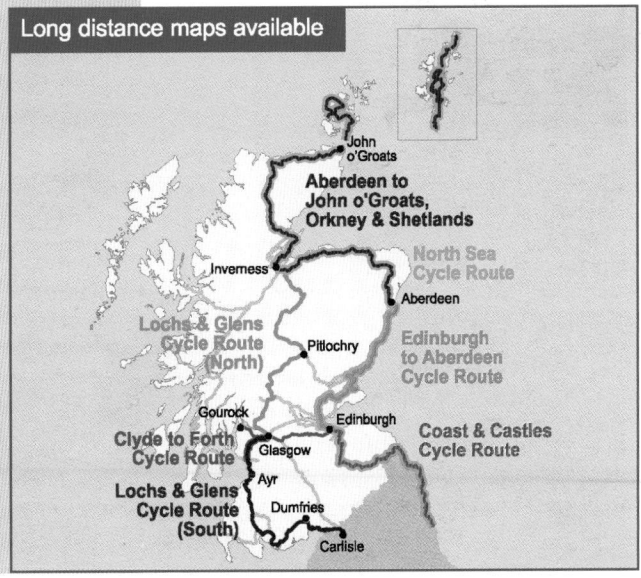

Long distance maps available

John o'Groats

Aberdeen to John o'Groats, Orkney & Shetlands

North Sea Cycle Route

Inverness

Aberdeen

Lochs & Glens Cycle Route (North)

Pitlochry

Edinburgh to Aberdeen Cycle Route

Gourock

Edinburgh

Clyde to Forth Cycle Route

Glasgow

Coast & Castles Cycle Route

Ayr

Lochs & Glens Cycle Route (South)

Dumfries

Carlisle

SCOTLAND

Loch Achray in the Trossachs.

Scotland is the most mountainous and spectacular region in the United Kingdom, and the National Cycle Network enables you to explore the area on a mixture of forestry tracks, paths alongside rivers and lochs, dismantled railways and quiet roads. The population of Scotland is concentrated in the Glasgow-Edinburgh corridor: outside this narrow strip lies one of the least densely populated areas of Europe, ideal for exploration by bike. Fewer people means fewer cars, and for anyone arriving here from the more densely populated parts of Britain there is a very pleasant surprise in store - many roads carry so little traffic that you can plan quiet, safe rides on B-roads and in some cases even on A-roads, except in the peak holiday period.

Sustrans' work started many years ago in Scotland and there are several traffic-free routes around Glasgow that date back to the 1980s, including the Glasgow to Loch Lomond route which is featured as a Day Ride (see page 186). The Lochs & Glens Cycle Route (from Carlisle to Inverness) was opened in 1995 and makes good use of many of these traffic-free routes. The Clyde to Forth Route crosses the country from the architectural masterpieces of Edinburgh to the vibrant atmosphere of Glasgow.

NATIONAL CYCLE NETWORK HIGHLIGHTS

Arran Ferry
A highlight of many journeys will be the ferry trips. The Arran ferry, shown here, can readily be reached from the Glasgow and Ayr cycle route at Ardrossan. The crossing leads to Brodick, and then you could take the Lochranza ferry to Kintyre.

Bell's Bridge, Glasgow
This key link across the Clyde was built for the Glasgow Garden Festival. It now leads to the Scottish Exhibition & Conference Centre and is becoming the centrepiece of redevelopment of the area.

Sluggan Bridge, near Aviemore
On the new offroad routes you'll find Sluggan Bridge standing in splendid isolation across the River Dulnain. The bridge was built 1729-30 on General Wade's military road to Inverness, substantially rebuilt 1830-40 and restored in 2001.

Kintyre to Oban
A view over Loch Sween and the Sound of Jura near Kilmory. Once away from the cities, Scotland abounds with spectacular open views which are a memorable part of every cyclist's journey through the Highlands and Islands.

Queen Elizabeth Forest Park
The Trossachs are close to Glasgow and provide wonderful wild countryside. The National Cycle Route follows forest roads from Aberfoyle, lochside paths past Achray and Venachar and the former main line railway to Oban from Callander to the Falls of Leny and eventually Glen Ogle – all marvellous!

John o'Groats
The culmination of many a challenge cycle ride from Land's End and elsewhere. The launch of the National Cycle Network was preceded by a Trailblazing Ride from John o'Groats to Dover during which support was pledged by each local authority along the course of the route. Catch the ferry to Orkney and keep cycling!

NATIONAL CYCLE NETWORK HIGHLIGHTS

Troon - Prestwick

This link has been some years in the making, and was finally completed in 2001, when it became instantly popular. This part of Scotland has quite high levels of cycle use, and through the National Cycle Network we expect many more people to be encouraged to cycle again.

Annan Bridge

This is just one of a series of fine new bridges built by Dumfries & Galloway to provide key links in the National Cycle Network.

Perth Sculpture Trail

The Sculpture Park is just a short detour from Route 77 and there is a long term plan to build a cycle bridge across the River Tay to link directly into the Park. Definitely worth taking a wander around.

Doon Bridge

This bridge takes the National Route southwards out of Ayr. The line of the railway to Heads of Ayr and Culzean has proved impossible to negotiate, although it could one day be developed to become one of Scotland's most spectacular routes.

Kingussie - Newtonmore

This is without doubt Scotland's premier section of new cycle track - smooth, continuous and set well back from the main road. It links the two villages for schools, shopping and all manner of everyday trips.

Millennium Link

This marvellous Millennium Project has re-opened the canal from coast to coast, with a new link into the Forth at Grangemouth. In addition to the construction of the modern boat lift, the towpath has been rebuilt to make an excellent cycle route.

CITY FOCUS

Maps & guides are available from National Cycle Network Information unless indicated otherwise. See page 185 for contact details.

Glasgow

The Clyde to Forth and *Lochs & Glens Maps*. Glasgow is a hub of the Network. Route 7 runs southwest from Bell's Bridge to Paisley where it joins a traffic-free route to Kilbirnie; to the northwest it follows a railway path through Partick, then the Forth & Clyde Canal through Clydebank towards Dumbarton. Route 75 runs west to east from Greenock to join Route 7 at Johnstone. To the east of Bell's Bridge it follows the course of the Clyde Walkway through Rutherglen towards Uddingston.

Glasgow CycleCity Map.

A-Z style map showing traffic-free, official and advisory routes, with plenty of extra information about cycle shops, cycling contacts, train services and relevant local publications. Covers the area bordered by Clydebank, Kirkintilloch, Newton and Barrhead. RC02 - £4.95

Edinburgh

The Clyde to Forth Cycle Route Map, The Coast & Castles Map and *The Edinburgh to Aberdeen Map.* Edinburgh is at the junction of Routes 1 and 75. Route 1, the Coast & Castles Route, enters the city along the Innocent Railway beneath Arthur's Seat and heads west through the city centre towards Queensferry and the Forth Road Bridge. Route 75 runs west alongside the Union Canal and east through the New Town to Leith.

SPOKES Edinburgh Cycle Map

(6th Edition) is an excellent street map covering the area between Musselburgh, Cramond, Balerno and Danderhall. On the reverse are maps showing recreational routes in Fife, Lothian and the Borders plus details of other publications and a list of bike shops. RPL05 - £4.95

SPOKES West Lothian Map

shows Route 75 and suggested routes in West Lothian, centred on Livingston. On the reverse are insets of Linlithgow, Winchburgh, Broxburn/ Uphall plus a wealth of useful information for cyclists. RPL65 - £4.95

SPOKES Midlothian Map

shows the Network and suggested routes to the south of Edinburgh, with insets for Dalkieth, Penicuik, Gorebridge and Bonnyrigg. RPL20 - £4.95

Aberdeen

The Aberdeen to John o'Groats Map and *The Edinburgh to Aberdeen Map* have insets showing Route 1 in Aberdeen. The route heads north to Dyce where it joins the traffic-free Formartine & Buchan Way. To the south Route 1 hugs the coast past the lighthouse and Nigg Bay to Findon. The southern map also shows the traffic-free Old Deeside Line which starts in Duthie Park Gardens.

NN7C - £5.99

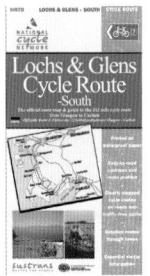

NN7B - £5.99

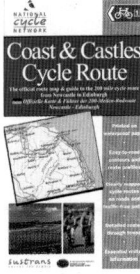

NN1C - £5.99

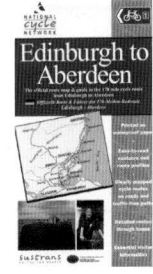

NN1D - £5.99

NN1E - £5.99

NN75 - £5.99

TRAFFIC-FREE PATHS PARTICULARLY SUITABLE FOR FAMILIES

7 🚲 Glen Ogle. 11 miles

This spectacular route follows General Wade's military road, then runs through birchwoods to join the Lochearnhead Branch. The route climbs 300ft for spectacular views over Loch Earn to join the former Callander Oban Railway, running on a ledge high above the valley floor. From the summit the route drops down to Killin on forestry tracks.

75 🚲 Airdrie & Bathgate railway path 14 miles

This trail across Scotland's central plateau follows the course of the old Airdrie and Bathgate Junction Railway which used to carry coal, ironstone and limestone. Many interesting sculptures have been erected along its course.

75 🚲 Johnstone to Greenock. 13 miles

This western section of the Clyde to Forth Cycle Route follows a railway path from Johnstone through Bridge of Weir and Kilmacolm to Greenock. The views from above Port Glasgow northwards across the Firth of Clyde to Ben Lomond and the Arrochs are stunning.

7 🚲 Aviemore to Boat of Garten 4 miles

This track quickly takes you out into wide open heather moors, seemingly miles from anywhere. At Boat of Garten, you have the chance of returning on the Speyside Railway, or continuing on forest tracks to Carrbridge, ending your trip at the newly restored Sluggan Bridge.

1 🚲 Dalkeith to Penicuik. 8 miles

The longest of the dismantled railways close to Edinburgh is also the most scenic, passing through many beautiful wooded cuttings and alongside the tumbling waters of the River North Esk. The trail runs south west from Eskbank (Dalkeith) to Penicuik.

1 🚲 Formartine and Buchan Way 30 miles

The trail follows the course of the old Great North of Scotland Railway from Aberdeen (Dyce) to Peterhead and Fraserburgh, which ran from 1865 to 1965. There are fine views of the mountains of Donside and Deeside including such famous ones as Bennachie and Lochnagar.

USEFUL MAPS & GUIDES

For details of the full range of maps, guides and other products available contact: **National Cycle Network Information, PO Box 21, Bristol BS99 2HA. Tel: 0117 929 0888. Or visit www.nationalcyclenetwork.org.uk** The range of National Cycle Network Maps is described in more detail on pages 218-237.

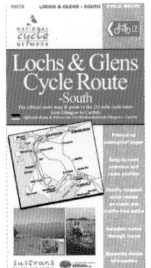  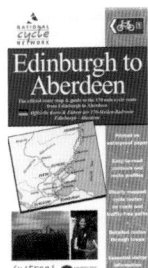  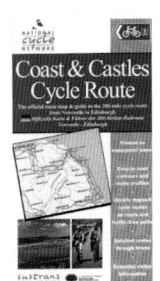 

7 *Lochs & Glens Cycle Route - South (Glasgow – Carlisle)* 212 miles. NN7B - £5.99

7 *Lochs & Glens Cycle Route - North (Inverness – Glasgow)* 214 miles. NN7C - £5.99

1 *Edinburgh – Aberdeen Cycle Route.* 170 miles. NN1D - £5.99

1 *Aberdeen – John o'Groats* 320 miles + Orkney/Shetland NN1E - £5.99

1 *Coast & Castles Cycle Route (Newcastle – Edinburgh)* 200 miles. NN1C - £5.99

75 *Clyde – Forth Cycle Route (Glasgow – Edinburgh)* 86 miles. NN75 - £5.99

In Scotland: The National Cycle Network Comprehensive guide to the Network in Scotland with details of routes currently open, mapping, direction tips and accommodation. RG98 - £9.99

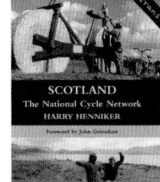

73 *The Isles & Highlands of Western Scotland* A guide to four outstanding circular tours from Arran to Cape Wrath and the major Hebridean Islands. RPL75 - £9.95

1 *The Border Loop Cycle Map* Stirling Survey Map covering 250-mile signposted route around the glorious Scottish Borders. RPR15 - £4.50

Ardrossan – Campbeltown Leaflet This stunning coastal section of National Route 73 takes in the Isle of Arran. RPN07 - £1.00

Douglas – Kettleholm Leaflet Covers this 42-mile section of Route 74. RPN01 - £1.00

1 *The Kingdom of Fife* Detailed map with directions describing over 100 miles of safe, signed routes circling the area between the Forth Bridge and the Firth of Tay RPL64 - £4.90

1 *The North Sea Cycle Route* A magnificent and visionary cross-border 3600-mile route linking Scandinavia, Germany, Holland Belgium and the UK. Available from Hull Tourist Information Centre, Tel: 01482 223559, or from Sustrans.

GLASGOW TO LOCH LOMOND

This ride out of Scotland's largest city starts from the Scottish Exhibition & Conference Centre, an important National Cycle Network junction of the Clyde to Forth Route (Route 75) and the Lochs & Glens Cycle Route (Route 7). Standing here one has the sense of Glasgow re-inventing itself: all around are new buildings with just the occasional one dating back to previous generations. After a short spell on a cycle path alongside the busy A814 you join a railway path, a green corridor through first an industrial, then a residential setting with many older buildings of red or yellow sandstone.

You pass John Brown's shipyard in the centre of Clydebank, where the great ships the *Queen Mary*, *Queen Elizabeth* and *Queen Elizabeth II* were built. Beyond Clydebank, the route joins the Forth & Clyde Canal on a broad, well-maintained towpath. The canal, built in 1790, and now reopened to boats, was the main route across Scotland linking the Clyde at Bowling, west of Glasgow, with the Forth at Grangemouth.

The ride becomes more open with green views of the Kilpatrick Hills behind Erskine Bridge. A second railway path starting at the end of the canal takes you through woodland and rocky outcrops to the outkirts of Dumbarton, the ancient fortress-capital of the Kingdom of Strathclyde. The route through Dumbarton is on quiet roads and soon you join the waterside path alongside the River Leven which leads to Balloch and the banks of Loch Lomond. It is worth stopping to read the information boards along the river with interesting background detail about the history and wildlife of the riverside.

The River Leven approaching Balloch.

Starting points

The Scottish Exhibition &
Conference Centre near Bell's
Bridge in the centre of Glasgow.

Distance

20 miles one way, 40 miles return.
For shorter rides there are good
turnaround points at the cafe at
Bowling Basin (20 miles round
trip) or Dumbarton (28 miles round
trip). There are railway stations
along the route if you wish to catch
the train back.

Grade

Easy.

Surface

A mixture of tarmac and gravel
paths.

Roads, traffic, suitability for young children

The route is traffic-free apart from
the section through Dumbarton
where quiet streets are used. There
are several road crossings, mostly
via toucan crossings or traffic
islands. The best sections for
children are the Forth & Clyde
Canal towpath between Clydebank
and Bowling and the stretch
alongside the River Leven north
from Dumbarton to Balloch.

Hills

None.

Refreshments

There is a cafe by the bike shop in
Bowling at the end of the canal
towpath.
Plenty of choice in Dumbarton
and Balloch.

Leaflets

*CycleCity's Glasgow Cycling Map
– City Centre and Suburbs* is an
excellent publication showing the
traffic-free paths, signposted cycle
routes, advisory routes plus a
wealth of other information. It costs
£4.95 and is available from Sustrans

Information Service, PO Box 21,
Bristol BS99 2HA. Tel: 0117 929
0888 or visit www.sustrans.org.uk

Nearest railway stations

There are stations along the route
from the Exhibition Centre in
Glasgow at the start to Balloch at
the end of the ride.

The National Cycle Network in the area

Glasgow is a hub of the National
Cycle Network: Route 7 runs north-
south from Inverness to Carlisle;
Route 75 (the Clyde to Forth Cycle
Route) runs west-east from Gourock
to Leith.

*Forth & Clyde Canal approaching
Erskine Bridge.*

Other nearby rides (waymarked or traffic-free)

1. Johnstone to Kilbirnie railway
path.
2. Johnstone to Greenock railway
path.
3. Airdrie to Bathgate railway path.
4. Clyde Walkway to the east of
Glasgow Green.
5. Forth & Clyde Canal.

Railway path near Clyde tunnel.

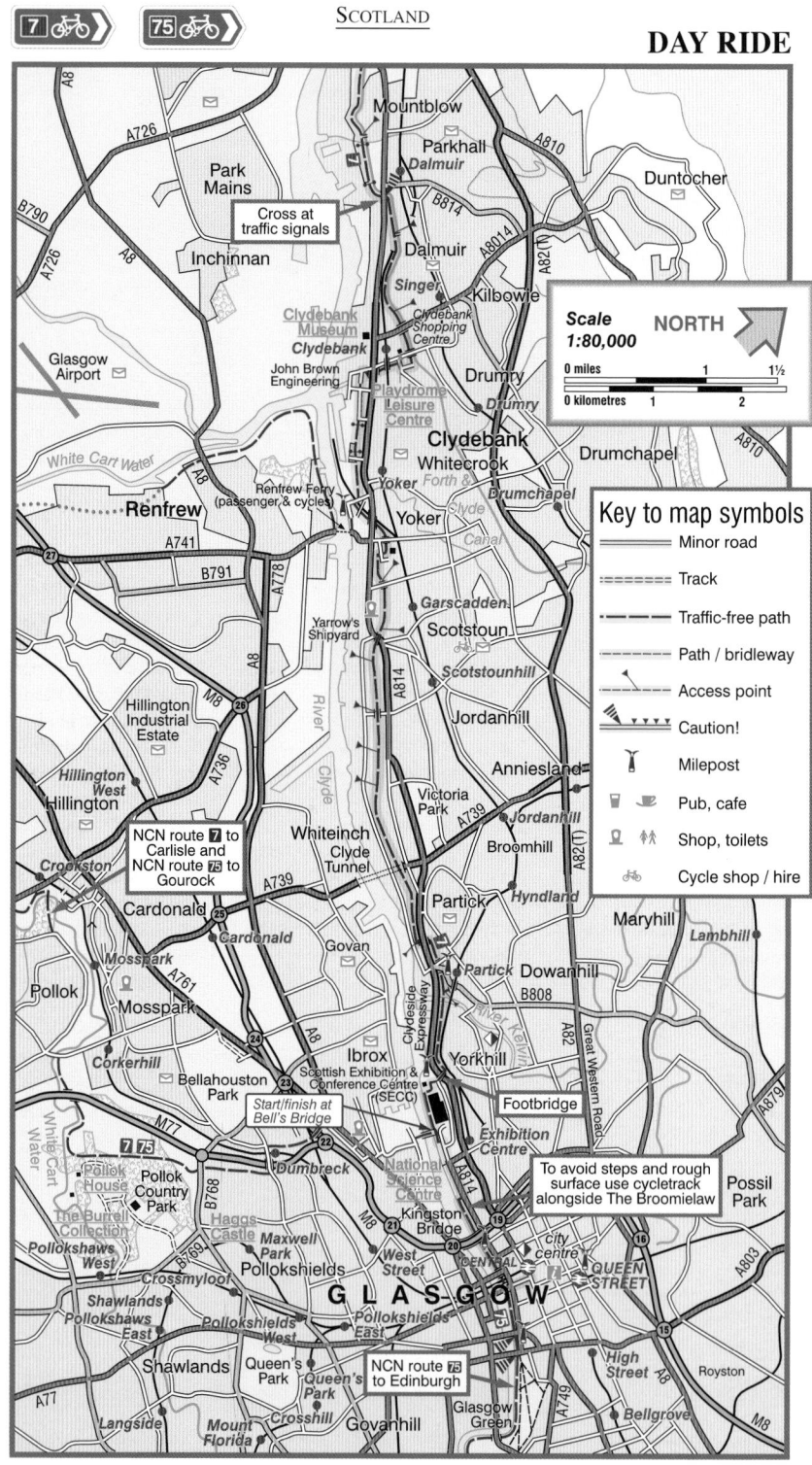

GLASGOW TO LOCH LOMOND

Cross at traffic signals

Scale
1:80,000

NORTH

0 miles 1 1½
0 kilometres 1 2

Key to map symbols

Minor road
Track
Traffic-free path
Path / bridleway
Access point
Caution!
Milepost
Pub, cafe
Shop, toilets
Cycle shop / hire

NCN route 7 to Carlisle and NCN route 75 to Gourock

Start/finish at Bell's Bridge

Footbridge

To avoid steps and rough surface use cycletrack alongside The Broomielaw

NCN route 75 to Edinburgh

Route instructions from Glasgow to Loch Lomond

The railway path through Whiteinch provides elevated green space through Glasgow.

1. From the Scottish Exhibition & Conference Centre in the centre of Glasgow, follow the paved promenade, with the river to your left. Follow the perimeter fence of the heliport, turn left onto Stobcross Road, cross the Clydeside Expressway via the footbridge then turn sharp left for the Glasgow to Loch Lomond Cycleway.

2. Follow the cycle path parallel to the Expressway. Shortly after passing the old red-brick Partick Fire Station, turn left into a subway, then right in the subway to join the railway path.

3. After three miles, at the end of the railway path turn right by a discount store and continue in the same direction towards Brown Engineering.

4. At Brown Engineering turn right to go through a subway, cross Stanford Street at the signals, then turn right and immediately left to join the towpath of the Forth & Clyde Canal.

Approaching Bowling on the Forth & Clyde Canal towpath with the Kilpatrick Hills in the background.

GLASGOW TO LOCH LOMOND

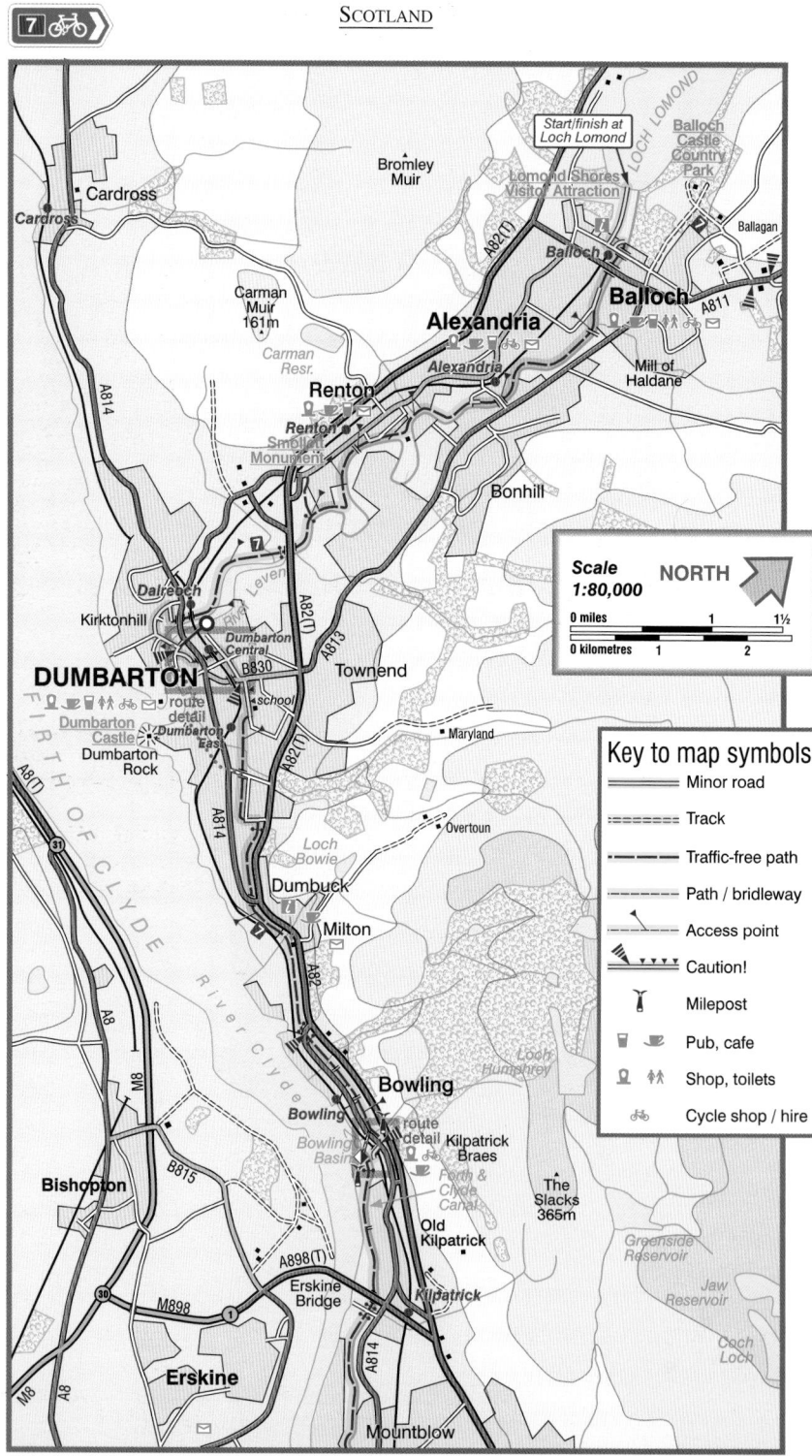

Start/finish at
Loch Lomond

LOCH LOMOND

Balloch
Castle
Country
Park

Lomond Shores
Visitor Attraction

Ballagan

Bromley
Muir

Cardross

Carman
Muir
161m

Balloch

Balloch

A82(T)

A811

Carman
Resr.

Alexandria

Mill of
Haldane

Renton

Alexandria

A814

Renton
Smollett
Monument

Bonhill

**Scale
1:80,000**

NORTH

0 miles		1	1½

0 kilometres	1		2

A82(T)

7

Dalreoch

Leven

Kirktonhill

A82(T)

Dumbarton
Central

Townend

A813

DUMBARTON

route
detail

B830

school

Maryland

**Dumbarton
Castle**
Dumbarton
Rock

Dumbarton
East

FIRTH OF CLYDE

A814

Loch
Bowie

Overtoun

51

Dumbuck

A8

M8

Milton

River Clyde

A82

Loch
Humphrey

Bowling

A814

Key to map symbols

━━━━	Minor road
════	Track
━ ━ ━	Traffic-free path
─ ─ ─	Path / bridleway
⊣	Access point
▼▼▼▼	Caution!
👤	Milepost
🥤 ☕	Pub, cafe
🛍 🚻	Shop, toilets
🚲	Cycle shop / hire

Bishopton

B815

Bowling

route
detail

Kilpatrick
Braes

Bowling
Basin

Forth &
Clyde
Canal

The
Slacks
365m

Greenside
Reservoir

Old
Kilpatrick

B815

30

M898

A8

M8

A898(T)

7

Erskine
Bridge

Kilpatrick

Jaw
Reservoir

Erskine

A814

Loch
Loch

Mountblow

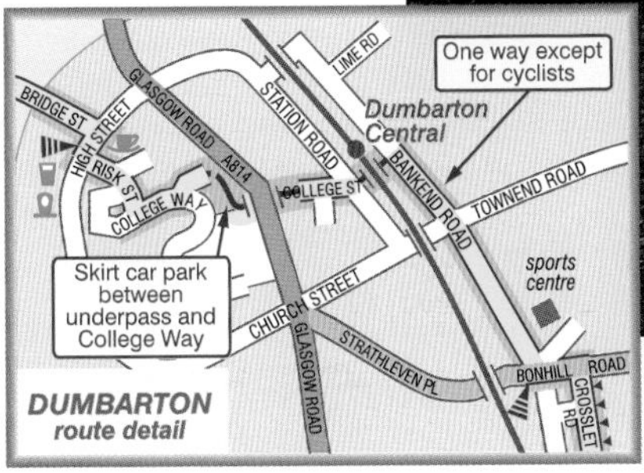

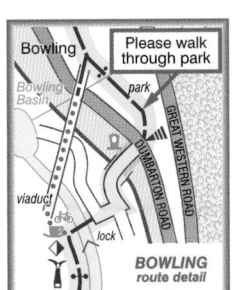

Bowling Tunnel.

5. Follow the canal through the Shopping Centre at Clydebank.

6. After four miles, at a large metal bridge over the canal by a bike hire outlet and small marina, turn right uphill, cross the road then turn left through the park onto a disused railway path.

7. Follow the railway path section for 2½ miles through woodland and exposed rocks. At the T-junction with Third Avenue on the outskirts of Dumbarton turn left and follow the excellent signposting for two miles through Dumbarton to the banks of the River Leven. (Follow the inset mapping.)

8. Join the path along the banks of River Leven and follow this for five miles to Balloch.

9. Cross the bridge and turn left into Balloch Castle Country Park to reach the shores of Loch Lomond.

The start of the River Leven route from Dumbarton to Loch Lomond.

CALLANDER TO KILLIN VIA BALQUHIDDER OR TO LOCH VENACHAR

A most spectacular setting of lochs and mountains forms the backdrop to these two rides north and south from the holiday centre of Callander. The ride north as far as Balquhidder runs along the course of the old Caledonian railway line which until 1965 used to run from Callander to Oban. Passing through broadleaf woodland alongside the swift waters and spectacular falls of the River Leny, the ride runs a parallel course to the A84 through the Pass of Leny, known as the entrance to the Highlands. There are fine views of Ben Ledi where it is said that 2,000 years ago the Druids lit fires at the top to celebrate the changing of the seasons. A quiet road is followed from the end of Loch Lubnaig to Balquhidder, where you may wish to visit Rob Roy's grave. You may wish to continue through the spectacular Glen Ogle to Killin and Loch Tay. This new route follows the old military road and the two disused railways which used to traverse the glen. Two listed viaducts are crossed, one of which has a fine new bridge span. There are excellent views of Loch Earn in places.

The shorter southern ride follows the shores of Loch Venachar past splendid isolated houses set above the water's edge, with views across to the mighty shape of Ben Ledi. You may well see colourful dinghies and windsurfers on the water. The loch ends at Blackwater Marshes, a Site of Special Scientific Interest. There are reeds, willow, birch trees and patches of bog myrtle. This special combination of plants and water provides home and food for Greylag Geese, Goosanders, Teal and Wigeons. The open territory is also excellent for birds of prey.

A short section on forest roads takes you to the refreshment stop/turnaround point at Brig o'Turk.

Falls of Leny on an ancient military road.

Starting point

The centre of Callander.

Distance

(a) Callander to Balquhidder
13 miles.
(b) Balquhidder to Killin
13 miles.
(c) Callander to Brig o' Turk
eight miles.

Grade

Moderate.

Surface

Mixture of tarmac and stone-based tracks. There are rougher sections at the north end of Loch Lubnaig and going into Killin.

Roads, traffic, suitability for young children

(a) Callander-Balquhidder. A traffic-free path starts from the Meadows car park in Callander. There may be a little traffic along the road serving the holiday chalets at the southern end of Loch Lubnaig. A very quiet road is used between Strathyre and Balquhidder. There is considerable holiday traffic between Balquhidder and Kinghouse. Take extreme care crossing the trunk road at Glenoglehead.

(b) Callander-Loch Venachar. There is a short section (½ mile) on the A81 south from the centre of Callander where care should be taken. You then join the minor road to Invertrossachs, which carries very little traffic. There is a three mile cycle path/forestry track between Invertrossachs and Brig o'Turk.

Hills

(a) Callander-Strathyre. There is a steady 200 ft climb from Callander past the Falls of Leny up to Loch Lubnaig. There are several other short climbs, including a steep one up a series of zig zags at the north end of Loch Lubnaig (fantastic views!).
(b) Balquhidder to Killin. There is a very steep climb from Lochearnhead to Glenogle, and a steep descent from Glenoglehead.
(c) Callander-Brig o'Turk. Generally rolling with the occasional short steep climb.

Refreshments

(a) Lots of choice in Callander.
(b) Cafe and pubs in Strathyre.
(c) Teashop at the museum in Stronvar just south of Balquhidder.
(d) The Byre Inn at Brig o'Turk.
(e) Lots of choice in Lochearnhead.
(f) Lots of choice in Killin.

Nearest railway station

The nearest is at Dunblane
(12 miles to the east).

The National Cycle Network in the area

1. From Killin, Route 7 follows Loch Tay, Pitlochry, Aviemore and Inverness.
2. To the south of Loch Venachar, Route 7 crosses the Dukes Pass via forestry tracks then passes through Aberfoyle and Drymen on its way to Loch Lomond and Glasgow (see page 186).

Other nearby rides (waymarked or traffic-free)

1. There are plenty of forest routes in Queen Elizabeth Forest Park (maps from Tourist Information Centres or the Visitor Centre north of Aberfoyle).
2. There is also a delightful ride on a traffic-free Water Board road along the northern side of Loch Katrine which can be continued on a minor road as far as Loch Lomond or Aberfoyle.

Southside Loch Venachar avoiding the main Dukes Road.

CALLANDER TO KILLIN OR TO LOCH VENACHAR

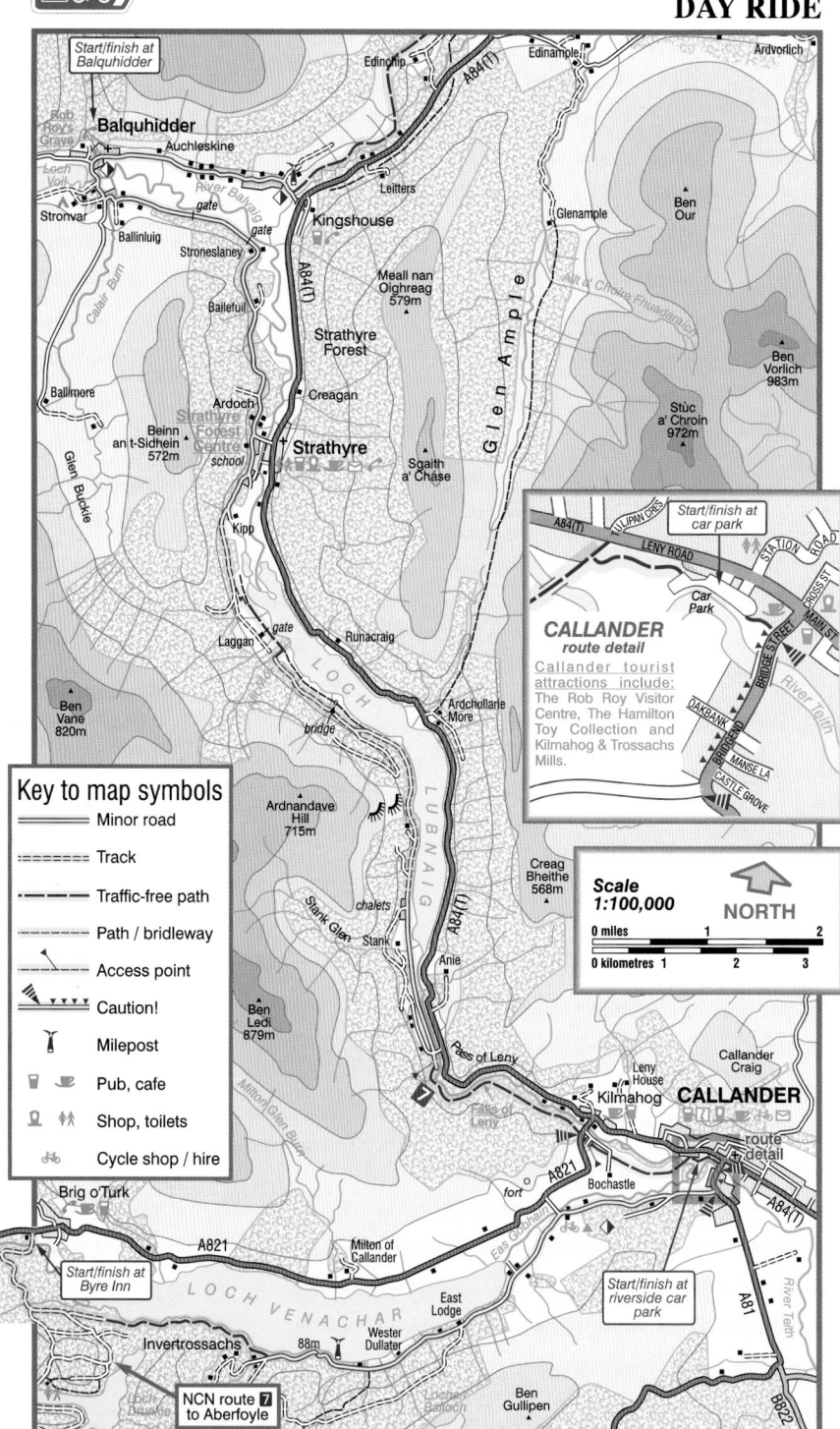

Start/finish at Balquhidder

Rob Roy's Grave
Balquhidder
Auchleskine
Edinchip
A84(T)
Edinample
Ardvorlich

Loch Voil
Stronvar
Ballinluig
River Balvaig
Kingshouse
Leitters
Glenample
Ben Our

Stroneslaney
Baileful
gate
gate
A84(T)
Meall nan Oighreag 579m

Cabar Barn
Strathyre Forest
Glen Ample
Allt a' Choire Fhuadaraich
Ben Vorlich 983m

Ballimore
Creagan
Ardoch
Strathyre Forest Centre
school
Strathyre
Sgaith a' Chaise
Stùc a' Chroin 972m

Beinn an t-Sidhein 572m
Glen Buckie

Kipp

Laggan
gate
Runacraig
LOCH

Ardchullarie More

Ben Vane 820m
bridge
LUBNAIG

Ardnandave Hill 715m
chalets
Creag Bheithe 568m

Scale
1:100,000
0 miles 1 2
0 kilometres 1 2 3
NORTH

Stank Glen
Stank

Ben Ledi 879m
Anie

Key to map symbols

— Minor road
===== Track
—·—· Traffic-free path
········ Path / bridleway
▲ Access point
▼▼▼▼ Caution!
⚲ Milepost
🍺 ☕ Pub, cafe
♒ 👫 Shop, toilets
🚲 Cycle shop / hire

Pass of Leny

CALLANDER route detail
Callander tourist attractions include: The Rob Roy Visitor Centre, The Hamilton Toy Collection and Kilmahog & Trossachs Mills.

Start/finish at car park
A84(T)
TULLIPAN CRES
LENY ROAD
STATION ROAD
Car Park
CROSS ST
MAIN ST
OAKBANK RD
BRIDGE STREET
River Teith
MANSE LA
BRIDGEND
CASTLE GROVE

Leny House
Kilmahog
Callander Craig

CALLANDER
route detail

Falls of Leny
Milton Glen Burn

Brig o'Turk

A821
A821
fort
Bochastle

Start/finish at riverside car park
A84(T)

Start/finish at Byre Inn
Milton of Callander
Eas Gobhain
A81
River Teith

LOCH VENACHAR
East Lodge
Wester Dullater
88m

Invertrossachs
Lochan Balloch
Ben Gullipen

Loch Drunkie
NCN route 7 to Aberfoyle
B8022

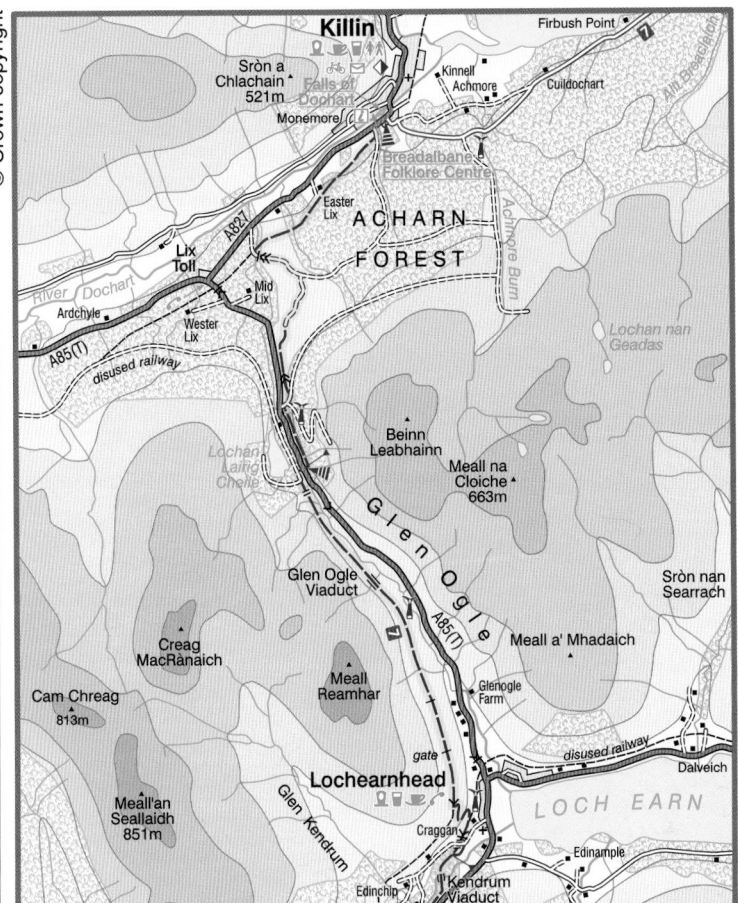

8. After crossing the new bridge over the Kendrum Burn, there is a link to the right leading to Lochearnhead. Then the path zig-zags steeply uphill with fine views over Loch Earn.

9. Cross the Glen Ogle viaduct to Glenoglehead. Take care crossing the trunk road. Follow the path into the car park.

10. Go through the gate and follow a new path steeply downhill to join forest tracks leading through Acharn Forest. Just before the A827 turn sharp right onto the disused railway which leads down to Killin. Return to Callander the same way.

B. Callander along the banks of Loch Venachar to Brig o'Turk

1. From the centre of Callander follow the A81 towards Glasgow for ½ mile, crossing the river bridge. Near the end of Callander, on a sharp left bend, turn right for 'Invertrossachs'.

2. Follow signs for Invertrossachs and Aberfoyle for 5 miles along this road.

3. At a 'Private Road. No cycling' sign ahead, bear right off the tarmac road onto a gravel path 'Aberfoyle'.

4. Follow this lochside path for 2 miles. At a T-junction with a wider forestry path turn right (or left for Aberfoyle). **Remember this point for your return.**

5. Keep bearing right, ignoring two turns to the left. At the major T-junction with 'Forest Drive' signposted to the left, turn right and go past Achray Farm to the Byre Inn at Brig o'Turk.

Route instructions:
A. From Callander to Balquhidder and on to Killin via Glen Ogle

1. From the western end of the Meadows car park in Callander, follow the cyclepath across the park signposted 'Balquhidder, Strathyre' to join the railway path.

2. Cross the river and after 1 mile cross the road (A821). **CARE!** Climb steadily beside the beautiful river.

3. The track turns to tarmac. Where the road forks take the right-hand branch, staying close to the water. The tarmac turns back to track at the end of the cabins.

4. After 2 miles bear left uphill then right following signs for 'Strathyre'.

5. The path descends to rejoin the railway path then shortly climbs again on a steep section of zig zags. At the T-junction with the forest road turn right. **Remember this point for your return trip.**

6. The track turns to tarmac. Follow this beautiful, narrow road for 5 miles through woodland to the junction in Balquhidder. Turn right onto the unclassified road to Kingshouse.

7. Just before the underpass, turn left onto the offroad path using the old military road towards Lochearnhead.

EDINBURGH TO THE FORTH BRIDGE

Riding across the Forth Road Bridge must be one of the most extraordinary cycling experiences in Scotland. Hundreds of feet above the waters of the Firth of Forth, with views to the east of the magnificent Forth Rail Bridge (the one where, as the saying goes, they start painting at one end the moment they have stopped at the other!) cyclists can cross from South Queensferry to North Queensferry in complete traffic-free safety along the cycle lanes that run either side of the bridge. The ride out from central Edinburgh uses a mixture of bus lanes, shared-use pavements, railway paths and quiet roads through Barnton, Davidson's Mains and over the lovely old Cramond Brig to cross the River Almond. You use quiet streets and new paths through Queensferry, named after Queen Margaret who used the ferry to cross the Forth in the 11th century. After crossing the bridge you have the choice of returning or dropping down into North Queensferry for refreshments, a visit to Deep Sea World and a train trip back to Edinburgh across the Forth Rail Bridge.

The Forth Road Bridge cycle track carries Route 1 into Fife.

Starting point
Haymarket Station, Edinburgh.

Distance
11 miles one way, 22 miles return.

Grade
Easy.

Surface
Tarmac.

Roads, traffic, suitability for young children
Quiet streets from Haymarket station are used until the start of the railway path. Care should be taken on the roads and crossings in Dalmeny. If you decide to visit North Queensferry there is a road section from the cycle path on the bridge down to the village. The most exciting section for children is the crossing of the Forth Road Bridge itself which has traffic-free cycle lanes on both sides.

Hills
Rolling.

Refreshments
Albert Hotel, Ferrybridge Hotel, Post Office Cafe, North Queensferry.
Cramond Brig Pub, Cramond.
The tearoom in Dalmeny House is open on Sunday, Monday and Tuesday afternoons in July and August.
The Forth Bridges Hotel, South Queensferry.
Various choices in South Queensferry village.

Leaflets
An excellent large map showing all the cycle facilities in Edinburgh is produced by SPOKES, the Edinburgh cycle campaign group, and is available from the National Cycle Network Information Service, PO Box 21, Bristol BS99 2HA. Tel: 0117 929 0888. Or visit www.nationalcyclenetwork.org.uk

Nearest railway stations
Edinburgh Haymarket, Dalmeny and North Queensferry.

The National Cycle Network in the area
1. Route 75, the Clyde to Forth Cycle Route runs across Scotland from Gourock to Leith.
2. Route 1 northbound connects Edinburgh with St Andrews and Dundee and continues along the coast to Aberdeen and Inverness.
3. Route 1 southbound runs east to Dalkeith then south through the Scottish Borders to Berwick-upon-

Princes Street, Edinburgh.

Tweed to join the Coast and Castles Route which follows the coast down to Newcastle upon Tyne.

Other nearby rides (waymarked or traffic-free)
There are many traffic-free trails in or near Edinburgh such as the Innocent Railway Path, the Water of Leith, the Union Canal, plus several sections of railway path in North Edinburgh.

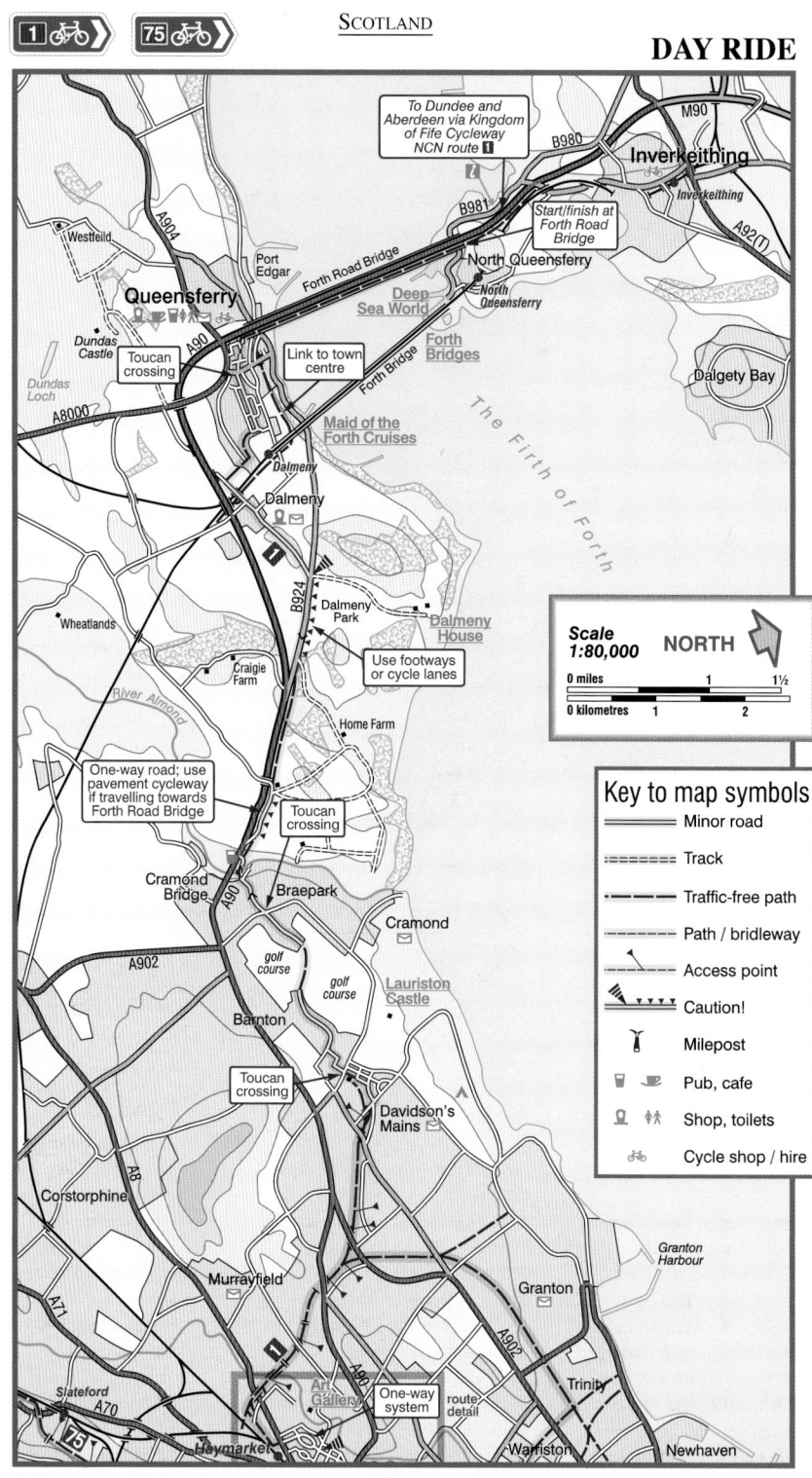

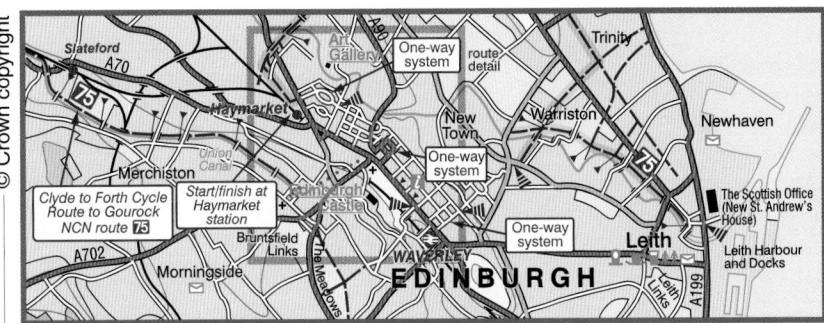

emerges onto Barnton Avenue West.

At the crossroads go straight ahead, using a toucan crossing, onto Brae Park Road signposted 'Cramond Brig, Queensferry'.

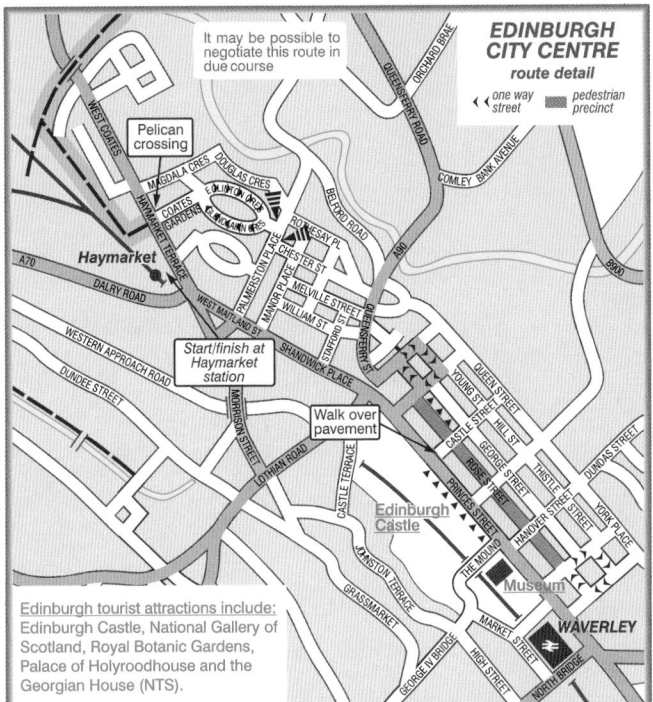

Edinburgh tourist attractions include: Edinburgh Castle, National Gallery of Scotland, Royal Botanic Gardens, Palace of Holyroodhouse and the Georgian House (NTS).

5. Cross the old bridge, climb, then immediately before the main road, turn right onto the pavement/cyclepath alongside the main road (A90).

6. Follow the same direction for two miles on the pavement along the one way road and the A90. Use the cycle lanes on the B924. Opposite the gates to Dalmeny House turn left to 'Dalmeny'.

7. At the end of Dalmeny village, at a sharp left-hand bend, bear right onto a no through road called The Glebe. Keep straight ahead and then turn right onto a steep path leading to Scotstown Road. Cross onto the opposite pavement. Turn right and follow signs past the high school to Rosebery Avenue. Turn left. At Kirkliston Road, use the toucan to cross and turn left into Viewforth Place, then Hugh Place, Ferrymuir Gate and onto the footway leading up to the Forth Road Bridge.

8. Alternatively, at the Glebe, follow the signs for South Queensferry onto the disused railway which leads to the village at the Scotmid Store. From here it is possible to access the bridge using Morrison Gardens. This brings you out under the bridge from where ramps lead up onto either of the cycleways.

9. Cross the Firth of Forth. At the end of the bridge return the way you came, or leave the bridge down steps and continue downhill for the pubs

Route instructions from Edinburgh to Forth Road Bridge

1. From Haymarket Station near the centre of Edinburgh turn left along the bus lane on Haymarket Terrace. Turn left into Haymarket Yards at Rosebery House. Follow the road through new offices onto a cycle track leading to Balbirnie Place. Follow the road around the housing near the railway line and turn left onto the disused railway. Follow this to the right.

2. Shortly, at the obvious fork of tracks (with Sainsbury's petrol station to the right) bear to the left.

3. At the second fork of tracks bear right and follow Silverknowes Drive and Terrace and at the right hand bend, a short path on the left leads to Cramond Road South. Cross into Barnton Avenue using a toucan crossing.

4. Go along Barnton Avenue. Ignore turnings as the road becomes a path then

Legend:
- National Cycle Network
- Selected traffic-free sections
- Network to be completed by 2005
- ⊙ Selected railway stations
- ⊙ Airport
- Route numbers
- 9 National

Carndonagh

Greencastle

Portstewart

Portrush

Giant's Causeway

B

Magilligan Point

Castlerock

3

4

Bushmills

2

B Coleraine

Ballymone

Limavady

Derry

96

Carrigans

Claudy

93

Portglenone

Strabane

92

Sperrins

Newtownstewart

Gortin

95

94

Cookstown

95

7

Omagh

Pettigoe

91

92

Fintona

Dungannon

9

Ballyshannon

6

95

Belleek

Lower Lough Erne

Portadown

91

Armagh

Enniskillen

8

Tynan

91

Upper Lough Erne

Clones

Ring of Gullion

91

Carrick-on-Shannon

20 miles

30 km

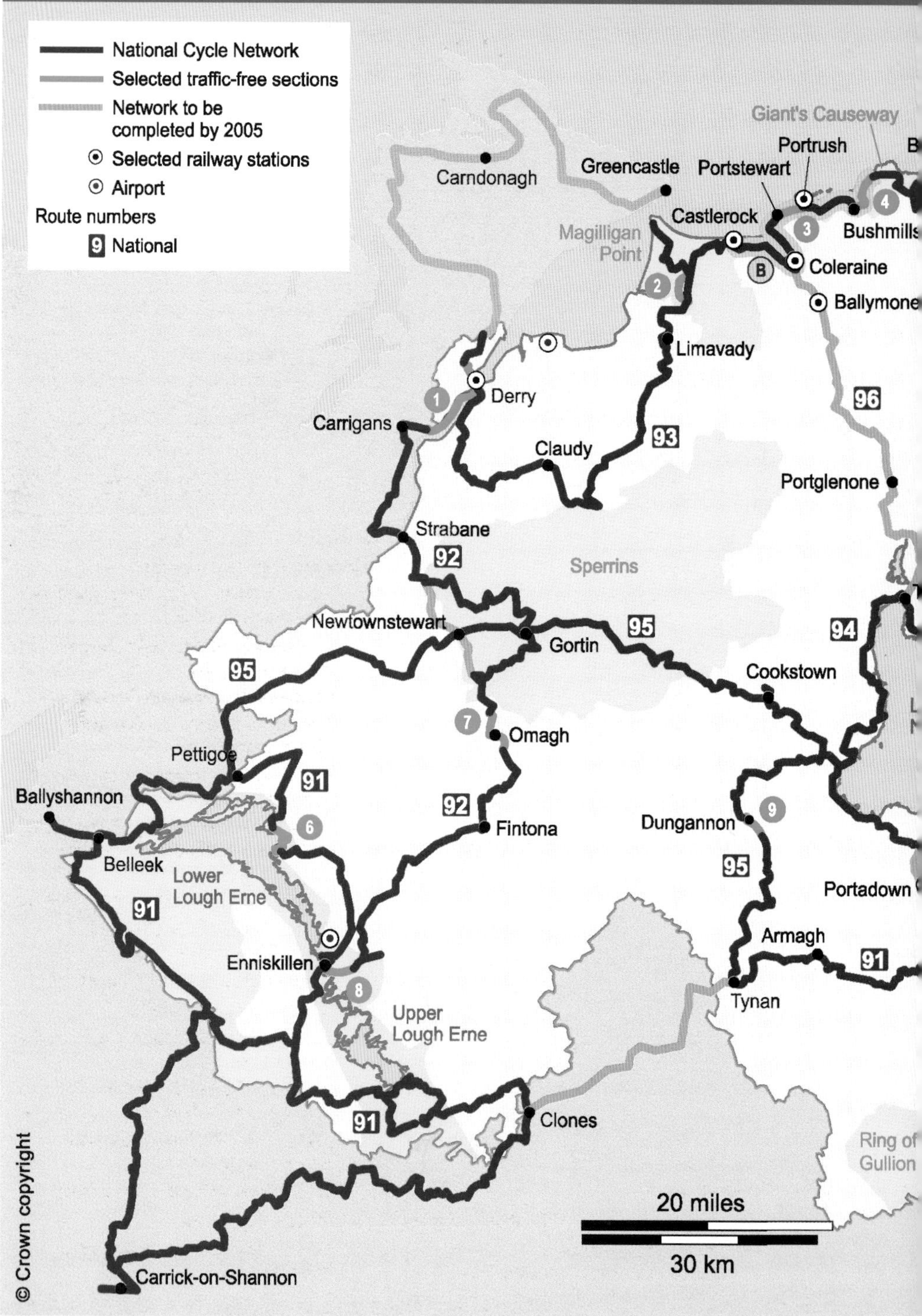

© Crown copyright

200

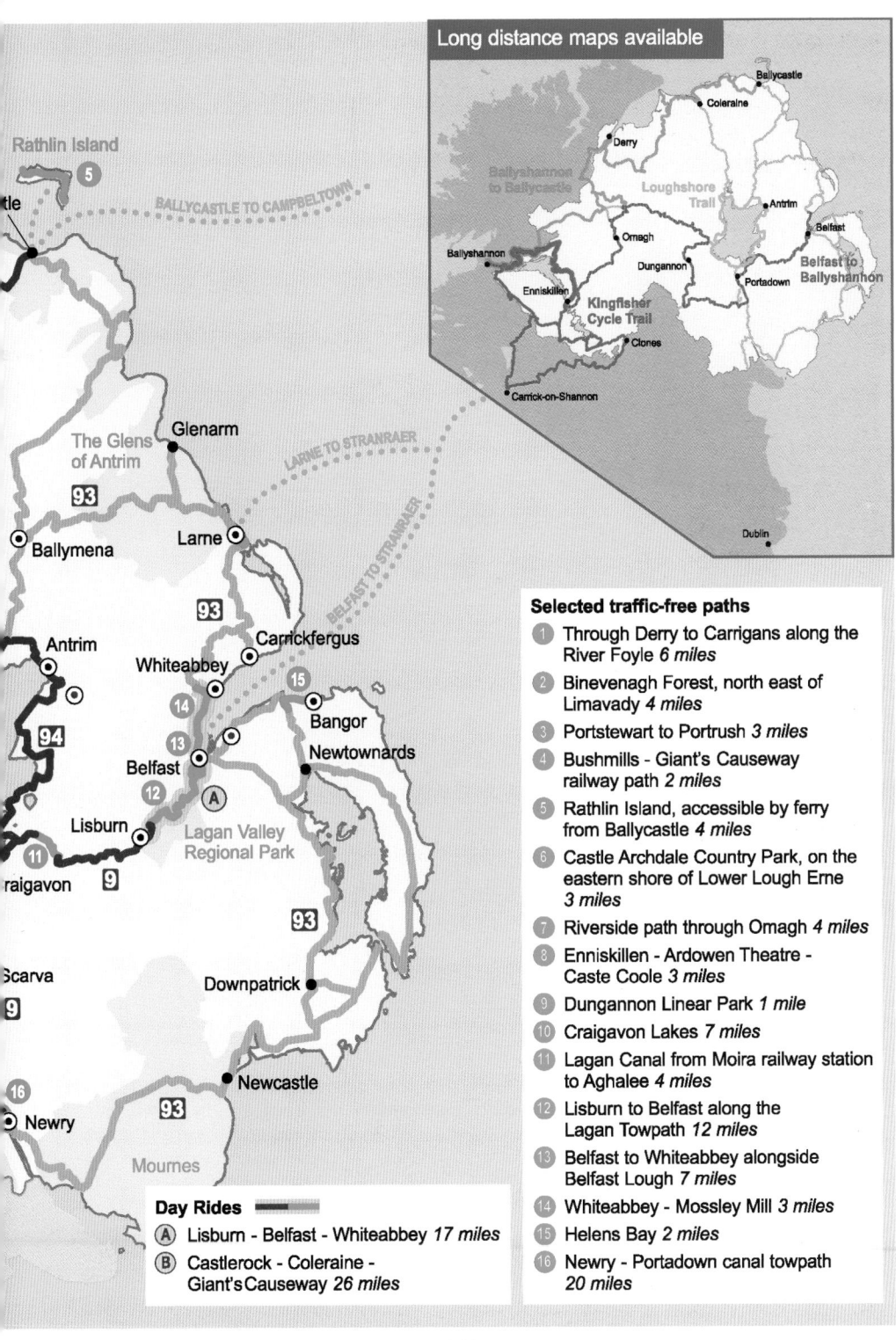

Long distance maps available

Selected traffic-free paths

1. Through Derry to Carrigans along the River Foyle *6 miles*
2. Binevenagh Forest, north east of Limavady *4 miles*
3. Portstewart to Portrush *3 miles*
4. Bushmills - Giant's Causeway railway path *2 miles*
5. Rathlin Island, accessible by ferry from Ballycastle *4 miles*
6. Castle Archdale Country Park, on the eastern shore of Lower Lough Erne *3 miles*
7. Riverside path through Omagh *4 miles*
8. Enniskillen - Ardowen Theatre - Caste Coole *3 miles*
9. Dungannon Linear Park *1 mile*
10. Craigavon Lakes *7 miles*
11. Lagan Canal from Moira railway station to Aghalee *4 miles*
12. Lisburn to Belfast along the Lagan Towpath *12 miles*
13. Belfast to Whiteabbey alongside Belfast Lough *7 miles*
14. Whiteabbey - Mossley Mill *3 miles*
15. Helens Bay *2 miles*
16. Newry - Portadown canal towpath *20 miles*

Day Rides ▬▬▬

A. Lisburn - Belfast - Whiteabbey *17 miles*
B. Castlerock - Coleraine - Giant's Causeway *26 miles*

NORTHERN IRELAND

The rural road network of Northern Ireland provides a range of cycling opportunities suitable for everyone from the occasional cyclist to the semi-professional. There are rich farmlands and a dramatic coastline. The area abounds in castles, iron age forts, prehistoric burial sites, cathedrals and churches, fine country houses and parks. The countryside is full of pleasant, relaxed towns and villages, and most important, there are Ireland's welcoming people, always glad of a chat, especially in the pub in the evening. The pub is also the best place to hear traditional Irish music.

Water is perhaps the dominant theme in defining the National Cycle Network in Northern Ireland. The route through Belfast runs alongside the River Lagan and Belfast Lough; likewise the River Foyle in Derry provides the best routes

Gad Tower, Upper Lough Erne. Ferry ride to the National Trust's estate at Crom on the Kingfisher Trail.

through the city; on the spectacular north coast the Network runs close to the sea from Magilligan Point to Giant's Causeway; the first mapped long distance route in Ireland, the Kingfisher Trail, explores Upper and Lower Lough Erne; the Portadown to Newry Canal towpath links both towns whilst the Camowen River in Omagh and the Callan River in Armagh offer traffic-free routes through the towns. Lastly the 'The Loughshore Trail' which is a route around Lough Neagh, the largest inland lake in the United Kingdom and Ireland, opened at Easter 2002.

NATIONAL CYCLE NETWORK HIGHLIGHTS

Scarva Visitors Centre

For the first time in years it is now possible to cycle the entire length of the Newry Canal towpath to Portadown. Halfway along the towpath is the village of Scarva where the Visitor Centre, bedecked with flowers, provides a welcome stop for tea and home cooking. A new bridge links directly to the towpath so avoiding traffic.

Causeway Coast

This beautiful and dramatic coastal route is one of the most visited attractions in Northern Ireland and has a wide range of tourist facilities. The route leads to the Giant's Causeway which is even more stunning.
A highlight in Coleraine is the stylish Millennium foot and cycle bridge across the River Bann.

Kingfisher Trail

The 230-mile Kingfisher Trail is the first long distance cycle trail in Ireland. It is a fully signed route and runs through the counties of Fermanagh, Leitrim, Cavan, Donegal and Monaghan. This is a beautiful rural area of quiet country roads well suited to cycling.

Lagan Valley Island, Lisburn

In 1998 the Island Valley was an overgrown derelict wasteland. Now, following a £25m transformation this area is a marvellous feature along the River Lagan, on National Route 9. A new civic centre, art gallery and restaurant are set among high quality riverside paths and cyclists and walkers can make use of the two new traffic-free bridges. The canal lock has been returned to working order and public art works include the dramatic '3D' towpath gateway.

Lough Neagh

The largest inland lake in the UK and Ireland is now encircled by a superb new cycle route – The Loughshore Trail. The route is 120 miles long and is almost entirely level, offering great views of the Lough. There are many attractions along the way such as the refurbished Randalstown Viaduct, the ancient Celtic Cross at Arboe, the new foot and cycle bridge over the Blackwater River at Maghery as well as the Lough Neagh Discovery Centre near Craigavon.

Sperrin Mountains

The Sperrin Mountains provide a marvellous area for leisure cycling, whether on the Coast to Coast routes or as a weekend activity break, based in the traditional, rural villages of Tyrone. The scenery is unspoilt, yet spectacular and the network of quiet country lanes provides cycling routes where cars are seldom seen.

TRAFFIC-FREE PATHS PARTICULARLY SUITABLE FOR FAMILIES

Craigavon Lakes 7 miles

Craigavon has a network of 30 miles of traffic-free paths. Route 9 runs along these paths from Portadown, starting at Edenvilla Park through to Oxford Island on the shores of Lough Neagh (there is a one mile section on a very quiet minor road). The route passes through the 250-acre City Park passing the Watersports Centre and Tannaghmore Gardens. Oxford Island is set in woodlands and meadows with refreshments and bird watching hides at the Centre. Good access from the train network to this route.

Foyle Valley Route 5 miles

This delightful path runs from the new Sainsbury's store alongside the River Foyle to Carrigans in Donegal. The route is a combination of high grade urban paths and a trail alongside the tourist railway line that runs south from Craigavon Bridge. When the path stops, the route links to the quiet Ballougry Road.

Newry Canal. 20 miles

This route links Newry to Portadown along the 20-mile towpath of the now, non-navigable Newry Canal. Half of the path is tarmac surfaced with future improvements planned to the remainder of the towpath. The villages along the way provide refreshments and the path is conveniently accessible by train from Belfast or Dublin.

FORSYTHE'S LOCK

NEWRY CANAL

Bushmills. 2 miles

The rock formation of the Giant's Causeway is one of the wonders of the world and the village of Bushmills is famous for its whiskey distillery. Now Route 93 links these two famous attractions, with a path that runs alongside the tourist railway and offers dramatic views of the Atlantic Ocean.

Dungannon Railway Path. 1 mile

The line of the old GNR railway line provides this short but attractive trail through Dungannon. The tarmac surfaced path includes a community sculpture piece, a Millennium Milepost and cycle racks. Join the path at the Tesco store or the bus station. Quiet urban roads also lead south to the Lake Park and more traffic-free cycling south of the town.

Lagan Valley Regional Park 10 miles

The delightful riverside towpath meanders through this well managed park from Lisburn to Belfast. The route is peaceful and flat and is home to birds such as swans, moorhens, ducks and kingfishers. Cyclists need to take care as this popular path is shared with many walkers.

USEFUL MAPS & GUIDES

For details of the full range of maps, guides and other products available contact: **National Cycle Network Information, PO Box 21, Bristol BS99 2HA. Tel: 0117 929 0888. Or visit www.nationalcyclenetwork.org.uk**
The range of National Cycle Network Maps is described in more detail on pages 218-237.

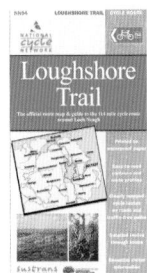

94 *Loughshore Trail*
120 miles
NN94 - £5.99

91 *Kingfisher Trail*
230 miles
NN9A - £5.99

NITB Guide to Cycling in Northern Ireland gives a useful overview of routes and includes contacts. RPL63 – 50p

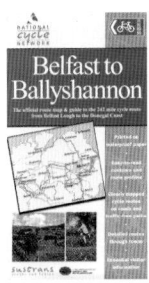

9 91 92 95 *Belfast – Ballyshannon Cycle Route*
231 miles NN9B - £5.99

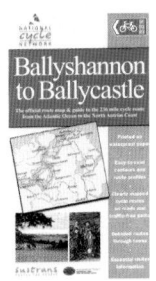

93 92 91 *Ballyshannon – Ballycastle Cycle Route*
236 miles. NN9C - £5.99

Newry Canal 20 miles of traffic-free towpath from Portadown to Newry. FPL41 – FREE

Omagh District shows National Route 92 through the region. FPR06 – FREE

Whiteabbey – Lisburn
The National Route through Belfast city centre. FPL20 – FREE

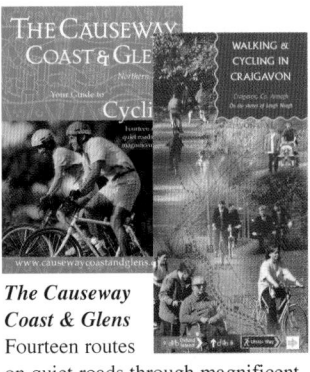

The Causeway Coast & Glens
Fourteen routes on quiet roads through magnificent scenery. FPL43 – FREE

Walking & Cycling in Craigavon
Shows the network of walking and cycling paths. FPL04 - FREE

Foyle Valley Cycle Route
21-mile cycle route, on traffic-free paths and quiet country roads. Connects Londonderry to the border towns of Lifford and Strabane. FPL42 – FREE

TOWNS AND CITIES ON THE NATIONAL CYCLE NETWORK

Maps & guides are available from National Cycle Network Information unless indicated otherwise. See page 205 for contact details.

Armagh

An ecclesiastic centre with two cathedrals and the oldest library in the country. The old cobbled city of Armagh is served by Route 91 with a new traffic-free riverside path alongside the River Callan linking to the Visitor Centre for Navan Fort, the famous old burial chamber.

In the east, a new urban riverside path connects the minor roads of Route 91 from the Portadown & Newry Canal to the Mall in the city centre.

Ballymena

The Ecos centre, a Millennium project, is situated off the A42 in Ballymena, and Route 93 links to the town centre by a new cycle and bridge. To the east, a cycle lane runs 3 miles to Broughshane, a village on the road towards remote moorland country, famous for its peat cutting, stone walls and quiet roads.

Belfast

The regeneration of the River Lagan has acted as a spur to create an attractive riverside route through the heart of Belfast, passing the Waterfront Hall, the Central Railway Station and the ferry terminals. Road space has been reallocated to cyclists to create continuous routes linking city with country along Belfast Lough to the

north and through the splendid Lagan Valley Regional Park to the south (leaflet available from Sustrans). NI Cycling Initiative is a campaign group lobbying for routes: contact Tom McClelland. Tel: 028 90 825279. Or website: www.niel.demon.co.uk/nici.htm. Guided cycle tours of Belfast take place daily with bikes provided. Contact Irish Cycle Tours on 028 9064 2222 or visit: www.irishcycletours.com

Coleraine

This university town in the north of the region was the first in Northern Ireland to install cycle lanes. A new Millennium Bridge offers a safe crossing of the River Bann for pedestrians and cyclists. The Network links the main shopping area, the newly-built Council Offices and the University

on the outskirts of town. It forms part of the scenic North Coast route from Castlerock to Portstewart, Portrush, the Giant's Causeway and on to Ballycastle. Contact Cycling Officer Jim Campbell on 028 703 41305.

Dungannon

A hilly market town served by a recently improved traffic-free route along the course of an old railway, offering a good connection to the west of town. Dungannon Lake Park is a very popular walking and cycling area. There is a network of flat, minor roads between Dungannon and Armagh, following the line of the disused Ulster Canal.

Limavady

Backburn Park uses the course of an old railway line to link Limavady's main street to residential areas. This traffic-free spine also serves the

town's main supermarket, council offices, schools and leisure centres. Route 93 connects with the Roe Valley Country Park to the south of Limavady and into the Sperrin Mountains. The National Cycle Network has helped develop what was already a healthy cycling culture in this flat town. To the north east there is a route planned through Binevenagh Forest with magnifcent views over Lough Foyle to Inishowen.

Lisburn

Two new bridges, one across the River Lagan and the other across a restored section of the Lagan Canal, put Lisburn's Civic and Arts Centres at the heart of Route 9.

This runs from Belfast through the Lagan Valley Regional Park to Union Locks. From here, via the Horseback Bridge, the National Cycle Network crosses the river and follows minor roads and the line of the old canal towards Lough Neagh. Links to the town centre and the Irish Linen Centre are being examined, possibly through Wallace Park or Castle Gardens.

Derry

The River Foyle is the focus of the National Cycle Network in Derry. A traffic-free riverside route runs for six miles right through the centre then alongside the Foyle Valley Railway towards Carrigans in Donegal. Several new retail, housing and office regeneration schemes along the river have incorporated cycle paths, giving easy access to rail and bus stations and the famous city walls. Signalled crossings have created a safe crossing of Craigavon Bridge, the city's famous double decker bridge. On the east side of the river, the path runs south to the residential areas of Prehen and New Buildings. There are monthly cycle tours of the city arranged by the campaign group Pedal Power website: http://homepage.mac.com/pedalpower/ For this and other queries contact the Cycling Development Officer, Eamonn Brown on 028 71 365151.

Newry

The river and canal (Portadown to Newry) run parallel down the valley through the centre of the town. The canal towpath provides Route 9 with an entrance into the town centre, whilst the route of the former Bessbrook tram line, under the spectacular Craigmore Viaduct, the highest in Ireland, will form the basis of a route towards Dundalk and Dublin. To the southwest of Newry is the Ring of Gullion, an Area of Outstanding Natural Beauty with signed local routes. There are plans for an improvement to the coastal route to the Mournes. Contact South Armagh Tourism Initiative. Leaflet available. Tel: 028 3086 8900.

Omagh

A market town and the county town of Tyrone. The traffic-free riverside route along the Camowen River links, via a bridge, to housing estates and schools, and goes past the leisure centre and health centre. A new path leads north past the council offices to Omagh's main tourist attractions: the Ulster American Folk Park and the Ulster History Park. Further north still is the attractive village of Gortin, a good base for exploring the Sperrins. Leaflet available from Sustrans.

Portadown & Craigavon

A cycle network connects Portadown to Oxford Island on Lough Neagh passing Craigavon Lakes.
In Portadown a traffic-free path runs past schools and the F.E. college. The canal towpath comes into the centre of town and will be improved south to Newry. For the time being, the Loughshore Trail (Route 94) crosses the River Bann in the town centre rather than at Bannfoot.
There is a leaflet available covering Craigavon Lakes. Contact Craigavon Borough Council. Tel: 028 3832 2205.

Portrush

The busiest holiday resort in Northern Ireland is well served with a traffic-free path running alongside the coast road offering stunning views of the Atlantic. The caravan and camping parks to the east of the town are linked to the town centre by cycle lanes. To the west the cycle route along the promenade leads to the magnificent Port to Port Path which offers a grand coastal experience as you travel to Portstewart. This area is well served by all sorts of accommodation.

Whiteabbey

The new coastal path coming north from Belfast links Hazelbank Park to Whiteabbey, serving the Rathcoole housing estate. A spur leads off to the University of Ulster at Jordanstown campus. The National Cycle Network turns inland from Belfast Lough where the Three Mile Water Route continues under some very impressive old viaducts to the new council offices at Mossley. An additional route runs from the coast via Glas-na-Bradan Glen linking Rathcoole to the Valley Leisure Centre which opens in 2003. Leaflet available from Sustrans.

CASTLEROCK TO GIANT'S CAUSEWAY

The Giant's Causeway is a World Heritage Site and a splendid destination for this scenic ride along the beautiful north coast of Ireland. You may well choose to break this ride up into several shorter sections, with Coleraine or Portrush as good starting points, both served by railway stations. North from Coleraine the ride links cycle lanes and segregated cycle tracks past the University of Ulster and onto two of the most popular resorts on the north coast – Portstewart and Portrush, linked by another length of cycle track with fine sea views across to the Mull of Kintyre. From Portrush to Bushmills, home of the famous Irish whiskey, the route follows quiet lanes parallel to the busy coast road. As the lanes climb to almost 300 ft you have all of the views with very little of the traffic – just the right combination! From Bushmills, a delightful section of railway path takes you almost to the door of the Giant's Causeway Visitor Centre. To the west of Coleraine, the route climbs steeply to almost 300 ft affording wonderful views out to sea over the sand dunes at The Barmouth. Once you have reached Castlerock railway station it is well worth the effort to explore the ruins of Downhill Castle and the dramatically located Mussenden Temple just to the west of the village.

NB For safety reasons (a steep hill with a blind bend and lots of pedestrians) you are NOT allowed to cycle the ½ mile down to the Giant's Causeway from the Visitor Centre. Please do not abuse this sensible safety precaution.

Views of the seven-mile Magilligan Strand from Mussenden Temple, Route 93.

Starting points
1. Castlerock Station.
2. The new Millennium Bridge over the River Bann in Coleraine.
3. West Strand, Portrush.

Distances
Castlerock to Coleraine: seven miles one way, 14 miles return. Coleraine to Portrush seven miles one way, 14 miles return. Portrush to Giant's Causeway: nine miles one way, 18 miles return.

Grade
Moderate.

Surface
All tarmac, with the exception of the railway path into Giant's Causeway which is a high-grade stone path.

Roads, traffic, suitability for young children
Most of the ride is on quiet roads, cycle lanes and segregated cycleways where the route runs (safely) alongside busier roads. The section between Portstewart and Portrush has fine views out to the sea. The final traffic-free section from Bushmills to Giant's Causeway is along the course of a disused railway.

Hills
There are several short hills and two longer climbs of almost 300 ft: one to the north west of Coleraine on the way towards Castlerock, the other between Portrush and Bushmills, both on very quiet stretches of road.

Refreshments
Pubs, cafe in Castlerock.
Lots of choice in Coleraine.
Lots of choice in Portstewart.
Lots of choice in Portrush.
Cafe at the Giant's Causeway.

Nearest railway stations
Castlerock, Coleraine, Portrush.

The National Cycle Network in the area
1. West of Castlerock, Route 93 climbs steeply on Bishop's Road to over 1,000 ft with magnificent views to the Inishowen Peninsula and, on a fine day, to the Scottish Isles of Islay and Jura. It then drops down to Limavady via Binevenagh Forest.
2. East of Giant's Causeway Route 93 continues inland towards Ballycastle and the ferries to Scotland and Rathlin.

Dramatic rock formations at the Giant's Causeway, World Heritage Site.

Other nearby rides (waymarked or traffic-free)
1. There are plans to create a ferry link from Magilligan Point to Greencastle on the Inishowen Peninsula, linking to the round-the-peninsula ride.
2. Rathlin Island, a ferry ride from Ballycastle, offers challenging cycling and walking to famous birdnesting sites and dramatic cliffs.

Railway path from Bushmills to the Giant's Causeway.

CASTLEROCK TO GIANT'S CAUSEWAY

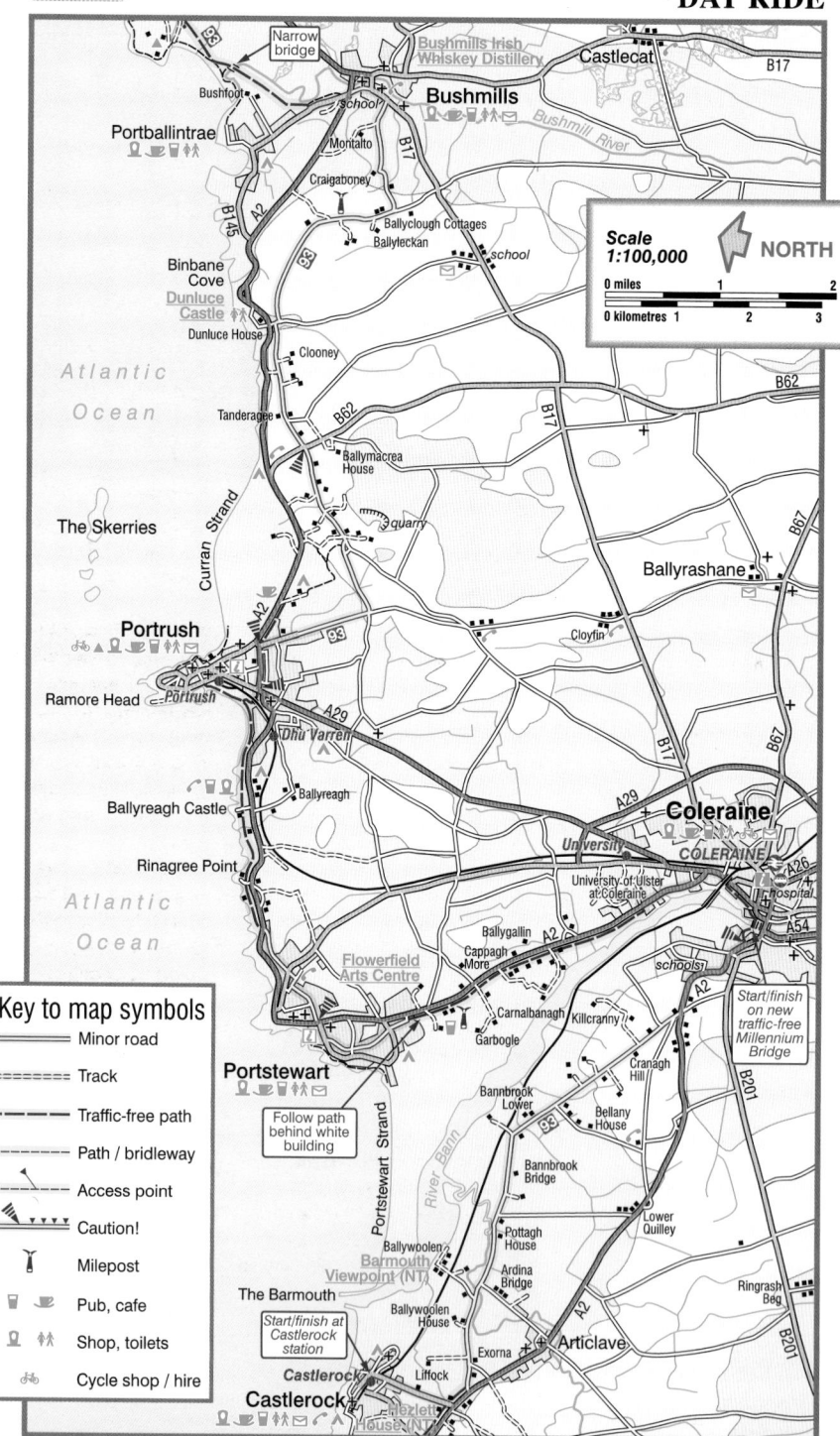

Narrow bridge

Bushmills Irish Whiskey Distillery

Castlecat

B17

Bushfoot

Bushmills

Bushmill River

school

Portballintrae

Montalto

B17

Craigaboney

Ballyclough Cottages

Ballyleckan

school

Binbane Cove

Dunluce Castle

Clooney

Dunluce House

Tanderagee

B62

B17

B62

Ballymacrea House

B67

Scale
1:100,000

NORTH

0 miles 1 2
0 kilometres 1 2 3

The Skerries

Curran Strand

quarry

Ballyrashane

Portrush

Cloyfin

Ramore Head

Portrush

A2

A29

Dhu Varren

Ballyreagh Castle

Ballyreagh

Coleraine

COLERAINE

University

Rinagree Point

University of Ulster at Coleraine

hospital

A29

A2

A26

A54

Atlantic Ocean

Ballygallin

Cappagh More

schools

B67

Flowerfield Arts Centre

Carnalbanagh

Killcranny

Start/finish on new traffic-free Millennium Bridge

Garbogle

Cranagh Hill

B201

Key to map symbols

══════	Minor road
======	Track
– – – –	Traffic-free path
·–·–·–	Path / bridleway
⊣	Access point
⚠ ▼▼▼	Caution!
⬆	Milepost
🥤 ☕	Pub, cafe
🛒 🚻	Shop, toilets
🚲	Cycle shop / hire

Portstewart

Follow path behind white building

Portstewart Strand

River Bann

Bannbrook Lower

Bellany House

Bannbrook Bridge

Lower Quilley

Pottagh House

Ardina Bridge

Ringrash Beg

Barmouth Viewpoint (NT)

The Barmouth

Ballywoolen

Ballywoolen House

Start/finish at Castlerock station

A2

B201

Exorna

Articlave

Castlerock

Liffock

Castlerock

Hezlett House (NT)

Atlantic Ocean

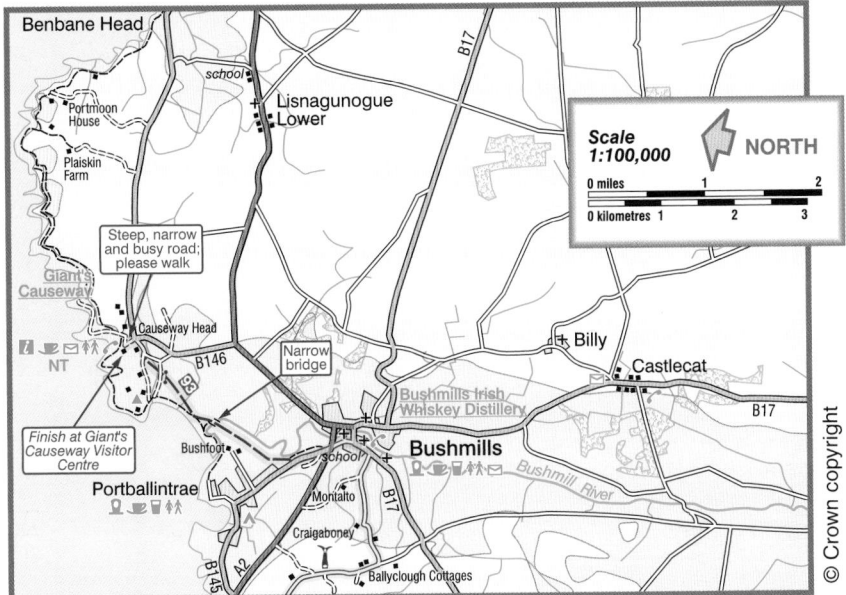

Route instructions from Castlerock to Giant's Causeway

1. From Castlerock Station, climb gently up the hill away from the sea and turn left along the segregated cycleway. Shortly, turn left down Ballywoolen Road at the school.

2. Follow this road for five miles, climbing 270 ft. At the T-junction with the A2 at the end of Cranagh Road, turn left on the cycle lane. **Easy to miss.** Halfway down the hill (after the second mini-roundabout) turn left onto a no through road, signposted 'Route 93'.

3. Follow National Cycle Network 93 signs through Coleraine, crossing the new bridge over the River Bann and following the cycle lane round to the left. Continue alongside the A2 towards Portstewart on segregated track.

4. **Easy to miss.** On the outskirts of Portstewart follow signs carefully, turning left and immediately right behind new white apartments.

Follow the waymarked route through the quiet residential streets of the town. (You may prefer to go along the main street of Portstewart with views out to sea – this is a more scenic route but obviously a lot busier with traffic.)

5. A segregated cycleway takes you from 'Port to Port' (Portstewart to Portrush) with fine views out to sea. On the outskirts of Portrush, the cycle track descends to the promenade. **Easy to miss.** At the bottom of the descent follow the promenade and after 100 yds turn right away from the sea and pass under the railway bridge.

6. Follow the signposted route through Portrush on segregated cycleways. On the outskirts of Portrush, just after the primary school turn right up the Ballywillan Road (a spur leads on to the caravan sites on the coast road) and after about 330yds turn left onto the Ballymacrae Road.

7. Follow the waymarked route for six miles along mostly quiet roads

parallel with the main coast road. You may wish to visit Dunluce Castle, a castle with a turbulent and fascinating history. There is one easily missed left turn on a fast descent just after a set of holiday cottages, about one mile before Bushmills. Look out for signs!

8. Soon after crossing the A2 onto the road towards Portballintrae, turn right at the Route 93 signpost onto the railway path and follow this for almost three miles to Giant's Causeway. You will need to retrace your steps as far as Portrush for a train station.

NB For safety reasons (steep hill, blind bend, lots of walkers, the shuttle bus) you are not allowed to cycle from the Visitor Centre to the Giant's Causeway itself. It is best to leave yourself enough time to do the full two-mile walk along the cliff top, down to the Giant's Causeway then back along the road.

LISBURN TO WHITEABBEY

Water is the linking theme of this ride as it makes its way along the River Lagan from Lisburn into the regenerated heart of Belfast, then out along the shores of Belfast Lough towards Whiteabbey and the Newtownabbey Way. Starting in Lisburn, on an island formed by the River Lagan and the canal, a long wooded, riverside section leads past old linen mills and right into the centre of Belfast via a safe crossing on the Ormeau Bridge. Many fine old stone buildings punctuate the riverside route through the city centre, and Clarendon Docks have been completely rebuilt, now boasting an attractive mixture of residential and commercial buildings. The Belfast Hills, particularly the dramatic outline of Cave Hill, form a fine backdrop to the second half of the ride. After passing the ferry terminals, a short section takes you on the narrow corridor between the docks and the motorway through Duncrue Industrial Estate where your nose will be assailed by a variety of powerful smells! This unavoidable section is soon over and you cross onto the north foreshore path that takes you all the way to Whiteabbey with the vast shimmering expanse of Belfast Lough away to your right. The fence alongside the first section has been erected to protect the wading birds from being disturbed by dogs and walkers.

Cyclists pass a Millennium Milepost on the Newtownabbey Way.

Starting points
1. The Waterfront Hall in the heart of Belfast.
2. Lisburn Borough Council Offices on the Lagan Valley Island, Lisburn.
3. Whiteabbey village, at the edge of Belfast Lough.

Distance
13 miles one way from Lisburn to the Waterfront Hall, Belfast (26 miles return).
Six miles one way from the Waterfront Hall, Belfast to Whiteabbey village (12 miles return).

Grade
Easy.

Surface
Tarmac surface throughout.

Roads, traffic, suitability for young children
There are two, traffic-free sections ideal for young children:
1. Civic Centre in Lisburn to Central Station in Belfast.
2. Dargan Road in North Belfast to Whiteabbey alongside Belfast Lough.

Hills
None.

Refreshments
Plenty of choice in Lisburn.
Cafe at Lisburn Civic Centre.
Tap Room, Hilden Brewery.
Cutters Wharf PH, Stranmillis.
The Stables Tearoom in Sir Thomas and Lady Dixon Park (just off the route, near Drumbeg).
Malone House Restaurant in Barnett Demesne (just off the route near Shaw's Bridge).
Lots of choice in the centre of Belfast.
Glenavna Hotel, Whiteabbey.
Ice cream and tea shops in Whiteabbey village.

Nearest railway stations
1. The route goes right past Belfast Central Station.
2. The best connection to Lisburn station takes you through Castle Gardens; or use Hilden Station.
3. Whiteabbey Station, across the busy A2, about ¼ mile to the west of the village.

The National Cycle Network in the area
1. West from Lisburn Route 9 continues over the newly-built Horseback Bridge at Union Locks and on towards Lough Neagh and Portadown to the Newry Canal towpath.
2. North from Whiteabbey, Route 93 follows Three Mile Water

Route 93 in Belfast passes the ferry terminals to England and Scotland.

Conservation Park under the spectacular Bleach Green Viaducts to the council offices at Mossley Mill before continuing towards the coast at Carrickfergus and Larne.
3. Route 93 will also run east, crossing the River Lagan via Queen Elizabeth Bridge and then fork with one route running north east to Bangor and the other south east to Comber, passing the Odyssey Millennium Project.

Traffic-free path along the River Lagan in central Belfast.

DAY RIDE

LISBURN TO WHITEABBEY

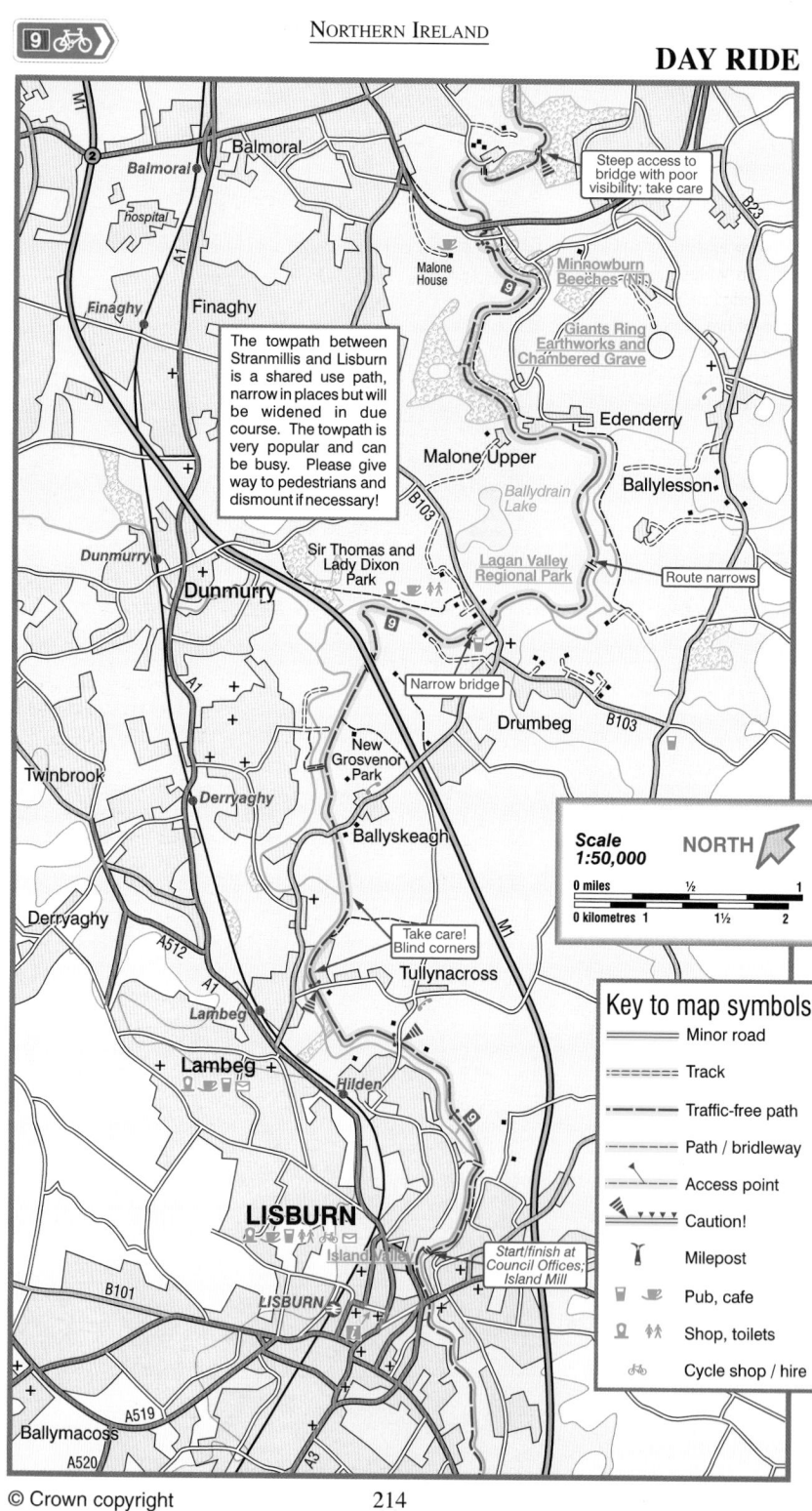

Balmoral

hospital

M1 · A1

Balmoral

Malone House

Steep access to bridge with poor visibility; take care

B23

Minnowburn Beeches (NT)

Giants Ring Earthworks and Chambered Grave

Finaghy — Finaghy

The towpath between Stranmillis and Lisburn is a shared use path, narrow in places but will be widened in due course. The towpath is very popular and can be busy. Please give way to pedestrians and dismount if necessary!

Edenderry

Malone Upper

Ballylesson

Ballydrain Lake

Dunmurry — Dunmurry

Sir Thomas and Lady Dixon Park

B103

Lagan Valley Regional Park

Route narrows

A1

Narrow bridge

Drumbeg

B103

Twinbrook

New Grosvenor Park

Derryaghy

Ballyskeagh

Scale 1:50,000

NORTH

| 0 miles | | ½ | | 1 |
| 0 kilometres | 1 | | 1½ | 2 |

Derryaghy

A512

A1

Take care! Blind corners

Tullynacross

M1

Lambeg

Lambeg

Hilden

9

Key to map symbols

====== Minor road

≡≡≡≡≡ Track

– · – · – Traffic-free path

– – – – Path / bridleway

Access point

▼▼▼▼ Caution!

Ⴖ Milepost

🍺 ☕ Pub, cafe

🛒 🚻 Shop, toilets

🚲 Cycle shop / hire

LISBURN

Island Valley

Start/finish at Council Offices; Island Mill

LISBURN

B101

A519

A520

Ballymacoss

A3

Route instructions

The route is well-signposted and once alongside either the River Lagan or Belfast Lough it is very difficult to get lost.

1. From the new Lisburn Civic Centre at Lagan Valley Island, follow the wooded riverside path on the east bank of the River Lagan north east towards Belfast for 10 miles, passing old linen mills and the relics of the old Lagan Canal.

2. Cross under Governor's Bridge (Stranmillis) to continue in the same direction along the newly-built segregated cycle lane along Stranmillis Embankment.

3. Cross the Ormeau Road (via controlled crossing) onto a continuation of the riverside route on a wide path. Go past Central Station, the Waterfront Hall, the Lagan Weir and the terminals for the ferries to England and Scotland.

4. Follow the waymarked route through Clarendon Dock and Duncrue Industrial Estate, across Dargan Road and onto the newly-built path alongside Belfast Lough.

5. Follow this for a further three miles, passing a tall fence on the right, the motorway to the left, then alongside Hazelbank Park as far as Whiteabbey village, following the coast the whole way.

Haulers Way Riverside Path, Belfast.

6. The Newtownabbey Way continues to Mossley Mill under the Bleach Green Viaducts.

The red bridge between Belfast and Lisburn in the Lagan Valley Regional Park.

LISBURN TO WHITEABBEY

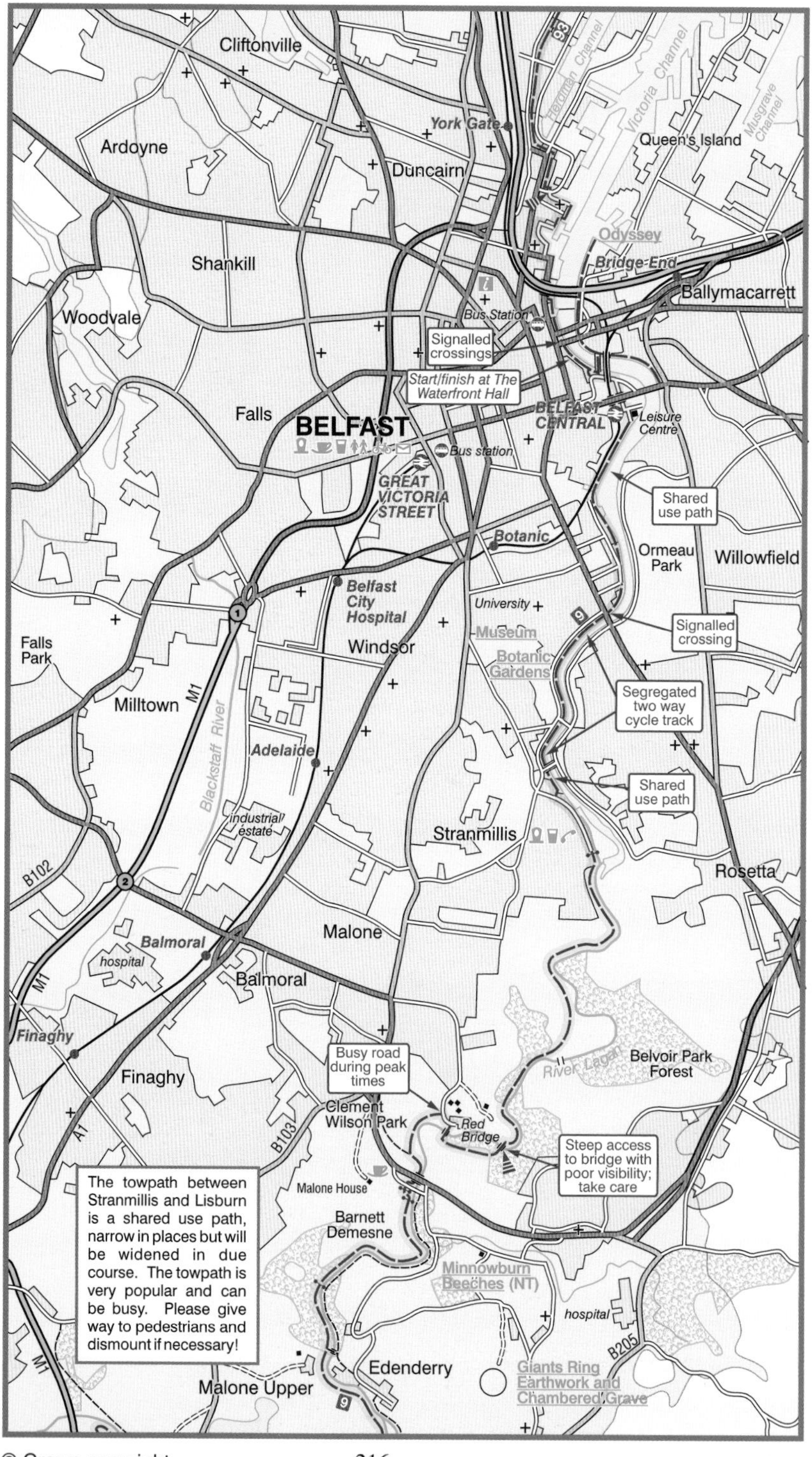

Cliftonville

Ardoyne

Duncairn

York Gate

Queen's Island

Odyssey

Bridge-End

Shankill

Ballymacarrett

Woodvale

Bus Station

Signalled crossings

Start/finish at The Waterfront Hall

Falls

BELFAST

BELFAST CENTRAL

Leisure Centre

GREAT VICTORIA STREET

Bus station

Shared use path

Botanic

Ormeau Park

Willowfield

Belfast City Hospital

University

Museum

Signalled crossing

Falls Park

Windsor

Botanic Gardens

Milltown

M1

Blackstaff River

Adelaide

Segregated two way cycle track

Shared use path

B102

industrial estate

Stranmillis

Rosetta

Malone

Balmoral

hospital

Balmoral

Belvoir Park Forest

Finaghy

Busy road during peak times

River Lagan

Finaghy

A1

Clement Wilson Park

Red Bridge

Steep access to bridge with poor visibility; take care

B103

Malone House

The towpath between Stranmillis and Lisburn is a shared use path, narrow in places but will be widened in due course. The towpath is very popular and can be busy. Please give way to pedestrians and dismount if necessary!

Barnett Demesne

Minnowburn Beeches (NT)

hospital

M1

B205

Malone Upper

Edenderry

Giants Ring Earthwork and Chambered Grave

216

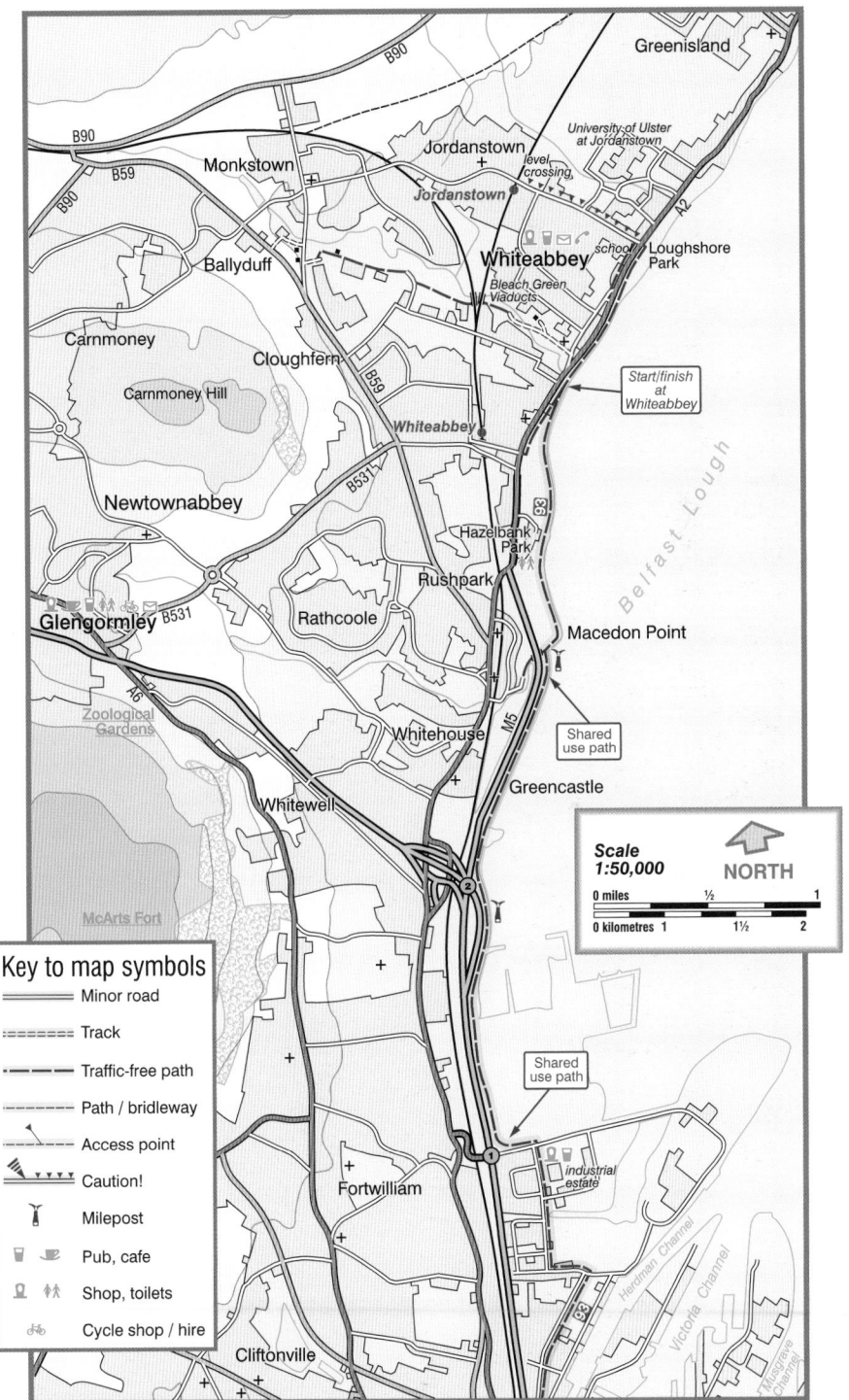

Greenisland

B90

University of Ulster
at Jordanstown

B90

Jordanstown

level
crossing

B59

Monkstown

Jordanstown

A2

Ballyduff

Whiteabbey

school Loughshore
Park

Bleach Green
Viaducts

Carnmoney

Cloughfern

Start/finish
at
Whiteabbey

B59

Carnmoney Hill

Whiteabbey

Belfast Lough

B531

Newtownabbey

B93

Hazelbank
Park

Rushpark

Glengormley   B531

Rathcoole

Macedon Point

A6

Zoological
Gardens

Whitehouse

M5

Shared
use path

McArts Fort

Whitewell

Greencastle

**Scale
1:50,000**

NORTH

0 miles   ½   1
0 kilometres   1   1½   2

Shared
use path

Fortwilliam

industrial
estate

Key to map symbols

———— Minor road

:======= Track

– – – – Traffic-free path

– – – – Path / bridleway

—▸– – Access point

🔺▾▾▾ Caution!

⚲ Milepost

🍺 🍽 Pub, cafe

♀ 🚻 Shop, toilets

🚲 Cycle shop / hire

Cliftonville

Herdman Channel

Victoria Channel

Musgrave Channel

LONG DISTANCE AND HOLIDAY ROUTES

National Cycle Network
shown on official maps

The Trans Pennine Trail (TPT) is a separately mapped,
funded and managed project

- Open and mapped
- Open and mapped TPT
- Open but not yet mapped
- Proposed routes

NATIONAL
cycle
NETWORK

M

A Millennium Commission
Lottery Project

This section of the book gives a brief description of each of the long distance routes which are available as maps from Sustrans and are shown on the map opposite. Several sections of the National Cycle Network make ideal challenges for a holiday lasting from a few days to a few weeks. The award-winning National Route Maps published by Sustrans show the routes in easy-to-use strip form with daily route profiles, mileages and details of Tourist Information Centres, for help in finding accommodation along the way. The routes are a mixture of quiet lanes and traffic-free paths including dismantled railways, canal towpaths and forestry tracks.

What sort of bike should I use?

You can use any type of bike to ride most parts of the Network. However, not all the surfaces are sealed, so the best sort of bike to use would be a hybrid bike, a mountain bike fitted with road tyres or a robust touring bike with strong wheels and a wide range of gears. Fit mudguards and carry your luggage in panniers on a rack – far more comfortable than cycling with a rucksack!

The Network keeps on getting better!

The partners in the National Cycle Network are determined to continue developing and improving the routes. For example, over time road junctions may be made safer; more traffic-calming measures may be introduced to slow down traffic on the road sections; better quality surfacing, drainage and regular maintenance of encroaching vegetation may be required on the traffic-free sections; in some cases entirely new traffic-free routes will be built to replace existing sections along roads. As the creation of the Network is an ongoing project, old maps will become out of date, so if in doubt, follow the signs.

 **GARDEN of ENGLAND CYCLE ROUTE (London-Dover-Hastings)**
Easy/Moderate - 180 miles NN1X - £5.99

 **DOWNS & WEALD CYCLE ROUTE (London-Eastbourne-Hastings)**
Easy/Moderate - 150 miles NN2A - £5.99

These two routes in the South East link London to the coast. The first route is arranged to suit those arriving in Britain at the gateway port of Dover. The main route follows the coast and its extraordinary chain of defences – Dover, Walmer, Deal and Richborough Castles – the last being the Romans' gateway to the country. Then inland to Canterbury before following as close as possible the whole length of the North Kent coast to Dartford, and then along the Thames Estuary to Erith, Thamesmead, Woolwich, the Barrier, the Dome and Greenwich.

South from Greenwich, the second map follows a route to Gatwick and Three Bridges, from where a series of railway paths and deep Sussex lanes reach the sea at Eastbourne. The route then follows the coast as closely as possible through to Bexhill and Hastings with a spur west to Newhaven, Brighton and north to Crawley.

Public transport
There are a number of convenient railway stations along the routes such as **Three Bridges**, **East Grinstead**, **Polegate**, **Sandwich**, **Canterbury**, **Whitstable** and **Sittingbourne**.

 HULL-FAKENHAM CYCLE ROUTE
Easy/Moderate - 206 miles NN1A - £5.99

 FAKENHAM-HARWICH CYCLE ROUTE
Easy/Moderate - 163 miles NN1B - £5.99

Easy gradients are a welcome feature of the Hull to Harwich route as it crosses the gentle countryside of eastern England from the Lincolnshire Wolds and Fens down into Norfolk and Suffolk. After the Wolds the route rarely rises above 200ft making it ideal for families or adults returning to cycling after a few years' absence. Linking the ports of Hull and Harwich, the route explores the cathedral cities of Lincoln and Norwich and visits many attractive East Anglian villages on its way through Constable Country to Harwich.

Public transport options

Kingston upon Hull: main line services via York, Leeds and Doncaster.

Harwich: main line services from London Liverpool Street. Local rail services from Ipswich, Colchester and Manningtree.

It is also possible to join the route from the following stations: **Market Rasen**, **Lincoln**, **Boston**, **King's Lynn**, **Norwich**, **Beccles**, **Halesworth** and **Ipswich**.

The coastal option in Suffolk uses three somewhat irregular ferries!

THE THREE RIVERS CYCLE ROUTE
(Newcastle-Sunderland-Middlesbrough)
Easy/Moderate - 135 miles NN14 - £5.99

The three rivers are the Tyne, the Wear and the Tees which together define the industrial North East. Following the decline of the shipbuilding, steel and coal industries, much derelict land has been regenerated into attractive parks and many old railway lines have become recreational paths. Put this together with the success of the riverside development along the Tyne through Newcastle, the attractions of the marina and National Glass

The Tyne Tunnel carries Route 1 from Jarrow to North Shields. Further east there is the alternative of the Tyne Crossing - spoilt for choice!

Centre in Wearmouth, and the barrage crossing of the Tees between Stockton and Middlesbrough, and you can see that the area offers far more to the cyclist than you might suppose! Circular rides can easily be fashioned by picking up the C2C route from Sunderland to Consett and thence northwards to the Tyne via Rowlands Gill and the magnificent viaducts of the Derwent Railway Path; or turn southwards to pick up the Lanchester Railway Path to the cathedral city of Durham and eventually the coast again at Seaham.

At the southern end of the Three Rivers Route a further circular trip can be made by using first the route through Hartlepool for the Middlesbrough Transporter, and then the Eden Valley railway path north from Stockton-on-Tees.

Public transport options
As the Metro does not take cycles, the start of the route is probably best reached by cycling along either the South or North Tyne Cycle Route from **Newcastle Central**. Further south **Sunderland**, **Seaham**, **Hartlepool** and **Middlesbrough** all lie very close to the route.

COAST & CASTLES CYCLE ROUTE
(Newcastle-Edinburgh)
Easy/Moderate - 200 miles NN1C - £5.99

This beautiful section of the National Cycle Network runs north from Tynemouth along the lovely coastline of Northumberland, England's least densely populated county. There are castles along the way at Warkworth, Dunstanburgh and Bamburgh, not forgetting Lindisfarne Castle and the Priory on Holy Island. The Scottish border is crossed soon after visiting the elegant Georgian streets of Berwick-upon-Tweed, England's northernmost town. The Scottish Borders are wonderful cycling country with little traffic and many fine, small towns – the route passes through Melrose, one of the most attractive in the region. After crossing the Moorfoot Hills, the River Esk Valley is followed through Dalkeith. The Innocent Railway Path takes you right into the heart of Edinburgh.

Transport
Apart from **Newcastle** and **Edinburgh** stations at either end, the East Coast Main Line Railway also stops at **Berwick** and **Alnmouth**, both squarely on the route.

EDINBURGH-ABERDEEN CYCLE ROUTE
Easy/Moderate - 170 miles NN1D - £5.99

From the beautiful city of Edinburgh the route crosses the famous Forth Road Bridge into the Kingdom of Fife and the historic town of St Andrews before continuing north along the coast via Dundee and smoky ol' Arbroath up to the granite city of Aberdeen.

Public transport options
Edinburgh Waverley: main line service from all parts of Britain.
Aberdeen: main line services from all parts of Britain including Edinburgh, Glasgow and Inverness.
It is also possible to join the route from the following stations: **Dundee**, **Arbroath**, **Montrose** and **Stonehaven**.

Cullen Viaduct has been restored to take cyclists on the spectacular coastal route between Banff and Buckie (Aberdeen-John o'Groats Route).

ABERDEEN-JOHN O' GROATS CYCLE ROUTE
(includes the Orkneys & Shetlands)
Moderate - 501 miles NN1E - £5.99

North of Aberdeen, 'the granite city with the warm heart', the route passes through the red-sandstone town of Turriff before reaching the Moray Firth at the fishing port of Banff. West from here you pass through the attractive settlements at Portsoy, Forres and Nairn. Beyond Inverness, 'capital' of the Highlands, the route continues north to Thurso, Wick and John o' Groats. The map also shows routes in the Shetlands and Orkneys.

Note that the northern half of this route is shown to a deceptively comforting small scale which belies the time distances!

Public transport options
Aberdeen: main line services from all parts of Britain including Edinburgh, Glasgow and Inverness.
John o' Groats: The nearest railway stations are either at **Thurso** (20 miles) or **Wick** (17 miles).

It is also possible to join the route from the following stations: **Elgin**, **Forres**, **Nairn** and **Inverness**, plus six stations between **Dingwall** and **Lairg**.

DEVON COAST TO COAST CYCLE ROUTE
(Ilfracombe-Plymouth)
Moderate/Challenging - 90 miles NN27 - £5.99

Cross beautiful Devon from the Bristol Channel to the English Channel, starting with a climb on a railway path from the seaside resort of Ilfracombe. Join the start of the traffic-free Tarka Trail in Braunton and follow the Taw and Torridge estuaries through Barnstaple and Bideford. From Petrockstowe, sunken lanes through rolling green countryside take you to Okehampton. Skirt the western edge of the vast granite mass of Dartmoor to reach the handsome town of Tavistock. The route finishes in Plymouth after a descent along the popular traffic-free Plym Valley Trail.

Public transport options
Plymouth: main line services from all parts of Britain including Bristol Temple Meads, Birmingham New Street and London Paddington. **Ilfracombe** has no railway station (but can often be reached by pleasure steamer from Penarth). The closest is at **Barnstaple** (accessed via Exeter).

THE CORNISH WAY CYCLE ROUTE
(Land's End-Bude)
Moderate/Challenging - 123 miles NN3B - £5.99

The Cornish Way runs the length of the county from Land's End to Bude. Significant sections of cycle route include Land's End to Sennen, the promenades around St. Michael's Bay, the fascinating Cornish Mineral Railways which pick up the remains of the once great tin industry, and a railway path for an easy route into Truro. From here the route divides into two, each equally hilly. The southern route crosses the Fal at King Harry's Ferry to generally follow the coast to Mevagissey, where it joins extensive new construction to Heligan Gardens and St. Austell. Again the route splits, either to follow a mineral route to the China Clay Museum at Wheal Martyn before joining the second at the Eden Project – Cornwall's monumental Millennium tropical gardens. North from here follow a maze of minor roads to Llanhydrock House, with its much needed new bridge over the A30 to Bodmin. At Bodmin the second route from Truro via some serious hills at Newquay eventually joins the easy Camel Trail railway path to Wenfordbridge, the wild open spaces of Bodmin Moor and finally the coast again at Bude.

Public transport
The route is well served by trains to **Bodmin Parkway**, **St. Austell**, **Truro**, **Redruth**, **Camborne**, **Hayle** and **Penzance**.

Right: Truro Cathedral welcomes the Trailblazing Riders on their way to Land's End (The Cornish Way).

King Harry's Ferry provides a crossing of the River Fal en route from Truro to Mevagissey.
Note: the very small (3 bikes) ferry at Malpas provides a delightful alternative (The Cornish Way).

Glastonbury Tor from the route to Wells. Nine incised standing stones are located between the Tor and Wells Cathedral (The West Country Way).

THAMES VALLEY CYCLE ROUTE (London-Oxford)
Easy/Moderate - 97 miles NN5A - £5.99

Starting at Putney Bridge, escape from London through Richmond Park and along the banks of the majestic River Thames, passing Hampton Court and Runnymede. After the vast splendour of Windsor Castle the route travels cross-country to rejoin the river at Wargrave, then threads its way through Reading. Glorious Chiltern beechwoods form a canopy over the lanes as you climb north past the Maharajah's Well at Stoke Row to historic Wallingford and Abingdon before reaching journey's end at Oxford.

Public transport options
London: main line services from all parts of Britain. Then cycle to the start of the route at Putney Bridge.
Oxford: main line services from London Paddington via Reading and from Birmingham.

It is also possible to join the route from the following stations:
Richmond, **Staines** and **Windsor** from London Waterloo.
Maidenhead, **Twyford**, **Reading** and **Didcot** from London Paddington.

THE WEST COUNTRY WAY CYCLE ROUTE (Padstow-Bristol/Bath)
Moderate/Challenging - 252 miles NN3A - £5.99

The West Country Way runs from the north Cornish coast to the historic cities of Bath and Bristol via a mixture of quiet lanes and popular traffic-free sections such as the Camel and Tarka Trails and the Bridgwater & Taunton Canal. On its West Country meanderings it takes in an exhilarating ridge ride over the roof of Exmoor, across the atmospheric Somerset Levels, to the mystical town of Glastonbury and the glory of Wells Cathedral.

Public transport options
Bodmin Parkway: main line services from Exeter, Bristol and London Paddington.
Bristol: main line services from all parts of Britain to Bristol Temple Meads.

It is also possible to join the route from the following stations:
Barnstaple (via Exeter), **Tiverton Parkway**, **Taunton** and **Bridgwater.**

SEVERN & THAMES CYCLE ROUTE
(Gloucester-Newbury)
Easy/Moderate - 128 miles NN4A - £5.99

Cross southern England from the cathedral city of Gloucester to the busy market town of Newbury. After the lush pastures of the Severn Vale, follow the railway path from Bristol into the beautiful city of Bath then onwards along the Kennet & Avon towpath with its spectacular viaducts and locks. The main route leaves the canal at Bradford-on-Avon to pass through Corsham, Chippenham, Calne, Avebury and Marlborough. A parallel route follows the canal to Devizes then diverts onto quiet lanes through Etchilhampton, Woodborough and Wootton Rivers. The north route (via Chippenham) and the south route (via Devizes) link up on the edge of Savernake Forest, to the east of Marlborough. From here, quiet lanes lead through the attractive town of Hungerford and a final canal section takes you into the heart of Newbury. Most of the remainder of the journey to Reading follows the course of the canalised river.

Public transport options
Gloucester: main line services from all parts of Britain including Bristol Temple Meads, Birmingham New Street and London Paddington.
Newbury: main line services from all parts of Britain including Bristol Temple Meads and London Paddington.

It is also possible to join the route from the following stations: **Bristol Temple Meads, Bath, Bradford-on-Avon, Trowbridge, Swindon** and **Hungerford,** as well as local stations to Reading.

The Severn & Thames Route passes right through the centre of Avebury Stone Circle.

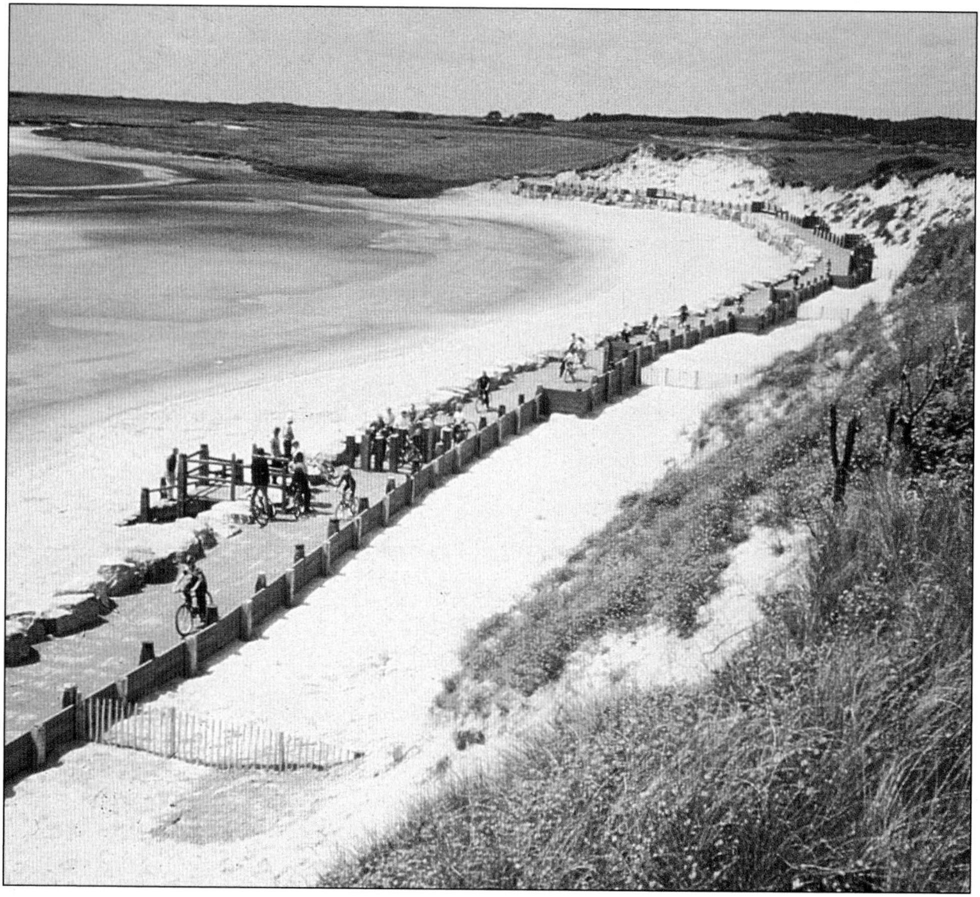

The new coastal path from Burry Port to Pembrey Forest doubles as coastal defence works (Celtic Trail).

4 47

CELTIC TRAIL WEST (LÔN GELTAIDD) (Fishguard-Swansea)

Easy/Moderate - 143 miles NN4C - £5.99

4 47 8

CELTIC TRAIL EAST (LÔN GELTAIDD) (Swansea-Chepstow)

Moderate/Challenging - 84 miles NN4B - £5.99

The route explores the beautiful Pembrokeshire coastline as far as St David's before turning southeast towards Pembroke Castle and Laugharne, home of Dylan Thomas. Beyond Carmarthen the route joins the Llanelli Millennium Coastal Park then follows the wide sweep of Swansea Bay. A tough forestry challenge on the High Level Route (climbing to 2000ft) takes you from Neath to Pontypridd.

Traffic-free paths lead southeast from Trelewis across the Hengoed Viaduct, through Sirhowy Valley Country Park and along the canal into Newport, leaving an almost flat ride to Chepstow and its magnificent castle.

Public transport options
Fishguard: occasional services from Swansea.
Swansea: main line services from London Paddington.
Chepstow: on the Cardiff to Gloucester line.

It is also possible to join the route from the following stations: **Haverfordwest**, **Pembroke**, **Carmarthen**, **Kidwelly**, **Burry Port** and **Llanelli, Neath**, **Port Talbot**, **Pontypridd**, **Cardiff** and **Newport**.

The National Cycle Network officially opened on June 21st 2000, when the whole 10,000-mile Network was ridden on this single day. 260 separate rides celebrated the event.

On the following few days the Network hosted the World's largest Cyclethon, when local authorities, community groups and charities staged events on routes throughout the country. Details available on the Sustrans website - www.nationalcyclenetwork.org.uk

WEST MIDLANDS CYCLE ROUTE
(Oxford-Derby via Birmingham)
Easy/Moderate - 162 miles NN5B - £5.99

Leave the Dreaming Spires of Oxford and pass through the historic town of Woodstock and a series of beautiful villages on your way to Banbury. A highpoint is reached at Sibford Ferris before the long descent down into the valley of the River Avon and Stratford. The route turns northeast through Redditch and Bromsgrove on its approach to Birmingham. The traffic-free Rea Valley Route goes into the heart of the city and the Birmingham Canal is followed out the other side. Further traffic-free sections either side of Walsall take you on to Lichfield with its famous cathedral. After visiting Burton upon Trent the route enters Derby via the Etwall-Mickleover railway path.

SOUTH MIDLANDS CYCLE ROUTE
(Oxford-Derby via Leicester)
Easy/Moderate - 148 miles NN6A - £5.99

Highlights along this route through the geographical centre of England include the old town of Winslow and the amazing cycle network in Milton Keynes. Traffic-free sections include the Brampton Valley Way between Northampton and Market Harborough, a riverside path through Leicester and the finish along the River Derwent into Derby.

Public transport options
Oxford and **Derby:** main line services from London

It is also possible to join the route from the following stations: **Milton Keynes, Northampton, Market Harborough, Leicester** and **Loughborough.**

The route of the East Midlands Cycle Route goes over the Grand Union Canal to Frog Island, Leicester.

The Birmingham Canal Network offers numerous traffic-free routes for cyclists. The Main Line to Wolverhampton takes Route 5 north (West Midlands Route).

Trans Pennine Trail

A national route for recreation and transport suitable for walkers, cyclists and (in parts) horse riders. It extends for 215 miles coast to coast, 350 miles in total, linking major towns and cities across the North of England from Liverpool to Hull, Leeds to Chesterfield. The TPT differs from the rest of the National Cycle Network as it is a separately managed and funded project. The multi-user nature of the TPT means that path surfaces are not necessarily of the same construction as the National Cycle Network. However the TPT forms an integral part of the Network and National Cycle Network route numbers are shown on TPT signs.

  TRANS PENNINE TRAIL WEST (Irish Sea-Pennines) RPN08A - £4.95

Southport, Liverpool, Warrington, Stockport, The Peak District and Penistone.

 **TRANS PENNINE TRAIL CENTRAL (Derbyshire & Yorkshire)**

RPN08B - £4.95

Barnsley, Leeds, Sheffield, Rotherham, Chesterfield and Doncaster.

 **TRANS PENNINE TRAIL EAST (Yorkshire-North Sea)**

RPN08C - £4.95

Doncaster, Selby, York, Hull and Hornsea.

  DERBY-YORK CYCLE ROUTE Easy/Moderate - 154 miles NN6B - £5.99

Exit Derby on the trail alongside the River Derwent, go right through the heart of Nottingham and into Robin Hood country, passing through Sherwood Forest Country Park and Clumber Park on a long traffic-free section. The route turns west from Worksop to Rother Valley Country Park where it joins the Trans Pennine Trail through Sheffield. Long traffic-free sections take the route east along the River Dearne then the River Don past the Earth Centre and Doncaster and into the Vale of York. The Selby - York Railway path and the Ouse riverside route lead right into the beautiful heart of York, one of Britain's most cycle-friendly cities.

Public transport options

York: on the East Coast Line with services from London King's Cross and Edinburgh.
Nottingham: main line services from London. It is also possible to join the route from the following stations: **Doncaster, Sheffield, Rotherham, Worksop** and **Hucknall.**

  THE WHITE ROSE CYCLE ROUTE (Hull-Middlesbrough)
Easy/Moderate - 123 miles NN65 - £5.99

Enjoy the splendours of Yorkshire between the bustling cities of Hull and Middlesbrough. You have a choice of two routes on leaving Hull: one runs west, parallel with the Humber, the other heads north across rolling wold country. They link in beautiful, historic York, one of Britain's most cycle-friendly cities. At Coxwold the route divides again: the easier western route runs through Sutton-under-Whitestonecliffe before crossing the North York Moors. The other option involves several challenging climbs through the spectacular heather-clad moorland.

Public transport options

Kingston upon Hull: main line services via York, Leeds and Doncaster.
Middlesbrough: main line services from York, Darlington and Newcastle.

It is also possible to join the route from the following stations: **York, Thirsk** and **Northallerton** are on the East Coast Line with main line services from London King's Cross and Edinburgh. Local services operate between **Selby** and **Kingston upon Hull** and intermediate stations.

The Naburn Swing Bridge took the East Coast Main Line railway from King's Cross to Edinburgh over the Ouse south of York. Now it is a key link in the Network.

   C2C (SEA TO SEA) CYCLE ROUTE

(Whitehaven/Workington - Sunderland/Newcastle)

Moderate/Challenging - 140 miles NN7AA - £5.99

Cyclists enjoying a rest on the C2C.

Sustrans' most popular long distance route crosses northern England from coast to coast. Enjoy the (relatively!) gentle ride through the Lake District before the challenging crossing of the Pennines. Your efforts are rewarded with a long downhill stretch to the coast at Newcastle or Sunderland, passing many magnificent sculptures along the way. For those seeking even more adventurous options there are some parallel offroad alternatives. For a return route from Newcastle back to Whitehaven why not try the Reivers Cycle Route? (Contact Sustrans for details).

Public transport options
It is best to buy a return ticket to Carlisle then catch a local train to get to the start and a local train back from the finish to Carlisle. This is a much cheaper option than buying two one-way tickets (one to the start and one back from the finish).

Carlisle: West Coast main line services from all parts of Britain.

Workington & Whitehaven: local train services from Carlisle.

Tynemouth: East Coast main line services to Newcastle from all parts of Britain. You will have to cycle back from Tynemouth to Newcastle via Route 72 along the north bank of the river as bikes are not allowed on the Metro (local train service).

Roker: Cycle from Roker to Sunderland then local trains to Newcastle (served by East Coast main line).

It is also possible to join the route from **Penrith.**

LOCHS & GLENS CYCLE ROUTE SOUTH
(Glasgow-Carlisle)

Moderate/Challenging - 213 miles NN7B - £5.99

LOCHS & GLENS CYCLE ROUTE NORTH
(Inverness-Glasgow)

Moderate/Challenging - 214 miles NN7C - £5.99

Ride south from Inverness, 'capital' of the Scottish Highlands, through spectacular mountain scenery to the bonnie banks of Loch Lomond. Riverside paths, dismantled railways and canal towpaths take you through Glasgow and southwest to the Ayrshire Coast with dramatic views across to the Isle of Arran. Pedal through the forested heart of Dumfries and Galloway to the Solway Firth coastline, across the border into England and journey's end at Carlisle.

Public transport options

Inverness: main line services from all parts of Britain via Glasgow Queen Street or Edinburgh Waverley.
Glasgow: main line services from all parts of Britain, services from south of Glasgow arrive at Glasgow Central and services north of Glasgow arrive at Glasgow Queen Street.
Carlisle: West Coast main line services from all parts of Britain.

It is also possible to join the route from the following stations: **Dumbarton** from **Glasgow, Pitlochry, Blair Atholl, Dalwhinnie, Kingussie** and **Aviemore** are on the line to Inverness; **Paisley, Johnstone, Lochwinnoch, Kilwinning, Irvine** and stations to **Ayr** as well as **Dumfries** are all on the route.

CLYDE-FORTH CYCLE ROUTE
(Glasgow-Edinburgh)

Easy/Moderate - 86 miles NN75 - £5.99

Cycle across Scotland from Gourock on the Firth of Clyde to the spectacular city of Edinburgh on the Firth of Forth. Savour the panoramic views across the Clyde to the hills behind Helensburgh before turning inland. Pass through the heart of Glasgow and on to the Airdrie-Bathgate railway path before linking with the Union Canal into the

Glen Oglehead viaduct prior to restoration (Lochs & Glens Route).

centre of Edinburgh. The map also covers several link routes: Glasgow-Loch Lomond, Glasgow-Kilmarnock (and Ardrossan), Edinburgh-Forth Road Bridge and Edinburgh-Musselburgh.

Public transport options
Numerous local stations on route are served from **Glasgow Central** or from **Queen Street.** From the latter you can catch the local train to **Drumgelloch** if you want to start at the end of the long railway path to **Bathgate.**
Edinburgh Waverley: main line services from all parts of Britain, and local trains to **Bathgate** and **Livingstone**.

It is also possible to join the route from many intermediate stations: there is an excellent network of railways around Glasgow operated by Strathclyde Passenger Transport – bikes are carried free of charge on all services.

LÔN LAS CYMRU SOUTH (Chepstow/Cardiff -Builth Wells)
Moderate/Challenging - 83 miles NN8A - £5.99

LÔN LAS CYMRU NORTH (Builth Wells-Holyhead)
Moderate/Challenging - 175 miles NN8B - £5.99

This spectacular route is the toughest in the National Cycle Network. It runs from the Bristol Channel to the island of Anglesey and frequently divides to offer challenging offroad options. Starting in either Cardiff or Chepstow, the route crosses several ranges of hills and mountains on its way through Wales, with east and west options linking at Builth Wells, Machynlleth, Dolgellau and near Porthmadog. North from here, the two routes become one, the gradients ease and railway paths whisk you north through Caernarfon and Bangor onto the gentle lanes of Anglesey.

Poured Metal by Jeremy Cunningham can be found on the Airdrie and Bathgate section of the Clyde to Forth route. Watch out for other sculptures along this route.

One of the high points on Lôn Las Cymru crossing the Gospel Pass, on the way to Abergavenny.

Public transport options
Cardiff: main line services from all parts of Britain.
Chepstow: on the Cardiff to Gloucester line.
Builth Wells: on the Swansea to Shrewsbury line. Get off at Builth Road then cycle to Builth Wells (1½ miles).
Llanwrtyd Wells: on the Swansea to Shrewsbury line.
Holyhead: on the Chester to Holyhead line.
It is also possible to join the route from the following stations: **Abergavenny**, **Merthyr Tydfil** (from Cardiff), **Machynlleth**, **Barmouth**, **Porthmadog** and **Bangor.**

 KINGFISHER TRAIL
Easy/Moderate - 230 miles
NN9A - £5.99

Based on the quiet lanes of the border counties of Northern Ireland, this route describes a figure-of-eight, crossing into the Republic of Ireland and the Leitrim Hills. A choice of shorter loops is shown making this an ideal family holiday.

Stunning views can be seen from Lôn Las Cymru North.

BELFAST-BALLYSHANNON CYCLE ROUTE

Easy/Moderate - 242 miles NN9B - £5.99

The first fully signed coast to coast route in Ireland takes in the Sperrins, the Lakes of Fermanagh and Leitrim and the beautiful sandy beaches of County Donegal.

BALLYSHANNON-BALLYCASTLE CYCLE ROUTE

Easy/Moderate - 236 miles NN9C - £5.99

Pettigo, Omagh, Newtown Stewart and Derry are among the places linked by this stunning route which counts the Port to Port Coastal Path and a link to the Giant's Causeway among its main attractions.

LOUGHSHORE TRAIL

Easy/Moderate - 120 miles
NN94 - £5.99

This route circles Lough Neagh, the biggest freshwater lake in the British Isles. The route can be followed in either direction and consists mainly of quiet, virtually traffic-free minor roads and lanes with stretches of forest track.

The Cott Ferry to Crom Estate crosses Upper Lough Erne on the delightful Kingfisher Trail.

National Cycle Network Route Maps

The National Route Map range is expanding all the time. The award-winning maps give easy-to-read contours, route profiles, mileages and essential visitor information. Latest editions are on water resistant paper.

Scotland

NN7B	Lochs and Glens - South: Glasgow - Carlisle	£5.99
NN7C	Lochs and Glens - North: Inverness - Glasgow	£5.99
NN75	Clyde to Forth Cycle Route: Glasgow - Edinburgh	£5.99
NN1D	Edinburgh - Aberdeen	£5.99
NN1E	Aberdeen - John o' Groats	£5.99

Wales

NN8A	Lôn Las Cymru - Welsh National Route South: Cardiff & Chepstow - Builth Wells	£5.99
NN8B	Lôn Las Cymru - Welsh National Route North: Builth Wells - Holyhead	£5.99
NN4B	Celtic Trail East: Swansea - Severn Bridge	£5.99
NN4C	Celtic Trail West: Fishguard - Swansea	£5.99

North of England

NN7AA	Sea to Sea (C2C) Cycle Route: Whitehaven/Workington - Newcastle/Sunderland	£5.99
NN65	White Rose Cycle Route: Hull - Middlesbrough	£5.99
NN6B	Derby - York	£5.99
NN14	Three Rivers Route: Newcastle, Sunderland & Middlesbrough	£5.99
NN1C	Coasts and Castles Cycle Route: Newcastle - Edinburgh	£5.99

Please ask for a free catalogue which includes over 150 items including accommodation guides.

Midlands

NN6A	South Midlands Cycle Route: Oxford - Derby, via Leicester	£5.99
NN5B	West Midlands Cycle Route: Oxford - Derby, via Birmingham	£5.99

East of England

NN1A	Hull - Harwich Cycle Route: Hull - Fakenham	£5.99
NN1B	Hull - Harwich Cycle Route: Fakenham - Harwich	£5.99

South East

LN001	London Thames Cycle Route	£4.99
NN2A	Downs & Weald Cycle Route: London - Hastings, via Eastbourne	£5.99
NN1X	Garden of England Cycle Route: Dover - London & Hastings	£5.99
NN4A	Severn & Thames Cycle Route: Gloucester - Newbury	£5.99
NN5A	Thames Valley Cycle Route: London - Oxford	£5.99

South West

NN3A	West Country Way: Padstow - Bristol/Bath	£5.99
NN3B	Cornish Way: Land's End - Bude	£5.99
NN27	Devon Coast to Coast: Ilfracombe - Plymouth	£5.99

Northern Ireland

NN9A	Kingfisher Trail: N & S Ireland	£5.99
NN9B	Belfast - Ballyshannon	£5.99
NN9C	Ballyshannon - Ballycastle	£5.99
NN94	Loughshore Trail	£5.99

NAME

ADDRESS

POSTCODE   PHONE

Phone 0117 929 0888 to place your telephone order

POCKX

Code	Product Name	Price	Total

☐ Mastercard   ☐ VISA   ☐ Delta/Connect

☐ Switch - issue no _____

Please EITHER enclose a cheque payable to Sustrans OR complete your credit/debit card number here and sign:

☐☐☐☐☐☐☐☐☐☐☐☐☐☐☐☐☐☐

SIGNATURE   DATE

CARD EXPIRY DATE ☐☐ / ☐☐

Order total _____

UK orders, add P&P 10% of total, minimum £2.50 _____

Non-UK order, add P&P 20%, minimum £3.50 _____

Total with P&P _____

Donation _____

GRAND TOTAL _____

Order online or find more info - visit our website at **www.sustrans.org.uk**

Please return this coupon with your payment to: Sustrans, PO Box 21, Bristol BS99 2HA. For UK orders, we aim to deliver within 10 days of receipt of order. Phone for express service.

Details from two mileposts. Above: Andrew Rowe's design is nautical whilst right: The Fossil Tree (by Jon Mills) shows the eventual demise of the motor car, fossilised as surely as the carboniferous plants which grew long ago to fuel it!

Stilwell's Britain Cycleway Companion

250-page guide packed with detailed accommodation listings for Britain's best known long distance cycle routes. Contains background information about the places to stop and stay along 10 National Cycle Network routes throughout the UK, including the C2C, Lôn Las Cymru, the West Country Way, Hull to Harwich and the Lochs & Glens route, plus 13 of England's regional routes. RG31A - £9.95

North Sea Cycle Route (Nordzee Route)

Opened in its preliminary form for the Millennium, this 3400-mile (5500 km) route is a continuous, signed route encircling the North Sea passing through seven countries: Scotland, England, The Netherlands, Germany, Denmark, Sweden and Norway. With many international ferry links along the way it can easily be divided into shorter sections. The North Sea Cycle Route will become one of 12 long distance routes in the EuroVelo network, a project initiated by the European Cyclists' Federation. A free route guide to the North Sea Cycle Route is available from Sustrans, or visit www.northsea-cycle.com for detailed route information.

Sustrans Stamping Scheme

First introduced on the C2C route, the popular stamping scheme now extends to all the mapped routes. As you cycle the Network, call in at the stamping points listed on the route card (enclosed with most maps) to get the card stamped. Collect six stamps and you can send for a commemorative T-shirt. Stamping points are marked on the National Cycle Network route maps but points do change from time to time, so visit: www.nationalcyclenetwork.org.uk or call the National Cycle Network Information Service on 0117 929 0888 for an up-to-date list. Additional cards for friends or family are available from Sustrans or at individual stamping points.

Millennium Mileposts

Standing just over two metres tall and made of cast iron, 1,000 Millennium Mileposts sponsored by the Royal Bank of Scotland are to be found all over the National Cycle Network. With four individual designs to choose from, you too can own one of these unique sculptures. Prices from £350 to £650. Phone 0117 929 0888 for a free information sheet (FF18).

THE TIME TRAIL

S ponsored by The Royal Bank of Scotland, the Time Trail is an exciting new puzzle that will add another dimension to your journeys along the National Cycle Network. It has been devised by artist Charlie Harrow.

One thousand tall cast iron Millennium Mileposts similar to the one pictured have been erected along the routes to mark the opening of each new section of the 10,000-mile National Cycle Network. On most you will find an embossed metal disc showing a Time Trail Symbol similar to the one shown here (not to scale).

Whoever cracks the Time Trail Code will win an exclusive Time Trail prize.

How far will I have to travel?
You won't have to cycle around the whole National Cycle Network – at least not to start with! The UK has been divided into nine regions, with at least two copies of each Time Trail symbol to be found in each. So, if you cycle from Penzance to Bristol on the National Cycle Network, you should find the five Time Treasures. Also, the mileposts have been arranged so that the first two sets of designs can often be collected during a single ride near a large town. But to tackle the final Treasure for the bronze reward you will have to travel further afield. Of course, you don't have to complete all the stages – you might simply decide to keep the pencil and paper rubbings as a memento of your trip!

See the order form on page 237 for details of how to order maps covering these routes.

How does the Time Trail work?
The metal discs show a series of pictures relating to the theme of Time surrounded by letters from a secret Code. There are over 60 different designs that have been divided into five themed sets. Each set relates to a Time Treasure.

This is what you do:
1. Collect pencil and paper rubbings of the discs as a record of your journey.
2. When you have collected rubbings of all the discs from a certain set, you can send for a Time Treasure. With the Time Treasure you can make a three dimensional sculpture of the rubbings you have collected. This will help you to crack the secret code in the design.
3. When you have collected all five Time Treasures, you can tackle the final Treasure.

How long will it take?
It all depends on how you cover the Network! As well as the 50 repeated designs, the year 2000 saw the addition of a few master Decoding Symbols which are needed to unravel the further mysteries hidden in the Time Trail. Only the originator of the Millennium Time Trail – Charlie Harrow – knows what these are, so please don't ask anyone at Sustrans because they don't know!

Further Information
For a free Time Trail information pack (FF19) or to order a kit (RG120 - £4.00) containing everything you need to start off contact the **National Cycle Network Information Service Telephone: 0117 929 0888 or visit www.nationalcyclenetwork.org.uk**

*A*round the kingdom and across the seas
Stand mileposts of iron with symbols to tease.
It's no race against time our TIME TRAIL quest,
With Treasures for all who succeed in the test.
Made neither from silver, diamonds nor gold,
But elements, common and ancient and old.

Either by foot or your bike wheels spinning,
Finding time to find Time is just the beginning.
Brass rub the designs of triangles and squares,
And pentagons too, with a few other spares.
Claim treasures to solidify time well spent,
Discovering, perhaps, what Time actually meant.

Four dimensional jigsaws found in groups of fives,
A sixth from them all makes it the Time of Our Lives.
Layers upon layers, a rainbow coded rhyme,
In a universe of stars we join up space and time.
The Millennium Time Trail works out for all to see
That Time in itself is still Time's mystery.

On the site of Consett's once renowned steelworks,
Tony Cragg's 'Terris Novalis' pays homage to the
surveyors' instruments which set out the railways and
the landscape of the industrial age (C2C Route).

sustrans

GOOD CYCLING CODE

KEEP SAFE, BE COURTEOUS AND ENJOY CYCLING ON THE
NATIONAL CYCLE NETWORK

By 2005 the National Cycle Network will be 10,000 miles of cycle routes, running right through urban centres and reaching all parts of the UK. It is designed to encourage people to start cycling again and to be a safe and attractive resource for families, novices and experienced cyclists. One-third of the National Cycle Network is on traffic-free paths providing a major new amenity for walkers and, in many places, people with disabilities.

On all routes..

Please be courteous. Always cycle with respect for others, whether other cyclists, pedestrians, people in wheelchairs, horse riders or drivers, and acknowledge those who give way to you.

On shared use paths...

One-third of the National Cycle Network is on traffic-free paths, such as disused railway routes. These are designed for shared use by cyclists and walkers. They are often suitable for wheelchairs and sometimes for horse riders.

Experience in the UK and abroad shows that such paths can benefit everyone and that they can be comfortably and safely shared if we show respect for others.

When cycling on shared use paths please:

- give way to pedestrians, leaving them plenty of room
- keep to your side of any dividing line
- be prepared to slow down or stop if necessary
- don't expect to cycle at high speeds
- be careful at junctions, bends and entrances
- **Remember that many people are hard of hearing or visually impaired – don't assume that they can see or hear you**
- **Ensure you have a bell on the handlebars of your bike and use it – don't surprise people**

- give way where there are wheelchair users and horse riders.

On roads...

Much of the National Cycle Network is on traffic-calmed or minor roads through towns and the countryside.

When cycling on roads:

- always follow the Highway Code
- be seen – most accidents to cyclists happen at junctions
- fit lights and use them in poor visibility
- consider wearing a helmet and conspicuous clothing
- keep your bike roadworthy
- don't cycle on pavements except where designated – pavements are for pedestrians
- use your bell – not all pedestrians can see you.

And in the countryside...

- follow the Country Code
- respect other land management activities such as farming or forestry and take litter home
- keep erosion to a minimum if offroad
- be self-sufficient – in remote areas carry food, repair kit, map and waterproofs
- try to cycle or use public transport to travel to and from the start and finish of your ride
- cycle within your capabilities
- match your speed to the surface and your skills.

Thank you for cycling!

The bicycle does not cause pollution or contribute to climate change.

Thank you for choosing this environmentally-friendly form of transport.

PRACTICAL ADVICE FOR CYCLISTS

'Oh no, not another section of patronising tips from some know-it-all. Why do they bother with them?' Well, may we apologise now to anyone who is quite competent at mending a puncture, planning a route and knowing what to take with them on a bike ride. We suggest you skip this chapter and get on with the rides!

For those of you who are a little less certain or a bit rusty after a few years' absence from your bike, the good news is that almost everything related to cycling is simple, straightforward and rooted firmly in common sense.

The bike

Don't be put off by all the hype about bikes with thirty gears, full suspension and frames made of exotic metals. A Tour de France winner on an old butcher's bike would probably be faster than most of us on a bike costing £2,000! Enjoying cycling is in the mind, not in the equipment. If you want to enhance your enjoyment of cycling then try to get out more regularly and get used to spending a couple of hours on a bike saddle. Try out other people's bikes and see if you prefer the saddle/riding position/feel of the bike.

The Network consists of a mixture of minor roads, railway paths, forestry tracks, canal towpaths, sections on roads through towns and specially-built cycle tracks. The surfaces are not all sealed and may vary in quality so, for the unsurfaced sections, it is wise to use a bike with strong wheels (ie not a lightweight racing bike!).

Thames Cycle Route – be prepared to give way to other users of the riverside path.

Children's bikes tend to be robust enough anyway, but adults should opt for a strong touring bike, a hybrid bike or a mountain bike fitted with smooth tyres.

What to wear

You don't need lots of expensive, specialist gear: several thin layers of ordinary clothing will normally do. However, if you do want to invest, the most important items are padded cycling shorts and padded gloves. Leggings or tracksters on top of cycling shorts are best for the legs. T-shirts, thermal vests, shirts or fleeces should be long enough to cover the back even when you are stretched forward. The ideal top layer is a windproof/showerproof top with zips to help adjust for changes in temperature. Your extremities are much more susceptible to cold on a bike than when you are out walking: take gloves and a hat. Tight, non-stretch jeans are about the worst thing to wear.

Helmets

See the 'Helmets' section in 'Cycling with children' on page 247.

Punctures

They do not happen that often (unless the hedgerows have recently been cut) but they are the most common form of breakdown and they can ruin a day out if you are not prepared. A pump, spare tube and puncture repair kit are the only indispensable accessories you should carry with you at all times. If you don't know how to mend a puncture, it is worth learning – punctures can happen anywhere, anytime, to anyone, however experienced you are and whatever sort of bike you are riding. There are lots of maintenance books but better still is to get an experienced cyclist to show you what to do.

What else to take?

Besides pump and puncture repair kit, consider the following: money, map/guidebook, energy snacks and water, spare clothes (especially hat and gloves), waterproofs and a lock. If there is any chance of still being out at dusk, take front and rear lights (check they work before you set off). A reflective belt takes up little space and is useful for being seen in murky conditions.

On those rare days when the sun is hot and bright take suntan cream and sunglasses. Drink much more water on hot days – you dehydrate far more quickly and are often not aware of it because your sweat evaporates in the breeze you create as you ride along.

Carrying equipment

What is the best way to carry equipment? For absolute minimalists, a water bottle and pump will fit on the frame, tools, keys and money will fit into a small bumbag. A larger bumbag will also carry a thin waterproof. More than this and it is best to carry food, spare clothing, waterproofs and lock in rear panniers rather than in a rucksack. Make sure the panniers are evenly loaded. If there is a chance of rain, put the contents of the panniers inside plastic bags. Handlebar bags are useful for easy access but they are not designed to carry heavy weights.

Cycling in a group

If you are cycling in a group of mixed ability and varying levels of fitness it is worth arranging regular rendezvous points for coffee/lunch/tea so that the slower people can catch up with the faster ones or so that the fitter people can do a longer route to get to the meeting point. The thought of getting to a good cafe, teashop or pub can do wonders in terms of encouraging people up hills! (It is worth checking the opening times of the refreshment stops to avoid disappointment).

More experienced cyclists can do their bit for the group by checking the bikes of the novices, helping mend punctures or making adjustments to the position of the saddle or handlebars and generally giving encouragement or advice at difficult junctions. A more experienced cyclist should always bring up the rear to prevent a novice from being stranded at the back with a problem beyond his/her ability to fix. In strong headwinds it is possible to help a weaker cyclist by getting them to follow closely behind you in your slipstream. Don't try this on unsurfaced sections – you need to keep an eye out for any rough patches!

Hownsgill Viaduct. A well earned rest on the C2C high above Consett.

CYCLING WITH CHILDREN

A successful family cycle ride can satisfy so many different needs and provide such rich and long-lasting memories that it is worth knowing in advance the ingredients that make up a good, safe ride that will encourage children to get hooked on cycling from an early age.

Children and Bikes

Children can be carried in a child seat on an adult bike, pulled along in a trailer behind the bike, ride a bike that attaches to the adult bike or ride their own bikes. Looking at the options from birth onwards:

0 - 9 months: until babies can hold their heads up by themselves they should not be carried on bikes. This may happen between six months and a year. It is a good idea to get the baby used to the bike seat as early as possible so that they are quite happy in this environment. The adult will also get used to carrying the increasing weight and learn how this affects the handling of the bike.

9 months - 4 years: the child can be carried in a specially designed seat fitted to the back or the middle of a bike. There are many different bike seats and means of attachment. Look out for reviews in cycling magazines and ask friends and cycle shops for advice about which seat they recommend.

18 months +: a toddler graduates happily from a push-along tractor / car without pedals to a tricycle or a bike with stabilizers and eventually to a bike without stabilizers. A child interested in cycling will probably be cycling without stabilizers by the age of 4 - 6.

The child seat

The two most important factors for parents' peace of mind and the child's enjoyment are safety and comfort. Can the seat be adapted for different sized toddlers and children? Is there adequate padding? Is the child firmly held in place by straps and safety bars in case they fall asleep and nod forward or in case you have to brake suddenly? There are some seats which recline which allow the child to sleep comfortably and help to stop the child's head lolling forwards. Other things to consider are how easily or frequently you may wish to remove the seat entirely: having a seat that can easily be switched

between the parents' bikes means that carrying the child can be shared during the course of a ride. Can the seat be used in conjunction with panniers?

There are some saddles which can be fitted to the crossbar. These give the child a much better view and allow conversation to take place, but obviously offer much less protection both from a safety aspect and from the wind and cold.

Trailers and trailer bikes

Trailers are a wonderful way to carry babies and children who are still too small to contribute pedal power. Babies as young as four months can be carried safely in a cycle trailer by fastening them in a small baby's car seat and then strapping that into the trailer. They can sleep when they wish and take a toy or a book with them. Trailers usually have accessible side pockets - children will enjoy disorganising their bits and pieces into them. The adult will find that towing a trailer affects bike handling far less than a child seat. Because of this, and despite the greater weight, cycling with a trailer can be less tiring than with a child seat.

Advantages to the whole family unit include the fact that a young child will be happier about longer excursions by bike (though it is still important to stop frequently to allow for play and leg-stretching). Another plus is that trailers are extremely conspicuous on the road and motorists tend to be overwhelmingly considerate. Also from the safety point of view trailers are designed so as to be very difficult to tip over – you can drop the bike horizontally without the trailer moving at all.

Having said that, drawbacks to trailer use are that they cannot be recommended in built-up areas. The extra length is obviously not helpful at busy junctions, and if you stop, and take the whole thing off the road, you block the pavement! However, on country lanes trailers are fine, though most weary parents will feel like avoiding very hilly areas. For peace of mind, it is worth avoiding the kind of countryside with twisting little lanes through dark woodland where drivers' vision is inevitably going to be restricted. Bought new, trailers are not cheap, but there is good availability of second-hand ones (try bike hire outlets selling stock at the end of summer).

Many railway paths are particularly suitable for wheelchairs and children.

Trailer bikes

Trailer bikes are the natural next step. By five years old, your child is going to be very burdensome either on a seat or in a trailer – yet is likely to have abundant energy! A trailer bike allows the child to contribute some pedal power without the responsibility for steering or braking. In effect the back half of a child's bike is attached to the adult's machine. There are various means of achieving this: the best are purpose-built trailer bikes which attach to a special frame you bolt to your own bike. This type works very well and adjusts with the growth of your child so that a single trailer bike will last them from around five years old to around nine. The worst are systems which encourage you to remove the front wheel from your child's bike and then clamp around its headset to attach it to your bike. These can wobble alarmingly – definitely try before you buy. As with trailers you get what you pay for. However, you are more likely to use a quality piece of equipment – and there is an avid second-hand market for purpose-built trailer bikes.

Helmets

Whatever your own views about wearing helmets, children should be encouraged to wear helmets for several reasons: until adolescence they are less able than adults to judge traffic speeds and distances and are thus more likely to be at risk when they are on their bikes in the presence of traffic (even if this is on quiet back streets or quiet lanes); they are more likely to try out stunts and tricks which may end in a fall; in the event of an accident when children are being carried on the back of a bike, they will not be able to prepare themselves for a fall in the same way as the adult.

One of the easiest ways to put a child off wearing a helmet is accidentally to pinch the sensitive skin under its chin while securing the clips on the helmet straps. Take great care to avoid doing this. Insert your forefinger between the clip and the chin so that your finger may be pinched, but not the child's skin. Encourage children to put on the helmet themselves – they should be able to do this from about the age of three. A helmet which is not done up is no use whatsoever: it will be thrown off in the event of a fall, exposing the head to injury.

It is important that the helmet is the right size, neither too big nor too small. Good cycle shops should help you select the right size. As with bikes, children are likely to grow out of several helmets between birth and adolescence. If a helmet has been involved in a serious accident or fall then **replace** it.

Children's bikes

It is better to buy the right size than buy a bike which is too large which the child can 'grow into'. Riding a bike which is too big is not only dangerous but is likely to put the child off cycling. Similarly once they have grown too big for a bike, think of passing it down or selling it secondhand. A child's first bike is better if it has no crossbar: this way the child falls through the bike and not off it. From the age a child can cycle, they should use and outgrow three bikes until they are old enough to ride an adult frame.

Hire bikes

At many of the more popular trails you can hire adult and children's bikes, kid seats, trailers and helmets. Look in the Yellow Pages or call the nearest Tourist Information Centre for details of hire centres. Ring in advance to book equipment, particularly on fine summer weekends. The hire centre staff are often the best people to ask about safe routes in the area.

Planning a ride: checking the bikes, what to take (food, drink, clothes)

Don't leave everything until the last moment: the evening before the ride check for punctures, check the brakes work properly, lubricate the chain and ensure that all the nuts on the rack and child carrier are tightly done up. Pack some food and drink (water or well-diluted squash is best). Oat bars, chocolate brownies and dried fruit travel well and give lots of energy, boiled sweets take up no room and are always good at stops. On cold days take something warm to drink (stainless steel thermos flasks are robust enough for the road). With regard to food and drink, little and often is better than one big midday meal. You don't need a pannier full of tools but you should have the equipment to mend a puncture (tyre levers, spare inner tube, puncture repair kit, pump). Other tools worth taking are a small adjustable spanner, a reversible screwdriver and Allen keys. It is worth carrying sticking plasters and a clean handkerchief in case there is a fall.

British weather is notoriously fickle and a child on the back of a bike generates no heat thus is much more likely to get cold quickly; even if it is a fine day take extra clothes (hat, gloves and socks) and something waterproof. There are waterproof covers available for children's seats which will keep the child dry. Don't forget nappies and a plastic bag to carry any used nappies (and other litter) back home.

Trailer bikes enable all the family to enjoy the route.

Planning a ride: when to go, where to go

The best time to go is when it is warm and dry with no wind blowing. If cycling through urban areas, Sundays are the days when there is least traffic. Country lanes can often be quieter during the week than at the weekend.

The options for where to go are much greater if the child is being carried in a bike seat (ie you are in complete control of their safety and the limits are when you get tired and/or the child gets bored). If the child is cycling rather than being carried, cycle paths on dismantled railways are ideal places for children to learn to ride and to gain confidence and stamina – the routes tend to be broad, flat, with a good quality surface and, most important, they are traffic-free.

Forestry Commission tracks are traffic-free but may be steeper and slightly rougher than railway paths. Certain Forestry Commission holdings have waymarked trails, some of which are promoted as suitable for families. Only a small percentage of canal towpaths are appropriate for family cycling. Some reservoirs have a cyclepath around their edge.

How far to go?

When deciding how far to go the best advice is: don't be too ambitious! It is better that everyone has a good time and wants to go out cycling again rather than coming back home exhausted and tearful and permanently put off cycling! If the children are on their own bikes, the ride should be designed around them and not the adults. They are likely to be bored by a long, non-stop ride. If there are things to look forward to such as a picnic, a playground, a castle, a sculpture, a stream or river, or a field full of animals then the children will be happier.

On a still day, on good, flat surfaces, 3-4 miles on a bike is equivalent to one mile walking so a 12-mile bike ride on a dismantled railway line is the same as a 3-4 mile walk. Hills, rough surfaces, wind and heavy loads all make cycling considerably slower and harder. 5-10 miles is about the right length trip for young children on their own bikes. 10-30 miles makes for a good day out for older children or for adults carrying children.

Getting to the start of the ride

The best rides are often those that start from home: children will recognise familiar places and there is far less hassle about getting everything organised. Catching a train with bikes and children is also possible, and children certainly like travelling on trains, but you will need to do some research to find out which trains carry bikes and perhaps make a booking in advance. Some trains only take one or two bikes, making a family trip with adults and children impossible. The National Rail Enquiry Sevice, Tel: 08457 484950, should be able to help with information about which trains are happy to carry bikes.

Cycling on roads with young children

Children must learn about the dangers of traffic and the need for safety whilst gaining confidence and stamina as they go out on longer rides. On the first few trips on quiet lanes it is worth teaching children to stop and pull into the side whenever a vehicle is heard. The best configuration is with adults ahead and behind. If there is only one adult, it is best to stay at the back to keep an eye on the children ahead. Always keep them in sight.

The most dangerous manoeuvre is a right turn from a main road on to a side road. Look behind you, wait for a gap in the traffic, indicate then turn. If there is a lot of traffic, pull in to the left and wait for a break in both flows of traffic. Teaching a child how to look behind them without wobbling and without veering into the middle of the road is one of the most important skills of cycling confidently.

If you are carrying the child on the back of your bike it is well worth pushing the bike up a steep hill that you might have tried to cycle up if you were on your own: it can be very difficult to dismount on a steep hill with the weight of a child on the back.

Teaching a child how to cycle

The proverb 'pride comes before a fall' could have been written specifically about learning to cycle. Just when children have proudly mastered one skill they will take a tumble and feel disheartened. Praise any progress and don't push the child too far or too fast. Cycling should be associated with fun, not just a task to learn. Confidence will be gained and lost a hundred times during the course of learning to balance on two wheels.

Most aspects of learning to cycle are common sense: children have to progress from a tricycle or a bike with stabilizers to balancing on two wheels; they have to learn how to stop by using their brakes, not their feet; they should learn to anticipate when to put their feet on the ground just before stopping; and they need to understand that they must keep their eyes on what lies ahead. All this can only be done after many sessions of trial and error with frequent falls and tumbles. It is vital that you choose somewhere safe, free from traffic with a good surface and if possible a very gentle downhill (it is easier to learn to balance freewheeling down a gentle slope). The child's hands, elbows and knees should be covered as there are likely to be a few scrapes and bumps. Children must be made aware of the dangers of traffic so they do not practice their newly-found skills in areas where they may unexpectedly come across traffic.

If a bike has stabilizers then gradually raise them off the ground so that the child begins to spend more time with the bike on the main wheels than on the small stabilizer wheels. An open frame enables the child to fall 'through' the bike rather than off it. Once the basics have been learnt, build up the child's confidence and stamina on traffic-free cyclepaths, before letting them loose on streets and roads.

Hampton Court Palace from the Thames Cycle Route.

HELPING CREATE THE NATIONAL CYCLE NETWORK

Help from volunteers at a local level is crucial to the development of the National Cycle Network. There are a variety of tasks which Sustrans needs help with – volunteering might only take a couple of hours a month or it might become one of your principal pastimes!

The Ranger Scheme was implemented in 1998, drawing upon people who are keen to look after sections of route or pieces of land near their home. The two types of Rangers are:
Route Rangers who look after route signing, Mileposts, Time Trail disks and sculptures, and perform some routine maintenance such as sweeping up glass and cutting back brambles. *Land Rangers* keep an eye on parcels of land which we are assembling for future use, but which for the time being lie fallow.

Trailblazing Works
Each year Sustrans runs a series of Trailblazing Work Camps throughout the UK. Volunteers can come along for the day or for the full 2-3 weeks and help build a key section of the National Cycle Network.

Other ways to help
Traffic counts, photography, administrative assistance, distribution of supporter recruitment leaflets and other work all rely on volunteers and we would be grateful for your help. Write to the Volunteer Co-ordinator, Sustrans, 35 King Street, Bristol, BS1 4DZ to receive further information.

Right: Volunteers on the 1998 Trailblazing Summer workcamp gather under Meldon Viaduct, Okehampton.

The route along the south side Loch Venachar, near Callander, was constructed entirely by volunteers.

OTHER PROJECTS

Although Sustrans has put a great deal of energy into creating the National Cycle Network, it has been a partnership project in which much of the work has been done by others, particularly a huge number of dedicated local authority officers, without whom the Network would still lie in fragments.

As well as the National Cycle Network, Sustrans works in a number of different areas.

Guardianship of Disused Railways
Over 10,000 miles of railways were abandoned at the time of the Beeching cuts in 1966. Although much of great value has been lost, the combined effort of local authorities and Sustrans has kept over 1,500 miles in public use. Sustrans owns about a third of these which it maintains against future transport use, and in the meantime uses for valuable walking and cycling routes.

Sustrans maintains over 700 bridges including some 40 railway viaducts. One of the invaluable roles played by our volunteers is that of Bridge Ranger where a volunteer can keep an eye on local structures.

Safe Routes to Schools
Safe Routes to Schools projects encourage and enable children to walk and cycle to school through a combined package of practical and educational measures. These projects involve the whole school community, local residents, local authorities, health and education workers and the police.

Safe Routes to Stations
This project involves developing safe and direct routes that link town centres and commercial, educational and residential areas with stations, giving cyclists and walkers priority over motor traffic.

Home Zones
A home zone is a street or group of streets where car users don't have priority over other users, with cars travelling at little more than walking pace. Sustrans is working in partnership with the Children's Play Council and Transport 2000 to encourage the development of home zones in the UK, both in existing communities and in new housing developments.

Rural Travel
Sustrans is involved in a range of new initiatives to help people get around the countryside without relying on private cars. The aim of these projects is to improve access for rural communities and visitors alike while tackling the growth in car use that threatens the quality of life for many in the countryside.

TravelSmart
The TravelSmart initiative uses a proven technique, called Individualised Marketing, to increase walking, cycling and use of public transport. It identifies people who are willing or able to reduce their private car use, and provides them with personalised travel information and incentives to encourage them to switch to public transport, walking or cycling or to other alternatives to driving a car.

International Liaison
For many years Sustrans has been involved in international projects and associations. Sustrans believes that the problems of congestion and pollution, of road danger, public health and global climate change can only be addressed at a world scale.
For more information about Sustrans' work visit www.sustrans.org.uk or call 0117 929 0888.

At Huntington School, York, the pupils redesigned their bike shed as part of their Safe Routes to Schools programme.

ACKNOWLEDGEMENTS

The National Cycle Network has been made possible by a huge co-operative effort over a period of years by hundreds of organisations and thousands of individuals. It is impossible to list all of them here. However, particular thanks are due to:

Nearly 500 local authorities who have developed local sections of route.

The Millennium Commission for its visionary lead grant of £43.5 million.

Government departments including the Department for Transport, Local Government and the Regions; the Scottish Executive; the Welsh Assembly; the Department of Regional Development (NI); and the Highways Agency.

Utility and statutory bodies including British Waterways; Forest Enterprise and Forest Service; English Regional Development Agencies (formerly English Partnerships); the Environment Agency; Ordnance Survey and Ordnance Survey of Northern Ireland.

Countryside and regeneration bodies including the National Trust; English Heritage; the Countryside Agency, Countryside Council for Wales; Scottish Natural Heritage; the Groundwork Trusts; and many national parks, countryside and heritage sites, tourism bodies and wildlife groups.

Railtrack, BRB (residuary) Ltd formerly known as Rail Property Ltd, British Railways Board and the Railway Heritage Trust.

Partner bodies representing cyclists, walkers, people with disabilities, horse-riders, anglers and other users of the routes.

Many local CTC and cycle campaign groups; the London Cycling Campaign.

Charitable trusts, in particular: The AIM Foundation; The Ashden Trust; A J Burton 1956 Charitable Settlement; C H K Charities Limited; The Freshfield Foundation; The Gannochy Trust; The Glass-House Trust; The JJ Charitable Trust; The Fanny and Leo Koerner Charitable Trust; The Mark Leonard Trust; The Manifold Trust; The Peacock Trust; The Pilgrim Trust; Rees Jeffreys Road Fund; The Ruben and Elisabeth Rausing Trust; The Serve All Trust; The L J Skaggs and Mary C Skaggs Foundation; R H Southern Trust; The Staples Trust; Vodafone Group Charitable Trust.

The cycle trade and industry, in particular the Bicycle Association and Association of Cycle Traders, and the contributors to the Cycle Levy Scheme: Brompton, Cycleurope, Dawes, Giant, H&J Supplies, Halfords, Madison, Moore Large, Professional, Raleigh, Saracen, SBC, Trek and Universal.

Sister Millennium projects that have created routes including the Trans Pennine Trail; the Kingdom of Fife Millennium Cycleways; Peterborough Green Wheel; the Millennium Coastal Park at Llanelli; the Earth Centre; Mile End Park; Changing Places; Turning the Tide; and others.

For corporate sponsorship particular gratitude is due to The Royal Bank of Scotland as well as to Halfords, Boots, and Madison.

And Sustrans' 40,000 Supporters, 1,300 Rangers, volunteers, trailblazers, route developers and letter-writers who have kept up the positive momentum throughout the period.

Sustrans would also like to extend thanks to all those who have generously contributed to the creation of the Network who we have not been able to list here.

Maps

Maps based on Ordnance Survey Strategi and OSCAR digital data with permission of the Controller of Her Majesty's Stationery Office © Crown copyright. All rights reserved Sustrans. Licence number GD 03181G0001.

Maps on pages 210, 211, 214, 216 and 217 based upon the 1984 Ordnance Survey of Northern Ireland 1:50,000 map with the permission of the Controller of Her Majesty's Stationery Office © Crown copyright. All rights reserved Sustrans. Permit No. 1493.

A-Z maps used on pages 69-77: Reproduced by permission of Geographers' A-Z Map Co. Ltd. Licence No. B1508. This product includes mapping data licensed from Ordnance Survey®. ©Crown Copyright 2002. Licence number 100017302.

Text & Research

Nick Cotton & John Grimshaw

Cartography

Stirling Surveys
Cycle City Guides
Sustrans

Project Co-ordination

Julian Holland
Sustrans

Design

Nigel White
Jeff Farrow
Lisa Bridge
Paul Taylor (original cover)
Sustrans

Photographs

Front cover Nick Turner
Spine Steve Morgan
Back cover Newcastle City Council

Principal contributors

Julia Bayne
John Grimshaw
Gareth Lovett Jones

Thanks also to

Robert Ashby
John Ashford
Ben Hamilton-Baillie
Graham Bell
J Bewley
Ray Blackwell
Borough of Poole
Nigel Brigham
Bristol Tourism & Conference Bureau
Bristol Tourist Information and Marketing Centre
British Waterways
Cadw: Welsh Historic Monuments (Crown Copyright)
Caledonian MacBrayne Ferries

Canterbury Council Tourism
Cardiff City Council
Bob Chapman
Nick Cotton
Michael Cutter
Patrick Davis
Richard East / City Design
Edinburgh & Lothians Tourist Board
Edinburgh City Council
Simon Elliott
Glyn Evans
Catherine Forrest
Gwynedd Council
Charles Harrow
Martin Harrow
Hawkeye
Herts County Council
Highlands of Scotland Tourist Board
Highways Agency
Ironbridge Gorge Museum Trust
Kai
Lucy Keeler
Keswick Tourism Association
Philip Lane
Grey Lipley
RJM
Jim Mackintosh Photography
Neil McNaughton
Ray Manley
Derek Marlborough
P Millmore
Jon Mills
Steve Morgan
NMR (Crown Copyright)
New Millennium Experience Company
Ken Nice
Grace Nicol
Chris Noble
Northumbria Tourist Board
Steve Patterson
Alan Pentland
The Perthshire Public Art Trust
Peterborough Photographic Society
Richard Robinson
Sandwell Metropolitan Borough Council
Roger Sinek
Toby Smedley
Ian Smith
Tim Snowdon
Pat Strachan
Suffolk County Council
Sunderland Association Football Club Ltd
Sustrans
Thanet Council
Richard Tibenham
Translink
Trans Pennine Trail
Andy Tryner
David Williams
Owen Wilson
Guy Woodland

Please photocopy this form

Join Sustrans

Sustrans (it stands for sustainable transport) is a charity that works on practical projects to encourage people to walk, cycle and use public transport. You can become a Supporter and help us to complete 10,000 miles of the National Cycle Network by 2005. You will receive a welcome pack with information about our work as well as regular newsletters updating you with progress during the year.

Give a donation of £3 a month or more by standing order and receive a voucher for a **FREE** National Cycle Network Route map worth £5.99 (30 to choose from). Give £10 a month or more and also receive a **FREE** copy of our 256 page Official Guide to the Network as a thank you.

1. YES I would like to support Sustrans

NAME

ADDRESS

POSTCODE

TELEPHONE   E-MAIL

2. YES I'll support Sustrans with a donation

£15 ☐   £25 ☐   £50 ☐   £100 ☐   £ other ☐   *(please tick)*   If other please state _____   ☐ Please send me a pack on leaving a legacy to Sustrans.
(£15 is the minimum rate)

Please EITHER enclose a cheque/PO/charity voucher payable to Sustrans OR complete your Access/Visa/CAFCard /Switch number here and sign: _____

SWITCH ISSUE NUMBER   CARD EXPIRY DATE

SIGNATURE   DATE

or YES I'll support Sustrans with a standing order

Your monthly standing order will provide us with vital regular income to help us complete the National Cycle Network and enable us to keep our administration costs to a minimum.

£3 ☐   £5 ☐   £10 ☐   £15 ☐   £25 ☐   £ other ☐   *(please tick)*

If other please state _____

REMEMBER: You can cancel this standing order at any time by informing us and your bank

NAME OF MY BANK

ADDRESS OF MY BANK

ACCOUNT NO _____   BANK SORT CODE __/__/ – /__/__/ – /__/__/

MY NAME   DATE

SIGNATURE

BANK INSTRUCTIONS: Please pay the above sum on the 8th next and **monthly** thereafter to **SUSTRANS**, Account number 01400978, Lloyds TSB Bank, 55 Corn St, Bristol BS99 7LE, Sort Code 30-00-01. **BANK PLEASE QUOTE REF:**

3. Gift Aid – Make your support go further at no extra cost to you

Sustrans can now claim an extra 28% from the Government! Please tick here ☐ if you want Sustrans to claim the tax back on all gift aid donations made from 6 April 2000 and complete today's date. ☐☐☐ I note that this declaration is valid until I tell you otherwise, and that I must inform Sustrans if I do not pay an amount of income tax and/or Capital gains tax at least equal to the tax the charity reclaims on my donations in the tax year.

4. Please return this coupon with your payment to Sustrans, PO Box 21, Bristol, BS99 2HA.

Charity Number: 326550